Blackwell Publishers
Oxford, UK and Cambridge, USA

Journal of the Association of Art Historians

Volume 17 Number 3 September 1994

Art History is published quarterly in March, June, September and December for the **Association of Art Historians** by **Blackwell Publishers**, 108 Cowley Road, Oxford OX4 1JF or 238 Main Street, Cambridge, MA 02142, USA. Registered charity no. 282579

Information for Subscribers: New orders and sample copy requests should be addressed to the Journals Marketing Manager at the publisher's address above. Renewals, claims and all other correspondence relating to subscriptions should be addressed to the Journals Subscriptions Department, Marston Book Services. PO Box 87, Oxford OX2 0DT. Cheques should be made payable to Basil Blackwell Ltd.

SUBSCRIPTION PRICES 1994	UK/EUR	NA*	ROW
Institutions	£77.00	US$128.00	£86.50
Individuals	£46.00	US$ 83.00	£56.00
Single copies (Institutions)	£23.00	US$ 38.00	£26.00
Single copies (Individuals)	£14.00	US$ 25.00	£17.00

*Canadian customers/residents please add 7% for GST

US mailing: Second class postage paid at Rahway, New Jersey. Postmaster: send address corrections to Art History, ℅ Mercury Airfreight International Ltd Inc., 2323 E-F Randolph Avenue, Avenel, NJ 07001, USA. (US Mailing Agent).

Articles for consideration to: Marcia Pointon, Editor, *Art History*, Department of History of Art, University of Manchester, Manchester M13 9PL, England.

Articles/Books for review to: Kathleen Adler, Reviews Editor, *Art History*, Centre for Extra-Mural Studies, Birkbeck College, University of London, 26 Russell Square, London WC1B 5DQ, England.

Membership of the Association of Art Historians is open to individuals who are art or design historians by profession or avocation and to those otherwise directly concerned in the advancement of the study of the history of art and design. The annual subscription, due on 1 January each year, is £34.00 (UK); £39.00 (Europe, including the Republic of Ireland); £45.00 or $80.00 (USA and Rest of the World), and includes four issues of both the journal *Art History* and the *Bulletin*. Student rates (UK) are available on application. Applications should be sent to Kate Woodhead, Dog and Partridge House, Byley, Cheshire CW10 9NJ. Tel: 0606 835517.

Back Issues: Single issues from the current and previous three volumes are available from Marston Book Services at the current single issue price. Earlier issues may be obtained from Swets & Zeitlinger, Back Sets, Heereweg 347, PO Box 810, 2160 SZ Lisse, Holland

Microform: The journal is available on microfilm (16mm or 35mm) or 105mm microfiche from the Serials Acquisitions Department, University Microfilms Inc, 300 North Zeeb Road, Ann Arbor, MI 48106, USA.

Printed in Great Britain by Hobbs the Printers of Southampton
This journal is printed on acid-free paper

 ISBN 0 631 194 754 ISSN 0141-6790

Art History Vol. 17 No. 3 September 1994 ISSN 0141-6790

CONTENTS

NOTES FOR CONTRIBUTORS

Art History provides an international forum for original research relating to all aspects of the historical and theoretical study of painting, sculpture, design and other areas of visual imagery. The journal is committed to the publication of innovative, synthetic work which extends understanding of the visual within a well-developed interdisciplinary framework and raises significant issues of interest to those working both within the history of art and in related fields.

(1) *Two copies* of manuscripts should be submitted; the overall word length should not normally exceed 9,000 words. They should be clearly typewritten, *double spaced* with generous margins. The title page of the script should indicate the author's name, institution, address and telephone number, together with accurate estimates of text and footnote wordlengths; subsequent pages should be numbered and should carry an identifying running head. The author should retain an up-to-date copy of the typescript. Photocopies of illustrations should be included with initial submissions and originals supplied only on the editor's request.

(2) English spelling conventions should be followed in the text (e.g. colour, centre); foreign-language citations should be given in translation in the main text, with the original appearing in full in an accompanying footnote. All quotations within the text should be enclosed within *single* inverted commas. More extensive citations should be indented without quotation marks. All new paragraphs should be clearly indicated by indentation.

(3) Footnotes should follow the text and be double spaced. References should be kept to a practical minimum and should avoid unnecessary digression or redundant displays of erudition. Bibliographical references should correspond to the following examples:

M. Baxandall, *The Limewood Sculptors of Renaissance Germany*, New Haven and London, 1980, pp. 20–1.
P.F. Brown, 'Painting and History in Renaissance Venice', *Art History*, vol. 7, no. 3, September 1984, pp. 263–95.

Titles in French should follow the capitalisation conventions adopted by the Bibliothèque nationale, Paris, as in the following example:

J.-C. Chamboredon, 'Production symbolique et formes sociales. De la sociologie de l'art et de la littérature à la sociologie de la culture', *Revue française de sociologie*, vol. 27, no. 3, July–September 1986, pp. 505–30.

(4) Illustrations should be used discriminatingly and should be confined to objects whose discussion forms a substantive part of the text. Good quality black-and-white plates should be provided upon acceptance of an article for publication. These must be clearly labelled and numbered, with accompanying typewritten captions on a separate sheet. Where indicated, measurements should be given in metric form; any details for reproduction from a larger image should be clearly indicated. Illustrations should be referred to as 'plate' in the text. All copyright clearance is the author's responsibility and full acknowledgement of sources should be included where appropriate.

(5) Corrections to accepted scripts should be kept to a strict minimum at proof stage. In view of the costs involved, the editor reserves the right to refuse any extensive alterations to authors' texts in proof. Prompt return of corrected proofs to the editor is essential.

(6) Manuscripts will not be returned to contributors.

Art History ISSN 0141-6790 Vol. 17 No. 3 September 1994 pp. 301–341

Erotic Revision in Thomas Eakins's Narratives of Male Nudity

Whitney Davis

To understand how subjective sexuality might be 'in' a picture or other representation — where it might be 'located' in the artefact itself and in the image that artefact relays — requires us to recall that desire and representation are partly outside one another. What achieves representation is not — or, at least, not wholly — what is desired. And what is desired is not — or, at least, not wholly — what is represented. Moreover, the conventional concept of desire as wanting what one does not have must be supplemented. Psychoanalytic metapsychology, for instance, suggests that desire, as we will see in more detail, is not-wanting what one *does* have.

I will allow the implications of this Freudian insight to emerge through an extended example. I will not ask how the American painter Thomas Eakins (1844–1916) wanted a 'homosexual' discharge of his fantasies, consciously or unconsciously, but instead how he did *not* want, at least wholly, a 'heterosexual' discharge. The on-going question of whether Eakins had 'homosexual' tendencies, then, is largely irrelevant here:[1] instead, we must ask how Eakins did *not* want, at least wholly, homosexual discharge. And I will not ask how Eakins's desire not to be heterosexual (or homosexual) was manifested in his art but how his desire not to be heterosexual (or homosexual) did *not* manifest itself in his art. In other words, I will ask how Eakins partly fulfilled his wishes by *retrospectively revising their repression toward a partial discharge in representation*. It will be useful to make some preliminary observations about this process.

The egoistic, sexual and aggressive wishes of human beings, Freud believed, have two sorts of history. Originating in perceptions, either they are discharged in motor action in the world — for example, in doing or saying something — or their discharge is delayed indefinitely, even permanently. Observing them in the forward direction of development — for example, from the theoretical moment of the 'origin' of a wish — we never know definitively whether they are on their way toward a complete discharge or toward a permanent reservation. But at a theoretical moment of absolute retrospection (identified with the psychoanalytic encounter itself), we can discover by reviewing the whole history of a wish that it has either been discharged or been reserved. Most likely, as Freud's model of the 'primary' and 'secondary' processes urged,[2] a wish will have been partly discharged, partly delayed or rerouted, and partly reserved, for wishes — as representations — can be *revised* to render passage toward discharge, the aim of mental activity, more possible.

For example, the most troubling components of a wish — what renders it personally unpleasant or socially objectionable — can be represented differently or eliminated from the dischargeable representation. Here Freud (a psychophysicist accepting the law of the conservation of energy) thought he also had to say that the 'original' content, now revised in the new representation of the wish, must be resituated somewhere in the mind. Conversely, a wish — however likely that it could be discharged readily — can always be partly delayed or reserved, for again, as a representation it can be revised to render its passage toward discharge more difficult. For example, because of a similarity that the dischargeable wish-representation bears to one which has already been delayed, it can be held back by an inertial drag.

These relations become indefinitely complex. A wish that has been revised on the basis of similarity with a delayed wish, rendering it more difficult to discharge, can always be *re*-revised — disentangling itself from inertial drag — on the basis of similarity to a readily dischargeable wish. And the wish that has been re-revised — escaping a 'repression', to use Freud's term for indefinite and permanent delays, to achieve 'sublimation', a dischargeable rerouting of the repressed — could always become the revision of a repression of yet another wish; all human wishes are likely to be represented in partly repressed, partly sublimated, and partly unmodified form. Freud conceived this 'total', but mentally distributed, representation to be largely 'unconscious': the wisher has no self-awareness of the wish to discharge the wish, or to delay it, and becomes aware of the representation of the wish itself only in its unrepressed — sublimated or discharging — forms. One might say, then, that we are only aware of our wishes when they are at least partly being fulfilled.

Moreover, the entire structure of human wishing must be relative to universal and to changing natural and social constraints. These set a criterion of probability, as it were, for each 'quantity' of wish — the 'Qn' in Freud's *Project for a Scientific Psychology*. In Freud's model, the wish for incest has a probability of close to zero, even though the psychic strength or potency of this wish must be high just because one's first sexual experiences are likely to be 'incestuous' ones. Other wishes, most notably 'homosexual' ones, supposedly approach this condition of maximum 'Qn' with minimum discharge: to use Freud's language in the *Project*, they have an 'unpleasant quality'.[3] Freud's sense of what confers a particular value of 'quality' — pleasant or unpleasant — on the 'quantity' of a wish reflects his evolutionary beliefs. Unrestrained incestuous and homosexual behaviour would lead, he thought, to the extinction of a species — an argument attuned to the facts of natural (but not necessarily of artificial) selection and thus of biological (but not necessarily of cultural) development. Later he saw the representation of the wish and the representation of its prohibition — a wish for the delay of another wish — as contending but equally unconscious dimensions of the human psyche. On this view, any representation of a wish must be seen as an attempt to revise, resist, or refute the representational possibilities at its polar opposite. This account has seemed to be a useful metaphor for the agonistic nature of social life or cultural production and for the tendency of representational styles to differentiate themselves. At a more profound level, it has seemed to acknowledge that no one's representations seem to him or her to be completely self-sufficient: our representation is always revision.[4]

Traditional rhetorical criticism allows us to use familiar terms — those of Aristotle, Quintilian and the grammarians — to describe the species of connection and contact between representations that supposedly account for their dischargeability or the need to delay or reserve them. When the representation of a wish, for example, is similar, as a whole image, to a part of a representation of a second, less easily dischargeable wish, it may increase the possibility that some proportion of the repression can be discharged through the 'metonymic' gateway. Forbidden wishes flow through representations that are similar to at least part of their content. At the same time, however, considering the 'metaphoric' potential in the same relation (the part evokes even as it replaces the whole), the presence of forbidden wishes may increase the possibility that some proportion of a dischargeable wish will be *prevented* from discharge. Forbidden wishes weigh down representations to which they are similar.

Many of the material assumptions embedded in Freud's model of psychic history are debatable. For example, human beings must be endowed at birth with a constant quantity of 'psychic energy', the 'Qn' of the *Project*, that must be totally conserved until discharge (that is, until transfer, through work, to another energy-conserving system). Using the famous metaphor of the 'mystic writing pad', Freud urged that all of the contents of undischarged wishing remain present somewhere in the mind despite ongoing revision.[5] In addition to depending on the nineteenth-century electromagnetic science, the model reflects nineteenth-century technologies of writing. When I delete a phrase in a text generated by my word processor, I am not preserving it in the Freudian sense; the text is just gone. And 'discharge', here, is occurring not only when I print out my text — the equivalent of Freudian discharge as motor action — but also throughout the process of writing as I eliminate material rather than delay or permanently reserve it. Whereas the 'mystic writing pad' has an 'unconscious', the word processor does not — at least not in the sense Freud imagined. To accommodate this technology of writing to the Freudian model, we would have to reconfigure Freud's conception of the initial point in a psychic process. The 'word processor'-psyche is not endowed with a *constant* 'Qn', despite the fact that a switch must be thrown; it draws irregularly on a fluctuating energy source. But if 'Qn' is not fixed from the beginning, it is not clear how to identify its supposed discharge, delay, or reserve — for making these distinctions depends on tracking a single value in its arithmetic fragmentation and reduction.

The Freudian model, then, runs into trouble when we track psychic processes in the 'forward' direction, from birth, the original configurations of egoistic, sexual and aggressive wishes moving toward discharge, and their 'primal' revisions in inaugural intersubjective 'scenes' of delay and reserve. But oddly enough, when tracking the same processes in *reverse* — starting from the *latest* configurations of apparent discharge, delay and reserve — the Freudian model seems to explicate actual patterns of revision in a subject's representations that we can identify historically.

There are several ways to handle this disjunction. Frequently psychoanalysis is said to fail as a science (for it does not produce teleological predictions) but to succeed as a hermeneutics (for it might offer retrospective means of understanding what has occurred). Some historians, including Freud himself, do try to track backward until the impossibility of any principled measurement of discharge, delay and reserve is encountered. At this point, multiple origins for the retrospectively observed psychic system — and the undecidability of selection among them — can be acknowledged.[6] Other historians, such as Michael Fried in his reconstructions of metaphoric and metonymic transfer in pictorial work, refrain from going back any distance in a subject's personal and social history. After all, psychic history is supposedly displayed all at once in the plane of representation, the topmost transparent page of the 'mystic writing pad'. In characterizing it, we need not invoke psychobiographical or social-historical speculations about its archaeology.[7]

Discontented with such principled 'formalist' refusal to speculate about the cause of representational revisions, other historians suppose that if the topmost plane of representation has been characterized subtly enough, then certain psychobiographical and social-historical explanations will be compelling. In fact, we might supplement the retrospective historical *understandings* of formalism with deterministic historical *explanations*; we can proceed in the 'forward' direction *from* causes suspected in advance on the basis of predictions about the necessary history of consciousness *toward* the constitution of the topmost plane of representation.[8] In this way we might describe the environment in which at least the topmost *few* planes of representation in the 'mystic writing pad' were built up.

This interaction between hermeneutic and historicist inquiry takes many forms. Most simply put, psychoanalytic interpretation enables us to identify the history of the discharge and delay of wishes; historicist interpretation enables us to explain why certain discharges or delays were more or less probable. To use the vocabulary of Freud's *Project* yet again, hermeneutic inquiry attends to the 'quality' and historicist inquiry to the 'quantity' of wishes. As these terms suggest, the two inquiries are inseparable: all wish-quantities — for example, of homosexual yearning, phobic obsession, or fetishistic denial — have specific qualities for the wisher, and all wish-qualities — for example, of excitement, anxiety, or disinterest — have some specific quantity. Most important, the values of quantity and quality evolve in reciprocal relation. For example, if the quantity of homosexual yearning that it is possible for the wisher to represent increases over time, its quality may shift from relatively unpleasant to relatively pleasant. The very fact that the quality is pleasant — readily dischargeable — may enable wishes that are still forbidden to flow through the new channel, establishing, in turn, a new quality requiring further mechanisms of discharge and delay. Freud coined the term *Nachträglichkeit* or 'delayed activation', to describe such historical structures of necessary reciprocal interaction between the quantities and qualities of wishes in psychic development.[9] He meant to emphasize that the latest value of a wish, as a representation in the topmost plane of representation, is the latest revision of its changing quantity and quality for the wisher; but the latest revision necessarily activates quantities and qualities that already exist both in the wisher's psyche and in his or her social environment: for example, if it becomes more possible to discharge homosexual yearning, it may be, for some wishers, that *other* wishes — perhaps masochistic or fetishistic — will flow through the metonymic and metaphoric gateways: the latest revision of the homosexual wish activates, after delay, the earlier or neighbouring wishes.

Stated in general terms, the latest quantity and quality of a wish always ties back to values established for wishes of which it is, in one respect or another, the metonymic or metaphorical revision. Despite the cliché that the Freudian psyche is radically fissured, discontinuous, or divided from itself, in fact — and this will be my main point of departure for an art-historical argument — *the Freudian psyche is radically continuous*: there is no possibility, in the Freudian psyche, that its own history is not its future meaning. Identifying the structures of *Nachträglichkeit* — which requires both hermeneutic and historicist inquiry — becomes, then, the essential project of any history of representation. No special procedures are needed beyond accepted methods of hermeneutic and historical analysis. In the example that follows, I will not justify such methods in themselves. In an attempt to describe an historical structure of *Nachträglichkeit*, my interest is in their necessary relation.

In the winter of 1882–83 Walt Whitman's *Specimen Days and Collect* was published in Philadelphia. It contained his new work, *Specimen Days*, a series of diary-like ruminations dating from the mid-1860s to the summer of 1882, and earlier texts, including his famous essay 'Democratic Vistas', first published in 1871.[10] We do not know if Thomas Eakins, Professor of Painting and Drawing at the Pennsylvania Academy of the Fine Arts, and, at thirty-nine years old, a well-known (if only modestly well-off) personality in the city, read the book in the first months of 1883. But he must have known a good deal about Whitman. The local papers had been reporting on the neighbouring poet's affairs (he lived right across the Delaware River in Camden, New Jersey) since the mid-1870s.[11] In 1882 Philadephia itself witnessed a movement to suppress the latest edition of Whitman's *Leaves of Grass*, paralleling a more notorious effort in Massachusetts. The debate was a good index of one's cultural sympathies. One was either for the Whitmanites, on the side of 'democracy', or for the anti-Whitmanites, on the side of 'decency'. Eakins did not personally meet Whitman until 1887,[12] but he probably felt a kinship with the poet when, in 1886, he resigned his position at the Academy in a controversy about teaching female students from the naked male model. Both men chose to wear common, rough clothing, out of place in the circles in which they sometimes moved; both were devoted to vigorous athletics; both loved the landscapes of New York, New Jersey and Pennsylvania, setting many scenes in locales they knew intimately. And both greatly enjoyed swimming at the shore or in local streams and ponds completely naked — a fact they cheerfully publicized.

In 'Democratic Vistas' Whitman had made an argument that could not fail to appeal to Eakins — not so much because of a shared political perspective (the painter's political views remain mysterious) but because Whitman's ideas applied to Eakins's profession as an artist, especially considering his uncertain financial success and precarious public acceptance. Despite tremendous progress in commerce and industry, the American states, Whitman asserted, still required an art that would exemplify — and in its very circulation help to promote — the ideals of American constitutional democracy and its theory of liberty. Only a cultural realization of 'man's free play of special Personalism' could assure the future growth of democracy, for only art gives the individual a coherent image of the ideal possibilities toward which he can struggle in the democratic process

— a process that will fail if not animated by each man's appreciation of his necessary fellowship with others in a free society. British critics doubted that America could rise above the confusion and ignorance of its voters. But Whitman urged that art would lift society by its bootstraps toward its own latent, inner ideal. He looked ahead a hundred years for the final appearance of an art 'for [the] general use of the manliness of the States'. Yet in 1871 he claimed to see its vague stirrings already, not least in his own work; he could sketch its 'basic model', the 'portrait of personality' it imagined. 'To our model,' he said,

> a clear-blooded, strong-fibred physique is indispensable: the questions of food, drink, air, exercise, assimilation can never be intermitted. Out of these we descry a well-begotten selfhood — in youth, fresh, ardent, emotional, aspiring, full of adventure; at maturity, brave, perceptive, under control, neither too talkative nor too reticent, neither flippant nor sombre; of the bodily figure, the movements easy, the complexion showing the best blood, somewhat flush'd, breast expanded, an erect attitude . . . [and] a general presence that holds its own . . . . Much is said, among artists, of the 'grand style', as if it were a thing by itself. When a man has health, pride, acuteness, noble aspirations, he has the motive-elements of the grandest style. The rest is but manipulation, (yet that is no small matter).[13]

For the moment, we will leave aside the question of 'manipulation', parenthetically noted to be 'no small matter'. In 'Democratic Vistas', Whitman gave no concrete example of 'grand' native style apart from his obvious *self*-description. But in the 1882 edition of *Specimen Days*, which included the 1871 essay, this gap was partly filled.

In April 1881, Whitman writes, he had visited Boston, where in Quincy Shaw's collection he saw Millet's masterpiece *The Sower*. Astounded by its 'sublime murkiness and original pent-up fury', he felt it displayed 'that last impalpable ethic purpose' he was seeking, telling the 'full story of what went before and necessitated the great French Revolution'. 'Will America', he wondered, 'ever have such an artist out of her own gestation?'[14] Back in New York that summer, he went to see *Custer's Last Rally* (plate 1), John Mulvany's recent painting produced 'on the spot, at the forts, and among the frontiersmen, soldiers and Indians'. He was favourably impressed. 'Altogether a western, autochthonic phase of America; a great lot of muscular, tan-faced men, brought to bay under terrible circumstances — death ahold of them. With all its colour and fierce action, a certain Greek continence pervades it; it has an ethic purpose below all.'[15]

Yet he was not wholly convinced. In the end the painting is just an example of American know-how — not quite the dream of 'Democratic Vistas' realized ninety years early. Indeed, the force of *Custer's Last Rally* appears to derive for Whitman partly from the lingering memory *of* Millet and partly from an event he dates to 10 August 1881, the day before he viewed it. He describes a stroll up the Harlem River:

1 Unknown artist, copy of John Mulvany, *Custer's Last Rally* (*c.* 1880, now destroyed), *c.* 1885?, oil on canvas, (unframed). Photo: courtesy of the Memphis Pink Palace, Memphis, Tennessee.

> [A]s I ramble by the more secluded parts or sit under an old cedar half way up the hill, many young parties gather to bathe or swim, squads of boys, generally twos or threes, some larger ones, along the sand-bottom, or off an old pier close by. A peculiar and pretty carnival — at its height a hundred lads or young men, very democratic, but all decent behaving. The laughter, voices, calls, responses — the springing and diving of the bathers from the great string-piece of the decay'd pier, where climb or stand long ranks of them, naked, rose-color'd, with movements, postures, ahead of any sculpture. To all this, the sun, so bright, the dark-green shadow of the hills the other side, the amber-rolling waves, changing as the tide comes into a transparent tea-color — the frequent splash of the playful boys, sousing — the glittering drops sparkling, and the good western breeze blowing.[16]

This scene, the 'good western breeze blowing', is like 'a western, autochthonic phase of America', like Custer's last rally — although Mulvany's 'muscular, tan-faced' men represent the end-point or extremity of the democracy among the 'naked, rose-color'd' boys. The poet sees the naked boys' fellowship as 'very democratic, but all decent behaving'; and this personality must be carried into the men's struggles on the frontier to establish Mulvany's 'ethic purpose below all', the meaning of his image as a rival of Millet's. As 'Democratic Vistas' put it, in a hundred years 'intense and loving comradeship, the personal and passionate attachment of man to man . . . which seems to promise the most substantial hope and safety of the future of these States, will be then fully express'd.' And in the famous footnote:

> It is to the development, identification, and general prevalence of that fervid comradeship (the adhesive love, at least rivalling the amative love hitherto possessing imaginative literature, if not going beyond it) that I look for the counterbalance and offset of our materialistic and vulgar American democracy, and for the spiritualization thereof. Many will say it is a dream, and will not follow my inferences: but I confidently expect a time when there will be seen, running like a half-hid warp through all the myriad audible and visible worldly interests of America, threads of manly friendship, fond and loving, pure and sweet, strong and life-long, carried to degrees hitherto unknown — not only giving tone to individual character, and making it unprecedently emotional, muscular, heroic and refined, but having the deepest relations to general politics.[17]

The quandary, of course, is that 'loving comradeship', by the poet's own terms, is to be the *product* of an American culture of the *future*. The swimming boys possess it naturally; Custer's soldiers possess it to the degree that they absorb and apply it; Mulvany's canvas is ethical because he presumes it for the legibility of the image itself. But a step is missing. The comradeship of the boys has to be 'carried to degrees hitherto unknown' for the soldiers to have acquired it as the cultural ideal that justifies their life and death, and any further image of them — but how is its *first* image to be created if what the boys do at present, is 'ahead', or in advance of, 'any sculpture'? The boys must learn through an image art makes of them that it is their own natural democracy and decency, their loving comradeship, that sustains the national order itself. But what artist will make the first 'sculpture'? On what grounds does he see in the boys what they themselves do not yet *see* but just *are*? In 1882 Whitman struggles with the profound *gap* between the naked boys swimming in the river and Custer's men falling on the frontier — as it were still awaiting the artist who will envision such 'portraits of personality' as the necessary images of and for one another.

Eakins, we might say, takes up the challenge. Irrespective of his actual experience of Whitman's thought, some of his most challenging work in the 1880s struggles to produce the essential mediating image that Whitman has implicitly imagined. We need not examine what might be seen as the historically inevitable nature of this struggle — especially for academically educated and professionalized

American artists between Lincoln and Teddy Roosevelt — and its sources and other expressions. Our interest is the structure of wish and revision in a few of Eakins's pictorial projects; the broad problem of the nature of an 'American' art — often seen by historians as the manifest content of American art's wish for a kind of America — would tell us little about Eakins's delayed activation of the terms. The striking formal similarity between the images with which both Whitman and Eakins envision the question and relay an answer suggests that Eakins partly replicated Whitman's sense of the problem. But the activations it sustained in him — particularly the status of their possible 'homosexuality' — were quite distinct from Whitman's. In the end Eakins was defeated by the contradiction, broadly true of Philadelphia or East Coast gentry society in the 1880s, between what is 'democratic', in the sense Whitman intended, and what is 'decent', at the mundane level on which poetic or pictorial images circulated. Whether he allowed himself to be defeated — whether he defended the contradiction which Whitman, shamelessly conjoining the 'fervid comradeship' of democracy and its supposed 'decency', poetically asserts he has surmounted — cannot be prejudged. If his art is essentially paranoid, as Michael Fried has urged,[18] we might expect it to disguise wishes that Whitman, the greater exhibitionist, more openly purveyed: whereas Whitman exhibits his desirability for others, Eakins might fear it, repudiating in turn (if we accept one Freudian interpretation), through projection, his own desire for others.[19] Whitman's and Eakins's 'homosexualities' — despite their socially unconventional, even socially proscribed *quantity* — have quite diverging *qualities*. Still, we can proceed from the hypothesis that the quality of the quantity of homosexuality in Whitman — the possibility that a truly substantial role for American art could be rooted in it — activated its complementary qualities in Eakins.

Perhaps made as early as 1883, two oil studies on the two sides of the same panel show the direction of his most literal-minded response to Whitman.[20] One depicts two naked youths on prancing horses, in the attitude of 'riders' from the Parthenon frieze, attributed in Eakins's day to Phidias, casts of which were in the Academy. The other (plate 2) depicts the same two riders, in the left background, and three foreground figures — 'Phidias' gesturing, a naked youth standing beside him, and another turning to the right. What Eakins visualizes, in fact, is the three standing figures in the middle of a riding *circle* with the horsemen moving around its perimeter. The viewer is situated as one of the riders, on our side of Phidias, looking across the circular ground at the other riders. In other words, Eakins both narrates and pictorially tries to construct the relations between art and society in Periclean democracy: the artist attends to the handsome boys (among whom the viewer implicitly has a place) in preparation for making their images (a half-finished temple can be vaguely seen on the horizon at right), and in turn they will accept such images as their own ideal — for the two youths beside Phidias are not his assistants but riders preparing to mount up in imitation of the ones Phidias indicates. Thus the natural democracy among the youths becomes — in the patently circular, self-fulfilling process Whitman imagined — the culture that sustains the state. 'The rest is but manipulation,' Whitman asserted. But in that lies the difficulty.

In Eakins's visualization, the sculptor's 'manipulation' is evident. Although

2 Thomas Eakins, oil study for a painting of 'Phidias' in a riding circle with four riders (two mounted, two unmounted) (*Phidias Studying for the Frieze of the Parthenon*), *c.* 1883–90, oil on fiberboard, present whereabouts unknown, reprinted from Lloyd Goodrich, *Thomas Eakins*, 2nd ed., Cambridge, Mass., 1982, vol. 1, p. 237, courtesy: Harvard University Press.

his gesture is ambiguous, either he commands the riders or he instructs the others, or both; in any case, he partly *creates* the very character that his image of the youths is supposed merely to recognize and return to them. But the political fantasy collapses if the 'special Personalism' of the youths is not present in them naturally — if it is imposed by authority. There is, moreover, the matter of Phidias's interest in the nakedness of the youths (on the frieze they are draped). In *Specimen Days*, Whitman is tactfully seated 'halfway up the hill', but Phidias/Eakins is in their midst, standing beside an almost ridiculously phallic stake marking the centre of the riding circle — a detail Eakins tried to over paint. Anyone who knew Phidias's biography knew that his 'decency' and 'democracy' were dubious.[21] 'Greek continence' did not readily emerge; the thematic difficulties were such — in order not to prejudge the case, I will not claim that the *Nachträglichkeit* was so troubling — that Eakins never completed a Phidias painting, although he hoped to do so.[22]

In the spring of 1883, however, another chance arose. Eakins's small but monumentally realized painting *The Swimming Hole* (to use the familiar title for what he may have labelled *Swimming*, the title under which it was first exhibited), usually dated to 1883–85, depicts six naked youths and men sunning themselves on a pier and swimming in a pond overhung by leafy branches (plate 3). Celebrated as 'the finest of Eakins's outdoor paintings',[23] modern critics have praised the solid fleshliness of the naked men, the subtle gradation of tone on the right side of the canvas, and the minute, almost finicky treatment of the sun's reflections on the ripples of the pond. The composition supposedly establishes what has been seen as the painting's 'complete unity'.[24] It creates an overall pyramid with its apex in the figure of the standing youth, whose vertical axis bisects the canvas, and locks one figure to the next: the reclining figure near the beginning of the pier to the seated man throwing something for the swimming dog, Eakins's setter Harry; to the standing youth at the end of the pier; to the diver plunging into the water; to the swimmer at the far right, Eakins himself; to his dog, paddling toward the shore; and back to the pier, where a wading boy closes the compositional triangle. In spite of this strong geometry, the scene appears strikingly natural, a result of Eakins's attention to the play of light, convincing shadow, and the minutiae of surfaces. For most viewers, the most notable weakness of the painting — the diving figure seems awkward, too thin, and foreshortened oddly — does not detract from the seeming 'unity' and 'realism' of the whole, favourite terms in modern Eakins studies.

But unity and realism are the last words that should be applied to it. It is, instead, an extraordinarily divided work based, it seems, on a series of fantasies and countering these, artificial views — naturalistic in procedure but certainly not 'realist' in origin — constructed to paper over its several fissures. It is easy enough to identify these. Formal evidence, such as the peculiar construction of the most active figure, and extrinsic facts — such as the painting's eventual failure to be accepted by its patron or, later, to be widely exhibited — suggest that Eakins and his first viewers immediately sensed its fissures. But in keeping with our emphasis on *Nachträglichkeit* as the *continuity* of eroticized revision in relation to earlier wishes, the issue is the specific *temporality* of the painter's self-revision. How did these fissures emerge in the process of conceiving and making the image? Only by establishing this sequence can we determine whether what seems to be a fundamental pictorial conception — for example, the strong pyramidal geometry of the composition — was subjected to later revision, implying that it carried troublesome meanings requiring such revision in order to be discharged, or, conversely, was itself a later revision of a troublesome meaning that had been partly suppressed (or both).

The painting was commissioned in 1883 by Edward Coates, head of a prominent Philadelphia family and on the board of the Academy.[25] Like Eakins on his mother's side, he had Pennsylvania Quaker roots, especially in the 'Welsh Barony', the settlements built up — or invented — as Philadelphia's 'Main Line' by the Pennsylvania Railroad in the 1870s and '80s. Whether Coates suggested the subject of the painting or whether Eakins did (possibly on the basis of studies he had already been doing in 1883), Coates surely knew the site of the 'swimming hole' (depicted as a fairly large pond) and perhaps had even swum there as a youth — as Eakins apparently did in the 1880s. It was very likely near Bryn Mawr, where in Lower Merion Township of Montgomery County several fine ponds could be found on Trout Run, half a mile from Haverford College (where Coates had gone to college), and on Mill Creek (running down to the Schuylkill

3 Thomas Eakins *The Swimming Hole* (*Swimming*), *c.* 1883–85, oil on canvas, 69.37 × 92.23 cm. Amon Carter Museum, Fort Worth, Texas (1990.19.1). Photo: courtesy of the Amon Carter Museum

River), a bit more than a mile from Bryn Mawr Station.[26] The ponds were set in gently rolling, wooded hills, with a few farms scattered round (a farm building can be seen in one of the photographs connected with the painting [plate 5h]); Lower Merion was locally known for its 'number of beautiful streams'.[27] But in the same breath as observers — county fathers and railroad and property developers — extolled its natural charms, they remarked on its 'valuable improvements'.[28] By the early 1880s, the township was grading roads, expanding mills and, by 1884, seeing the first big granite buildings of Bryn Mawr College itself. On the railroad, the new station at Bryn Mawr 'might well be cited as a model of taste and beauty', as railroad public relations had it; 'beautiful and comfortable station houses were built, followed by a superb hotel.'[29]

The rapid suburbanization of west Philadelphia and the Main Line created their own enclaves of reserve — chiefly Fairmount Park in the city itself, proudly shown off at its Centennial Exhibition in 1876. Here the city fathers hoped to preserve, or to recreate, the natural condition of the watershed of the Schuylkill, like 'Devil's Hole', a deep pond on Cresheim Creek draining into the Wissahickon, 'a spot frequented first by the superstitious in the early days, and now by artists and all lovers of nature',[30] and, during the Revolutionary War, stained by blood in the Battle of Germantown. Although its more specific personal associations and contemporary social uses remain to be explored, Coates's and Eakins's swimming hole was another such place, at least for the boys and men who went there even after the new station opened and the county's creeks and ponds were being dammed and drained.[31] As the poet of the Wissahickon hills, Cornelius Weygandt, put it, there one 'could hear again the cattle of the Quaker farmers coming home at evening',[32] memorialized in John Greenleaf Whittier's famous *Pennsylvania Pilgrim* of 1872. Whittier expressed the sentiment — the local pride, quiet religiosity, civic-mindedness — that Coates may have brought to his memories of the swimming hole and presumably expected from Eakins's painting of it:

> Was it caressing air, the brooding love
> Of tenderer skies than German land knew of,
> Green calm below, blue quietness above,
> Still flow of water, deep repose of wood
> That, with a sense of loving Fatherhood
> And childlike trust in the Eternal Good,
> Softened all hearts, and dulled the edge of hate
> Hushed strife, and taught impatient zeal to wait
> The slow assurance of the better state?
> . . . Be it as it may: within the land of Penn
> The sectary yielded to the citizen,
> And peaceful dwelt the many-creeded men.[33]

Of course, the 'still flow of water, deep repose of wood' may never have actually existed for either patron or painter. But both, in the mid-1880s, could take the image of such a place as the nostalgic horizon — the rural, racial and religious point of reference — for cultivated, urban Quaker gentry. It expressed the continuity of a family's local history, at least in Coates's case; ambivalence about the rush to suburbia; idealization of a supposed preservation of the land, retaining the owner's rights to move through it; respect for one's social bonds; and a wish to memorialize dutiful manhood, whether building a railroad or a park, in the terms that city men took seriously. *The Swimming Hole* was at least partly an image of a place where remembered, imagined and claimed masculine innocence — about nature, property, industry, companionship, change — could be reconstructed and reflected back to a man as a picture of what, supposedly, he really wants. And indeed, what *does* a man want?

If Eakins's larger project lay midway between Whittier and Whitman, his vehicle in the painting — a concentrated image of the naked male body — lay midway between academic classicism, referring itself to Greek sculpture, and a more recent American visualization of male physical 'self culture'.[34] Many Philadelphian men of Eakins's generation were hearing how badly off they were — an alarm sounded by one of the city's best-known citizens, the emigrant Scottish physician Silas Weir Mitchell. In *Wear and Tear, or Hints for the Overworked*, Mitchell bemoaned the debilitation of American manliness caused by the demands of city and commercial life. 'The worst instances to be met with', he declared, 'are among young men suddenly cast into business positions involving weighty responsibility, stricken down in the moment of triumph.'[35] For wealthier patients, Mitchell advised a long trip out West. But ordinary clerks and managers would have to make do with a brief 'constitutional' (later organized as a form of bodily self-culture by Bernarr Macfadden and other leaders of the movement).[36] The city, urged Mitchell's epigones, was dirty and hot, its homes stuffy and cramped. 'The great mass of our people shut out the sunshine,' wrote one proponent of self-culture, 'while the vagabond newsboys, half-clothed and half-fed, but moving about in the open air all day, are comparatively well.'[37] Such observers saw that American boys and men — even the middle-class youths the physical-culture movement addressed — were far from being the lithe and sleek, or strong and manly, creatures imagined by poets and painters. Whitman's epiphany on the Harlem River would have mystified William Blaikie, a leader of the physical culture movement from the 1870s through the '90s; 'not one American boy in five is well built,' he complained in 1879.

> Go down to the public bath-house; and look at a hundred or two of them as they tumble about in the water. He will see more big heads and slim necks; more poor legs, skinny arms, and lanky, half-built bodies than he would have thought the town could produce. . . . Strip adults, and the stream of walking skeletons or clumsy fat objects would disgust you.[38]

Throughout the north-eastern United States, social response to these alarms, medical, economic and moral, was forceful, conjoining nostalgia for the generation of young men lost in the war, anxiety provoked by the new Darwinian picture of managerial occupations in market capitalism, hysteria whipped up by hucksters for medical, travel and sports products, and more rational responses to tuberculosis. City baths were improved; the Y.M.C.A. was formed; at

Harvard's new Hemenway Gymnasium, and at Yale, Amherst and elsewhere, college athletic courses were created. Recalling the injunctions of Benjamin Franklin, who had insisted in 1749 that youths at his Institute 'be frequently exercised in Running, Leaping, Wrestling, and Swimming',[39] the University of Pennsylvania opened a new Department of Physical Culture in May 1883, the same spring or early summer in which Eakins apparently began work on his picture.[40] Many of the earliest physical directors in municipal or college athletics were brought over from exhibition careers as gymnasts and weight trainers. They hoped to transform what they called 'weaklings' into 'well-built' young men: they cajoled and exhorted, held up poor bodies to ridicule, made impossible claims, and played on every boy's desire — as they believed — to be better than his fellows. 'I was born a weakling,' declared Edwin Checkley, an early bar-bell enthusiast.

> Nobody thought I was really worth rearing. Today I can lift three men, each weighing one hundred and fifty pounds and trot with them for a hundred yards. If you are what you are, it is scarcely an exaggeration to say that you can become what you wish to be.[41]

Enabling boys to 'become what they wish to be', the physical directors' image of a manly physique was a very specific one. They disliked the distorted bodies produced by manual labour, developing ways for young men aspiring to managerial positions to construct their bodies differently. Many of them even saw no virtue in established sports like rowing, which Eakins had been painting in the 1870s. (That Eakins's rowing imagery — not despite but because of its many personal and local connotations — relayed homoerotic wishes is obvious enough, but it is not my topic here: in the *Nachträglichkeit* of Eakins's erotic revision, the eroticism of the rowers, their beauty and desirability, was under a general cultural assault in the early 1880s — and the *revised* homoeroticism that emerges in Eakins's visualizations of the mid-1880s should not be conflated with it. By the same token, the eroticism of the still later boxer and wrestler images further revise the revision.) Indeed, the physical directors liked to compare the oarsmen's chests and arms, the so-called 'greyhound look', to the new ideal — the torso of a Greek sculpture or a weightlifter's hefty frame, created on new machines devised to pack and puff a youth's 'lanky' or 'stringy' physique (hitherto associated with the spareness of heroes like Lincoln) with new muscles. Publishing pictures of famous rowers, Blaikie noted the 'flat, slabsided, almost hollow, look about the upper chest and front shoulder, and the small upper arms'. Men should just 'compare these', he urged, 'with the full and well-rounded make' of the man he depicted (plate 4), 'Mr Roberts' (i.e. Robert J. Roberts) of the Y.M.C.A. in Boston; 'a statuette of him in each gymnasium and gallery of art would be eloquent of the best type of physical manhood.'[42]

Blaikie's picture showed Mr Roberts from the back, not the front, emphasizing his rounded, protruding buttocks — a part of the new, physically cultured anatomy that none of the early manuals explicitly considered, subsuming its development under the 'loins', 'sides of the waist' and 'upper thighs'. In 1879, when Blaikie's book appeared, it was inappropriate to put a barely dressed man

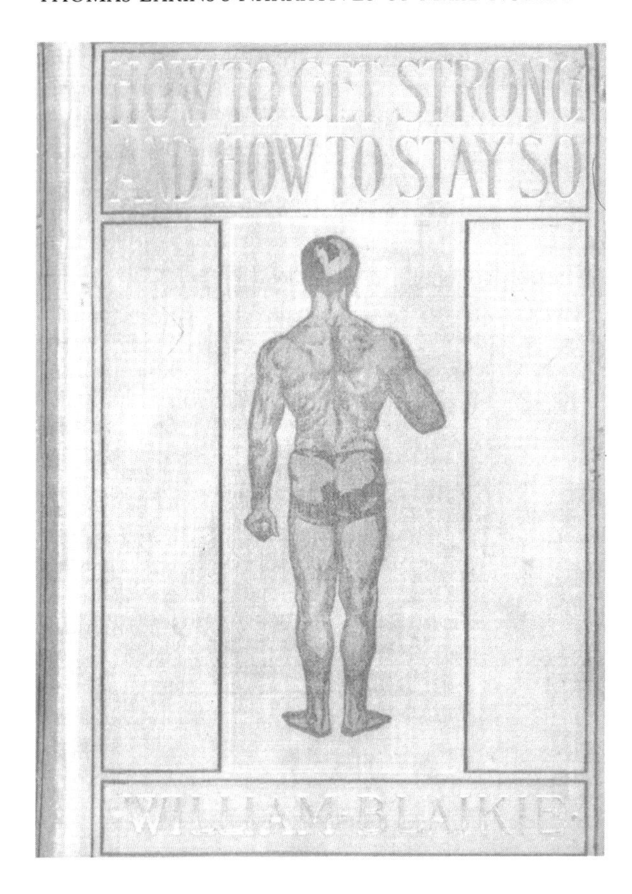

4 'Mr Roberts' (Robert J. Roberts, Physical Director, YMCA, Boston), from William Blaikie, *How to Get Strong and How to Stay So*, New York, 1879.

(covered only at the loins) on the front of a popular book. Even in the 1890s Comstock's Society for the Suppression of Vice, in New York, confiscated photo posters of Eugen Sandow, William Muldoon, Bernarr Macfadden and other physical-culture stars.

In the same vein, Blaikie's imitator Richard Proctor unfavourably compared an eminent oarsman with the 'wonderful diversity of chest development' visible in the Parthenon sculptures. As he went on, 'a man seen in the bathroom [i.e. the bathhouse] with such muscles as the Greeks show at either side of the waist' — his way of designating a well-developed rear end — 'would be at once recognized as a professional athlete.'[43] Needless to say, however, among a 'hundred or two' youths 'tumbling about in the water', this 'professional athlete', in order to make his physique visible, would have to *make* himself visible — for what other reason do men have to look at him but the fact that he makes it impossible for them not to notice his special new body? Unlike the labourer seen resting on his shovel, or the oarsman resting in his scull, or even the swimmer tumbling about, the physically cultured man must *pose*, sculpting himself in and for the vision of others. His attraction of a look — carving out a stable place in visibility for his body to be seen — is his confirmation that he is ideal.

Several men at Eakins's swimming hole have countered the 'wear and tear' Mitchell identified. At a place evoking ideal boyhood associations in stressful new times, they rest in fresh air and sunshine. The broad shoulders and chest of the reclining figure, the muscled arms of the thrower, and the well-developed buttocks of the standing figure show that they are physically cultured men, at least in part.[44] As Eakins's palpable references to sculpture suggest, they are not only resting but *also* posing — even though none of them, with a single exception, is looking at any other. But in the *Nachträglichkeit* of erotic revision — Eakins reproduces the newly established image of a physically cultured man in terms of established desires he brings to that image — the artist pushes further than the visibilities physical-culture posing had clarified and heightened, if not introduced, in American erotics. In his revision of the image, Eakins approaches the point of immodesty and sexualization. He and Coates almost certainly adopted the theme of naked young men for its many local connotations — not for its connection with homoerotic physique photography of the 1890s, still to be established on the very basis of Eakins's and similar visualizations; the painting is closer to Blaikie's cover drawing of 'Mr Roberts' in 1879 than to Checkley's frontispiece in 1890, among the first images to picture a solemn weightlifter frontally, skimpily clad, making the quasi-masturbatory gesture that became *de rigueur* in a thriving visual genre.[45] Physical-culture images fell on the contemporary line, in other words, between decency and indecency. Although they depicted nakedness with a pretence of neutrality — offering information, like a medical drawing — this nakedness was itself seen to be created only *for* looking. But male nudity had to be constructed as innocent, a conventional Adamic nakedness that a viewer *happens* to see rather than the new nakedness oriented toward the viewer *in order* for him to see it.

As I will try to show, it was this sight that Eakins *already* desired, the wish he brought to the physical-culture images already responding to it. But it was also precisely the sight that contemporary society prohibited whenever its masturbatory homoerotic connotation — its 'homo*sexuality*' — was dramatized. In Eakins's painting, then, the physical-culture image was drained of its erotic teleology, rerouted in pictorial revision: to the very degree that the naked figure, especially a 'well-built' one, turns toward the viewer to solicit his (or her) look, it had to be turned away again. Yet this condition was at odds with his claim to be a well-built body in the first place — for the claim depended on display, the admiring and envious looking of others, an essential or constitutive *im*modesty. In completing his painting in this culturally conflicted scene of representation, Eakins went much further than Coates expected, delving into the patron's fantasy with (for Coates) shocking realism, and crafting his own 'realism' in the image of a shocking fantasy — so shocking he could not sustain it through pictorial revision. Coates could not accept it even in revised form; he eventually refused the painting.[46]

A good deal of evidence bears on Eakins's production of the painting — many photographs and several oil studies. The chronology and relations of these productions remain to be fully clarified. The sequence I reconstruct is consistent with the available information and resolves certain contradictions in it (for example, in dating the photographic expeditions and in identifying some of the people photographed and painted). One group of ten photographs was almost certainly made in the good weather months of 1883, soon after Eakins received the commission (or perhaps even suggesting the theme *for* the commission when received). Oil studies were made in 1883 or '84 and more, probably, in 1885. A second group of photos was made beginning in July 1884. Eakins worked on the canvas itself from 1884 until at least August 1885 — but he dated the painting '1883', perhaps because that was when the first photos, the basis of the painting, were taken. To the extent that the completed painting of 1885 revises the previous studies of 1883–85, as we will see, the date '1883' might be serving as a revision of the revision — that is, a denial that the painting *is* a revision.[47]

The status of the photos, especially those I just called the 'first' group, has not been clear to date. Three of them show naked youths (and, in one, Eakins) swimming at the site itself. Seven show naked youths in the woods. It has never really been recognized, however, that all the boys in all ten of these 1883 photos are the same — that is, that all ten photos show the same group of boys at the swimming hole and in the woods, which must have been quite near the pond. The photos of 1884–85, however, show *different* youths and men. They were taken during the *second* stage of the painting's production, partly outdoors (probably returning to the site near Bryn Mawr) and partly in the studio at the Academy.

We should begin, then, with the *first* stage of production, in 1883 — the so-called 'naked horseplay' photos.[48] Each of these shows either seven or six 'boys' (that is, young men aged between approximately fourteen and twenty years old, or what would later be called 'adolescents'), apparently students and friends of Eakins. At various points, one of the boys was presumably helping Eakins move the camera — its vantage point shifts several times — and thus he does not appear in the image. With one exception, Eakins was almost certainly the photographer. Indeed, the ten photographs form a coherent narrative, quasi-cinematic *series* — for our purposes here, the most important fact about them — although Eakins scholars have always published them out of order and there is still plenty of room for debate, not essential to my main point, about the details of sequence, entrances and exits, and the significance of gestures and glances. This series seems to depict a specific series of events. As photographer, Eakins, like 'Phidias' in the unachieved painting (plate 2), probably stage-managed the scene, giving directions. But it is possible that he merely took pictures of pre-existing friendships and feelings among the boys disposing them towards one another in predictable ways. Either way, the series is not 'random', a 'raw slice of life', as the photos have been described.[49] It was partly 'scripted' in advance, if only in an implicit mutual understanding — or, more important, what could be seen as such an understanding — among most or all of the participants.[50] The actions of the eight participants, the seven boys and Eakins himself, *can be understood as* the interaction of four 'couples' which establish themselves, divide, and recouple in other permutations, but with an underlying stability to the four pairs represented at the beginning. Each of the four 'couples' can be seen to have a distinctive way of behaving. Such understandings, needless to say, should not be conflated with an identification of what actually occurred or even what the photographs did or do, in 'fact', depict. It is the partly *retrospective* eroticization of the photographs in the historically emergent images derived partly from them — the oil studies and final canvas — that constructed the narrative we can identify, not necessarily 'in' the photographic sequence itself, as a kind of 'primal scene', but in the consciousness of emergent significances the painter retrospectively trains on it. For the moment, then, I begin with the way in which the photographs *can* be understood; my evidence that they *were* so understood is, of course, derived in part from the *later* history of the *Nachträglichkeit* of their replication. That this is a hermeneutic rather than a strictly historicist procedure poses no problem, in itself, for a psychoanalytic 'history' of erotic consciousness.

Considering the relatively smooth unfolding of the depicted action, the actions that would seem to have had to have transpired *between* the surviving photos (such as undressing [from plates 5a to 5b] or shifting locales [from plates 5e to 5f]), and the length of time it would have taken to move and reset the camera, the action photographically depicted in the ten images was probably in part a *re*-enaction or staging — a (re-)performing of actions that would have happened too fast for the photographer to capture them the first time through. In turn, this fact of the 'timing' of a potentially narrative text, the actual series of photos, in relation to a narrative 'fabula', the actual unfolding of events in order, leaves room for possibly missing photos of other stages of the action. But the narrative 'story', the unfolding of events *as* they are presented *in* the photos, is causally quite continuous. The intended photographic 'text' for the historical 'fabula', then, is probably *more or less* complete. As the narratological term 'fabula' suggests, however, fabulation — or fantasy — enters narrative at its supposed point of origin in 'history' itself; it is representation that 'retrospectively', but prospectively as well, produces it. To shorten the exposition, I do not directly consider the ways in which the actions presented in the photos are already revisions of actions carried out earlier. But it is important to stress again that the photos are not mere documents of what actually occurred at the swimming hole, something we will never know. Indeed, as we will see, they apparently *failed* to document — or, more exactly, successfully to represent — what the photographer–painter later took, in ongoing retrospective revision, to be revealing events. Because there is no evidence for these events in anything but their later representation, we may choose to call them constructions of fantasy. But that does not rule out the ways in which they might have been propped on gestures, glances, or other events which did transpire. If I begin my analysis of the sequence of revisions which produced the final painting with the photos — we have to start somewhere — it is only an heuristic device, and misleading. Revision itself has no beginning and no ending, and constructs its meanings in transit.

The events 'begin' in a circular forest clearing, where the camera is set up in the centre but in the next nine 'takes' will both move a few feet from it and point in different directions. Six boys have stripped naked and, divided into two 'teams', play tug-of-war standing and then seated (not illustrated here). In the third 'take' (plate 5a), the two teams fissure into three pairs. 'Albert' and 'Bob', the first couple, begin wrestling while 'Charlie' and 'Dave', the second couple, laughingly make the calls, and 'Edward' and 'Fergus', the third couple, stand by amused. (Rather than labelling them A, B, C, etc., I provide fictitious names

5a ?Thomas Eakins, or unidentified photographer, photograph of Eakins's students in a forest clearing, with two wrestlers (possibly the first in a series of photographic studies of wrestlers for *The Swimming Hole*), *c.* 1883.

5b Thomas Eakins, photograph of Eakins's students in a forest clearing, with six wrestling (possibly second in a series of photographic studies of wrestlers for *The Swimming Hole*), *c.* 1883.

5c Thomas Eakins, photograph of Eakins's students in a forest clearing, with two boxing (possibly first in a series of photographic studies of boxers for *The Swimming Hole*), *c.* 1883.

5d Thomas Eakins, photograph of Eakins's students in a forest clearing, with two boxing (possibly second in a series of photographic studies of boxers for *The Swimming Hole*), *c.* 1883.

Plates 5a–d all 10.16 × 12.7 cm, copy negatives from dry-plate negatives. Pennsylvania Academy of the Fine Arts, Charles Bregler's Thomas Eakins Collection, purchased with the partial support of the Pew Memorial Trust (1985.68.2.1020, 1021, 1025, 1023). Photos: courtesy of the Pennsylvania Academy of the Fine Arts.

5e Thomas Eakins, photograph of Eakins's students in a forest clearing, with two boxing (possibly third in a series of photographic studies of boxers for *The Swimming Hole*), *c.* 1883, after Gordon Hendricks, *The Photographs of Thomas Eakins*, New York, 1972, no. 12 (reversed).

5f Thomas Eakins, photograph of Eakins's students at the site of the swimming hole (possibly first in a series of photographic studies of swimmers for *The Swimming Hole*), *c.* 1883, 8.25 × 9.52 cm.

5g Thomas Eakins, photograph of Eakins's students at the site of the swimming hole (possibly second in a series of photographic studies of swimmers for *The Swimming Hole*), *c.* 1883, 7.78 × 9.84 cm.

5h Unidentified photographer (?'Albert'), photograph of Eakins and his students at the site of the swimming hole (possibly third in a series of photographic studies of swimmers for *The Swimming Hole*), *c.* 1883, 15.4 × 19.84 cm.

Plates 5f–h all albumin prints on paper. Hirshhorn Museum and Sculpture Garden, Smithsonian Institution, transferred from the Hirshhorn Museum and Sculpture Garden Archives, 1983 (photographer: Lee Stalsworth). Photos: courtesy of the Hirshhorn Museum and Sculpture Garden.

for the boys; 'Fergus' was actually Eakins's student Benjamin Fox, but otherwise the boys are unidentified. Although this narrativizing device, of course, promotes an interpretation of the photographs *as* narrative, we should not forget that the boys in the photographs *were* known to Eakins as individual people; a psychoanalytic 'history' must always take care to personalize, whether or not it also narrativizes, events.)

In the fourth 'take' (plate 5b), the camera moves to get a better view of the wrestlers and reveals 'Gordon' at the left. Albert and Bob continue to struggle, almost falling to the ground, and Charlie and Dave throw themselves at each other, Dave thrusting his knee into Charlie's groin. Edward and Fergus jokingly menace one another but do not come together.

In the fifth 'take' (plate 5c), the camera moves back again and a little to the right. Edward and Fergus have sat down on the left, joined by Gordon, now stripped naked. The wrestlers have reoriented their interests. Charlie challenges Albert to a boxing match. Bob sits languorously beside the other observers. Dave, watching intently, sits in front of the boxers on the right.

In the sixth 'take' (plate 5d), the match does not go well for Albert, on the defensive. Bob now sits forward while Dave relaxes. The other boys have moved; Gordon stands up directly behind the boxers. In the seventh 'take' (plate 5e), Albert's defeat is certain. Bob now stretches out on the grass on Charlie's side, where Edward talks with him. Fergus, still in the same position, raises himself on his elbows to watch the end of the bout. Dave has left the scene altogether, not because the camera changed position — it did not — but possibly because his partnership with Charlie is now disturbed by Charlie's defeating Albert for Bob's attention. Dave may be sulking.

In the next, eighth 'take' (plate 5f), the camera has been set up by the swimming hole; again, Eakins's helper Gordon does not initially appear in the scene. (Although it is perfectly possible that Gordon's entrances and exits merely record the fact that he was occasionally occupied outside the scene with entirely unknown affairs, their correlation with the camera movements is too strict to be *seen as* fortuitous; what is outside the depicted scene is not, of course, necessarily outside the 'scene' of representation.) In the foreground, Dave sits by himself absorbed in playing with debris at the bank of the pond. Victorious Charlie stands proudly on the rocks of the pier, watching Albert's partner Bob, who is about to enter the water. In the background, Albert, the loser, stands with hands on hips looking across the pond, taking no notice of the others. Edward and Fergus are paddling in the pond.

In the ninth 'take' (plate 5g), Bob has dived in and now pulls himself back out, joining Edward, still in the water, and Fergus, who has climbed out and sits looking down at Bob. Gordon reappears, standing partway out on the pier. And Dave makes a vigorous reappearance — getting over his sulk, he administers the *coup-de-grâce* on behalf of his mate Charlie, and restores his own status by running from the shore out to the end of the pier and shoving Albert into the pond. Charlie and Bob do not form a pair, after all; instead, Bob makes friendly talk with Edward and Fergus.

In the final, tenth 'take' (plate 5h), Gordon sits down at the far left. Fergus rejoins Edward in the water and the two cling to the side of the pier. Dave crosses from the far to the near side of the pier and tests the water, while Charlie stands beside him and, looking down, laughs at the latest arrival, Eakins himself. Bob, also laughing, helps pull Eakins out of the water. Hapless Albert, tossed by Dave into the water, has swum to the shore and takes the photo. The artist has traded places with Bob's comrade, and Bob welcomes him; Charlie and Dave, athletic masters of the pier, pose and preen before him.

Much more could be said about this sequence. Any verbal description is necessarily tendentious; it will somewhat misjudge the nature and tone of the depicted action and the balance of its motivations. But an overall coherence roughly like the one I have just identified seems clearly to be present. Some plan set up a framework for the boys's actions — for example, someone had to bring boxing gloves (plate 5c) — but it need not have assigned particular roles, gestures, or glances. Nonetheless, the series of photos, once printed, readily depicted the highly personalized social structure of the naked horseplay; perhaps the horseplay was only visible as telling a story about comradeship among the boys once it *had* been printed. The choreography of the boys' play was distinctly erotic in the broad sense: they display specific attachments and attitudes in relation to one another. And it is more narrowly sexual: their eroticism, their 'fervid comradeship', displays a fully visible narration of their intimacies, judgements, rivalries, piques, indifferences, humiliations, triumphs and displays, the whole ballet carried out fully naked and in close physical contact with one another. Threading through the ramified relations, there appears to be a tale of competition and conquest among and between two couples, two pairs of comrades. All the boys are aware of and take part in this minuet. Several boys are aware of the camera and show off for it. For his part, Eakins follows — and constructs — the events partly by keeping a centred focus on the frontal nudity best visible at each point: the maximum visibility of the boys's genitals to the camera is essentially the same thing as the maximum visibility of social relations in their hierarchically organized, erotic and sexual aspect. Or to put the point in terms of *Nachträglichkeit*, reviewing the photographs for the evidence of frontal genital nudity — unacceptable, perhaps, to a potential audience — enables the construction of an erotic or sexualized narrative of the boys' social relations.

Far from being the 'decency' and 'democracy' Whitman saw among the boys swimming in the Harlem River, this boy society, despite its fun, is on the verge of being a *non*-decent, *non*-democratic one — as the first 'boy workers' at the Y.M.C.A., for example, quickly found out, and as G. Stanley Hall, Freud's great predecessor in America, tried to interpret in his huge treatise on *Adolescence*.[51] Equally important, the photos — if the maker was thinking ahead to an audience — become evidence that *from the beginning* Eakins put the boys up to something he already hoped he could see. Reviewing the sequence, 'fervid comradeship' among the boys could seem to have been 'carried to degrees hitherto unknown' as a *result of* Eakins's 'manipulation' — the predictable outcome for Phidias standing in the centre of a circle of boys intending to produce an image of their desirability for their own present and future imitation but also generating an image of their desirability *for him*, for what *he* sees is their aggressive sexuality. Thus the naked horseplay is not only the evidence of the boys' not-so-decent not-quite-democracy — anyone who knew 'adolescent' boys did not need photos to prove this — but also for the *artist*'s lack of decency and democracy in making the photos in the first place. The Whitmanian ideal and Phidian method have backfired. In this Edenic setting and this Adamic condition, everyone's natural innocence — central to both Whitmanian and Whittleresque fantasy — has potentially been lost. Can a painting be rescued from this unwanted result?

In the so-called 'Arcadian' works, made in the same years, Eakins tried: instead of starting from naked, adolescent youths, he went back to earlier childhood to depict an innocent, quasi-Edenic/Adamic and quasi-Hellenic society containing both amativeness and adhesiveness in Whitman's sense.[52] But his models for the 'Arcadian' images are not, in themselves, a wholly convincing image of *culture* (if that is, indeed, the overarching theme) — despite, for example, his metaphor of music as the spiritual glue of the group, a dematerialized, ethereal substitute for the older boys' sexualized games. In fact, the painter's exposure of childhood nakedness raises suspicions of pedophilic prurience somewhat different from, but with the same result as, the potentially homoerotic connotations evoked by the 'naked horseplay' series. In the second stage of work on the *Swimming* picture, in 1884 and '85, Eakins tried to revise what he had seen about the boys' society.

In late August of 1884 Eakins's student Thomas Anshutz told another student and friend, J. Laurie Wallace, that Eakins was 'painting a picture for Mr Coates of a party of boys in swimming'. He was probably referring to Eakins's oil study now in the Hirshhorn Museum (plate 6).[53] Eakins need not have *begun* the Hirshhorn study in August 1884. It could have been started shortly after the first photos were taken, that is, in the spring or summer of 1883. But it is consistent with the revision effected by the study that nearly a full year might have elapsed between the first photographic expedition and Eakins's completion of the study. In any case, it was clearly made *after* the photos: although it absorbs the photos, it does not transcribe them. Instead, it combines, rearranges, and eliminates elements of the earlier series — a selective, synthetic memory of what had transpired at the swimming hole.

The study establishes much of the armature Eakins finally used in the painting (plate 3). Whether he reviewed the photos or not, he decided that Gordon was not on the pier; he eliminated the figure who was the least important to the overall action, as well as the most visible reminder of his own role as photographer. In the study, the swimmer replicates Edward's movements, and, of course, Eakins's, and the youth pulling himself out of the water replicates Fergus's movements and, again, Eakins's; the figures in the water, then, revise the observers in the photos — Edward, Fergus and Eakins. The standing figure partly replicates Charlie, with shoulders back and hands on hips, in the ninth 'take' (plate 5g), adding his almost sculptural *contrapposto* in the tenth 'take' (plate 5h) — one of the most vivid (because pictorially familiar) images from the series. But this figure is tall, well built and brightly lit. His physique is actually less like Charlie's, slender and wiry, than like his mate's: Dave is a broad-shouldered fellow with the best-defined chest and well-muscled thighs and buttocks, the only physically cultured boy in the group. A synthesis of the two leaders among the boys, the standing figure in the Hirshhorn study is the focus of Eakins's interest and obviously the fulcrum of the scene.

6 Thomas Eakins, study for *The Swimming Hole* (*Swimming*), *c.* 1884–85, oil on fiberboard, 22.22 × 27.3 cm. Hirshhorn Museum and Sculpture Garden, Smithsonian Institution, Gift of Joseph H. Hirshhorn, 1966 (66.1510). Photo: courtesy of the Hirshhorn Museum and Sculpture Garden.

Behind the standing figure are two more mysterious figures. One is stretched out full-length on his belly, propping his head in his hand. He seems to be looking up at the standing boy or watching the diver. He has no prototype in the swimming photos — in none was any boy lying on the pier — but replicates Bob watching the end of the boxing match (plate 5e). The leftmost figure is seated in a peculiar position, possibly with one knee up and an arm around it, like observers of the boxing match (plates 5d and 5e). But he seems hunched forward, recalling Dave at the edge of the pond before his sneak attack on Albert (plate 5f). He appears to pass a hand over the upper thighs, just below the buttocks, of the reclining figure. It is possible that Dave had actually done so; in the seventh 'take' (plate 5e), he is out of view, as are Bob's buttocks. In making the oil study, did Eakins remember a gesture he saw out of the corner of his eye? Or does the touch emerge in the study as a retrospective pictorial fantasy? (As it is difficult to decipher unambiguously, it raises the possibility that it is a pictorial slip; if so, it would express a forbidden view rather than reproduce a vague one.) At any rate, neither of these figures extracts a single memory-image from the swimming excursion. Instead they gather up, at the end of the pier in a place that was never really occupied, a complex of more scattered images. The passage as a whole carries a good deal of the erotic narrative of the photographic series — off to one side, of course, but in clear relation to the standing figure, continuing the story of hierarchy and subtle mutual affections, admirations and assaults.

In the initial performance, Bob jumped or dived into the water, watched by Charlie. As the photos revealed, Bob's relations with the other boys are the most complicated, or, more exactly, most open of the group — he is the wrestling comrade of Albert, who boxes with Charlie, who solicits his attention and watches his doings, but he goes his own way, friendly with Edward and Fergus and piquing Dave, who takes him as his rival for Charlie's friendship, or perhaps, if Dave wanted to fight Albert, as the friend Dave really wants. Despite Charlie's preeminence in the hierarchy, his status as the leading character or *subject* in the boys' society, Bob is the leading *object* of desire — the one with whom everyone, including Eakins himself, has some kind of attachment. Although his dive was not actually photographed (it transpires in the ellipsis between plates 5f and 5g), the study takes it as the main event of the excursion — locating it in the centre of the composition.

As one of Eakins's students remembered, the diver was 'the most difficult to paint'.[54] Eakins therefore made a wax model to study the figure. Another student who saw this object noted that Eakins 'put a spindle through the middle of the figure so that it could be turned upside down and hold the pose.'[55] Perhaps the spindle went through the model's navel to its lower back, but this could easily break when turned. More likely, the spindle ran up the model's anus through its head. This way it could be 'turned upside down', and its arms or legs moved around, to construct the form. But making such a model of the diver — the image of the boy's socially and erotically appealing comrade, the object of much of their interest — would put the final retrospective seal on the erotic meaning of the photographs, even as it was revised in the oil study. Indeed, the artist's sodomization of the model replicates the sexual dimension of the images, and the earlier events, at their smuttiest level. In the lurid light of a dirty joke, the standing figure in the Hirshhorn study staring right at the anus and hidden genitals of the diver brings 'fervid comradeship' into a visibility that is merely salacious — reintroducing the troubling question of the artist's own Phidian role as inventor or instigator of this indecency.

Despite its condensations, the Hirshhorn study translated the eroticism of the photos as a retrospective image of what had transpired. In the retrospective light thrown, in turn, by the model, the study became not only a synthesis of the photos but also an image of what the photos had not even seen — gestures and looks that combine meanings inherited from the photos and introduced by the model to become suffused with a significance that is specifically *homosexual*. That last term can be used advisedly. In the early1880s, American doctors were beginning to identify it 'amid the lowest forms of bestiality and sensuousness exhibited by debased men', as an editorial declared in the New York *Medical Record*. But it is probably immaterial whether Eakins had heard of this new concept as such. Pennsylvania had long prohibited sodomy and his student and friend Laurie Wallace engaged in transparent evasions to avoid suspicion.[56]

7 Thomas Eakins, *Rock Thrower* (?Jesse Godley's brother posing as a rock thrower, probably a photographic study for *The Swimming Hole*), *c.* 1884–85, albumin print on paper, 9.52 × 6.35 cm. Hirshhorn Museum and Sculpture Garden, Smithsonian Institution, transferred from the Hirshhorn Museum and Sculpture Garden Archives, 1983 (photographer: Lee Stalsworth). Photo: courtesy of the Hirshhorn Museum and Sculpture Garden.

Two other studies show that Eakins quickly shifted ground. On one side of a small panel, Eakins painted the left side of the pier with the reclining figure only, dropping the crouching figure. On the other side, he opened a new chapter in the narrative; he sketched the head of his dog Harry swimming in the pond, suggested, perhaps, by some ripples in the Hirshhorn study.[57]

On 31 July 1884 Eakins, the sculptor Jesse Godley and Godley's brother went out to the boathouses at Bryn Mawr. Photos taken there, and probably throughout the next year, were used — with the new oil studies — to reconfigure the painting's conception. In two photos, a man who is probably Godley's brother poses as a rock-thrower (plate 7) and in a third as a thorn-puller, all recalling well-known ancient statuary.[58] These photos are preparations for a new figure in the final painting (plate 3) — the seated man in the middle of the pier, with close-cropped, slightly greying hair and moustache (clearly marking him as five to fifteen years older than the boys in the first photos), who throws a ball for Harry. His lower body is taken over from the crouching figure in the Hirshhorn study (plate 6), but the upper body brings in the new action and wholly orients him to the dog in the water. In another photo, Godley stretches out on a wooden platform. Flipped over, he becomes the reclining figure in the painting, who no longer looks up and toward the standing figure but also down at Harry, while his brother tosses the ball. Like the standing and throwing figures, he suggests ancient statuary,[59] but Eakins's changes in his pose required the additional photo work. In still other photos, made with Academy models, different poses were investigated.[60]

Many viewers have noted that the painting rearranged the poses adopted by the boys in the first photos (plates 5a–h) to hide any frontal genital nudity, supposedly unacceptable to Eakins's audience. But the Hirshhorn study (plate 6) had already solved that difficulty — and yet the *painting* is as different from the *study* as the study is from the first photos. The painting's reorganization in 1884–85, then, was not merely the elimination of frontal nudity. It was, more important, a resetting of the narrative. Specifically, I think, Eakins attempted to transform 'fervid comradeship' into 'general politics', revising the indecency of the boys's hierarchical society toward the democratic decency imagined in acceptable fantasies.

The painting (plate 3) breaks apart the story of desire and aggression narrated in the first photos (plates 5a–h) and condensed in the Hirshhorn study (plate 6). Introducing the dog Harry, for example, adds a new, more trivial focus. The two figures on the left of the Hirshhorn study have been disentangled from each other and from the standing figure; now they both orient themselves to the dog. The figure pulling himself from the water in the study, expressing the roles of the observers in the first narrative, switches direction in the painting; the red-haired boy, the latest image of Fergus/Fox, lowers himself into the water near the dog. Eakins, swimming, seems to be looking at them. In other words, a *foreground* compositional triangle, with Harry at its centre, creates a new zone of interaction, running from middle left to right bottom, turning the interaction on the pier itself, in the Hirshhorn study, a full ninety degrees. Despite the pyramid that encompasses all the figures, in relation to this frontal zone the two other figures, standing and diving, become *background*, set in another spatial plane. We see them *through* a web of glances and gestures in the foreground plane — a scene of peaceful, harmless relaxation in which all figures, not touching one another, develop a mutual bond only through their relation to a common object of affection, the dog Harry.

Standing figure and diver are turned away. Compared to the standing figure in the Hirshhorn study (plate 6), in virtual profile, in the painting he turns his back, like 'Mr Roberts' (plate 4). What he is looking at is practically on the *other* side of the pier, as the diver's foreshortening suggests. The diver's face, despite facing us, is obscured; although still above water, it is painted in dark streaks. It is hard to see his full head of dark brown hair and dark moustache and beard. In fact, it is a deft portrait, which Eakins probably painted by turning the canvas upside down, of his student George Reynolds, who appeared in a series of Marey-wheel photos made in 1884: whatever Eakins did with his wax model of a diver, the *painted* diver is clearly based on photos of Reynolds running and jumping.[61]

Like Jesse Godley, Reynolds was an older man, about Eakins's own age. A regular in M Company of the 9th New York Cavalry Regiment in the Civil War, he won the Congressional Medal of Honor for capturing the state flag of Virginia at the third Battle of Winchester (Opequon) on 19 September

8 Thomas Eakins, *The Veteran* (George Reynolds), *c.* 1884–88, oil on canvas, 56.51 × 38.1 cm. Yale University Art Gallery, Bequest of Stephen Carlton Clark, B.A. 1903 (1961.18.20). Photo: courtesy of the Yale University Art Gallery.

1864.[62] As his commander put it in the dispatch, this was a day when 'the glorious old First Division [to which the 9th Cavalry belonged] was never in better condition; officers and men, as they saw the sun appear bright and glorious above the horizon, felt a consciousness of renewed strength, a presentiment of fresh glory to be added that day to their unfading laurels.'[63] Twenty years later, in the mid-1880s, Reynolds was the model for Eakins's painting *The Veteran* (plate 8).[64] In 1883, in fact, the first history of Winchester had been published and recalled the horrifying losses, estimated at 12 per cent of the Union command and twice that for the South.[65] Reynolds's brother Ned expressed the feelings of the veterans in a poem written in memory of their boyhood friend in Russell, New York, Bill Clark of the 60th New York, killed at Gettysburg:

> A soldier of the Sixtieth lay dying on Culp's Hill:
> There was lack of tender nursing, there was dearth of surgeon's skill;
> For the battle hot was raging, and each moment added one
> To the thousands that lay dying in the hot midsummer's sun.
> A comrade, fighting near him, bent to hear what he might say —
> To receive his latest message to the dear ones far away.
> The dying soldier faltered: 'Ned, I'll never more, alas!
> See my home and friends in Russell, dear old "Russell on the Grasse"!
> . . . Tell my brothers when they gather round, the story of to-day —
> How gallant Greene's New York Brigade held Ewell's hosts at bay,
> And tell them that 'twas at that point where foemen turned and fled
> That their brother "Bill" was found, among a score of Rebel dead.'
> . . . He paused — the comrade lower bent to hear his latest word;

> The swelling roar of battle was the only sound he heard;
> The wounded heart had ceased to beat, the spark of life had fled;
> Another happy home was filled with sorrow for the dead.[66]

In this light, Eakins's painting of the swimming hole — its evocation of classical images of warriors and dying heroes — depends on resetting the tone of the scene to evoke struggles, victories and defeats not in the sense the earlier images had documented, a story of contests native to a society of boys, but in a sense appropriate to the world beyond the boys' horizons — for instance, to Custer's command of the 25th New York Cavalry in the Civil War or to his death in the more recent battle depicted by Mulvany and described by Whitman. On the twenty-fifth anniversary of Gettysburg, the veterans of the 9th New York were addressed at their battleground cenotaph by Colonel Wilber Bentley, who rendered what Eakins, I think, tried to suggest in the painting:

> We rear this monument . . . to bear witness to the faithful service and the terrible sacrifice that was made to perpetuate a government whose benign influences provide for its subjects as no other under the sun has done. . . . Men who shuddered at the thought of war, who had never, perhaps, seriously asked themselves how much they loved their country, laid aside at once every consideration and offered their lives upon its altar. . . . The Ninth New York was pressed close against the enemy. . . . Well do we remember that beautiful summer morning, July 1st, 1863. The sun rose in its splendor and brilliancy as if it was ushering in another day of peace to the honest farmers who lived in peace in this beautiful valley [recall, here, the Pennsylvania Quaker farmer of Whittier's elegy]. The sun-kissed hills reflected back the brilliant orb of day, and stood in their silent grandeur, giving no sign of the armies who at that very moment were preparing for conflict under cover of the beautiful forests. . . . We glance back through the intervening years between this reunion and those terrible days when the dirge of death and the song of victory mingled and blended. Today we hear the trumpet of glad jubilee sounding in another year of peace. As we gather closer and feel the pulse-beat of each other's sympathy, we remember to-day, with a peculiar tenderness, the missing ones, the honored dead, the heroic men who helped to make our beloved land great and true.[67]

In the context of such sentiments, the mood of the *Swimming Hole* is not, as commentators suppose, a delightful innocence — even if this would have been a successful revision of the earlier indecencies. Despite its pictorial ancestry, the finished painting is not an image of boys, all in fun, imitating the ambitions and struggles of men. Instead, it is a fantasy of men setting aside care to become, once more, like carefree boys. The disparity of ages and the mutual independence of the characters indicates that this is not a gang of boys but a happenstance meeting of men who have met up at the swimming hole, perhaps just for the hour, their bond created by a rambunctious dog. For this group, the fresh air of the pond is fresh precisely because here there is no smell of death. The painting discovers a decent homoeroticism (for example, Bentley's 'sympathy' and 'peculiar tenderness') by routing its primal fantasies — of aggressively sexual hierarchy and contest — toward discharge in the *recognition* of an actual history of war and death, in relation to which the painting overtly stages it scene. But this dischargeable homoerotic fantasy revises the preceding, more homosexual one — itself a fantasy constructed, I have suggested, in retrospective reviewing.

Whether Eakins succeeds in producing the very image of the inner relation between Whitman's swimming boys in the Harlem River and Mulvany's drama of *Custer's Last Rally* remains doubtful. If the painting hopes pictorially to visualize the relation, it ends up avoiding it. Moreover, compared to the earlier photo of Dave pushing Albert into the water (plate 5g) or the still earlier images of dying warriors, both 'fervid comradeship' and 'general politics' have been substantially muted in order to bind them together. In fact, adhesiveness *and* citizenship — the role of the men as self-cultured, free-standing citizens and defenders of democracy — are joined together only because they are seen to occur apparently in the same place at the same time; in the painting, adhesiveness, the zone of interaction between standing figure and diver, is literally *seen through* the foreground zone, the zone of democratic decency. But they have no inherent, causal relations, as Whitman urged they should: in the manifest story — the calculated space — of the painting, the two narratives subtend at right angles to each other. Although there are two webs of gazes and gestures taken in by us all at once, no gaze and no gesture passes *between* the webs. Thus, if we see the story and means of the painting as 'unitary' and vividly 'realistic', as commentators would have us believe, it is only because we have been browbeaten by the massive, artificial compositional pyramid. Fixed on the abstract domain of the picture plane itself, it smashes together two meanings in a single revisionary act of erotic-political fantasy at the same time as it forbids their original social and sexual union.

I cannot conclude without noting, however, that if the homosexual past of *The Swimming Hole* has been broken apart, turned aside, or reversed in the painting, it returns in the painting's imaginary dimension — in the most literal sense. It is Jacques Lacan's sense of unconscious — delayed or permanently reserved — wishing travelling from perception toward motor realization ('the Imaginary') that it operates at the level of the 'letter', rather than the conventional meaning, of representation; until motor realization or intersubjectively intelligible speech begins to materialize, the wish subsists in the most literal, material dimension of the signifier.[68] It is doubly fortunate (but not, of course, necessary) that 'the imaginary' in Eakins's painting should apparently break out in the actual depiction of images in the most literal sense — that is, in the pictorial visualization of reflections. From the early 1870s through to the end of the 1880s, Eakins displayed exacting concern for perspective and reflection. To study light effects for his rowing paintings, he put cut-outs and coloured bits of cloth on a wet roof in the bright sunlight.[69] In his lectures at the Academy in the mid-1880s he expounded 'the principles governing the different reflections on the near side of a wave, the far side, and the top', insisting that 'there is so much beauty in reflections that it is well worth while to get them right.'[70] In *The Swimming Hole* (plate 3), the wading boy, Fergus/Fox, is a bravura performance.

His reflection captures both the foreshortening of the figure and the refraction of its image. Likewise, the reflections of Harry's and Eakins's heads are completely rational and convincing.

But the reflected figure of the *diver* openly revolts against the painting's science, order and unity. In theory, 'Reynolds' is far back from the picture plane, diving away from the viewer toward the middle of the pond, as his dramatic foreshortening implies. He should be reflected, then, in a curve running from his point of entry into the water to a point no closer to us than the forward edge of the pier. But instead a ghostly image, outlined with bluish stripes, extends from his head in a long arc coming far forward toward the picture plane to a point almost touching Eakins's outstretched hand in the water and continuing, reflected in a series of smaller ripples, to the very bottom edge of the canvas. The reflected image of the diver's upper thigh is placed inches from Eakins's hand. And in fact Eakins is not looking straight at Harry, in front and actually slightly to the left of him, but rather at a reflection in the water, about a foot away from his outstretched hand, where a slight perturbation, two circular strokes placed side by side, indicates where the diver's genitals are reflected — an effect much more obvious when the painting is turned upside down.

The curving image of the reflected diver reconnects the two sundered narrative domains of the painting placed at right angles to each other in a way that the abstract compositional pyramid cannot. At the same time as it recalls, perhaps even restores, the homosexual relations of the swimming hole — the diver, the object of desire every boy wants to touch, was also the boy who at last welcomed Eakins to the pier — it places them on the other side of what Eakins thinks he wants the viewer to see, the reflection of 'fervid comradeship' *into* 'general politics'. Thus, homosexuality is not simply reversed or rejected — that would produce an *in*visibility which the painting, in many respects a paean to pure visibility, does not attempt — but rather *re-reversed*, the upside-down of its turning-away. In the delayed activations of erotic revision, the retrospectively emerging fantasy — that Eakins might see, even touch, the penis of the most desirable boy — survives its narrative dramatization, its repetition and simultaneous rejection, and its rerouting in metaphorical substitutes and replacements. This fantasy is not the 'origin' of the painting; as we have seen, it emerges pro- and retrospectively as a representation propped upon events and meanings, and whatever desires organize them, outside representation. And it is not the sole content of Eakins's sexualized consciousness in producing the painting — for that is no more and no less than the *entire* network of revisions in transit from the desires that are being partly fulfilled to the desires *not* to be so fulfilled. The painting itself is, finally, not the 'end' nor resolution of this sequence. The painter does not know what resolution he desires until, retrospectively, he sees what his prospectively surging desires have enabled him to achieve; and then, of course, he does not want it. The painting is merely the relay that permits him to hold together and go on.

Whitney Davis
Northwestern University
Illinois

Notes

This essay was begun while I was Visiting Scholar at the Stanford Humanities Center; aspects were presented in lectures at Stanford, University College, London, and Barnard College. I thank Martin A. Berger, Doreen Bolger, Ronald C. Brister, Wanda Corn, Michael Fellman, Robert Haywood, Christine Hennessey, Margaret Iversen, Jonathan Katz, Michael Leja, Cheryl Leibold, Richard Meyer, Alex Nemerov, Michael Plante, Alex Potts, John R. Sellers, Ken Silver, Marc Simpson, Todd Smith and Bill Stern for assistance, references and suggestions. Research in the Library of Congress, the National Library of Medicine, the New York Public Library and the New York Academy of Medicine Library was supported by a Guggenheim Fellowship; research in the Kinsey Institute for Research in Sex, Gender, and Reproduction was supported by Northwestern University.

1 For a recent judgement on this point, seen as a substantive one, see Kathleen A. Foster and Cheryl Leibold, *Writing About Eakins: The Manuscripts in Charles Bregler's Thomas Eakins Collection*, Philadelphia, 1989, pp. 110–11. I place 'homosexual' (and 'heterosexual') in scare quotes to recall that it is an open question whether 'homosexuality' — in the sense partly due to Freud's conceptualizations of 1905–15, building on late nineteenth-century sexological inquiries — can be identified in homoeroticisms of earlier periods. The peculiar term itself dates to the 1870s. I will not explore this issue directly. Note, however, that some American physicians of the early 1880s and '90s were familiar with the emerging terminology and its technical meaning (see note 56 below).

2 Sigmund Freud, *The Interpretation of Dreams* (1900). James Strachey (ed.) et al., *The Standard Edition of the Complete Psychological Works of Sigmund Freud*, 24 vols., London, 1951–74 (hereafter *SE*), vol. 5, pp. 509–621 (i.e. chap. 7).

3 Sigmund Freud, *Project for a Scientific Psychology* (1895), *SE* 1, pp. 305–43.

4 Some writers urge that the history of the discharge of a person's egoistic, sexual and aggressive wishes must possess the structure of language itself, a social formation into which a 'subject' is supposedly 'inscribed', for it is in language that relations among representations — their similarities and differences — are supposedly produced. We need not accept this account in its most simplistic form. It remains unclear what wish — except perhaps a universal wish for 'difference' itself? — produces the language if it is the language that produces wishes. In fact, despite the claims of some 'semiotic' thinkers, it is probably untrue that language consists of a structure of arbitrary similarities and differences in the first place. (And if similarity and difference are non-arbitrary, then they are not produced strictly by relations among representations. Instead, they are brought into such order in the process of using the language to refer to the world and to accomplish tasks — including the attainment of wishes.) Nevertheless, a more modest form of this view, broadly associated with the later work of Jacques Lacan, can be a helpful way of elaborating the basic Freudian point. We will simply *define* a person's 'language' as the effects of similarity and difference among representations in continuous discharge and delay. The probability of discharge is set by intersubjective conventions in force (or enforced) when the language is used. (The Lacan of the 'Rome Discourse' and other essays gathered in *Ecrits* [trans. Alan Sheridan, London, 1977] is still excessively influenced by a simplistic Saussurean model of language; I refer to the *Four Fundamental Concepts of Psychoanalysis* [trans. Alan Sheridan, New York, 1978] and especially texts like 'Clivage du sujet et son identification', *Scilicet* 2/3 [1970], pp. 103–36, for the more nuanced model.) Genuine Lacanian analysis recognizes how wishes produce language intersubjectively in actual relations among speakers who provide metaphorical and metonymic representational possibilities for one another — at the same time as such communication necessarily adopts linguistic conventions. (If this were not the case, the Lacanian model could not tackle one of its most important clinical tasks — namely, the description of novel or non-conventional 'languages' produced in the schizophrenias.) By contrast, spurious 'Lacanian' analyses merely assert that language, a social formation embodied in a 'culture', produces wishes — confusing Lacan's with the structuralists' or Althusser's mechanical theories of consciousness.

5 Sigmund Freud, 'A Note Upon the "Mystic Writing Pad"' (1923), *SE* 19, pp. 227–34.

6 See especially Sigmund Freud, 'From the History of an Infantile Neurosis' (1919) (the 'Wolf Man case'), *SE* 17, pp. 1–222; see Whitney Davis, 'Sigmund Freud's Drawing of the Dream of the Wolves', *Oxford Art Journal* no. 20, 1992, pp. 70–87.

7 See especially Michael Fried, 'Representing Representation: On the Central Group in Courbet's *Studio*', Stephen Greenblatt (ed.), *Allegory and Representation*, Baltimore, 1981, pp. 94–127, and 'The Structure of Beholding

in Courbet's *Burial at Ornans*', *Critical Inquiry*, no. 9, 1983, pp. 635–83. This is my description of Fried's procedure; he might not endorse it. Notice the essential relation (in the essays cited) between, on the one hand, Fried's use of a psychoanalytical vocabulary of condensation and displacement (not accompanied by an identification of the 'primal scene' itself) to describe pictorial phenomena and, on the other, his claim to conduct an analysis that is analytically prior to the so-called contextualization practised by social historians: Fried nominates the topmost plane of representation — what he calls the 'scene of representation' (it includes the painting and the beholder's perceptual, bodily and motor relation to it) — as the site of history in the representation. But the causal connection between the 'primal scene' and the 'scene of representation' is unexplored. Possibly we can see through the topmost page of the 'mystic writing pad' to the bottommost page, something informative in itself. But we know nothing about the *forward* constitution of the pages in their retrospectively identified historical order. This is not a methodological problem, however, and certainly not a theoretical deficiency. In forensic history, we must always identify the stratigraphy before we speculate about the causes of the sequence it exhibits. In this light, Fried's occasional diagnostic hypotheses — his analysis of the cause of the structure of the 'scene of representation' he describes — are superfluous.

8 Of course, Freud offers deterministic predictions about the *structure* of consciousness — but its history, its actual content and development, is left for an interpretive, retrospective hermeneutics. By contrast, Marxism offers deterministic (essentially non-retrospective and unhermeneutic) predictions about these contents and developments as such. Thus, a Freudian hermeneutic of formal structures explicated by Marxist or similarly historicist determinism has some appeal for those who hope to write total histories.

9 'From the History of an Infantile Neurosis', *SE* 17, pp. 1–222. For the structure of *Nachträglichkeit* in the intrapsychic constitution of a particular subjective sexuality, see my 'HomoVision: A Reading of Freud's "Fetishism" ', *Genders*, no. 15, 1992, pp. 86–118.

10 Walt Whitman, *Specimen Days and Collect*, Philadelphia, 1882.

11 See Scott Giantvalley, *Walt Whitman, 1838–1939: A Reference Guide*, Boston, 1981, pp. 37–66 (including Philadelphia press citations for the period 1875–83).

12 See William Innes Homer, 'New Light on Thomas Eakins and Walt Whitman in Camden', in Geoffrey M. Sill and Roberta K. Tarbell (eds.), *Walt Whitman and the Visual Arts*, New Brunswick, N.J., 1992, pp. 85–98. See also Lloyd Goodrich, *Thomas Eakins*, 2nd ed., Cambridge, Mass., 1982, vol. 2, pp. 28–38; Henry B. Rule, 'Walt Whitman and Thomas Eakins: Some Variations on Common Themes', *Texas Quarterly*, no. 17, 1974, pp. 7–57; Elizabeth Johns, *Thomas Eakins: The Heroism of Modern Life*, Princeton, 1983, pp. 144–69.

13 Whitman, 'Democratic Vistas', *Specimen Days and Collect*, op. cit., pp. 232–3.

14 Whitman, *Specimen Days and Collect*, op. cit., pp. 181–2. See further F.O. Matthiessen's seminal speculations on 'Whitman's landscapes and the realism of Millet and Eakins' in *American Renaissance: Art and Expression in the Age of Emerson and Whitman*, Oxford, 1941, pp. 599–613.

15 Whitman, *Specimen Days and Collect*, op. cit., pp. 187–8. For the enthusiastic reception of this painting in the 1880s, see Robert Taft, *Artists and Illustrators of the Old West 1850–1900*, New York, 1953, pp. 134–41. The original painting was apparently destroyed in a fire in London, where Mulvany exhibited it. I illustrate it with a copy made by an unknown artist.

16 Whitman, *Specimen Days and Collect*, op. cit., pp. 186–87. The obvious comparison with Whitman's 'Twenty-Eight Young Men Bathe by the Shore' in *Song of Myself (Leaves of Grass*, Philadelphia, 1883, pp. 29–78) might be made.

17 Whitman, 'Democratic Vistas', op. cit., pp. 247–8. For Whitman's concept, see Michael Lynch, ' "Here is Adhesiveness": From Friendship to Homosexuality', *Victorian Studies*, no. 29, 1985, pp. 67–96; Michael Moon, *Disseminating Whitman: Revision and Corporeality in Leaves of Grass*, Cambridge, Mass., 1991; and Byrne R.S. Fone, *Masculine Landscapes: Walt Whitman and the Homoerotic Text*, Carbondale, Ill., 1992. Matthiessen and subsequent Whitman and Eakins scholars have observed a relation — aesthetic, philosophical, and perhaps political and personal — between Whitman's bathers and Eakins's young athletes and swimmers. I follow — and extend — this analysis because I do believe it retrieves one of the most important determinants in Eakins's image-making. But other relations deserve elucidation as well; they have been obscured because of the perceived aesthetic superiority and, more recently, the political interest of Whitman's art. For example, some of Bayard Taylor's poems — extremely popular in Eakins's time, and more likely to have been read by Eakins's Philadelphia patrons than Whitman's writings — describe naked male beauty in more con-

ventional but equally erotic ways (see, for example, 'Hylas', *Romances and Lyrics* Boston, 1882, pp. 72–5). Their pederastic interests are often greater than Whitman's, at least in the manifest narrative or imagery itself. In fact, Whitman's revision of pederastic homoeroticism in the direction of a more general 'masculine' eros — also notable in Eakins and in post-Whitmanian homosexualists such as Carpenter — was a major shift in Euro-American homoertic representation since Winckelmann. As we will see, however, at the 'deep' level of the image, Eakins's interest in the bodily integrity and beauty of 'men' may revise, by repressing, the *continuing* salience of specifically pederastic wishes. These wishes — at least in the 'Platonic' or 'ideal' expressions — had long been permitted a place in public image-making, so long as they never required a depiction of the pederast's arousal and the youth's desiring sexual response to it organized as a mutually determined teleology (even though this was, I have argued elsewhere, the central desire of a specifically 'homosexual' modern homoeroticism: Whitney Davis, 'Winckelmann's Homosexual Teleologies', Natalie Kampen, et al., [eds.], *Sexuality in Ancient Art* [forthcoming]). But it is also this instant toward which Eakins's fantasy partly moves.

18 See Michael Fried, *Realism, Writing, and Disfiguration: On Thomas Eakins and Stephen Crane*, Chicago, 1987.

19 Fried identifies Eakins's imagination of the vulnerability of the naked male body to a devastating anal assault by an idealized male authority — graphically depicted, only lightly revised, in *The Gross Clinic* of 1875 — as 'homosexual' (*Realism, Writing, Disfiguration*, op. cit., p. 68). On the paranoid repudiation of homosexuality in projection, see Sigmund Freud, 'Psycho-Analytic Notes on an Autobiographical Account of a Case of Paranoia (Dementia paranoides)' (the 'Schreber case'), *SE* 12, pp. 1–84: homosexual wish and its complementary prohibition split the subject in the projection. Eakins's repudiation, of course, is sublimatory rather than psychotic: he is no Judge Schreber.

Considering the De Manian origin of elements in Fried's terminology (see Paul De Man, 'Shelley Disfigured', *The Rhetoric of Romanticism*, New York, 1984, pp. 93–124), it is interesting that he interprets psychologically — as Eakins's discharge of a 'homosexual wish-fantasy' — what De Man would consider to be purely 'linguistic.' In fact, there are 'linguistic' — pictorially conventional — forerunners for Eakins's image at just this site of metaphorical transfer. Gruesome chromolithographs of war wounds in the thighs and buttocks were printed in Philadelphia in the mid-1870s to illustrate the medical history of the Civil War, in which Eakins's future colleague at the Academy, the anatomy instuctor Dr W.W. Keen (appointed in 1876), had served; see Silas Weir Mitchell, George R. Morehouse and William W. Keen, *Gunshot Wounds*, Philadelphia, 1864; George A. Otis (ed.), *The Medical and Surgical History of the War of the Rebellion*, part 2, vol. 2, *Surgical History*, Washington, DC, 1877, for example, pl. 9; and W.W. Keen James (ed.), *The Memoirs of William Williams Keen, M.D.*, Doylestown, Pa., 1990, pp. 40–1. No contradiction obtains between Eakins's supposed 'homosexual wish-fantasy' (and its possible paranoiac projection), embodied in *The Gross Clinic*, and the existence of available cultural productions, such as the chromos, which activated this fantasy after delay. Indeed, we should always seek such relations as the actual mechanism of *Nachträglichkeit*. But Fried ignores the routing and thus cannot see the topmost plane of representation as other than 'disfigured'; he cannot quite identify the structure of its erotic revision or *re*-(dis)figuration.

20 See Goodrich, *Eakins*, vol. 1, pp. 236–7; Gordon Hendricks, *The Life and Work of Thomas Eakins*, New York, 1974, p. 192. The earliest date (adopted by Goodrich) is established by the general appearance of 'Greek' themes in Eakins's work (see Marc Simpson, 'Thomas Eakins and His Arcadian Works', *Smithsonian Studies in American Art* 1, no. 2, 1987, p. 92), but the studies could have been done as late as 1890 (so Elwood C. Parry, III, 'The Thomas Eakins Portrait of Sue and Harry', *Arts magazine*, vol. 53, no. 9, May 1979, p. 151), when Eakins apparently discussed them with his friend Sadakichi Hartmann, who later praised Eakins's 'unbridled masculine power' and 'manly' painting ('it has muscles') (*A History of American Art*, Boston, 1902, vol. 1, pp. 203–04). The exact date of the studies does not affect my point here.

21 The ancient sources for the life of Phidias — recounting his political alliance with Pericles's governing clique, the supposed embezzlement charge, and the scandal of his lover's portrait — would have been well known (for the ancient testimonia, see Andrew Stewart, *Greek Sculpture: An Introduction*, New Haven, 1991, vol. 1, pp. 257–63). For Phidias's art as seen at the time, see Charles Waldheim, *Essays on the Art of Pheidias*, Cambridge, 1885.

22 Goodrich, *Eakins*, op. cit., vol. 1, p. 236.

23 ibid., p. 94.

24 Simpson, 'Eakins and His Arcadian Works', op. cit., p. 93.

25 I am grateful to Doreen Bolger for the opportunity to read her paper 'No "Sweetness and Light" from Thomas Eakins: Edward H. Coates and *Swimming*', to be published in *Thomas Eakins and 'Swimming'* (Fort Worth, Tx., forthcoming 1996) and originally presented at the College Art Association, 6 February 1993; she investigates Coates's decision to refuse the painting and take another in its stead. The following considerations can be added to her account. Bolger says that Coates had commissioned the painting 'by the summer of 1884'. As we will see, there are reasons to believe it was conceived the year before.

26 My tentative identification of the site has yet to be confirmed. With the vast expansion of the Philadelphia suburbs in the twentieth century, these sites have vanished. But they are clearly visible on the 1894 U.S.G.S. survey of the Norristown Quadrangle, Pennsylvania (and cf. *Combination Atlas of Montgomery County, Pennsylvania*, Philadelphia, 1877). According to the survey, the pond upstream from Dove Lake on Mill Creek seems to have possessed the 'boat houses' noted in Eakins's record of his excursion in July, 1884 (see note 53 below).

27 William J. Buck, *History of Montgomery County within the Schuylkill Valley*, Norristown, Pa., 1859, pp. 28–9.

28 ibid., p. 29. see also Eli Bowen, *The Pictorial Sketch Book of Pennsylvania: or its Scenery, Internal Improvements, Resources, and Agriculture*, Philadelphia, 1852, p. 56, and F.C. Hobson, William J. Buck and Henry S. Dotterer (eds.), *The Centennial Celebration of Montgomery County*, Norristown, Pa., 1884.

29 William B. Sipes, *The Pennsylvania Railroad: Its Origin, Construction, Condition, and Connections*, Philadelphia, 1875, pp. 79–80.

30 Charles S. Keyser, *Fairmount Park and the International Exhibition at Philadelphia*, Philadelphia, 1876, pp. 117–18, with engraving; Devil's Hole was painted by Henry A. Frey in 1886 (see T.A. Daly [ed.], *The Wissahickon*, Philadelphia, 1922, frontispiece).

31 The swimming and skating places in the city neighbourhoods were rapidly being lost and much lamented by older inhabitants (see John F. Watson, *Annals of Philadelphia, and Pennsylvania, in the Olden Time*, Philadelphia, 1881, vol. 1. pp. 495–6).

32 Cornelius Weygandt, *The Wissahickon Hills*, Philadelphia, 1930, p. 41; Weygandt roamed the watershed as a boy in the 1880s.

33 John Greenleaf Whittier, 'The Pennsylvania Pilgrim', *Complete Poetical Works of John Greenleaf Whittier (Cambridge Edition)* Boston, 1894, pp. 108–09; see Weygandt, *Wissahickon Hills*, op cit., p. 39. Augustus Saint Gaudens's *Pilgrim*, made in 1904 to recall *Puritan* of 1887, was moved to Fairmount Park in 1920.

34 See generally Anita Clair Fellman and Michael Fellman, *Making Sense of Self: Medical Advice Literature in Late Nineteenth-Century America*, Philadelphia, 1981; James C. Whorton, *Crusaders for Fitness: The History of American Health Reformers*, Princeton, 1982; Donald J. Mrozek, *Sport and American Mentality, 1880–1910*, Knoxville, Tn., 1983; Harvey Green, *Fit for America: Health, Fitness, Sport, and American Society*, New York, 1986. For considerations somewhat parallel to the ones I develop below, see Michael Hatt, 'Muscles, Morals, Mind: The Male Body in Thomas Eakins' *Salutat*', in Kathleen Adler and Marcia Pointon (eds.), *The Body Imaged: The Human Form and Visual Culture since the Renaissance*, London, 1993, pp. 57–70. The painting Hatt considers was painted in 1898, considerably later than *The Swimming Hole*. In my view, the particular dimensions of Eakins's erotic revision at that point are different from the formations of the mid-1880s considered here, let alone the formations of the mid-1870s considered by Fried (see note 19 above). Although all are well within the very (perhaps overly) general system identified by some 'queer theory' as the mutually constitutive interrelation of 'homosociality' and 'homosexuality' (that is to say, within the field of 'masculinity' as such), the quantities and qualities of egoistic, aggressive and sexual wishes in continuous replication are constantly revised. A full-scale narrative of this history is far beyond my scope here. See also Robert Haywood, 'George Bellows's *Stag at Sharkey's*: Boxing, Violence, and Male Identity', *Smithsonian Studies in American Art*, vol. 2, no. 2, 1988, pp. 1–15, and compare John Wilmerding, 'George Bellows's Boxing Pictures and the American Tradition', *American Views: Essays on American Art*, Princeton, 1991, pp. 305–27.

35 Silas Weir Mitchell, *Wear and Tear, or Hints for the Overworked*, Philadelphia, 1871, pp. 46–7.

36 For a thorough account, see Green, *Fit for America*, op. cit.

37 James Freeman Clarke, *Self-Culture: Physical, Intellectual, Moral, and Spiritual*, 15th edn., Boston, 1880, pp. 55–6; see also Felix L. Oswald, *Physical Education: or, The Health-Laws of Nature*, New York, 1883, pp. 158–9. Throughout the last third of the nineteenth century, the 'vagabond newsboys', like tramp boys, were frequently the object of thinly veiled homoerotic interests, perhaps because they were willing to have sex with men, whether paid or not.

38 William Blaikie, *How to Get Strong and How to Stay So*, 2nd edn., New York, 1899 (first

published 1879), pp. 14, 89.

39 For Franklin's *Proposals Relating to the Education of Youth in Pennsylvania*, see Horace Mather Lippincott, *Early Philadelphia, Its People Life and Progress*, Philadelphia, 1917, p. 147.

40 Edward Potts Cheyney, *History of the University of Pennsylvania, 1740–1940*, Philadelphia, 1940, pp. 312–17.

41 Edwin Checkley, *A Natural Method of Physical Training: Making Muscle and Reducing Flesh Without Dieting or Apparatus*, New York, 1892, p. 146.

42 Blaikie, *How to Get Strong*, pp. 20–3, 84–92. Roberts was 'the most outstanding Y.M.C.A. physical director of this period' (Emmett A. Rice, *A Brief History of Physical Education*, New York, 1929, pp. 193–4). His philosophy of 'B.B.H.' — 'breast bone high' — is succinctly stated in his 'Health Hints for Men', *American Gymnasia*, no. 1, Oct. 1904, p. 24. Compare Whitman's 'breast expanded, an erect attitude' (*Specimen Days and Collect*, op. cit., pp. 232–3).

43 Richard A. Proctor, *Strength; How to Get Strong and Keep Strong*, New York 1889, pp. 33, 51.

44 Indeed, the standing figure appears to possess the exact neck, arm, chest and other measurements of the manly ideal Mr Roberts described to interviewers (quoted in Blaikie, *How to Get Strong*, op. cit., p. 88). But notice that the lower body of the thrower, for example, has another basis, it seems, than physical-culture imagery; we will return to the ways in which each figure, in fact, is actually a complex palimpsest of forms. Eakins is not necessarily attempting to illustrate physically cultured bodies for their own sakes; rather, he evokes them, along with other imagery, for other purposes — a point to which we must also return. Elizabeth Milroy ('Thomas Eakins' Artistic Training, 1860–1870', Ph.D. dissertation, University of Pennsylvania, 1985, pp. 333–4) implies that Eakins's sporting pictures of the early 1870s were already interested in physical-culture theory. The pictorial evidence, however, is not convincing. The rowers, it is clear, were not 'physical-culture' ideals in Blaikie's sense; they had social status of a different kind.

46 See generally Peter Weiermair, *The Hidden Image: Photographs of the Nude Male in the Nineteenth and Twentieth Centuries*, trans. Claus Nielander, Cambridge, Mass., 1988; Allen Ellenzweig, *The Homoerotic Photograph: Male Images from Durieu/Delacroix to Mapplethorpe*, New York, 1992, pp. 6–64; compare James Crump, *George Platt Lynes: Photographs from The Kinsey Institute*, Boston and New York, 1993. I am grateful to Todd Smith and the Kinsey Institute for the opportunity to examine rare homosexual pornographic photographs of the 1890s, chiefly French and German. The Comstock records suggest that America had its share of such images too.

46 Bolger, 'No "Sweetness and Light" from Thomas Eakins', suggests that the picture may have violated Coates's sense of propriety and of a Hellenizing painting. The difference between painter and patron, then, would fundamentally be a matter of conventional aesthetic attitudes and conflicts. A painting of nude bathers by Alexander Harrison exhibited at the same time as Eakins's, Bolger observes, roused no opposition; she infers that it was not the nudity — or implicit eroticism — in the Eakins that disturbed Coates. But Harrison's painting is lost; we cannot gauge its specific eroticism. Moreover, Coates, other evidence suggests, had a highly moralistic conception of the art to be produced in the Academy. 'In conducting the schools [of the Academy],' he declared in 1890, 'the Direction aims that study shall be on the broadest, most liberal and highest plane, still believing, in the face of denial, that there is a conscience in art, and that earnest sincerity and genuine purpose are the proper conditions, as well as the justification of its pursuit. . . . "Nothing, not even art itself, is of any worth to man, invested as he is by the whole army of evil, unless it is the deepest and highest sense good"' (Edward H. Coates, *The Academy of the Fine Arts and Its Future: Address Delivered Before the Arts Club of Philadelphia, January 24, 1890*, Philadelphia, 1890, printed transcript in the N.Y.P.L). The principal 'denial' Coates must have had in mind was surely Eakins. But the exact reasons for Coates's denial of the 'denial' that is Eakins's final painting are not my main concern here.

47 As a point of methodological interest, we can reconstruct the sequence of pictorial revisions independently of psychoanalytic assumptions about erotic discharge and representational *Nachträglichkeit*. Indeed, we should do so. Narratological analysis, for example, helps to establish sequence — as, of course, does close attention to formal and stylistic relations and contextual information. A perspective on the analysis of pictorial narrative is offered in my *Masking the Blow: The Scene of Representation in Late Prehistoric Egyptian Art*, Berkeley, Calif., 1992, esp. pp. 234–55, 271–8.

48 The term is Gordon Hendricks's in *The Photographs of Thomas Eakins*, New York, 1972, p. 6.

49 Goodrich, *Eakins*, op. cit., vol. 1, p. 241.

50 The full sequence in one of its narratively coherent orders is as follows: (1) [or (2)] Olympia 15 (Ronald J. Onorato, 'Photography

and Teaching: Eakins at the Academy', *American Art Review*, no. 3 [July–August, 1976], p. 136) (not illustrated here);
(2) [or (1)] Olympia 16 (Onorato, 'Photography and Teaching', op. cit., p. 136) (not illustrated here);
(3) Hendricks, *Photographs of Thomas Eakins*, no. 125 (my plate 5a);
(4) Hendricks, no. 122 (my plate 5b);
(5) Hendricks, no. 124 (my plate 5c);
(6) Hendricks, no. 123 (my plate 5d);
(7) Hendricks, no. 126 (reversed — my plate 5e);
(8) Hendricks, no. 42 (my plate 5f);
(9) Hendricks, no. 43 (my plate 5g);
(10) Hendricks, no. 44 (my plate 5h).
Apparently we do not possess prints actually produced by Eakins himself, a fact ultimately responsible for certain errors and variations in the corpus of existing prints.

In the early 1880s, Eakins was doing motion-sequence studies, using the Marey wheel and collaborating with Muybridge (see Hendricks, *Photographs of Thomas Eakins, passim*; cf. Ellwood C. Parry, III, 'Thomas Eakins's "Naked Series" Reconsidered: Another Look at the Standing Nude Photographs Made for the use of Eakins's Students', *American Art Journal*, vol. 20, no. 2, 1988, pp. 53–77). William I. Homer and John Talbot, 'Eakins, Muybridge and the Motion Picture Process', *Art Quarterly*, no. 26, 1963, pp. 194–216, dispute the 'myth' that Eakins was a significant 'inventor' in this domain; they chiefly refer, however, to technical — rather than pictorial or conceptual — innovation. The *Swimming* preparations have so far not been seen as part of Eakins's motion-photography enterprise. In their narrative dimension, however, they were a more profound exploration of the possibilities of a photographic tracking of motion than those of Marey or Muybridge, who produced more simple arrays which Eakins, as we will see, folded into his final non-photographic image.

51 G. Stanley Hall, *Adolescence: Its Psychology and Its Relations to Physiology, Anthropology, Sociology, Sex, Crime, Religion and Education*, 2 vols., New York, 1904. For Hall's recollections of the homosexual practices rampant in a New England school he attended in the late 1850s, see his *Life and Confessions of a Psychologist*, New York, 1923, pp. 133–4. On the boy workers, see the fundamental bibliography, covering the preceding thirty years, in William Byron Forbush, *The Boy Problem: A Study in Social Pedagogy*, Boston, 1901, pp. 180–6. The sexuality of all-boy society was a major concern — for example, the Y.M.C.A.'s hope for 'self-government' among boys was a rhetorical antidote to their 'self-abuse' — but was rarely addressed explicitly until the early 1900s.

52 See Simpson, 'Thomas Eakins' Arcadian Works', op. cit., for a fine account.

53 See Phyllis D. Rosenzweig, *The Thomas Eakins Collection of the Hirshhorn Museum and Sculpture Garden*, Washington, DC, 1977, no. 40. Anshutz might have been referring to what became the final painting itself, thus showing that it was begun in summer 1884, although completed as late as summer or fall 1885. As we will see, however, Wallace (like Anshutz himself) was involved in the revision effected by the final painting — and thus Anshutz would have had no need, if he was speaking of this work, to draw Wallace's attention to it. He may have meant to designate other studies, now lost; but the Hirshhorn study is the only surviving one depicting a 'party' of boys.

54 Charles Bregler, 'Thomas Eakins as a Teacher [Pt. 2]', *The Arts*, no. 18, October 1931, pp. 38–9.

55 Adam Emory Albright, 'Memories of Thomas Eakins', *Harper's Bazaar*, August 1947, p. 139. About 1930, Susan Macdowell Eakins recalled that 'Eakins modeled the diving figure in wax and then painted from it, making sketches on the spot [of the site?], for color of flesh, the green, the water and the sky, on a sunny day' (Rosenzweig, *Eakins Collection*, no. 40).

56 George F. Shrady, 'Editorial', *Medical Record*, no. 4, 1884, p. 70. It is not known whether Eakins had heard stories reported about boys in a Baltimore reformatory who had contracted gonorrhea in 1883–4 through anal sex (described for Philadelphia readers in Ralph Winslow, 'Report of an Epidemic of Gonorrhea Contracted from Rectal Coition', *Medical News* [Philadelphia] no. 49, 1886, pp. 180–2) or whether he was aware that between about 1878 and 1884 'several arrests' had been made in Philadelphia of men 'wearing female attire' (see 'Correspondence', *Alienist and Neurologist*, no. 5, 1884, pp. 351–2; at this point, there was a common, but highly unstable, correlation between 'homosexuality', effemination and transvestism, to which homosexualist culture itself frequently responded by emphasizing conventionally 'masculine' attributes and emotions). Among other sources, Havelock Ellis's and John Addington Symonds's representation of homosexual activities in American cities (first published in German in 1896; see Ellis, *Sexual Inversion* 3rd edn., Philadelphia, 1915, pp. 176–7, 351–2) apparently draws on information, or oral tradition, running back into the 1880s and including 'Joseph Flynt's' narrative of homosexual society among American tramps (pp.359–67). By the 1930s, swimming pools, bathing houses, gymnasia and Y.M.C.A.

buildings were widely understood, among homosexual men, to be places where sex could be had; see especially Thomas Painter, *Male Homosexuals and Their Prostitutes in Contemporary America*, New York, 1941, 2 vols. (unpublished MS. in Kinsey Institute), vol. 1, pp. 185–9. Although Painter was reporting life in New York, Boston, Philadelphia and other East Coast cities during the Depression and the first years of the war, he speaks several times of a long tradition. Indirect evidence — for example, the rhetoric of 'self-government' and related advice manuals for boys (see note 51 above) — would date the practices to the 1890s at the latest.

The first medically observed case of 'contrary sexual instinct' in America was published in 1879; Richard von Krafft-Ebing's *Zur konträren Sexualempfindung* was reviewed in 1882 ('Progress in Neurology', *American Journal of Neurology and Psychiatry*, no. 1, 1882, pp. 323–5); and by 1883, a former Surgeon General, William A. Hammond, had collected several more cases and combined them with an historical review and survey of the European literature (*Sexual Impotence in the Male*, New York, 1883). For these early concepts and attitudes, see also William Dickinson, 'A Case of Sodomy', *Saint Louis Medical and Surgical Journal*, no. 40, 1881, pp. 196–7 (anal intercourse is 'frequently committed' among boys); Edward C. Spitzka, 'A Historical Case of Sexual Perversion', *Chicago Medical Review*, no. 4, 1881, pp. 378–9 (on the transvestite Lord Cornbury, an early British governor of New York; Eakins later painted Spitzka's portrait, but it is not known whether they were acquainted in the 1880s); G. Alder Blumer, 'A Case of Perverted Sexual Instinct', *American Journal of Insanity*, no. 39, 1882, pp. 22–5; J.C. Shaw and G.N. Ferris, 'Perverted Sexual Instinct', *Journal of Nervous and Mental Disease*, no. 10, 1883, pp. 185–204; James G. Kiernan, 'Perverted Sexual Instinct,' *Chicago Medical Journal and Examiner*, no. 48. 1884, pp. 263–65; Bernard S. Talmey, 'Notes on Homosexuality', *New York Medico-Legal Journal*, vol. 34, no. 8, 1917, pp. 3–4 (case of a man pursuing homosexual encounters since 1855). For 'homosexuality' in Victorian America, see further Vern L. Bullough and Martha Voght, 'Homosexuality and its Confusion with the "Secret Sin" in Pre-Freudian America', *Journal of the History of Medicine and Allied Sciences*, no. 28, 1973, pp. 143–56; Vern L. Bullough, *Sexual Variance in Society and History*, New York, 1976, pp. 587–93; and a thoughtful and judicious analysis by Bert Hansen, 'American Physicians' Earliest Writings About Homosexuals, 1880–1900', *Milbank Quarterly*, no. 67, Supplement 1, 1989, pp. 92–108. (Apparently the first writer to canvas this material, however, was Painter, *Male Homosexuals in Contemporary America*, op. cit., esp. vol. 1, pp. 58–124, an extremely important work, deserving full publication, to which I acknowledge a great debt.) Even after the First World War, however, many Americans refused to credit the idea that men might have or desire sex with one another; see, typically, Perry M. Lichtenstein, 'The "Fairy" and the Lady Lover', *Medical Review of Reviews*, no. 27, 1921, pp. 369–74 (responding to the popular query 'does the "fairy" or "fag" really exist?').

In 1905, William Held published the autobiographical narrative of a Hungarian immigrant to America, born in 1844, whose 'effemination and dual personality' gradually led him, apparently by the mid-1870s, to adopt feminine lifeways, including the feeling of menstruating (*Crime, Habit or Disease? A Question of Sex from the Standpoint of Psycho-Pathology*, Chicago, 1905, pp. 89–109). But it is not clear whether such narratives should be understood as representing 'homosexuality'. Although they likewise may not have conceived the acts as 'homosexual', army medical officers in the Civil War became well aware that men sometimes introduced objects — including the penis of other males — into their rectums, although the purpose of such acts was tactfully not mentioned. (The *Index-Catalog of the Library of the Surgeon-General's Office, United States Army*, Washington, DC, 1892, s.v. 'Gonorrhea, Rectal', 'Rectum, Foreign Bodies in', 'Sodomy', 'Unnatural Coitus', lists several dozen studies from the 1830s on.) In one of the first items of evidence for Eakins's own visual and thematic interests, his good friend of boyhood, Max Schmitt, wrote a letter to him enclosing a drawing of himself swimming on (or diving onto) his back and lifting his legs, displaying his anus directly to the viewer's (Eakins's) eyes (Letter of 1 May 1866; see Rosenzweig, *Eakins Collection*, op. cit., no. 10).

For Laurie Wallace's ambiguous sexuality, see Hendricks, *Life and Work*, op. cit., p. 156. In 1895, the circle of Eakins's male friends was described by one member to another as 'us Whitman fellows' (William Innes Homer, *Thomas Eakins: His Life and Art*, New York, 1992, p. 116), a phrase that certainly had coded meaning by this point in the American and European reception of Whitman. Note again, however, that my point is not to show that Eakins was, or could have identified himself as, 'homosexual'. Rather, the existing judgements both on 'homosexual' sexual actions and on 'homosexuality' — as well as the established view of 'sodomy' — provided reference points which Eakins's desire, in ongoing erotic revision, took account of and moved away from.

The earliest references Freud gave for his fundamental concept of 'bisexuality' (*Three Essays on Sexuality, SE* 7, pp. 143–4) were to American physicians — such as Kiernan, cited above — writing in the early 1880s, although significantly, Freud strongly misread them. (If he read them at all; possibly his knowledge was obtained through reviews published in German in the early 1900s.) For reasons of his own, it was important for him to date the scientific lineage of the concept to a time well before the mid-1890s, when both he and Wilhelm Fliess became familiar with it. I have argued that it was actually cultural production such as Eakins's reimagination of homoeroticism, in turn inherited and mediated by homosexualist culture of the 1890s, to which Freud responded in his theory (dating to his work of 1905–10) of the psychosexual etiology of homosexuality (see Whitney Davis, *Homovisibility: Male Homosexual Desire in the Visual Field, 1750–1920*, The Harris Lectures in the History of Art, University College, London, May 1993). This raises the methodological difficulty of using Freudian theory to explicate precisely what must explain the emergence of that theory itself. I will address this matter in another context.

57 William Innes Homer (ed.), *Eakins at Avondale and Thomas Eakins: A Personal Collection*, Chadds Ford, Pa., 1980, no. 8. Harry first belonged to Eakins's sister Margaret; she died at the end of 1882. He was painted at least two other times (*A Personal Collection*, op. cit., no. 3; Theodor Siegl, *The Thomas Eakins Collection*. Philadelphia, 1978, no. 104). His role in the revision of Eakins's image should not necessarily be seen as utterly unerotic, although his connotations remain mysterious. Another study for *Swimming*, with empty landscape on one side and a sketch for the standing figure on the other, has been published (*Nature and Focus: Looking at American Painting in the 19th Century*, Houston, 1972, no. 27) and a third panel also exists (*A Personal Collection*, op. cit., no. 9). They probably date to this period of revision.

58 Rosenzweig, *Eakins Collection*, op. cit., nos. 47A–C; cf. Hendricks, *Photographs of Thomas Eakins*, op. cit., nos. 49, 50.

59 Garnett McCoy, 'Some Recently Discovered Thomas Eakins Photographs', *Archives of American Art Journal*, vol. 12, no. 4, 1972, p. 17, bottom. The Pergamene *Dying Gaul* has been offered as a parallel for the reclining figure in the painting, but Alex Potts has noted the reference to the dying warrior on the Aegina pediment — a parallel with more stylistic and thematic plausibility.

60 For example, Onorato, 'Photography and Teaching', op. cit., nos. 0–11, 0–12. McCoy, 'Recently Discovered Photographs', op. cit., pp. 16 and 17, top, publishes two photographs with Wallace and Jesse Godley or Godley's brother as the models.

61 Hendricks, *Photographs of Thomas Eakins* op. cit., nos. 94–100, 101 (?), 102 (?). Eakins's student Charles Bregler later correctly identified the diver as Reynolds (see Rosenzweig, *Eakins Collection*, op. cit., no. 40) but because it has not been recognized that this figure was a very late addition to the narrative composition his statement has caused some confusion — for Reynolds cannot, of course, be found among the boys and men in the photographs.

62 Daniel S. Lamont, George B. Davis, et al. (eds.), *The War of the Rebellion: A Compilation of the Official Records of the Union and Confederate Armies*, series I, vol. 43, Washington, DC, 1893, part 1, p. 551; Newel Cheney, *History of the Ninth Regiment, New York Volunteer Cavalry, War of 1861 to 1865*, Poland Center, NY, 1901, p. 291. The statement that Reynolds was a 'cavalry officer', repeated in the Eakins literature (e.g., Goodrich, *Eakins*, op. cit., vol. 1, p. 298), is incorrect; his regiment, service, and decoration have not previously been identified.

63 Report of Brigadier-General W[esley] Merritt, 12 October 1864 (*Official Records*, op. cit., series 1, vol. 43, part 1, pp. 444–5). Merritt's more considered (but still one-sided) story of the Battle of Winchester was related in his contribution 'Sheridan in the Shenandoah Valley', in Robert U. Johnson and Clarence C. Buel (eds.), *Battles and Leaders of the Civil War*, New York, 1888, pp. 500–21 (the capture of the flag is noted on p. 509).

64 The exact date of the painting is uncertain (see Goodrich, *Eakins*, op. cit., vol. 1, p. 297); it was probably made between 1884 (date of second swimming hole excursions) and 1888 (anniversary of Gettysburg).

65 George E. Pond, *The Shenandoah Valley in 1864*, New York, 1883, p. 171; the figures are established by Jeffry D. Wert, *From Winchester to Cedar Creek: The Shenandoah Campaign of 1864*, New York, 1987, pp. 101–04. As Wert shows, many of the soldiers — at the time or in later recollections — saw Winchester as the bloodiest battle of the war.

66 Edward Reynolds, 'Russell on the Grasse', *Dedication of the Monument to the 60th New York Volunteer Regiment* [1 July 1888], *New York at Gettysburg*, vol. 1, Albany, NY, 1900, pp. 453–4.

67 Lieutenant-Colonel Wilber G. Bentley, 'Address at the Dedication of Monument, 9th

Regiment Cavalry — "Westfield Cavalry"', *New York at Gettysburg*, op. cit., vol. 3, New York, 1901, pp. 1149–56.

68 'The Agency of the Letter in the Unconscious or Reason since Freud'. *Écrits*, op. cit., pp. 146–78.

69 See Rosenzweig, *Eakins Collection*, op. cit., nos. 18, 19, 22, 56, 57; Homer, *Eakins*, op. cit., pp. 60–5, 139–40.

70 Goodrich, *Eakins*, op. cit., vol. 1, pp. 102, 105, cf. 184; for the lectures, see Siegl, *Eakins Collection*, op. cit., no. 56E; Foster and Leibold, *Writing About Eakins*, op. cit., p. 187.

Art History ISSN 0141-6790 Vol. 17 No. 3 September 1994 pp. 342–382

'With my own eyes': Fetishism, the Labouring Body and the Colour of its Sex

Griselda Pollock

In 1886, in an anonymous letter to the *Wigan and District Advertiser* (30 January 1886: 2), Arthur Joseph Munby (1828–1910) wrote, 'for my own reasons, I have for more than thirty years, studied the subject of female labour, not merely in books and at second hand, but *with my own eyes and on the spot* (my emphasis)'.[1] Having thus looked, Arthur Munby then rehearsed this proximity in writing detailed accounts in diary notebooks, complete with verbatim conversations recorded in a transcription of Lancashire dialects. (There are nine notebooks devoted to his sixteen visits to the mining districts around Wigan between 1853 and 1887.) He also recaptured his visual encounters in photographs of women miners he bought locally or arranged to have taken in one of the many photographic studios operating in Wigan.[2] In one such image, taken on 11 September 1873 at Little's studio in Clarence Yard, Wigan, Munby is also photographed (plate 9). It is a rare occurrence, unique as far as I know. The photograph, therefore, represents a moment of proximity. The woman in the photograph is the Wigan miner Ellen Grounds, who appears in several photographs and is described in the diaries which Munby kept (plate 28). In his diary entry about the studio session with Ellen Grounds (11 September 1873), Munby writes that he stood beside her 'to show how nearly she approached me in size'. While the photographic collection and the diaries of Munby have become quite well known since the opening of his archive at Trinity College, Cambridge in 1950, the fact that Munby also made sketches and watercolours is less publicized. This article sets out to explain why.

I seem to have been working on this archive forever. It is central in my research project on 'working women and bourgeois men in visual representation in the nineteenth century'. The archive solicits different readings. None exhausts the possibilities and complexities of its word–image relations, its class–gender hierarchies, or race–sexuality axes. So far I have published on the theoretical issues it raises around class and gender in feminist analysis and on the nature of 'the secret' it contained that required its being sealed for forty years.[3]

Attempts to explain Munby's 'secret' as his personally perverse sexual fantasies about large, working-class women have fallen before the theoretical revisions to histories of sexuality offered by Foucault, who argues that Victorian sexuality was endemically 'perverse',[4] and by the deployment of psychoanalysis in contemporary feminist theories of subjectivity and culture. Yet again, photographs

9 Robert Little, *Ellen Grounds, aged 22, a broo wench at Pearson and Knowles's Pits, Wigan, taken 11 September 1873 (and Arthur Munby)*, 1873. Munby Collection, Trinity College, Cambridge. Reproduced by kind permission of the Master and Fellows of Trinity College, Cambridge.

of women miners, acrobats, milkmaids and servants are regularly used now as merely useful documentary images of Victorian 'female labour' and are not read as sites of private pornography. Finally, Lee Davidoff has shown how Munby's interest in and relationships with working women can be read in relation to the symbolic meaning of bodies in bourgeois ideologies of class and gender, that were shaped in childhood through the specificities of childcare in the bourgeois household.[5]

I want, however, to argue against this 'normalizing' trend. The 'secret' that is part of this archive is indeed a shocking one. But it can only be discerned if we track the relations, or rather the relays, between the three instances of representation which compose the archive — writing, photographs and drawings. As an art historian, I am drawn specifically to the unpublished album of sketches from which a few examples have been extracted and reproduced. But there has been a polite, and thus a political, oversight of many of them. It is not that they contain a 'truth' disguised in diary and photographic collection or that they 'express' Munby's feeling or views on working-class women more directly. I aim rather to develop my argument around drawing and visualization, drawing and both the represented and the representing body. This allows us to see both the 'dangers of proximity' and the defence mechanisms incited against that moment of *'with my own eyes'*. It was intense psychic conflict that necessitated the compulsive writing and the tedium of the repetitious collection of photographs. It is necessary to reconstitute the economy — social, symbolic and psycho-sexual — within which the various acts of representation interact.

One of the sketches represents Munby's encounter with Eliza Hayes, aged twenty-five, on Rose Bridge (plate 10). Like the diaries, it is a recollection of a meeting. It is, however, a 'reconstruction' drawn by an amateur draughtsman. This fact of non-professional, untrained image-making is what makes it interesting, and revealing when read in the way I propose to do. An orthodox art-historical analysis might merely be embarrassed by its obviously untutored awkwardness, its trite composition and crude delineation. What we see in the sketch is an aesthetically unmanaged exposure of the significance of that encounter for the person who wanted to commemorate it by a drawing *with his own hand*.

It is a shocking image. What has been attended to here and made *visible* could hardly be even implied in the photograph showing Munby and Ellen Grounds together in one space (plate 9). It is the radical disjunction between two images with similar components that alerts us to the different meaning, purpose and effect of various media in this economy of representation. The sketch does not aim to create the potential similarity between Munby and the woman miner that the photograph could stage for him to contemplate at a later date, in his rooms in London. Instead, the use of ink and added colour demarcate a radical difference between the two figures which is not reducible to any simple statement of conventions for representing gender. The key measure of difference between the two figures is, in fact, colour. 'She' is black-ened. We could also note that he is tall and lean and she is large and square, that his features are sharp, his hands delicate and his feet petite, while her hand is almost bigger than her almost featureless face. In that crucial phrase, all we can see are the whites of her eyes — his terror projected on her terrorizingly illegible face — and her

10 Arthur Munby, *Eliza Hayes, aged 25, Rose Bridge (and Arthur Munby)*, Munby Album (unpublished). Munby Collection, Trinity College, Cambridge.

full lips. Taken together, these distinctions cast what is at once an encounter between a man and a woman, a bourgeois and a working-class person within a racializing and racist stereotypology. The strangeness of the confrontation with an example of 'female labour', her sex anchored by the linguistic message giving her a name, Eliza Hayes, is being represented as both a disordering of gender difference and the construction of racial difference at the point where gender difference breaks down. Yes, this 'Eliza Hayes' dresses, stands and is as big as a 'man'. This disturbance of the order of sexual difference experienced simultaneously as the site of class is visualized through the [European bourgeois] semiotics of racial difference produced within the cruelties of colonial discourse.[6]

The developed state of the figures in the foreground means that the encounter and the detailing of this seesawing of sameness and exaggerated difference are the chief attractions for the producer of the drawing. Yet nothing in a drawing should be ignored. Its being there demands at least cursory consideration. So what of the faintly indicated mining buildings in the background, which cannot escape being described as crudely phallic? They occur on 'her' side of the drawing narrating the place she has worked 'all the days of her life' (see handwritten inscription under the drawing). Balancing the 'male' figure on the left, they also frame the 'female' miner within a doubling of masculine signs. As their minimal form invites us to read the image formally, we note the correspondence between the shadow 'he' casts and the phallicized shape of the lift shaft with its rounded top; the wheel for the cage can, in fact, in contrast to the way the shadow of the 'woman' miner — the part that is cast on the wall — be read as a woman in profile in conventional female garb. Note too that the shadows reverse their respective sizes. This secondary version of the manifest drawing stages an encounter between a mature woman and a large phallus.

As a semiotician inspired by Mieke Bal's notions of 'reading', I should handle all of this evidence.[7] But what I am interested in is what is happening in this drawing notionally *before* the restitution of a phallic masculinity indicated so crudely by the industrial towers and his phallic shadow. I want to concentrate on the fantastic scenario in the foreground — where difference is both suspended and aggressively inflicted, where a white man's race becomes a critical term in the interplay of 'class and gender'.

There is, of course, a common sense explanation. Work around coal mines begrimes the workers. Furthermore there were probably miners of African descent in an area so close to Liverpool, where there had been a considerable black community since the eighteenth century.[8] But blackness, however derived, acquires a symbolic function in these images. Munby does comment repeatedly on the miners' 'blackness' in his diaries. But the sign, *black*, does not only stand for dirt, and dirt for sexuality; it signifies difference at the point where both dirt and sexuality — alluded to as a matter of colour — are caught up in the troubled field of subjectivity, sexuality and vision in a bourgeois imagination that is white, colonial and masculine by virtue of the way these terms coincide and mutually inflect each other.[9]

In this article I shall focus — eventually — on photographs and writings which result from Munby's encounters with Ellen Grounds and on the album of sketches from which the Eliza Hayes drawing is taken.[10] The main point I shall argue is this. The Munby archive has been selectively studied at a cost. Examining the relations *between* diaries, a photographic collection and an album of sketches will suggest that different media, forming the basis for different practices of representation, service different psychic needs which determine for each element, writing, photograph, or drawing, a specific place and role in *an economy of representation* which is both an economy of desire and an economy of power. We cannot read the several kinds of textuality as the unified and unifying expression of their coherent author, Arthur Munby. They are an index of the fractures within an historically positioned subject whose discontinuous psychic interests, desires, narcissistic and sadistic impulses will be spread across an interrelating but fissured field of representations. These furthermore belong to a discursive formation in whose spaces we can find a dispersed range of texts and images: the work of canonical artists and writers, travel literature, governmental inquiry and working-class militancy. Thus, to escape from the kind of fetishizing of Munby as a quirky individual or a psycho-sexual oddity, I will try to establish a broad field in which these images from the Munby archive may be seen to operate — a field that I would define by the terms sexuality and surveillance. Sexuality and surveillance stake out a terrain for a feminist historical analysis of nineteenth-century visual culture opposed to the dominant modes of art history — monograph, movement, style, descent, work of art. The terms sexuality and surveillance propose a project informed by, but not contained within, the major formulations about the social and psychic construction of subjectivity and of sexual and cultural difference provided by the theoretical writings of Michel Foucault and Sigmund Freud. Their theories address common themes — the gaze, sexuality, the subject, discourse/representation — but in incompatible ways. As a result, and despite what they appear to share as topics, each produces a distinct theoretical object. The gaze of mastery is not at all the same as the gaze of desire, for instance. The social subject produced in discourse is not the split subject created psycho-symbolically by language and the unconscious. But as analytical discourses shaped by the historically specific material of nineteenth-century bourgeois society which they theorized, 'Freud' and 'Foucault' converge upon the question raised by my larger project: under what conditions and with what effects did working-class women enter the spaces of bourgeois representation in the nineteenth century?[11] Labour and the labouring body fall into Foucault's analysis of the bourgeois technologies of discipline, surveillance, knowledge and, hence, power, which colonized the social as well as individual body in the nineteenth century. Foucault further argued that in the specifically bourgeois construct of 'sexuality', sex became the cornerstone of a class identity. From that source, the discourses of sex saturated, with perverse sexualities, the bodies of those in all classes the bourgeois system aimed to discipline and those it feared as transgressors of its regime. Foucault's theories are, however, indifferent to questions of gender and hence to the ways class and gender interface in this bourgeois regime of sexuality. Sexual difference figures only momentarily, in its absence, in his study of discourses surrounding the loss of fixed sex, such as his case study on the hermaphrodite Herculine Barbin.[12] Yet his theories of bourgeois sexuality do note its implicit racism.[13]

But what happens if the labouring body is sexed and implicitly raced as in the case of Ellen Grounds or Eliza Hayes? Within regimes of bourgeois representation, can that body be sexed? Is racialization the sign of the conflict? Does it not produce levels of contradiction that then provide spaces for masculine fantasy or feminine pleasures? While it is important to acknowedge women's pleasures and meanings in labour and its costumes, they are not available for study through this archive. The reference should function to mark the possibility of a different class and gender meaning for the bodies which are the topic of Munby's fascination and curiosity.[14] My purpose here is to reverse both the gazes of mastery and of desire which motivated the formation of the Munby archive, making its subject, the white bourgeois man, the object of a feminist re-reading. This repositioning implies a solidarity with the women represented and refigured in the images, in the knowledge that there existed a chasm between what Munby *saw* and what the women whom he scrutinized, photographed, drew and wrote about 'imagined' about themselves.[15]

The marking of the body as a site of sexual difference, however, invokes a different theoretical corpus, psychoanalysis, which theorizes the body as a representation. The body is not a given but is produced as a figuration, and is invested with conflicting meanings and potentialities because it both provides the materials — in the form of the drives — for the figuration of psychic subjectivity and is, in the same process, organized by psychic representations of that materiality.[16] Questions concerning the sexed labouring body in representation might then be framed as follows: what were the pleasures for bourgeois men in looking at representations of labouring bodies which were also female bodies? Did these bodies fall simultaneously, or contradictorily, under the incommensurate gazes of surveillance and of desire? The labouring woman's body appears to escape, or at least, to deviate from the bourgeois semiotics of the visibly gendered and fixed different bodies of Man and Woman, as the very sign and confirmation of the naturalness of difference, hierarchy and masculinity with its privileged status. Did images of labouring women's bodies circulate from Parliamentary report (plate 11) to popular journalism (plate 12), to the walls of official galleries (plate 13) and pages of private albums (plate 10), as elements of the bourgeois deployment of social technologies regulating the body of the proletariat? Were they not also exciting in their defiance of intended discipline, in their total disordering of the visibility of difference, inching across the field of law to that of desire so as to offer, for a moment, erotic, if not pornographic pleasures, in that most unlikely terrain, knowledge? Finally what light could we throw on bourgeois racism by noting the conjunctions in these spaces of gender and colour, of sexuality and blackness?

Other Times, Other Places, The Same Thing?

The singularity of the Arthur Munby archive has directed undue attention to his psycho-sexual peculiarity. I want to point out simply that Munby was not unique in his fascination with the complex of dirt, bodies, sex and female labour. Indeed, there is a range of material from literature to painting, from illustrated journalism to political discourse in the nineteenth century which inhabits this tropic territory. At the intersection of surveillance and sexuality, mining and its communities solicited a range of representations which both throw light upon the Munby archive and create a continuity that allows us to think historically about sexuality and desire in classed, gendered and racializing formations. The mining industry provided the bourgeois tourist with sights/sites that were at once socially peripheral yet fascinating, that were imagined as dark and nether regions, that were places the bourgeois encountered abjection *and* arousal, where black and white were freighted with overdetermined symbolic and psychic loads. In Zola's novel *Germinal*, published in 1884, these materials are presented in a highly developed literary code. Character allows Zola to distinguish the femininities and sexualities played out in bourgeois stories of mining communities. There is the adolescent girl, Catherine, dressed as a boy, who is the focus of

11 Anon *Woman Miner Working Underground* engraving from *First Report of the Commissioners of the Children's Commission on Mines*, Parliamentary Papers, 1842 vol. 15.

12 Anon *Wigan Colliery Girl at Work* from the *Pictorial World*, 18 April, 1874.

13 Constantin Meunier, *Haulier from the Borinage at the Pit*, 1881, oil on canvas. Musée communal des beaux arts, Charleroi.

masculine desire:

> Catherine was ready first. She stepped into her miner's trousers, put on her coarse linen jacket and fastened her blue cap over her knot of hair. In these clean, Monday-morning clothes she looked like a little man, and the only trace of her sex was a slight swing of her hips. (p. 31)[17]

She is contrasted with the overblown and sexually saturated young woman, Mouquette, who, 'shaking with giggles, strutted about among them in her indecent attire. The bulges of flesh, exaggerated to the point of deformity, were both comical and exciting.' (p. 42) Finally there is the mother, Maheude: 'the shapeless body of a female worn out with bearing young, all flabby under her cotton coat and trousers'. (p. 494)[18] Zola's story is set in a mining community in northern France in the 1860s when women still worked underground. (They were excluded in 1874.) Early in the novel, he writes of his outsider hero, Etienne Lantier's disturbing realization of this fact.

> As he turned round, Etienne once more found himself pressing against Catherine. But this time he became aware of the curve of her young breast, and suddenly understood. 'So, you are a girl?' he murmured in amazement. She replied in her gay, straightforward way: 'Yes, of course! What a time it has taken you to find out.' (p. 49)

In 1880 Vincent van Gogh, a later reader of *Germinal*, chose to begin his proposed career in art with a scene drawn from what he had seen *on the spot and with [his] own eyes* in the mining district of the Borinage in Belgium (plate 14). For all its beginner's awkwardness, the drawing comprises the key components of a clichéd visual *phrase*, and it is hence typical of what I have elsewhere defined as Van Gogh's copybook apprenticeship.[19] Dating from August–September 1880, Van Gogh's drawing mimics the illustrated journalism of English magazines like the *Graphic*, to which he hoped to sell his work (plate 15). This straggle of miners going to work in the early dawn tramping through a wintry landscape made cold by snow, and painful through the sharply pointed branches of bare thorn bushes, quotes Jean François Millet's *Going to Work* (1851–3, Cincinnati Art Museum), and through that image, the medieval scenes of seasonal peasant labour and the theme of the Expulsion from the Garden of Eden (Masaccio's famous fresco would make the point here). The selection by artists of the tramp to and from work as a setting for pictures of working people has more mundane origins. These were the only occasions when underground workers were visible to the artistic tourist or travel journalist as can be glimpsed in two related images: one a much later photograph by Gustave Marissiaux (1872–1929) *Return from the Horloz Mine, Tilleur* 1904 (plate 16), and the other a painting by Van Gogh's Belgian contemporary Constantin Meunier (1831–1905), *Return from Work*, 1881 (plate 17). Zola also invoked this sight:

> And all along the road from the silent village to the panting Le Voreux a line of shadows tramped slowly through the blast. The colliers were

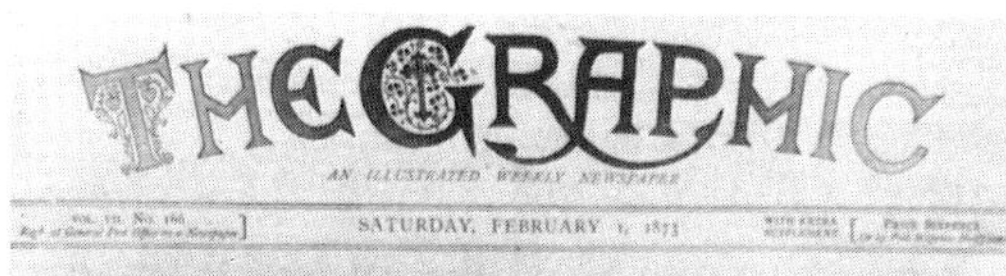

14 Vincent van Gogh *Miners Going to Work*, 1880. Rijksmuseum Kroeller-Mueller, Otterloo.
15 *The Graphic* 1874.

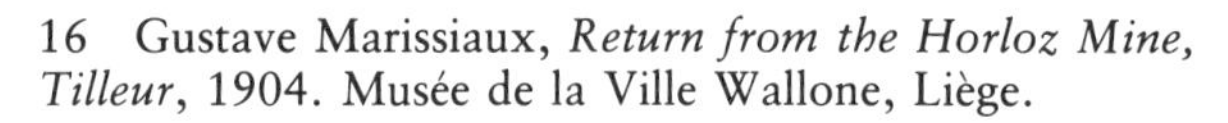

16 Gustave Marissiaux, *Return from the Horloz Mine, Tilleur*, 1904. Musée de la Ville Wallone, Liège.

17 Constantin Meunier, *The Return from Work*, 1881. Musée Constantin Meunier, Brussels.

> off to work with shambling gait and folded arms, for they did not know what else to do with them. Each one had his *briquet* on his back. Though they were shivering in their thin clothes, they did not quicken step, but plodded on, strung out along the road like a trampling herd . . . The miners squared their shoulders, folded their arms, and set off in a straggling line, with a rolling gait which made their big bones stand out through their thin clothes. As they went along in broad daylight, they looked like a band of Negroes who had fallen in the mud. (p. 74)[20]

Meunier's painting alerts us to what is only tentatively present in Van Gogh's drawing — the *women* miners. Belgium was one of the last European countries to forbid women's labour underground. Van Gogh's drawing includes both the conventionally dressed women surface workers, wearing skirts with a shawl and bonnet, and the women who went down into the pits like Catherine Maheu — 'dressed like lads'. Their costume included short knee-length breeches and jackets which attracted a variety of kinds of attention and interpretation as the quote from Zola above indicates, and paintings and drawings by Meunier and Cécile Douard further demonstrate. Douard (1866–1941), a French artist who worked in Belgium, made these women the subject of major paintings and drawings which alternated between deviance and sexualization. In some works she stressed the size and strength of women doing heavy labour underground, pushing and hauling the coal-laden trucks from the cutting face to the collection depots (plate 18), while other drawings feature scenes of women waiting to descend. These images

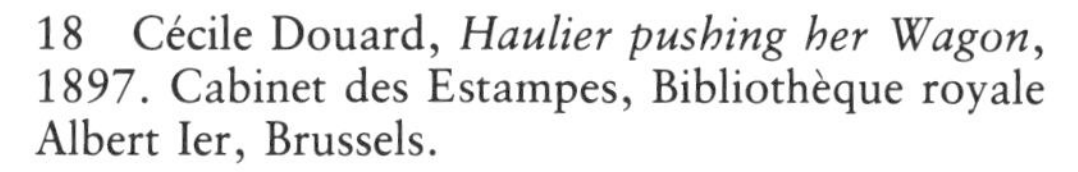

18 Cécile Douard, *Haulier pushing her Wagon*, 1897. Cabinet des Estampes, Bibliothèque royale Albert Ier, Brussels.

19 Cecile Douard, *Hauliers awaiting the Descent*, 1892. Cabinet des Estampes, Bibliothèque royale Albert Ier, Brussels.

show the costume exposing a more conventionally feminine body, which, in pose and viewpoint, becomes almost coy (plate 19).

However feebly realized, Van Gogh's drawing includes the key components of a dispersed discourse on the mining communities as exemplars of the radical alienness of industrial labour while not locating that alienation as a social effect in and of capitalism. The inclusion of the betrousered women miners, however, is the least developed element of this work. These trousered women in the drawing are unemphatic, in direct disproportion to the anxiety they aroused. In Meunier's painting, by contrast, attention is drawn to the young woman miner by narrativizing the scene. She turns 'in her gay and straightforward way' towards her companions and thus towards the viewer. She holds her clogs in her hand which in turn makes the viewer notice the nakedness and size of her bare feet and calves. None the less, the uncertain inclusion of the underground women workers in Van Gogh's beginner's attempt underlines the critical point of fascination which motivated the repeated gaze of the bourgeois tourist at this industrial site: the labouring body and the problem of its sex — or shall we say the problem that a labouring woman posed to a regime of sex whose privileged sign and ideological foundation was a specific and gendered body, believed to secure that regime by the 'natural' and given character of its difference.

Let me introduce now a written text, *The Belgians at Home*, published in 1911 (the date of the exclusion of women from Belgian pits) by an Edwardian novelist and travel writer of no great distinction, Clive Holland. Holland's is a mundane text, balancing the factual with the picturesque, the exotic with the frankly horrific. It shares with many other texts, both painted and written, a way of constituting an object for investigation and consumption, a system for establishing 'truth' about labour, the body and sexuality.

The text is a tapestry of several orders of discourse which collectively produce social knowledge for an authoritative, bourgeois gaze. The passage that interests me narrates the journey to Mons, part of the industrial south of the country. It begins with a **socioeconomic** discourse which supplies a way of knowing strangeness through official facts and figures. The region has been transformed by the rapid impact of industrialization which now conditions its character and appearance. Unfettered and sudden industrialization of a region crudely exploited the work force and its natural resources. This is, according to Holland, a now historical fact which it is safe to know in 1911 because the text can reassure the readers that this harsh face of capitalism has been transcended. Conditions have now been much improved and are better managed. The acknowledged evils of the system in 'the bad old days' have been transferred, however, to the gene pool of the local workers. Their bodies have internalized the past; their physical appearance bears traces of those 'hard times'. Social and economic relations are thus distanced through an **anthropological** discourse. This transition is the site of a bourgeois process of *racialization* of its social others. The workers in the mining industry form a physiognomic type. They have become a 'race':

> . . . The effect of this almost unremitting, arduous and unhealthy toil has been the production of a race dwarf-like in stature. . . . This strange weird type, which chiefly comes of the third and fourth generation of miner is particularly noticeable.[21]

The body is thus a key sign for the displacement of social relations and its effects, in Lenin's phrase overwork and underconsumption, and for the emergence of the strategy of racialization of the working class. History and society evaporate before the concrete physicality of appearance and its apparently genetic foundations. Upon this basis, a **sociological** discourse can once again operate because the workers have been othered so radically, racially, that they can no longer implicate the bourgeois readers, despite their incomes supplied by shares in the great mining companies. The text can then discuss the social customs and habits of this 'race' apart. They are, we are then told, illiterate and irregular, their marital and sexual arrangements frankly deviant. Local cultures cannot be imagined as specific customs within the diversity of human populations. The implicit judgement according to an unspoken norm introduces a **moral** discourse through which the culture of this race is roundly condemned: 'It is the habits and customs to which we have referred which make Hainault a dark blot upon the map of Belgium, a district notorious for its immorality, crime and brutalised population.' (p. 125)

Kinship systems specific to a particular community, which were determined by economic factors related to methods of payment and employment current in the mining industry, are represented as deviations which indicate the corrupted and criminalized character of the people. An unspoken norm generates both a national and a transnational class identity for its non-mining, and non-Belgian readers. For the mining communities, marriage meant the removal of a son's or daughter's wages from the parental household, and was often delayed until younger children could replace their older siblings' earning capacities. Miners were often paid for teamwork, and family labour ensured that scanty wages remained in the household rather than being shared out with subcontracted labour. The specific cultural and social forms of the mining communities were negotiated responses to specific economic conditions. Poor wages caused hardship and suffering, but the typical kinship arrangements could not be said to brutalize, demoralize or criminalize a population. As Angela Davis has argued about the specific strategies of resistance in slave households, the management of interpersonal relationships and sexual mores was at least one space in which the dehumanization of enslavement and exploitation of the worker could be resisted.[22] That the miners can be imagined as 'brutalized' reveals the presence of the laws of sexuality governing the bourgeois social and subjective constitution. The text reveals unconscious motivations precisely at the point at which the sociological and economic discourses give way to a moralizing yet fascinated exploration of sex in the life of the mining community. The implicit assumptions of Holland's text, its baseline for nature and truth, articulate the ideological formations of bourgeois society fixated on female chastity as a necessary corollary of the maintenance of private property, which can only be secured through legally contracted heterosexual relations and legitimated reproduction. It is only the absence of the bourgeois law as the regulatory condition for 'sexuality' (used here in Foucault's sense of a specifically bourgeois construct) which renders the practices of other populations illicit or transgressive. This text, like Munby's, perpetually summons up the opposing but normative term of the binary opposition in order to position the reader in relation to the fascinating but ultimately abnormal social other.

The fictive landscape of work and degradation which the text has been sketching is finally populated with its most lucid and overdetermined sign — the body of labouring women:

> As one cycles along the road on the way to Mons . . . one meets at sundown the stunted generation of miners flowing in their hundreds and thousands out of the colliery gates, dull with fatigue and often bemused with the effects of the *schnick* they have been drinking all day. Nor are the women and girls more pleasant figures: perhaps even less so. One passes hundreds of them, low of stature, with bare arms grimed with the dust of the coal they have been hauling and tipping out of huge wicker baskets upon railways sidings into the awaiting trucks, *faces hard with the degradation of unfitting toil*, arms and figures like those of prize fighters — masses of muscle, almost denuded of any curve or softness. At first one may mistake them for gangs of boys or

> lads . . . Often their muscular legs are bare, and their feet merely thrust into wooden sabots. Often their feet are shoeless. Beings which those gifted with the kindliest charity can scarcely look on save with disgust. (p. 126)

We seem at first to be in Van Gogh's landscape, but at twilight not dawn, when stunted miners flow out, exhausted and drunk. But as the gaze distinguishes the women and girls, we are precipitated into Douard's frank confrontation with a woman haulier (plate 20). Despite their low stature, the effect of this labour is not to stunt women but to turn them into prizefighters. (Recall Munby's interest in Ellen Grounds's stature.) Size then becomes the sign of their deviance, which proliferates all over their bodies — grimy arms, bared legs, roughly shod feet. A fictive body is aggressively assembled from these overcharged parts. We cannot sufficiently stress both the familiar (in the sense that it is still with us) and the alien nature of the nineteenth-century bourgeois man's obsession with women's exposed legs. Apart from the regulated trope of the nude, women's legs were never represented unclothed. Abigail Solomon-Godeau's important study of a French archive, in which a countess aberrantly presented her naked legs to the photographer, significantly titled 'The Legs of the Countess', argues that even in pornography the exposed was always related to the stockinged in the art of dressing or undressing.[23] While dancers and other performers may not have worn skirts, their revealed legs were sheathed in tights to ensure what she calls 'the transformation of carnal flesh into the sublimated sculptural form of aesthetic, albeit eroticised, delectation' (plate 29). It may be that the obsessional interest in the mining woman had something to do with a costume which covered the groin but 'revealed' the legs, an inversion of the bourgeos lady, who wore no underclothes but hid her legs. We can fairly certainly surmise that the issue of blunt nakedness of the leg worked *metonymically* in regard to the masculine erotic gaze moving from leg to genitals, but that it equally functioned fetishistically as defence and disavowal in relation to men's fantasies and fears about the sight of women's sex.

To return to the passage quoted from Holland's text, the imaginary traversal of the body is concluded with the equally troubling disorder of the face: 'hard with the degradation of unfitting toil'. Face and body signify paradigmatically in relation to a chain whose other pole contains idle and curvaceous bodies, softened faces and elevated or fitting occupations. The structuring absence of the text is the bourgeois/feminine body, maintaining through its absolute difference from the masculine body, a gender division which is at the same time a hierarchy of the sexes. The bodies of the labouring women throw into confusion this feminity and unravel the signifying chain which secures bourgeois masculine identity and authority.

These bodies disorder a world of visible knowledge and transparent difference: at first sight, they can be mistaken for boys. In the art form of the female nude, the feminine body was configured as if a soft, pink bonelessness and undulating curvaceousness were natural, that is, nature as only culture could reveal it, and simply coincident with the form and skin of woman (see, for instance, Alexandre Cabanel's *Birth of Venus*, 1863, Paris: Musée d'Orsay). Holland's text uses the

20 Cecile Douard, *Haulier, Seated Resting*, n.d. Université de travail Paul Pastur, Charleroi.

word 'denuded', which means to be made naked, for bodies which are in fact fully and often coarsely dressed. The paradox indicates a loss of the confidence normally secured by the aesthetically constructed nude when sexuality entered the field of vision. The erotic charge of the female nude, the obverse of its function as the truth of woman, is displaced here by the anxiety about a costume which is a state of undress, which covers and exposes in equal proportions. In bourgeois culture, we find the ironic pairing of the artificially fashioned form of the female nude and over-costumed lady, hatted, gloved, corsetted and so swathed in metres of heavy cloth that scarcely a trace of the body was visible. The female body in both seemingly opposite instances is rewritten through fetishism, of art form or of costume, both of which signify the masquerade, that is femininity as artifice appearing as merely acculturated nature. The sight of working women wearing trousers, which so insists upon the fact of bipedalism, thus signifying women's similarity as humans to men, and yet, simultaneously inviting the viewer/reader to imagine the specificity of what happens between their legs, exposes the bourgeois fiction and fetishization of woman through what I have to dare to call an insistent and unmediated exposure to physical nature. Nature here does not signify an essence, but an undifferentiated territory, which like Kristeva's semiotic, is the recalcitrant materialism of which signs are made. There are their legs, muscled, dirty, walking, unavoidably visible, factual. Like the little boy in Freud's legend of sexual difference, when encountering the genitally specific female body as what seems an uninscribed nature, the male does not know what he has seen. Later the semiotic frame of phallocentric culture names what was seen as absence and makes it the very sign of lack. But in the case of these evidently powerful, unswathed, unveiled, uncorsetted bodies, the fascination lies precisely in the suspension of that law of difference with its expulsion of the masculine subject from its pre-Oedipal fantasy of oneness or likeness to the grand, powerful and mercifully as yet undifferentiated maternal body.

Seesawing across this unregulated body of the labouring woman, the text represents the women miners of Belgium as a transgression of femininity, and this is as much a question of class as of gender. They have too much, and are too visible. The idle feminine lady has to be summoned by the text to define the deviance of women workers and as the consolation for the dreadful sight of what labour has done to them. Here a sketch from the Munby album might serve as illustration of the unfixing of 'femininity' which this text struggles to contain by invoking the culturally invented 'natural' woman as opposed to these deviants (plate 21). These coincidences between Zola, Van Gogh, Meunier, Douard, Holland and Munby, serve not to trace a descent, or a set of influences, but instead to produce a Foucauldian genealogy for the bourgeois fantasy of the labouring body and its problematic sex. Rigidly encased in a costume which physically inhibits her movements and renders her the mannequin of a femininty she is required to perform in person and in daily ritual, the lady is excluded from labour and money, from mobility in the public realm, from locations of power. There on the roads of Mons, Holland shows his readers the blatant lawlessness of women who walk like sailors along public roads, bodies half-exposed, on their way to and from the work which earns them precious little, but money all the same. In this context, the evocation of this tiny, white, delicate, rarefied femininity is part of the signification of bourgeois masculine power, racially as well as in terms of class and gender. Proletarian women such as these miners defied this order, neither confirming the visual axis of sexual difference, nor exhibiting through their bodies and gestures a powerless deference. In baring and bearing the signs of work and exploitation upon a body which should signify female gender precisely through the absence of both, these working women confused the field of vision by configuring class and yet defying bourgeois codes of gender by their physical size. This conjunction of labour and sexuality disturbs the regime of truth upon which the touristic vision was premised. Yet it exercised sufficient fascination to solicit both extended scrutiny and the most energetic and compelling prose, even if the desire to see and traverse every deviant element must finally be disavowed as too disgusting to contemplate. The text assumes its distance from the deviant configurations, dirt and moral corruption, only after it has truly rubbed its readers' noses in it. Here we can see the labouring

21 Arthur Munby, 'Miner and Lady' (untitled), n.d.. Munby Album (unpublished), Munby Collection, Trinity College, Cambridge.

woman's body, particularly that of the miner, as the point at which the forces of surveillance (regulation, mastery and discipline) and sexuality (fascination, mystery and desire) converge to overdetermine the presence of these troubling bodies in bourgeois representation.

Masquerade and Fetish: the Semiotics of Appearance and Difference

There are photographs of the Belgian women miners in the Munby archive. But the majority of his photographs are of a group of about 1,300 British women miners, living within a ten-kilometre radius of the town of Wigan, Lancashire. They were surface workers — known as pit-brow lasses (plates 22–25). Women had been banned from underground employment in British pits by an act of parliament in 1842. During a British parliamentary commission on the employment of children in the mines, men from elite social groups in government visited the coal-mining districts of the country and 'discovered' that women as well as children were labouring underground in this industry. The wealth of first-hand evidence from the women themselves recorded by the commissioners

22 Robert Little, *Female Collier from Rose Bridge Pits, height about 5 feet 9, taken 10 August 1869*, carte-de-visite. Munby Collection (112-7-c), Trinity College, Cambridge.

23 Robert Little 'Pitbrow Worker, Wigan', 1866, carte-de visite. Munby Collection, (III-5-c), Trinity College, Cambridge.

24 Robert Little 'Pitbrow Worker, Wigan', 1866, carte-de-visite. Munby Collection (III-19-a), Trinity College, Cambridge.

25 Louisa Millard 'Pitbrow Woman', 1869. Munby Collection (Album II-112-10-c), Trinity College, Cambridge.

insists upon the hardship of the labour in terms of conditions, hours and pay. The conclusion drawn by those advancing a bill for the sudden and absolute abolition of this labour with all its attendant hardships on working people in single-industry communities, was couched in terms of shame, terror and moral panic at this 'evil'. All the argumentation against the vested interests of capital were couched in highly gendered terms and required a constant assertion of the unnatural character of this labour for women and of the moral dangers which threatened further to denature woman as they worked long hours in mixed company, unsupervised, deep in the darkness of the earth.

Bodies were crucial signifiers in this struggle. Commissioners described the dress or rather undress of the mining women. They crawled along tunnels dragging heavy wagons of coal dressed only in a pair of breeches, with a leather belt around the waist to which was attached a chain which, passing between their legs, attached them like horses to their loads. One commissioner noted, 'The chain, passing high up between the legs of the girls, had worn through large holes in their trousers, and any sight more disgusting or indecent or revolting can scarcely be imagined as these two girls at work — no brothel can beat it.'[25] The 1842 report contains one of the first instances of graphic illustration as opposed to technical diagrams accompanying a parliamentary document (plate 11). Despite its gauche simplicity, or rather, because of its evident lack of artistic skill, it provided convincing visual evidence to corroborate the horrors imagined in the verbal report. Because it could not be accused of using artistry to fabricate the scene, the drawing appeared to offer vicarious yet vivid access to both the site and the sight of the immoralities hitherto shielded in darkness and distance. This illustration was also independently circulated in London salons, and its currency, as proof of the 'pornography' daily enacted in the mines, contributed to the build-up of pressure which assisted the rapid passing of Lord Shaftesbury's bill to remove women from the mines.

Women continued to work in British mines out of economic necessity because there was often no other employment in their region. But they did so in disguise, dressed in clothes borrowed from brothers and fathers, while others accepted work thus dressed on the pitbanks. In 1863 the House of Commons received a petition from the National Association of Coal, Lime and Ironstone Miners of Great Britain, in which, amongst other demands for protection against the unfair practices of the coal owners, the Union stated: 'That the practice of employing females on or about the pitbanks of mines and collieries is degrading to the sex and leads to gross immorality, and stands as a foul blot on the civilisation and humanity of the kingdom.'[26]

During the hearings of the Select Committee of the House of Commons set up to examine the miners' complaints, evidence was taken about women's labour at the pits. The costume of the women regularly featured as a symptom of the evil female labour caused to the femininity (read domesticity) of the women as potential wives and mothers; it was called 'a man's dress' and one witness added, 'I believe in some cases it drowns all sense of decency betwixt men and women, they resemble each other so much.'[27] Thus the erosion of visible difference is held responsible for a deviation from a desired mode of behaviour which here found the labour aristocracy attempting to enlist the governing bourgeoisie in

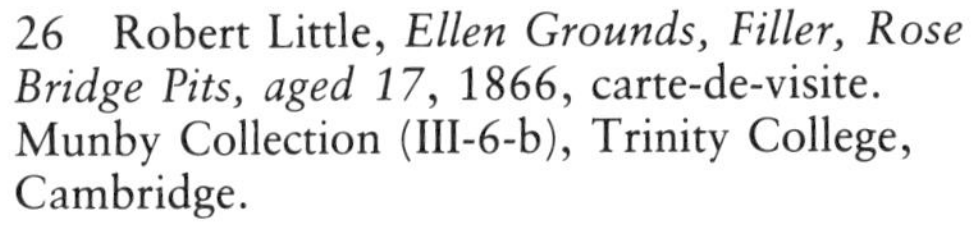

26 Robert Little, *Ellen Grounds, Filler, Rose Bridge Pits, aged 17*, 1866, carte-de-visite. Munby Collection (III-6-b), Trinity College, Cambridge.

27 Robert Little, *Ellen Grounds, Collier in Sunday Dress*, 1866, carte-de-visite. Munby Collection (III-6-d), Trinity College, Cambridge.

disciplining working women into a cultural and social ideal of feminine domesticity.[28]

Evidence for the 'peculiarity of dress' and hence the moral danger was supplied by photographs — the first time that photographs were submitted as evidence to a parliamentary inquiry. Given the date of this photograph of Ellen Grounds aged seventeen made by Robert Little in 1866 (plate 26), it is possible that her image was placed before the Committee as typical of the working costume of the Wigan pitbrow workers. While indicating the development of discourses linking vision and truth, with which photography was becoming implicated in the new disciplinary technologies, their appearance indicates the belief that degradation and immorality would be visible in the physical appearance of the body — a moral and spiritual lack would be there for all to see. What is there to be seen in the photographs is, however, only clothes and studio props — presenting a striking incongruity between the pastiche of country house grandeur serving as the cheap studio backdrop with the crudely patterned carpet, and the roughly dressed and booted woman, leaning against a just visible wooden body prop, and awkwardly handling an out-of-date riddle and spade. The costume of deviance, however, is supplemented by the rhetorical devices of posture, gesture and position of the body in relation to the photographer's and hence the viewer's gaze. This involves frontality, feet spread apart, and often hands on hips or otherwise firmly placed. Photography does not record a body in representation but produces a symbolic body for and through representation (plates 22–26).

Representatives of the mine owners opposed to any further curtailment of their access to cheap female labour arranged for the Committee to see another set of photographs of the same women. Mr Gilroy, manager of one of the major mining concerns in Wigan, had his 'girls' photographed in their Sunday dresses, meant to signify not costume, but the outward and visible signs of an inward and invisible femininity (plate 27). Again Ellen Grounds appears in the archive, dressed in Sunday clothes, seated now on a velvet upholstered chair, resting her elbow elegantly on the table with its decorative plant. This second series of photographs of miners in Sunday dresses tries to argue that working clothes are only that, a costume, garments placed on an essentially feminine body. This second image is offered as a truth and its artifice is less immediately evident for this is the prevailing fiction, a class ideal of a feminine body, without muscle, grime, or signs of labour. These two sets of photographs allow us to compare the equal but opposing fantasies which I suggested structured Clive Holland's much later text and which are constantly re-enacted across the Munby archive.

If we look at a series of *carte-de-visite* photographs of Wigan women in their working gear (plates 22–27), we can identify a recurring rhetoric in which the sitters are positioned for the viewer. Women stand or sit, always frontally posed, face to camera, with all its resultant awkwardness, legs planted firmly apart, holding studio props of shovels and sieves. Hands resting on shovel hilts, or arms on hips, the body is opened out for the viewer and acquires a solid facticity as a body. Yet, in an important and historically precise sense, it remains hard to sex the body according to contemporary codes. In the Sunday photographs (such as plate 27), the women sit in a quite different fashion, legs erased in the sweep of the flowing skirt, hands gracefully and inertly placed in laps, elbows elegantly resting on a table, bodies turned gently off-centre to make inclined heads and arms a part of a continuous flowing line with softened contours. It is superfluous to talk frankly of bodies. These are the codes of the representation of femininity in which the body is absented and a more immaterial 'condition' — femininity — is substituted through textures of fabric and the cut of costume, the fall of wrist and fingers.[29]

The specific appeal and pleasure of photography resides in its power to provide such credible figurations of fantasy by constructing with equal conviction such different bodies. In the one group, sexual difference is seemingly suspended by bodies which are known to be women's but which look like men's — muscled, direct, tough. The women have bodies but no strong signs to sex them, that is, to make them signify a specific construct of sexual difference. I am perhaps overstating this, for the Munby archive contains many images which show women with earrings and frilly blouses or wearing a hat. But I suggest that we cannot now read these images at all as they would have signified in the nineteenth century for such combinations of what were once men's work clothes, namely jeans, with make-up and earrings are now a common feature of Western codes of femininity. We have to realize how very recently Western women began to wear trousers and how rapidly it has become normalized so that what we may be seeing in these images as clear indexes of feminine decoration and fashion were then overwhelmed by anomaly of their trousers and clogs or by something else about the combination of clothes, which I shall come on to later.[30]

In the other set of photographs, sexual difference is confirmed, paradoxically through the evasion of the body and the proliferation of rhetorical signs of difference coded through costume, posture, gesture and overall harmonious effect, which coalesces into the naturalism with which photography seduces us into accepting the world as transparently present: see, here is woman. The photographs from these two albums reveal that difference is an inscription on the body, a play of signs, and not a matter of given facts, or self-evident identity. It further shows that disordering a given system of inscription has unpredictable pleasures which need to be analysed at the level at which they may be operating — psycho-symbolically.

In twentieth-century psychoanalysis femininity has been theorized precisely as *masquerade*, that is, as not so much a veiling of a real or essential femininity as an effect of signification of difference for men within a phallic economy of signs and bodies which make femininity always a pose, and a fiction. Femininity is defined in relation to the phallus which one can either pretend to be or to have, while of course never acceding to either condition. Woman disguises her lack *vis-à-vis* the phallus by appearing to be it for men, identifying with the lack it ironically signifies, and hence becoming a signifier for masculine desire. Desire desires that which is impossibly lost, and it is occasioned by submission to the law which makes one subject to language and a sex. This account is the highly abstract and symbolic Lacanian reworking of Freud's thesis which, in fact, has a much more nineteenth-century feel to it. Freud writes of the absence and presence of a penis. The masculine subject's own sense of precarious subjectivity — his narcissism — is protected by a game played out on the body of woman whose apparent physical difference, registered as a lack, is disavowed by *fetishism*, the logic of substitution which allows the fetishist to maintain incompatible knowledges:

> A narcissistic relation to the male body image as phallic is at stake, but it is secured by reference to the mother's body. The fetish represents the desired but absent maternal phallus. It is a compromise formation between the traumatic perception that the mother has no penis and the continuing wish that she should have one.[31]

The fetish protects the son against narcissistic injury to his own body image as phallic — that is the obligatory acknowledgement of his own lack. The mother's apparent lack is itself fetishized so that the son appears to lack lack. Difference is, therefore, not a categorization, a, b, c, etc., but a relational effect, **a** and **non-a**, in which imaginary, symbolically inscribed bodies become signs within a system that is asymmetrical *vis-à-vis* **a** (masculine) and **non-a** (feminine) subjects, but which is no less traumatic for both **a** and **non-a** as a result of the precarious hierarchies it arranges. Its very instability and fictionality generates specific anxieties and intensities at the level of its constant repetition in representation. Whichever formulation of the masquerade one turns to, and there are several within the psychoanalytic debate — Freud, Lacan, Rivière, Johnston, Doane — the basic issue is that 'woman'/femininity signifies what she is not — whatever that might be, for it is not assumed to be knowable within the phallocentric economy which uses woman as a means to erect a difference whose positive effect is the illusion of 'man'.[32] John Fletcher, summing up Lacan's contribution, concludes:

> In Lacanian theory a series of lacks and losses, of the object in the drive, of the subject in relation to language, are overlaid and signified by the phallus and the woman in so far as she assumes the position of the phallus. As man's missing part, as substitute for what he has had to sacrifice or mortgage to the Law, the woman-as-phallus for the man comes to signify in Lacan's terms 'what he has to renounce, that is, **jouissance**'. Just as [Claire] Johnston's account insists on the woman's radical heterogeneity that is excluded or repressed by the phallic system of the male and the not-male, so Lacan's account recognises 'a rejection of an essential part of her femininity' entailed by the woman's position as phallus-for-the-man. In his later formulations, her position as 'not all' (*pas tout*) is supplemented by 'something more' (*en plus*), a *jouissance* beyond the phallic function. The masquerade comes to signify the alienation involved in the substitution of 'appearing' for 'having'.[33]

These photographs seem to give us some access to the anomalies of this process when confronting the emergent rhetorics and technologies of photographic representation. Heavily indebted to existing visual conventions and practices, photography, none the less, offered a new kind of visuality when it restaged those poses and gestures in its own, emergent semiosis. Through the index of a proper name, these images appear to give us simply two views of Ellen Grounds in 1866. Both — or some pair like them — lay on the table in the House of Commons, and both were then made part of Arthur Munby's private collection. Their use was in the movement of a gaze between them — and the impossibility of using either in the presence of the other to fix a meaning for what they purported to represent. The Sunday dress image provides the 'appearance of femininity', while signifying 'femininity as appearance' — *masquerade* — which is as much a veiling and a displacement as any kind of showing. The poses and presentation of the women in their work-clothes signify a kind of blunt presence where hands go out of shape as they are used to grasp shovel hilts or stretch to encompass wide riddles, and an apron is tucked up to reveal two legs ending in firmly shod, large feet. These images are figuratively naked — revealing not the body of woman, as we wrongly assume the nude does. They offer the prosaic conjunction of the signs of the artifice of sexual difference, as the conventional signs of both masculinity and femininity cohabit a single form. Can these details be managed as fetishes — to disavow the maternal lack by finding bodies that seem to promise to be both *pas tout* (the feminine lady as lack which ensures a coherence of masculine mastery of the phallus), and *en plus* (the phallic mother beyond the law of difference where the boy can also be the phallus for her whose desire he wishes to fulfil)?

It is impossible for us now to register an erotic if not a pornographic charge in what were then shocking and exciting transgressions of the regimes of sexual and social order. If we were to see them only within the Foucauldian system of surveillance, exhibiting as part of their utilization in parliamentary investigation, the disciplinary impulse in which a union of working men collaborated with the bourgeoisie to domesticate women, we would miss their productivity in relation to sexuality. The existence of these photographs in the Munby archive indicates not only their polyvalence, but also the fact that they offered an unstable visual field which was fractured by other — psychic — exigencies precisely because of their specificity as images, participating in what Jacqueline Rose has called, 'sexuality in the field of vision'.[34]

Fetishism, Writing and Drawing

Let us turn now to a diary entry, which records Munby's visit to the home of Ellen Grounds, Wednesday 10 September 1873.[35]

> I reached Wigan . . . and walked up to Scholes, the main street of the colliers' quarter of Wigan, to call on Ellen Grounds, the nearest of my friends, and learn from her the news of the pits. . . . Here I knocked: and opening the door whom should I see but Miss Ellen Grounds, wiping the deal table in the middle of the brick floor. Miss Ellen who is now four and twenty, was in woman's clothes, this time: a decent brown stuff frock with sleeves, and a white apron: and her light brown hair was knotted up simply behind, and brushed smooth against her comely cheerful face. She looked up with a puzzled smile. 'What, Ellen dun yo known ma?' — 'Yea, Ah do — why yo' was here better than three years sin!' she answered: and gave me her hand, which was clean, and in spite of her manly work was neither coarse nor very hard. A fire was blazing in the grate, of course: and one side of it sat Ellen's father the brooman, who was fresh from work and was black; on the other, her handsome old mother, in a blue striped kirtle and a close frilled cap. And by the window with his feet on the settle, sat her younger brother, a collier; who never spoke a word the whole time I was there, except Yes and No — in answer to me. 'Sit ye doon,' said the damsel, handing me a woodenseated chair; and the old couple added 'Aye, sit ye doon.' But why did Ellen wear this *effeminate* dress? Why was she so *exasperatingly clean*, and the coal dust gone from her hands? Because she has been playing all week, stopping away from the pit, to attend her mother, who is unwell. . . . And has Ellen got a sweetheart? 'Naa, Ah lost him,' said Ellen calmly enough. 'He died o'smallpox,' said

her father, 'but he's left her summat to remember him by.' 'What, that two year old child on the floor?' 'Yah!' said Ellen taking up the lad and fondling him, which indeed she had done before: and added in reply to what I said, 'But Ah never had a chance to marry him, yo know.' Neither she nor her parents were ashamed of the matter, though they are all decent folks. Her father was evidently fond and proud of the child . . . Then we talked about being 'drawed aht' [photographed]. Ellen said she had been 'draw'd aht twice in my pit claes' and had seen her own picture hanging up for sale. It is not good however; and I asked her if she could not come tomorrow, as she is 'playing'. Her father and mother both concurred; and Ellen never thought of objecting to walk through the town in her pit dress; which indeed dozens of pit girls do daily, and go of their own accord to be drawed aht in that attire, in order that they may send the picture to absent friends. So Ellen promised to come tomorrow in her pit clothes . . . The only question was, whether she should come with a black face or a clean one. She observed that one often looks just as well with *a black face*: I left the point to her discretion: but asked to see her working dress. 'Here's t'bonnet,' she said bringing out of the scullery the pit girls' wadded hood bonnet, sound and fairly clean: 'and here's mah bedgoon'; which was of pink cotton, patched with bits of blue. And the breeches? 'Naa,' said Ellen, with creditable shamefastness, 'Mah breeches is oopstairs. Ah cannot fotch 'em dahn.' Her father and mother, however, both counselled her to bring them: and *I was glad of the opportunity of examining this unique garment*. So Ellen went upstairs, and came down with her trousers over her arm. 'Them's mah breeches,' she said: 'they're patched that Ah connot tell t'maan piece on 'em: they was a pair o' men's owd breeches when Ah gat 'em, and Ah've wore 'em t'nahn year at Ah've worked at pits.' And they were still good: a pair of trousers made up of patches of cloth and cotton and linen of various colours, but toned down by coaldust to a blackish brown. They were warmly lined and wadded, especially at the knees, to protect them when kneeling among the coals or crawling up the shoot: a garment well fitted to keep warm the legs of a woman doing outdoor work. *And (which spoke well for the fair wearer) the inside of the trousers was* ***clean***. They had button holes round the top. How do you keep them on? I asked. 'Well,' said Ellen in mere simplicity and not coarseness, 'there's many a wench ties string around their waist: but Ah've getten a good backsahd, at keeps me breeches op!' She who made this dreadful speech is a fair and comely English girl: homekeeping, industrious, and virtuous according to her lights.[36]

This passage merits more attention than I can give it here. Its length is important, as is its detailed recreation of the setting and the dialogue. It is typical of the writing in the diaries about the women miners — tedious, detailed, anxious to miss nothing, mundane and yet, at moments, deeply shocking. As a text it reveals much through the pace of the writing. The time it took to write down, and then to be read, is what alone conveys the timing of the drama it *commemorates*. I use the word advisedly: Freud writes of the fetish:

> Something else has taken its [the maternal penis'] place, has been appointed its substitute, as it were, and now inherits the interest which was formerly directed to its predecessor. But this interest suffers an extraordinary increase as well, because the horror of castration has set up a *memorial* to itself in the creation of the substitute.[37]

I want to touch on a few elements, which relate to the argument I have tried to develop here. Munby is disappointed to find Ellen 'exasperatingly clean' and dressed in woman's clothes. He calls these *effeminate*, a significant inversion. Working clothes were condemned by the miners' union as being masculine, yet Munby treats them as the norm he desires while femininity in this space has become disappointing, if not deviant. Most crucial is the examination of Ellen's clothes themselves. Munby wanted direct, physical and visual contact, *on the spot and with my own eyes*. Fetishism is a necessary part of the process. The diary text in which the encounter is recorded is longwinded, and boringly so, preparing us for the ultimate sight by prolonged foreplay composed of professional observation, the socio-economic disclosure of facts and figures. The pattern is not dissimilar to that which I traced in Holland's prosaic tourist guide to Belgium. We are told what the clothes are made from and how they have worn; information here services an unacknowledged erotic agenda. The discourse on cleanliness — his initial disappointment at finding her white and not black with coal dirt — now signifies in another, sexual, register when we are made witness to his peering into the crotch of her trousers for signs of dirt, which is, of course, a sign of sexuality, examining that area which would have touched the sexual parts of her body, looking directly at which might prove psychologically traumatic. The fact that the trousers are clean, that is without evident signs of sexual or other bodily functions, produces a prosaic relief following the excitement and danger of having dared indirectly to look at a woman's sex. 'Nothing to see' is, paradoxically, comforting. We are thrown back to that moment in Freud's story of the little boy when he 'first catches sight of a girl's genital region, he begins by showing irresolution and lack of interest; he sees nothing or disavows that he has seen, he softens it down, or looks about for expedients for bringing it into line with his expectations.'[38] There are many levels in which fetishism operates here and I am not wanting to reduce all masculine sexuality and all problems of sexuality and vision back to this one process. In this instance of one passage from Munby's diary, there is fetishism in the displacement of viewing 'woman' onto scientific investigation of the *inverted* masquerade of femininity, a woman's body and its masculine costume.[39] The trousers which metonymically signify the woman's sex by contiguity then become a fetishizing displacement of the absence that is in the end both so traumatic and yet necessary for this masculinity.

Another level of fetishism is, however, the writing, and in the writing. This involves a re-staging of this '*with my own eyes, on the spot*' proximity to the visual object, but softened down, muffled by expedients for managing the confrontation with a series of differences which are at once utterly threatening and yet the object of always unacknowledged yearning. Once he has peered and found no sign, he can reclaim his mastery, his fixity as 'Man', rational, speaking, naming, the subject of the discourse *but only through the act of writing which frames the 'seeing' with the fetishism of discourse.*

Both writing in ink on paper and photography work by tonal contrast, producing what we call black and white. Black and white tonalities available to photography at this date, however, could not capture 'dirt'. We know this from another part of the Munby archive which involved Hannah Cullwick, who wanted to be photographed 'in her dirt'. She was advised that to 'come out black' she should be rubbed with *yellow*.[40] It was hard for the photograph to signify the play on dirt and sexuality to which we have indirect access through the writing. This may mean two things: that the photographs function as an antidote to the dangers of proximity and seeing because they freeze and hold vision in a comforting opacity — a media greyness in which no cat is black or white, clean or dirty; or that there is another form of fetishism to be discerned in the photographs. If the latter were the case, scale would be the device.

On 11 September 1873 Munby went to Little's studio in Wigan, where he had arranged to meet Ellen Grounds for a photo session (plate 28).

> 'Hes yon wench coom?' 'Yea, hoo hes,' said Mrs Little and she and her grown-up daughter wore a puzzled smile, as if they were about to show me some *strange creature*. A moment afterwards, Ellen herself came out of the kitchen: and she was in her pit clothes, as she had promised. 'Well, Ellen, yo've coom!' 'Yah. Ah's coom, Sir!' said the collier-lass who looked vastly better and also *bigger* in her working dress than she did last night in her woman' clothes. She wore her wadded bonnet, the front part tied tight over her forehead, and the hood encircling her head like an aureole; her loose bluepatched cotton bedgown made her full bust and broad shoulders look *larger* still: below it came a striped skirt *gathered up round the hips; and under* that her breeches — the pair she showed me last night — and her iron clogshoon. She had forgotten to bring her topcoat: and first she tried on a coat belonging to Mrs Little's son, a big lad, but it was too small for her; so she tried a rough coat, like her own, of *Mr* Little's; and it fitted her well. Then she was furnished with a spade to represent her great pit shovel. She shouldered the spade in workmanlike fashion, buttoned her coat, and stood readily and well, *as I posed her*, and she was taken, first in that guise, and then without the coat: I standing beside her, to show how nearly she approached me in size (*my emphases*).[41]

One other photo exists in the collection of Ellen Grounds in work-a-day woman's clothes holding a broom (plate 28a). The backdrop appears the same as in these last two suggesting perhaps Mr Little's studio on this same occasion. Her bonnet is differently tied and her striped skirt has been let down and covered with an apron. But both photographs make her seem very tall, by contrast to the scale of the photographs of Ellen Grounds in 1866 (plates 26 and 27). Either they

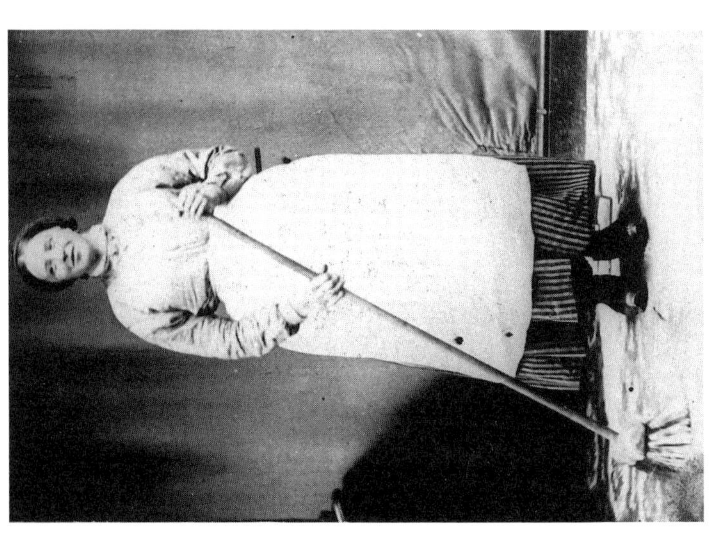

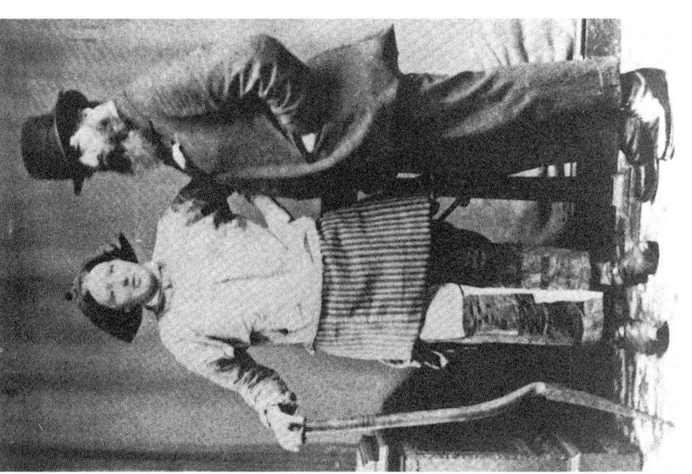

28 Robert Little, Triptych of three photographs:
a) *Ellen Grounds, Collier Girl, 108 Schofield Lane, Wigan, aged 22, taken in my presence, 1873, 11 September*, further annotated: 'Eh! it favours as Ah were sweeping the hahse'. Munby Collection (112-20-d), Trinity College, Cambridge.
b) *Ellen Grounds, aged 22 a broo wench at Pearson and Knowles's Pits, Wigan, taken 11 September 1873*, carte-de-visite. Munby Collection (113-1-c), Trinity College, Cambridge.
c) *Ellen Grounds, taken in my presence, 11 September 1873*, carte-de-visite. Munby Collection (113-1-a), Trinity College, Cambridge.

have been cropped or Munby, choreographing the photo-session, insisted on this lowered position of the camera and its proximity to the subject, so that she fills the space while there are no objects to indicate scale.

This triptych of images creates an interesting narrative if we frame the duet between Munby and Ellen Grounds with her 'workmanlike' image and her 'effeminate' one — the two encountered over two days in real time but fabricated in discontinuous space by the photographs (plate 28a, b, c). The diary entry suggests a desire to see Ellen Grounds in her pit clothes. This is the locus of a pleasure, which is not to be found if the same tall woman wears a dress; then she appears less large. The working costume has specific effects; it creates an illusion of size, which, in a sexual binary, we might say made her more masculine. But that is not said. Hard hands are described by Munby as 'manly'. It is probable that size also signifies or allows the trace of another kind of body, the maternal body, that is a female corporeality marked in the dramas of sexual difference but registering a condition that is not yet subjected to the law of difference, castration, symbolic or otherwise. What it is can only be hunted down through a disjointed series of moments of vision, through staged sites ('as I posed her'). These sights allow him to glimpse a fantastic body which is only poorly described by the Freudian term, the phallic mother.

> The pre-Oedipal, phallic or archaic mother must be understood as a Fantasy — the child's fantasy of an omnipotent, absolutely powerful, sexually neutral figure. Freud argues that the child (presumably a boy) bestows on the mother what he attributes to himself . . . The phallic mother is the fantasy of the mother who is able to grant the child everything, to be its object of desire, and in turn to be the subject who desires the child as her own object.[42]

In this diary entry the striped skirt is mentioned as 'gathered up round the hips', giving rise to an opportunity to speak of body parts. The description of the clothes is a displaced allocution of the body. It is not precisely the female body. Its confusion of strict codes of gender makes it a curious exemplar of something akin to the 'sexually neutral body' that houses a longing for a specifically maternal body. It has a bust for sure which suggests this mature, maternal body (Ellen Ground had had a child). At the same time this gathered up skirt suggests that we redefine what the Wigan miner women were wearing. To say they wore trousers is to miss the point entirely. They walked about in public with their skirts hitched up — and although their legs are encased in rough men's trousers, these function as a sheath, like the tights worn by ballet dancers and acrobats (plate 29) which drew attention to the legs while also veiling them — maintaining precisely the 'almost-but-not-quite' quality so essential to the structures of fetishism. In between these two bodies — one boringly veiled and contained and a parody of the femininity of women of his own class — the other partially revealed and transgressive of the strict codes demarcating sexual difference within Munby's bourgeois world — where is Munby, or shall I ask *what is he*? What is he trying to get at with this paradoxical proximity, this repetitious search for some kind of primal seeing? What's the point of having images like those of

29 London Stereoscopic Company, *Azella*, 1868. Munby Collection (114-14-d), Trinity College, Cambridge.

himself and Ellen Grounds in one frame, fixed as a matching yet disparate pair (plate 9).

But let me pause here. Whatever markers of difference I suggest we can read in these images will appear to be wilful, or, at best a hypothetical reading of how these images might signify according to the theoretical models with which I have framed them. The photographs maintain discretion. They are as obvious as they are in the end opaque in relation to what motivated their production and collection and sustained their appeal to this one owner. There is another kind of evidence, however, upon which I can call. It is available precisely because it is so different from the dead-pan of early photographic representation. That is in the album of sketches in which Eliza Hayes is represented (plate 10).

Drawing is closer to writing. It is also graphic. Yet drawing does not provide the fetishizing mastery produced in writing. Drawings invite a symptomatic reading of inclusions and exclusions, resistances and hesitancies, attentions and investments. Photography takes the pre-photographic material, already coded by choices of pose, gesture, setting, lighting, usually framed by inherited conventions of picture-making. It then 'translates' it, which is at once a loss and a conversion. The result is quite different from the created drawing which registers pressures from the Imaginary in more inadvertent ways.[43] In the finished work, these become the very substance and effect. Drawing involves the body which traces on the fictive space of the paper fantastic bodies the drawing subject

30 Arthur Munby, *Boompin' Nelly (Ellen Meggison), John Lancaster's Pits, from life*, n.d., pen and ink sketch. Munby Collection (110-17-folio 7-recto), Trinity College, Cambridge.

conjures up, often unconsciously through this activity. Through the movements of a hand, the drawing registers interest, anxiety, significance. Colour, scale, size, proportion, pose and gesture are the result of decisions, in which conscious selection and intention are *overdetermined* by a multiplicity of unconscious choices and desires.[44]

If we go back to Eliza Hayes (plate 10), might it be possible to suggest that this is what Munby ‘saw’ in this Freudian version of the ‘mind's eye’ when he looked at Ellen Grounds too? Are the other sketches of the women miners with whom Munby cultivated such ‘friendships’, as his class and money permitted, to be read also as a more revealing index of what motivated his observation of female labour ‘*on the spot and with [his] own eyes*’? Another named miner who appears in the album is Ellen Meggison, known affectionately in her community as ‘Boompin' Nelly’, a mother of eight children. Munby first met her in 1853 and she is recorded in the diaries over thirty years. Munby drew Ellen Meggison seated, legs apart, elbows resting on her knees while she holds the paws Munby has drawn as her hands (plate 30). Her face and arms are black,

31–33 Arthur Munby, untitled sketches, n.d., pen and ink. Unpublished album, Munby Collection, Trinity College, Cambridge.

and more, he has traced in her features the racist caricature of the facial type associated in nineteenth-century Britain with colonial otherness, be it Irish or African.

'With my own hands' . . .

I want to conclude with yet more extreme images from this truly riotous album (plates 31 and 32). Despite their shared lack of signs of professional expertise, Munby's drawings are a frightful contrast to Van Gogh's beginner's exercise, as well as to photography's reassuring, freeze-frame stillness, its dead-pan nonchalance. Munby's unschooled but striking drawings of Lancashire pitbrow women are charged with the evident intensity of the hand that held the pen to create on the page such vividly imagined faces and bodies. Unchecked by having internalized the rules of art, the aesthetic disciplines which regulate and manage the psychic drives which play across all tracings of the body, these images brutally create the components of a white bourgeois's repertoire of the fantastic body.[45]

Nothing in the measured tones of the diary entries, with their careful recapitulations and verbatim records of conversations and encounters with generous, friendly, warm-hearted and intelligent pitbrow women prepares us for these raw and abusive visualizations of working-class women. Grotesque racist caricature slips towards overt bestialization along a chain of Eurocentric signifiers from coal dust, dirt, skin colour, race, savage, beast, animal. My argument is, therefore, simply this: that the compulsive writing of the diaries and the notebooks, the collecting of hundreds of almost identical photographs, can now be read as a defence, indeed a necessity, a self-imposed submission to the safety of discourse and the opacity of the photograph. Here, in the sketches, we glimpse what they veiled, and thus at last see what 'vision' constituted the secret that Munby wanted kept when he ordained that his diaries and collection were not to be opened until forty years after his death. Writing above all secured for Munby a stable subject position producing the distance of surveillance to control the dangers of proximity, which, like the sleep of reason, produced monsters. The copious diary texts were a defence against the breakdown and excess incited by the proximity he obsessively sought all those years from 1853 through to 1882 to these 'not-quite-female bodies', which appealed to him as transgressively indifferent, and yet would also be aggressively punished in his own representations as indecipherably other. In the drawings there is a vivid and almost literal figuration of what was verbally evoked in Holland's text, stunted prize fighters, with grotesque paws for hands and huge clubs for feet, with faces not merely hard from unfitting toil, but so other in relation to the white femininity they oppose (plate 21), they can only be imagined in the racist stereotypes created by an imperial bourgeoisie for its enslaved and abused African other (plate 33). Here, in terms of a visual shock that it is hard to tolerate, and cruel to inflict on a viewer who has any investment in African identity, we can see the interface of race, class and sexuality. While affirming the centrality of racism to the imperial bourgeois imaginary, this drawing indicates the transpositions and mutual inflections of race, class and gender in the constructions of white bourgeois masculine subjectivity in the nineteenth century.

Only as the subject of a mastering enunciation, as an author in a pseudo-scientific discourse of social investigation, was this white masculinity secure against itself, that is to say, only when 'surveillance' mastered a psychically constructed 'sexuality'. Thus, we find that a splitting of the subject, registered theoretically in the different concepts of the gaze in the work of Foucault and Freud, managed the superimposition of the one over the other and identified the gaze of mastery with the Oedipal formation of the Law while the gaze of desire found a way to hold on to a pre-Oedipal fantasy. There, in discourse, the man could verbally affirm what he found when his curious and eroticizing gaze *penetrated* beneath the coal dust, the dirt, the muscle. There, in *écriture*, he could conjure back again the maternal womanliness his look would pursue to the limits of visibility. In finding nothing to see, he saw the lack that secured the difference upon which his sexual superiority, his social and self-mastery 'as a man — a white, bourgeois man' depended. Yet in the encounter that had been risked, proximity to something *en plus*, something that had to be signified through size, through excess in relation to the fetishized image of the castrated feminine lady, could be momentarily glimpsed, offering a pleasure which almost created a space in which that 'become-man' and that 'lost-woman' were 'alike', that is, where the rule of sexual difference and the expulsion of the male child from a universe made secure and dominated by a 'maternal' figure could be fantastically and, for a moment only, joyfully suspended in an imaginary visuality. Yet finally, that law of difference had to be sadistically reimposed as the pen covered the page, drawing its 'blackened' veil over such dangerous visions.

Language, being still so phallocentric, makes this difficult to articulate. Constant encounters with the images are necessary to keep in mind the possibilities which only the different kinds of visualization could manage to keep in tension. 'The maternal figure' is not a happy phrase. It is used here to try to signal that fantastic body invented retrospectively by the child as it accedes to the Symbolic and thus acquires the means to signify both the loss and memory of plenitude, which the Symbolic inflicts and articulates. *The mother*, a linguistic term, is not the mother except in relation to the linguistic signifier, *the father*. These two terms are produced in relational difference by language which then articulates symbolically, as linguistic difference, a field of meanings, affects, fantasies and desires which were hitherto complex, transitive and unfixed and, in Lacan's terms 'imaginary', that is premised in the mirror image of visualized bodies and scenes.[46]

The maternal thus refers to an undifferentiated or pre-differentiated parent figure comprising many persons who fill that space in the early social and psychic life of a child. Parents of both sexes are part of this primary figure, and in social and historical conditions of childcare, non-related adults may participate — wet nurses and other class or race childcarers.[47] In my work on images produced by European bourgeois men in the later nineteenth century, Van Gogh or Toulouse-Lautrec, I have used the writings of another man of that generation and class, although socially and culturally differentiated by being Jewish in an anti-Semitic Europe: Sigmund Freud.[48] In the problems some of his male patients experienced with their adult sexuality, Freud discerned the traces of the conflict initiated by the Oedipal crisis which forbade to them their primary sexual object: the maternal figure. The taboo against this incestuous choice was, however, fractured by the internal, social and gender divisions of the 'maternal figure'. In adult life the aggression inspired by the forced submission to the Law of the Father was displaced from the Mother through the idealization of an almost inaccessible, incorporeal femininity. The aggression and anxiety created by this prohibition and loss could be inflicted through sexual or other practices on the bodies of working-class women, which while female, and thus other, were not registered or treated as completely feminine. The feminine then signified the incestuously forbidden but idealized and 'loved'. In order to be desirable and sexually used, another female body was needed. To be erotic it had to be debased and it was debased by being eroticized. In the paintings and drawings by the artists mentioned above, this division is articulated clearly in terms of the quite distinct visual rhetorics which are used: on the one hand, for the representation of ladies, and especially the artists' mothers, and, on the other, for prostitutes, urban working-class and peasant women. These 'other' bodies are figured to emphasize not so much difference from men, as difference from the lady — the Symbolic representative of the Mother with its unconscious freight from a pre-Oedipal relation to the son. Paradoxically, this differencing occurred through exaggeration of maternal features such as hips and breasts, or through extreme difference from an idealized feminine face and phallicized body. The trope most often used was *bestialization*, which stands for both sexualization and sexual use. But bestialization goes beyond sexuality with the added weight of horror and abjection. In the drawing of Eliza Hayes (plate 10), the male figure appears — on a conventional axis of difference — almost feminized, with the delicate features, dainty hands and little feet. It is as if this figure internalizes aspects of the loved feminine as both class identification and a means of access to the forbidden bourgeois mother. Before him stands not an other, a working-class woman, but his psychic projection that is legible only in terms of the way it manages his white masculinity's profound ambivalence. In characteristically fetishizing fashion, all the signs work both ways. She is large and comforting; she is large and threatening. She is like me; she is repulsively different. She is like a man; she is not-woman, not the sign of femininity. She is a *neither-nor* figure. The excess that the recalcitrant otherness of a non-phallically inscribed femaleness threatens to present to the precarious masculine subject — signified after Oedipalization as the phallic mother — is inscribed all over her body in colour, in scale, in a face that sports only eyes and lips and a body with multiple nipples and a huge hand. Nothing I say can trap this fantasy within the mastery of language. As a Freudian reader of the image, I want what I say about it to sound odd, disturbing, rude, crude, excessive and extreme, shocking us by confronting us with what we try not to know about our fantastic psychic life. According to Freud, the unconscious works, in dreams for instance, by depositing its 'hot' material into bland and puzzling images or scenarios whose meanings begin to unravel and proliferate as one is forced to 'say' what you imagine you saw in that 'mind's eye'.[49] I am, therefore, not describing a supposed fact *there* in the drawing, but reading, i.e. verbalizing, the image's materials for the psychic ambivalence it stages. My interpretation depends, furthermore, on drawing in conjunction with other kinds of inscription — writing — and other kinds of imagining — photography — as part of the complex process of an historical but not idiosyncratic subjectivity to which the Munby archive provides access.

Munby's archive, as representative of the broader field of representation with which I have tried to link it, could, therefore, be read in Oedipal terms, except for compulsions which have so far been foregrounded in studies of Munby — the diaries and the photographic collection. These do not reveal as starkly either the contradictions or the sadism. Rather, they instance the defences against them. By setting the diaries and photographs in conjunction with the overlooked album — or the repressed album, which has only been selectively reproduced — another trope can be identified for this paradox of white bourgeois masculinity: its self-definition and its conflicted structures of desire are premised **not** on a binary opposition man/woman which appears so publicly at the ideological level in Victorian discourses. A more intricate pattern of fractured femininities had to be constructed where difference was never only sexual. It was figured through the constant relay of social and racial difference, colonizing each other's tropes to visualize the psychic dramas of an historically specific masculine subjectivity and its confrontation with, and formation by, difference.

The Munby archive is riven with these fissures. In the diary-writing there is frequently a moment when, however much he reports on his peering and seeing anarchic signs of many differences written in working women's bodies (they look like lads, they walk like sailors, they are as black as can be, their hands are hard as men's and so forth), he can ultimately reclaim what he calls 'womanliness'. This is always a relief because it signals the absence of sexuality, which, I suggest, signifies in his texts, autonomous, female power where the phallic mother is not just his fantasy but what women really might be: more powerful — and '*en plus*' than men.

> Ellen flung herself into a chair and Jane leaned against the drawers, panting, and wiping the beaded sweat — and with it some of the blackness — from her red face . . . those two young women in men's clothes, as black and grim as fiends and as rough and uncouth in manners as a bargee, and yet, *to those who looked deep enough* not unwomanly or degraded (Munby Diary, 29 September 1860).

Womanliness, like femininity, has a comforting sound in most languages. Its phonetic largesse disavows the aggression toward, and terror inspired in 'men' by, a naked 'woman', woman in her female specificity, her specific (i.e. not phallically masquerading) corporeal presence which offers to phallocentric 'vision' a field of radical undecideability, and thus defies its logic and its logos. Munby's figures are not nude, of course. But they registered as brute nature, uncivilized, unpolished, untransformed because they did not emit the signs of phallic culture — feminine deference and femininity as absence of an equal, contending power. They did not display the masquerade that is white bourgeois femininity. Trousered, these women disturbed the protective shield of costume which both aestheticizes and fetishizes sexual difference in a phallocentric culture. Without that artifice of fixed but veiled difference, the masculine imaginary ran riot, revealing some images of what such a subject desires, which the law forbids, and the fetish disavows: the archaic phallic mother who, on this side of the Oedipal complex, can only be signified by men as raw, uncooked, unassimilable, abject and yet who, beyond its law, beckons almost majestically. For while I would define fetishism as a process of containment within a semiotics of phallically defined gender, I want also to stress the pressure of what it tries to hold onto by freezing, substituting, displacing and yet commemorating. Fetishism is a memorial to another set of relations to and feelings about femaleness and its other, 'unfeminine', yet irreducibly female, and maternal bodies. The Munby drawings, however, expose a perpetual regress. Even if we find a condition in which the surveilling bourgeois man 'desired' a controlled proximity to that which appeared to suspend the phallic law of difference, and liberate him from the social and sexual structures forming his gender and class, that imagined moment is itself censored. The contradictions of gender and class were visualized through yet another semiotics of power, the demonized fictions of the colonial imaginary which these images suggest were as critical to that psycho-symbolic formation as those of gender and class. These matters were, it would seem, black and white.[50]

Griselda Pollock
University of Leeds

Notes

1 Arthur Joseph Munby was interested in many forms of heavy labour performed by women. In this article I shall focus on his major preoccupation — women in mining. Munby had trained as a solicitor but worked as a civil servant for the Ecclesiastical Commission in London. His investigations into 'female labour' were both amateur and private. He was forced by circumstances to 'come out' but very late on. For instance, in 1887 he attended a delegation to the Home Secretary in defence of woman's right to work. His papers were donated to Trinity College Library at his death in 1910 with the proviso that they were not to be read for forty years. Since that date interest has been attracted to this archive, resulting in a number of publications: D. Hudson, *Munby: Man of Two Worlds*, London, 1972: this reproduces selections from the diaries linking Munby with contemporary Victorians; M. Hiley, *Victorian Working Women*, London, 1979: this focuses on the photographic collection of working women also using extracts from the diaries about Munby's amateur research; L. Davidoff, 'Class and Gender in Victorian Britain', in J.L. Newton (ed.), *Sex and Class in Women's History*, London, 1983: this deals with Munby's relation with Hannah Cullwick, the maidservant whom he married, in the context of class and gender hierarchies in the bourgeois family and household; H. Dawkins 'The Diaries and Photographs of Hannah Cullwick', *Art History*, vol. 10, no. 2, 1987, p. 154–87: this develops a feminist analysis of the archive focusing on Hannah Cullwick, whose diaries and images form a major part of the collections.

2 T.G. Dugdale, Louisa Millard, Robert Little, John Cooper are the names that occur most frequently in the Munby collection. John Hannavy and Chris Ryan, *Living and Working in Wigan*, Wigan, 1986, gives a complete listing of over thirty photographic studios in Wigan from the 1850s to the 1930s.

3 The theoretical and methodological issues have been discussed in 'Feminism and Foucault', to appear in *Theory and Interpretation in the Visual Arts*, Keith Moxey, Michael Ann Holly and Norman Bryson (eds.), Wesleyan University Press, 1994. A reading of Munby's 'secret' and issues of the closed archive are discussed in 'The Dangers of Proximity: The Spaces of Sexuality in Word and Image', *Discourse*, vol. 16, no. 2, 1993–4 (published by Center for Twentieth-Century Studies, University of Wisconsin, Milwaukee).

4 'Nineteenth-century "bourgeois" society — and it is doubtless still with us — was a society of blatant and fragmented perversion. And this was not by way of hypocrisy, for nothing was more manifest and more prolix, or more manifestly taken over by discourses and institutions'. Michel Foucault, *History of Sexuality: Volume One — An Introduction*, Harmondsworth, 1978, p. 47.

5 Davidoff, 1984, see note 1.

6 The term and its further meanings are taken from Homi Bhabha's work, especially 'The Other Question: The Stereotype and Colonial Discourse', *Screen*, vol. 24, no. 6, 1983, pp. 18–36. Bhabha develops a field of analysis in which Foucault's theories of power/knowledge and Freud's theories of fetishism are set into play to define the ambivalence of colonial discourse: 'Nor would it be possible, without the attribution of ambivalence to relations of power/knowledge, to calculate the traumatic impact of the return of the oppressed — those terrifying stereotypes of savagery, cannibalism, lust and anarchy which are the signal points of identification and alienation, scenes of fear and desire, in colonial texts. It is precisely this function of the stereotype as phobia and fetish that, according to Fanon, threatens the closure of the racial/epidermal schema for the colonial subject and opens the royal road to colonial fantasy.' (p. 25).

7 Mieke Bal, *Reading Rembrandt: Beyond the Word-Image Opposition*, Cambridge, 1992.

8 Peter Fryer, *Staying Power: The History of Black People in Britain*, London, 1984.

9 I am working implicitly with Lacanian categories of the Imaginary and Symbolic. These constitute two registers of representation as well as two levels of subjectivity. For fundamental definitions see J. Laplanche and J.B. Pontalis, *The Language of Psychoanalysis*, London, 1973, and for an analysis of the terms relative to cultural theory, see F. Jameson, 'Imaginary and Symbolic in Lacan: Marxism, Psychoanalytic Criticism and the Problem of the Subject', *Yale French Studies*, nos. 55/56, 1977, pp. 388–95. 'The Imaginary may thus be described as a peculiar spatial configuration whose bodies primarily entertain relationships of inside/outside with one another, which is then traversed and reorganised by that primordial rivalry and transitivistic substitution of imagoes, that indistinction of primary narcissism and agressivity, from which our later conceptions of good and evil derive.' (p.357). This quote captures the ambivalence of the many dualisms which characterized the fantasies shaped by the imaginary which is principally a spatial and visual syntax in contrast to the Symbolic's

alienation of the subject in language — sequences, signifying chains, words, substitutions.

10 The Munby archive is in Trinity College, Cambridge. I am grateful to Diana Chardon of the Library, who has catalogued the album of sketches.

11 This project is part of a book, *Sexuality and Surveillance: Working Women and Bourgeois Men*, London: Routledge (forthcoming 1994).

12 Michel Foucault (ed.), *Herculine Barbin Being the Recently Discovered Memoirs of a Nineteenth-Century French Hermaphrodite*, trans. Richard Dougall, New York, 1980. For a critical reading of Foucault's thesis, see Judith Butler, *Gender Trouble: Feminism and the Subversion of Identity*, London and New York, 1990.

13 Foucault, *History of Sexuality*, op. cit., p. 125.

14 In a remarkable undergraduate dissertation (University of Leeds, 1982) Sally Walker, a costume historian, attempted to argue for the meanings of this working costume for the women who wore it in the political struggles around women's right to work.

15 These women have left little documentation about themselves — autobiographies, diaries, etc. At least in the 1842 Parliamentary Commissions we can find reported speech of women miners. But they are always spoken for in later texts and never called to give evidence in their own voice. Ironically, it is Munby's compulsive recording that gives us the only access to these women's account of their experience of work and family. This is the topic of another paper.

16 Two further psychoanalytical models should be noted: that of Lacan in which the body is achieved as an effect of the internationalization of an imago, see 'The Mirror Phase . . .' in *Écrits*, London, 1977, and that of Julia Kristeva, whose thesis on the subject's relation to language is premised on the constant struggle between *the semiotic* — the remnants of the drives present through traces such as sound, rhythm, colour, etc. — and *the symbolic*, the attempted fixing of meaning and temporary construction of unity by means of which the subject may recognize itself in the signifying positions offered by language. Both theories suggest states of both discontinuity and precarious unity in constant play, in which 'the body' refers to both the grounds of representation and the represented. See Julia Kristeva, 'The System and the Speaking Subject', in Toril Moi (ed.), *The Kristeva Reader*, Oxford, 1986.

17 Emile Zola, *Germinal* [1884], Harmondsworth, 1954. Page references are to this edition.

18 Maheude is finally forced to return to work underground at the end of the novel having lost many of her family. Earlier in the text, when she is working at home, Zola repeatedly draws attention to her sagging breasts.

19 G. Pollock, '*Van Gogh and Dutch Art: Van Gogh's Notion of the Modern*', PhD, London University, 1981, which will be published as *The Case Against Van Gogh: The Cities and Countries of Modernism*, London, 1995.

20 Zola, op. cit., p. 37.

21 Clive Holland, *The Belgians at Home*, London, 1911, p. 124.

22 A. Davis, *Women, Race & Class*, New York and London, 1982.

23 A. Soloman-Godeau, 'The Legs of the Countess', *October*, no. 39, 1986, pp. 65–107.

24 Ibid., p. 74.

25 *British Parliamentary Papers*, First Report of the Commissioner on the Mines vol. 15, 1842, p. 24: Session 3 February–12 August, 1842.

26 *British Parliamentary Papers*, vol. 13, 1867: p. xiii.

27 *British Parliamentary Papers*, Evidence of P. Dickenson, 19 March 1866, question no. 651.

28 We should not minimize the gender conflict within working-class politics. But we should also not ignore the class difference in the motivation of working-class men and bourgeois men in relation to the ideals of feminine domesticity. The point is that in both cases men abrogate to themselves the power to define women's social roles and identities in ways which effectively shore up their power and position as 'men'.

29 There is a detail in this photograph which unsettles the image — her fingernails. I shall be dealing with that in another study of these images which relates to a different strategy of reading for class and gender focusing on an unexpected site of their signification: hands. See my forthcoming articles 'The View From Elsewhere: The Politics of Female Spectatorship' about hands in Manet's *Bar at the Folies Bergère*, in Penny Florence and Dee Reynolds (eds.), *Media, Gender, Subject*, Manchester, 1994, and another analysis of a similar problem in Bradford Collins (ed.), *Current Methodologies: Thirteen Approaches to Manet's Bar at the Folies Bergère*, Princeton, 1995.

30 Lisa Tickner, 'Women and Trousers', Paper given at the conference *Leisure in the Twentieth Century*, published by the Design Council, London 1977, pp. 56–67. Before the Second World War women wearing trousers fell into a few categories — military (and these were often cross-dressers), the stage, sport, the beginnings of the bicycle, and glamorous evening or leisure wear. The major nineteenth-century instance was 'bloomerism' which has its own complex history in relation to middle-

class women's politics, dress reform and the suffrage. See Angela Kingston, '*Bloomerism*', unpublished MA Thesis, University of Leeds, 1984, on the representations of women in bloomers in the British press in 1851.

31 John Fletcher, 'Versions of the Masquerade', *Screen*, vol. 29, no. 3, 1988, p.50.

32 Claire Johnstone, 'Femininity and the Masquerade: *Anne of the Indies*', in Claire Johnstone and Paul Willemen, *Edinburgh Film Festival: Women's Cinema*, London, 1975; Joan Riviere, 'Womanliness as Masquerade' [1929], in Victor Burgin et al., *Formations of Fantasy*, London, 1986, pp. 35–44; Jacques Lacan, 'The Meaning of the Phallus', in Juliet Mitchell and Jacqueline Rose (eds.), *Feminine Sexuality*, London, 1982, pp. 74–85; Sigmund Freud, 'Fetishism' [1927], in *On Sexuality*, Penguin Freud Library, vol. 7, Harmondsworth, 1977, pp. 351–7; Mary Ann Doane, 'Film and the Masquerade: Theorising the Female Spectator', *Screen*, vol. 23, no. 3–4, 1982, pp. 74–87.

33 John Fletcher, p. 52–3.

34 Jacqueline Rose, *Sexuality in the Field of Vision*, London, 1986.

35 This is a long quotation but it is necessary to present the full text to stress the excess of 'the scene of writing' where an event is restaged. The pace and detail of the writing indicates much more than a mere record of the visit. It is a dramatization, playing with delay and carefully building up to a final revelation and release of tension. And finally, only when it is read in its entirety, does the full force of the fetishism of writing emerge. For a comparable analysis of diary writing, sexuality and the body see Francis Barker, *The Tremulous Private Body*, London, 1984.

36 *The Diaries of Arthur Munby*, unpublished manuscripts, Cambridge: Trinity College, vol. 41.

37 Freud, 'Fetishism', op. cit., p. 353.

38 S. Freud, 'Some Psychical Consequences of the Anatomical Distinction between the Sexes' [1925], in Penguin Freud Library, vol. 7, *On Sexuality*, Harmondsworth, 1977, p. 336.

39 On the relation between fetishism and scientific investigation/curiosity and its socially acceptable sublimations see Freud's writings on Leonardo da Vinci: S. Freud, 'Leonardo da Vinci and a Memory of his Childhood' [1910], in Penguin Freud Library, vol. 14, *On Art & Literature*, Harmondsworth, 1985.

40 *The Diaries of Hannah Cullwick*, Liz Stanley, (ed.), London, 1984, pp. 75–7, describes Hannah Cullwick's visit to the studio of Mr Stodart of Margate in 1864.

41 Cited M. Hiley, op. cit., p. 92.

42 Elizabeth Grosz, in Elizabeth Wright (ed.), *Feminism and Psychoanalysis: A Critical Dictionary*, Oxford, 1992. This figure can also become the source of persecutory fantasies. The difficulty lies in the fact that the terms in which this fantasy is represented remain exclusively phallic so that the body of the maternal fantasy is still to be articulated through Oedipal castration anxieties. A more polymorphous sexuality seems to be insisting through the kind of body imagery we are discerning in the Munby archive — where size of hands, feet, shoulders and busts engage attention.

43 See Jameson, op. cit., on the Imaginary.

44 *Overdetermination* is a Freudian term: 'Formations of the unconscious (symptoms, dreams, etc.) . . . [are] related to a multipicity of unconscious elements which may be organized in different meaningful sequences, each having its own specific coherence at a particular level of interpretation.' Laplanche and Pontalis, op. cit., p. 292.

45 I am indebted here to Heather Dawkins's work on Degas for this concept of the 'fantastic body'. See H. Dawkins, '*Sexuality, Degas and Women's History*', PhD, University of Leeds, 1991.

46 Jacques Lacan, 'The Mirror Phase as Formative of the "I" ', in *Écrits*, London, 1977, pp. 1–7; for a useful account of Lacanian concepts and their use in cultural analysis see Frederic Jameson, op. cit., 1977.

47 I go into the role of the social division of childcare in relation to Munby and bourgeois masculinity in 'The Dangers of Proximity', *Discourse*, vol. 16, no. 2, 1993. The discussion is indebted to Lee Davidoff's founding article on this archive, 'Class and Gender in Victorian England,' in Judith L. Newton et al. (eds.), *Sex and Class in Women's History*, London, 1983, pp. 17–71.

48 'Fathers of Modern Art and Mothers of Invention', in *Differences: Trouble in the Archives*, vol. 4, no. 3, 1992, pp. 91–132 on Toulouse-Lautrec. On Van Gogh see my forthcoming *The Case Against Van Gogh*, 1995. The key text by Freud is 'On the Universal Tendency to Debasement in the Sphere of Love' [1912], *Standard Edition*, James Strachey (ed.), vol. 11, pp. 177–90.

49 S. Freud, *Interpretation of Dreams* [1900], Penguin Freud Library, vol. 4, Harmondsworth, 1976, or for a more concise presentation of the theory, see *Introductory Lectures on Psychoanalysis* [1916], Penguin Freud Library, vol. 1, Harmondsworth, 1973. Note that 'unconscious representation . . . neither reflects nor signifies the subject and its objects. It is a pure cathexis of the word as such . . . the unconscious representation is only a text. But the text produces effects; since sexuality is organized as we have seen, not according to some instinct, some "tendency", but according to what has been said.

Consequently, discourse makes impossible any direct and peaceable relation to the body, to the world and to pleasure. It turns away from *jouissance*; it is in this sense that it is castrating.' Michele Montrelay, 'Inquiry into Femininity', *M/F*, no. 1, 1978, pp. 87–8.

50 Toni Morrison, *Playing in the Dark Whiteness and the Literary Imagination*, Cambridge, 1992, offers an extended analysis of the phenomenon in the formation of 'American' literature.

Art History ISSN 0141-6790 Vol. 17 No. 3 September 1994 pp. 383–417

Marat/Sade/Picasso

Neil Cox

The title of this paper extends that of a play by the German writer Peter Weiss: *Marat/Sade*.[1] The Marquis de Sade (1740–1814) infamously provides the name for the love of brutal persecution, torture and violence which characterizes one kind of human activity and, more problematically, sexual desire. Jean-Paul Marat (1743–1793) is known as the most virulent spokesman of the Jacobin faction in the French Revolution: a proponent of the generous use of the death penalty and mob violence as means to socio-political change. Marat was assassinated by one Marie-Anne-Charlotte Corday (1769–1793).

Weiss wrote a note to accompany the play, by way of explaining where he had departed from historical fact:

> Sade's encounter with Marat, which is the subject of this play, is entirely imaginary, based only on the single fact that it was Sade who spoke the memorial address at Marat's funeral. Even in this speech his real attitude towards Marat is questionable, since he made the speech primarily to save his own skin; at that time his position was in danger, his name on the list of those marked out for the guillotine.[2]

This paper deals with the same speech which had inspired Weiss to imagine Marat and Sade in debate.[3] Like Weiss, I will be pursuing not much more than a coincidence. The claim which Weiss makes concerning Sade's motives is slightly mistaken as to the circumstances of the speech, which may have involved not so much political expediency as a case of mistaken identity.[4] Mistakes — or confusions — or elisions — of identity play an important role in the images I will discuss, as well as in their historical subject.

Some thirty-five years before Weiss wrote his play, another artist took an interest in Marat's assassination. The artist was Pablo Picasso (1881–1973), and this paper is built around the possibility that Picasso also knew and exploited the content of Sade's speech. Picasso was certainly not the first artist to take Marat's assassination as his subject: the first and greatest picture in the series was of course *The Death of Marat* (Musées royaux des beaux-arts, Brussels), by Jacques-Louis David (1748–1825).

I want to draw connecting lines between these players: Marat, Sade, Picasso, David and — the odd one out — Corday. In so doing, I also hope to counter several commonly held views of Picasso.

Firstly, and not so controversially, I disagree with those commentators who argue that Picasso's work is consistently inspired by autobiographical themes. At worst this encourages the view that Picasso's art is a reflex response to stress or delight in his private life.[5] At best this view restricts the possibilities of interpretation to a considerable extent.[6] As the persistence of autobiographical readings would suggest, Picasso's work is indeed invariably narrative in its concerns. It is dependent however on a use of imagery which is easily but not *sensibly* verbalizable according to some simple key — the artist's private life, for example. Picasso's extreme reluctance to offer extended commentary on his work, and his preference for the pun over the proposition, have meant that the intellectual breadth of his work has often been underestimated. Since the location of Picasso's intellectual life was in visual imagery rather than words, much of his argument has been missed.

The *Marat* pictures are my case in point: for, secondly, I will argue that Picasso produced these misogynistic tableaux in reflecting upon aggression and surrealist notions of the *femme-assassin*, rather than to exorcise his own female demons. I want to elucidate the transformative and mutative dimension of Picasso's ongoing narratives, and especially his tragi-comic fascination with the reversal and substitution of 'roles'.

Finally, I will show how Picasso's fascination with 'convulsive identity' owes much to his involvement with the Surrealist intellectual circle. It has been argued that Picasso was a reluctant Surrealist as a result of his excessive attachment to 'the object'[7] — meaning both the object-world and, more loosely, his own biography. I will demonstrate that Picasso's *Marat* pictures and other related works are, on the contrary, explorations of psychological and psychoanalytic claims made in Surrealist journals.

Thus far my art-historical aims, but I would not want to obscure the sheer fascination of the works which Picasso produced in the five or so years with which I am concerned, and which testify to the intellectual richness of the Surrealist movement for an art rooted in psychological narratives. Even less would I wish to forget the connectedness of this art to real, perhaps endemic, modern anxieties.

I

Before discussing Picasso or Sade, the circumstances of Marat's assassination by Corday, and David's commission to paint it should be recounted. Marat was born in Neuchâtel in Switzerland, and like his father was destined to become a doctor. He attended the University of Bordeaux, received an honorary degree from St Andrews, spent much time in London and visited Dublin, Amsterdam and the Hague during the ten difficult years of his medical training. He began publishing radical political tracts in London in 1773. In 1779 he was appointed physician to the troops of the King's brother, the Comte d'Artois, and he was in great demand as a court doctor. During this period he published a few notable scientific papers. It was in 1789 that Marat's public career really took off with the publication of a newspaper entitled *l'Ami du peuple*; in September 1792 the name was changed to *Journal de la République française*. Marat, elected to the Convention, was by now known as 'the people's friend'. He was particularly strident in his criticism of the monarchy, but also accused the Girondin faction of treason. Marat played an important role in the riots of 31 May and 2 June 1793 which led to the fall of the Girondins. At this stage Marat's skin disease — 'une lèpre' — was advanced, and for this reason he spent much of the time immersed in a cloth-lined bath of tepid water.

Charlotte Corday, a provincial convent-educated royalist, travelled alone from Caen to murder Marat. This lurid account is borrowed from Anita Brookner:

> On 23 April 1793 she obtained a passport for Paris, giving as the pretext for her visit a need to consult someone at the Ministry of the Interior on behalf of a friend. On 11 July she arrived in Paris. She asked at the stage coach office for the name of a hotel and was directed to the Hotel de la Providence, 19 rue des Vieux Augustins, where a servant told her that Marat had been ill and was confined to his apartment in the Rue des Cordeliers. This was bad news, for she had intended to stab him in the National Convention. On Saturday 13 July she bought a kitchen knife with a long blade from Badin, in the arcades of the former Palais-Royal. She took a cab to Marat's house, where his mistress Simone Evrard refused to admit her. She returned to her hotel at noon and wrote a letter to Marat promising to reveal details of plots in Caen and the Vendée, this of course being precisely the sort of thing that Marat liked to denounce. She posted her letter and waited in her room for an answer. To while away the time she summoned the hairdresser, then changed into a spotted muslin dress with a pink fichu. A tall black hat with a green cockade and black tassels completed her outfit. She wrote another note and put it into her pocket to deliver personally. Into her bodice she put her birth certificate, an address to the French people, and the knife. At seven in the evening she took another cab to Marat's house. Simone Evrard again refused to admit her but Charlotte Corday took advantage of the arrival of a newspaper seller and a printer to slip into the apartment. Marat, who was in his bath, sheeted to prevent the scaly sores on his body coming into contact with the copper lining of the wooden tub, and a turban soaked in vinegar round his head, overheard angry voices and called out to have Corday admitted. She entered the room, on the wall of which she could have seen two crossed pistols with the legend 'La Mort', took a sheet of paper, and dipped a pen in ink to write the names of the plotters of Caen. She then pulled out the knife and stabbed Marat in the right lung. Marat called out to Simone Evrard, 'A moi, chère amie, a moi', then lost consciousness. His body was lifted from the bath by two members of the household who knocked Charlotte Corday to the floor. She made no attempt to resist. Marat was pronounced dead at a quarter to eight in the evening by a member of the Collège de Médecine who lived on the floor below. Because of the heat of the night and the unhealthy state of Marat's blood, embalming was begun immediately.[8]

Corday was tried and guillotined within a few days of the murder.

The story of David's painting is equally well known. David had, in fact, visited Marat the day before the assassination (presumably the painter was acting in his capacity as president of the Jacobin Society), where he saw him working in the bath and using an up-ended packing case as a desk. David seems to have sketched Marat soon after the murder, in order to produce the well-known commemorative print of the 'friend of the people'. He also took charge of the funeral arrangements, which were problematic because of the poor state of Marat's body. These arrangements set the tone for the powerful analogy which David drew between Marat and Christ in the painting:

> In the disaffected church of the Cordeliers, at the end of Marat's street, the body was exhibited on a dais, above the bath and the packing case . . . . A smoking incense burner was placed before the body and the only lighting was artifical. The funeral, which lasted six hours, took place at five o'clock in the evening of 16 July to the accompaniment of muffled drum-beat and cannon. The body was laid on a bier drawn by twelve men. Girls in white with branches of cypress surrounded it, and they were followed by the entire Convention, the municipal authorities, and the people of Paris. There was a full panoply of cardboard trees and mountains, but an eerie innovation was the improvised canticle — 'O coeur de Jésus, O coeur de Marat' — chanted by the crowd. Marat was buried in the garden of the Cordeliers club; his heart placed in a porphyry urn, was suspended from the club's ceiling.[9]

David was in effect invited to produce a commemorative painting of Marat on the day after the assassination. One Deputy asked: 'Where are you, David? There is a painting for you to do,' to which David promptly replied 'And indeed I shall do it.' David's painting shows Marat at the moment before expiry, pen still faintly gripped in his fingers. The still life in the foreground contains Charlotte Corday's introductory letter, another note bearing testimony of Marat's charitable activities, and a rather modest murder weapon.

The clear message of the David painting is that of the sanctification of Marat in death. If we are to believe the accounts of Marat's skin condition, it seems clear that the figure in the bath is in rather better shape than he should be. Furthermore his pose, as has often been noted, derives directly from Renaissance depictions of the dead Christ. In particular the Michelangelo *Pietà* in St Peter's, and the Raphael *Entombment* of 1507, also in Rome, were both known to David and provided excellent models for the tragically lifeless arm of Marat. Two other features of the painting which are worth noting are the depiction of the vertical mouth of the dying Marat, slightly parted, and analogized with the wound on his chest — 'la blessure *sacrilège*'[10] — together with the extraordinarily erotic presence of the corpse. Both features were important to Picasso, as was the foreground still life.

David's painting appeared before the French public on 16 October 1793, which was declared a public holiday. It was exhibited in the Louvre courtyard alongside that of another revolutionary martyr, Le Peletier de Saint-Fargeau, in a kind of makeshift chapel.

Between the original funeral of Marat in July, and this appearance of the David painting a considerable, politically motivated, cult of Marat had grown up. Several of the revolutionary councils of Paris, the *Sections*, had announced holidays and organized processions in honour of Marat, Le Peletier and others.[11] These processions usually included the unveiling of portrait busts, and speeches on the subject of the heroes. So it was that the Marquis de Sade, who had with remarkable good fortune escaped the Bastille and succeeded in joining the revolutionary administration of the Section des Piques (first as its Secretary, then as its President), came to pronounce a 'Discourse to the spirits of Marat and Lepeletier' on 29 September 1793. The speech contained the usual rhetoric about Marat himself,[12] but it is the passage on Corday which makes it particularly interesting from the perspective of the imagery of other *Marat* paintings:

> Sweet and timid sex, how can it be that your delicate hands grasped the dagger which seduction sharpened? . . . Oh! your eagerness to come and throw flowers on the tomb of this true friend of the people makes us forget that the crime could have been committed by one of your number. Yet Marat's barbarous assassin was one of those hybrid beings of indeterminate sex, spewn up by the flames to the despair of both, belonging completely to neither. A black veil should forever enshroud our memory of this creature! Above all we must ensure that she is not represented as an enchanting symbol of beauty, as some have dared to do! Oh, you gullible artists, shatter, invert, disfigure the features of this monster! Do not even offer her to our indignant eyes unless surrounded by the Furies of Tartary . . . [13]

Picasso's painting known as *Woman with Stiletto* (plate 34), dating from 19–25 December 1931, produces remarkable echoes of Sade in rendering the figure of Corday as a formidable terror.[14] By way of enhancing our sense of what Picasso is doing in this image, I want briefly to look at a couple of other examples of Marat assassination paintings.[15]

David excludes the murderer herself. An interest in painting Corday grew directly and perhaps morbidly out of her own request to be painted before her death. Corday portraiture developed into a recognizable salon subject during the nineteenth century, when the dominant view of Marat was as a ruthless and bloodthirsty demagogue. Thus Corday became a pure and courageous heroine, the subject of several successful plays. One such image occurs in a painting by Paul Baudry (1828–1886) of 1861 (plate 35). Corday appears as a stern but grandiose missionary, in a scene of some chaos, merging with a map of France on the wall. Marat on the other hand is disallowed the dignified death which David had granted him, and is represented as struggling to pull himself out of the bath, the handle of a rather more impressive knife sticking out of his chest. The obscure angle from which the revolutionary is seen contributes to his bizarre form in this painting, and makes the antiquarian respect for many aspects of the David painting all the more striking. It is nevertheless not credible that the scene Baudry depicts is merely an earlier moment in a narrative which would

34 Pablo Picasso, *La Femme au stylet* [Paris], 19–20 & 25 December 1931, oil on canvas, 46 × 61 cm. Musée Picasso (no. 136), Paris.
35 Paul Baudry, *Charlotte Corday*, 1861. Musée des beaux-arts, Nantes.

lead to the still calm of the David: the knife, the board over the bath, the chair, the shelf and the newspaper all distinguish Baudry's account. I will return later to this interest in the accoutrements of the crime.

A far more ambivalent depiction of both Marat and Corday is to be found in two paintings by the Norwegian Edvard Munch (1863–1944) (plate 36). Munch's pictures abandon, as we might expect, the realist ambitions of David and Baudry, and instead concentrate on the existential, literally naked dimension of the relation between Marat and his assassin. If the first reflects David's stark frontal image, the second of these paintings from 1907 is closer to Baudry. In both cases Munch's Marat retains — in contrast to Baudry's — a resemblance to Christ in his cruciform pose. Corday is now bolt upright, naked, and as if in a trance. Marat is not clearly a murder victim, and seems to look at Corday from his bed. Even more strange is the implication in the second image that the hands of the two figures touch. Certainly it would seem that the moral choice between the figures of Marat and Corday is tipping back in Marat's favour here,

36 Edvard Munch, Death of Marat I, 1905–08. Munch Museum, Oslo.

but it is doubtful whether that was out of compassion for Marat's politics on Munch's part, and more likely that Corday provoked in Munch a fine example of the Nietzschean dread with which women in general filled him. The historical pretensions of these paintings do little to divert Munch from his imagery of the erect, ghostly, destructive virgin.

I think it is clear that Picasso's picture is the one which most closely approximates to Sade's view of the proper depiction of Corday, whilst it also plays on David's theatrical setting. Corday's grotesquely invertebrate naked body does exhibit two breasts, but there are few other signs of gender — not usually absent for Picasso, even in so remote a creature as the 1929 *Woman in a Red Armchair* (Musée Picasso, Paris). Picasso's Corday enters a claustrophobic attic room like an enormous worm. Shrieking — like a 'Fury of Tartary' — at the pin-headed Marat, she sticks the stiletto into his heart, from which floats an amoebic cloud of blood. As in the David, Marat drops his quill, and his left hand appears to clasp what must be another piece of paper: Corday's letter of petition? Picasso retains David's muddy green for the bath-tub drapery and background, but adds a fluttering tricolour at the elephantine foot of his victim.

It must be asked whether the similarity between two images of Corday — one from Picasso and one from Sade — is just a coincidence? In section III I will present some evidence in favour of a circumstantial connection: Picasso's involvement with Surrealism meant an awareness of a cult of the *femme-fatale* and the *femme-assassin*. As we shall see, the fantastic androgynous imagery conjured up by Sade, although motivated by propagandist fervour, captures in advance much of the gloating publicity given to notorious female assassins in the press of the 1930s, a publicity taken up and inverted by Surrealism.

Secondly, it seems reasonable to wonder whether Picasso's choice of Marat and Corday was motivated in the same way as Munch's: out of a Nietzschean dread of woman?[16] Such a view seems supported by the fact that the visual vocabulary of the *Woman with Stiletto* seems to originate in paintings of 1928–9, when, as has often been pointed out, Picasso's relationship with Olga Koklova was deteriorating. The *Woman in a Red Armchair* is a life-size example of this misogynistic development. The meaning of this imagery will be shown to change in the context of the broader Surrealist interest in female psychiatric patients and female murderers of a specific psychological type.

The third and most urgent question which arises as this stage is why precisely Picasso should pick upon *David's* painting as his model at this point in time?[17] An examination of other instances of the same imagery in Picasso's work of the period reveals that, whilst it is true that the first Marat picture, *Woman with Stiletto*, certainly employs a female figure much like that in *Woman in a Red Armchair*, this figure also occurs in Picasso's small but highly worked painting of the Crucifixion (plate 37). Thus, in the next section, I will look at Picasso's interest in the crucifixion theme as a prelude and companion to the Marat variations. It is plausible to think that this relationship between the two groups of pictures exists, as it reflects Picasso's appreciation of the religious model which David adopted for his martyr, and the potential combination in the crucifixion theme of violence and latent sexuality. In pursuing what could loosely be termed 'ritual sacrifice' in this different way in 1930, Picasso was responding to the layers of meaning which he found in David's painting: of religious and erotic presence.

II

The crucifixion variations in which I am interested seem to go as far back as 1926 (plate 38). This sketch, isolated in the Zervos catalogue, mixes an image from the bullfight — the mounted Picador as centurion — with the biblical narrative. The identities of other figures are unstable: also present are an amorphous female figure to the left, and a collapsed naked woman at Christ's feet. As a compositional idea it relates to two drawings from the period 1930–31. When this composition was worked up, the traumatized woman reappeared in detail on 25 May (Z.VII.279) and 26 May 1929 (plate 39), as well as in three sketches for a different composition which introduced another element from the bullfight: the transfixed crowd in a roman-type amphitheatre (plates 40 and 41). A man climbs a ladder at the left; the traditional gaming drum, die and cup rest in the foreground, and left of centre the feet of Christ are surrounded by the delirious women mourners. This was the composition which Picasso painted, in oils on wood, 7 February 1930. Two further drawings belong to this compositional project (plate 42 and Z.VII.316]. In both Picasso has moved towards a Romanesque or Byzantine Christ, although retaining many of the

37 Pablo Picasso, *La Crucifixion*, [Paris], 7 February 1930, oil on wood, 50 × 65.5 cm. Musée Picasso (no. 122), Paris. (Z.VII, 287)

characters from the earlier drawings. The unreliable dating given by Zervos[18] suggests that these two drawings were made after the oil painting had been completed.

In an illuminating article on Picasso's interest in the crucifixion theme, published over twenty years ago,[19] Ruth Kaufmann analysed the *Crucifixion* of 1930 in terms of Surrealist preoccupation with 'primitive' rites:

> Such Surrealist journals of the late '20s and early '30s as *Documents* and *Minotaure* contain numerous articles about these primitive rites and art forms by such friends of Picasso as Michel Leiris, Georges Bataille and Robert Desnos. The importance of these Surrealist interests is reflected also in the leading general art magazine of the period, *Cahiers d'art*, edited by Picasso's great friend and the future compiler of his works, Christian Zervos. The art that received particular attention in these journals was Christian art that was demonic or heretical, European art of the archaic periods, and the arts of the primitive peoples of Africa, Oceania and Pre-Colombian America.[20]

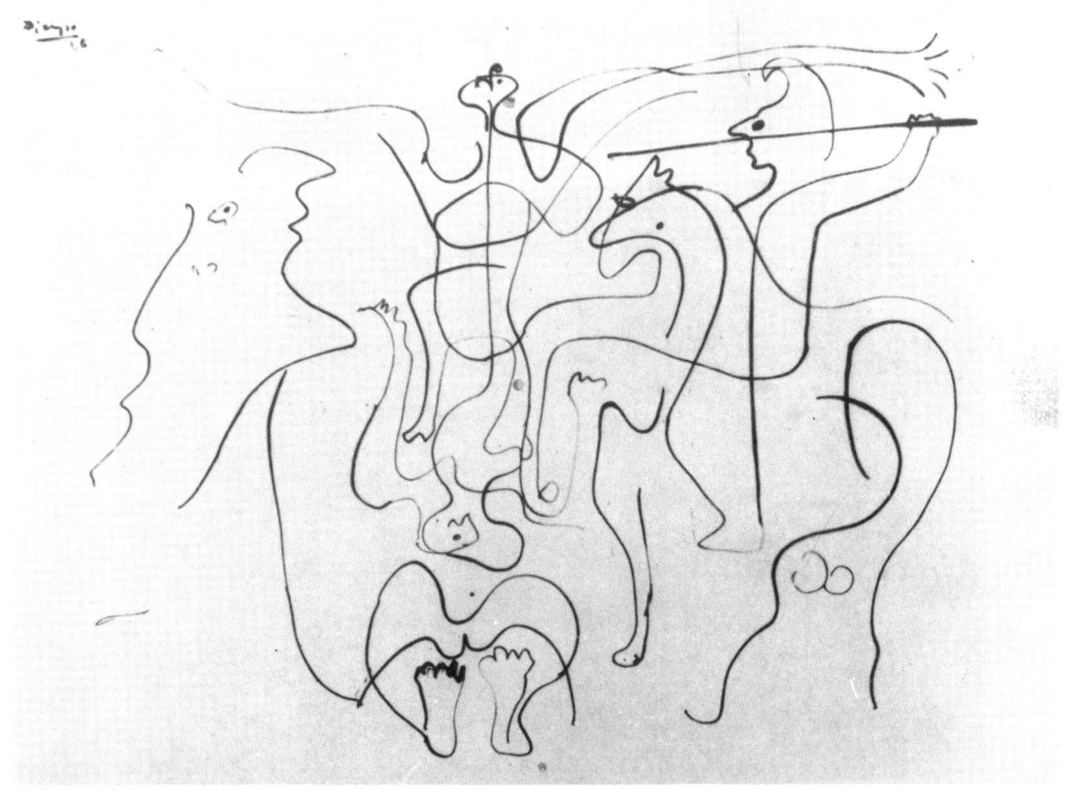

38 Pablo Picasso, *Le Christ en croix*, 1926, drawing, 41 × 50 cm (Z.VII,29)

Kaufmann shows how Picasso might have built upon the striking combination of Christian imagery and destructive 'dionysian' energy to be found in the *Three Dancers* of 1925 (Tate Gallery, London), by attending to the ritual aspects of the crucifixion narrative as well as its corporeal and psychological extremity. Thus Kaufmann argues that two of the 1929 compositional drawings (in her order, plates 41 and 40) focus not on the symbolic figure of Christ but on the 'responses of the participants and onlookers'.[21] The naked woman at Christ's feet is identified as the Magdalen, 'whose facial features are confounded with her genitalia'[22] in testimony to her base sexuality. The centurion to the right and the 'naildriver' ascending his ladder to the left are seen as detached, a judgement which in the latter case is less than secure: rather the open mouth and bulging eyes may reflect the strain of climbing the ladder, and this kind of realism has many precedents in both Northern and Italian painting.[23] Similarly, the mindless nonchalance of the horse chewing the cud may have precedents in anecdotal passages from earlier crucifixions.[24] A character unmentioned by Kaufmann enters from the far right in both drawings, in one to be repulsed by the centurion, and in the other to make the typical *ecce homo* gesture — complete with *repoussoir* gaze — of an attendant St John. In plate 41 there are as many as six figures in the immediate area of Christ, and as many as three in plate 40.

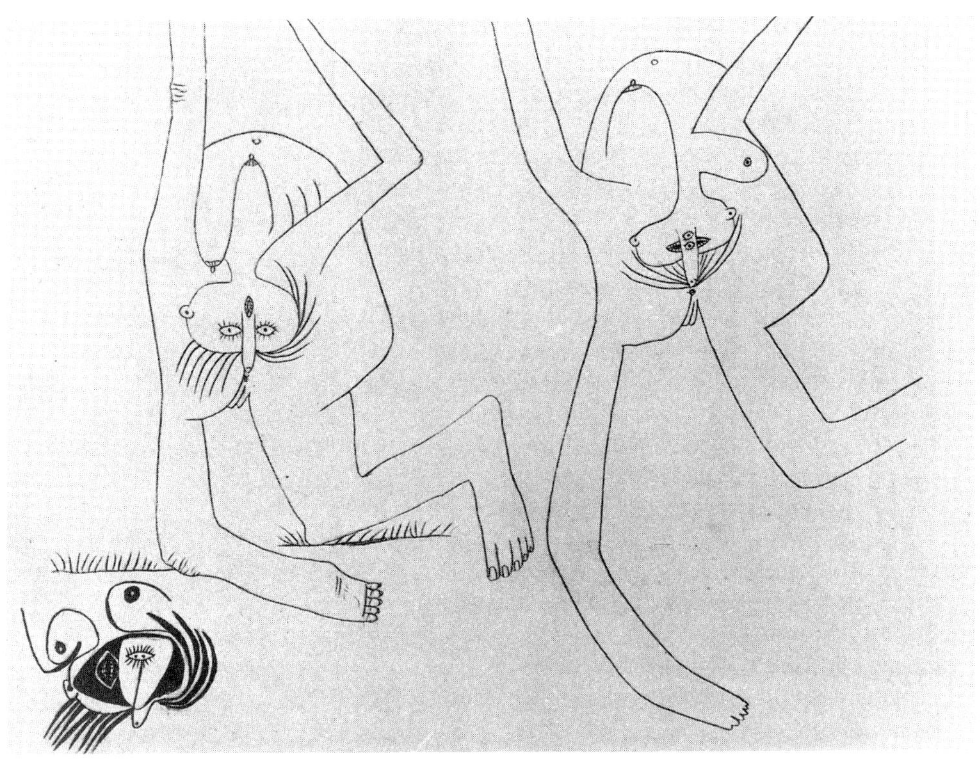

39 Pablo Picasso, *Untitled*, 26 May 1929, Pencil drawing. (Z.VII,280)

40 Pablo Picasso, *Untitled*, pencil drawing. (Z.VII,281)

41 Pablo Picasso, *Untitled*, pencil drawing. Musée Picasso (no. 1875–45), Paris. (Z.VIII,283)

42 Pablo Picasso, *Untitled*, pencil drawing, 1930–31. (Z.VII,315)

The arena in which the spectators appear is convincingly associated with the bullring. In Z.VII.282, not discussed by Kaufmann, it is clear that Picasso uses grisaille to create faces where one side is brightly lit and the other in a deep shadow. Kaufmann shows that this kind of face type belongs to the sun/moon imagery of the crucifixion theme, recalling the eclipse described in two gospels,[25] and again often represented in paintings of the subject.

The elements of the sun/moon figure and the bullfight occur in the finished painting. The sun/moon character is to the immediate right of Christ, and a picadoresque centurion shrinks into a miniature on the left. The bullfight quite explicitly relates the crucifixion to public sacrifice. As Kaufmann points out, Georges Bataille in particular was well aware of the origins of the Spanish spectacle in the archaic Roman cult of Mithras,[26] which also has its significant sun imagery, and in the latter connection she cites Bataille's 1930 article 'Soleil pourri', which appeared in the *Hommage à Picasso* issue of *Documents* in 1930.[27] Written with a mixture of bravura and academic laconicism, this 'notice' contrasts the elevated symbolism of the noonday sun with its real emasculating and disturbing effect on the human eye and mind. The unobserved sun appears an object of great beauty, the observed an ugly and horrifying tormentor. Bataille equates the beautiful sun with Mithras the executioner, or with the 'vulture' devouring the liver of Prometheus, or finally with a self-mutilator or a headless man.[28] For Bataille, the significance of these figures, or rather these actions, is in their psychological purity.[29] Although this precludes any easy analogies with the practices of painting, Bataille concludes:

> However, it is possible to say that academic painting more or less corresponded to a lofty cultivation of the spirit. In contemporary painting, by contrast, the search for a conclusive rupture in this elevated culture, and for an almost blinding revelation, has a part to play in the creation or in the destruction of forms. This search is truly perceptible only in the painting of Picasso.[30]

Kaufmann makes use of another of Bataille's publications: an analysis of *L'Apocalypse de Saint-Sever*,[31] an eleventh-century French version of an eighth-century Spanish manuscript by Beatus of Liebana (Bibliothèque nationale, Paris). She identifies the collapsed figures at the bottom left of Picasso's painting — generally acknowledged as the two deposed thieves — with the contorted figures of the victims of *Le Déluge* in the manuscript. Certainly Bataille's text draws attention to the 'déformations arbitraires' of the medieval figures. Kaufmann's other interesting suggestion, that the large green form in the top left of the *Crucifixion*, usually identified as the vinegar-soaked sponge, should instead be seen as an apocalyptic Nebuchadnezzar's stone,[32] is certainly more speculative. It is possible to read this form as a plume on the bizarre helmet of another centurion (compare the helmet in plate 40 with the painting of a *Head in Profile*, dated 26/1/30, Z.VII.298); if not, as the sponge. This problem has obvious consequences for the identification of the left-hand figure — centurion or another hysterical female mourner? Kaufmann's treatment of the peculiarly comic creature to the right of the sun/moon figure as a ritualistic presence is also speculative.

The other two important identifications which Kaufmann makes seem correct: the left-hand Mantis-headed figure as the Magdalen,[33] and the central figure before Christ as the Virgin.[34] What is peculiarly interesting about the latter identification is, of course, the close similarity of the Virgin's physiognomy to that of the *Woman in a Red Armchair* of 1929. Picasso's practice of recasting his characters in this way will take on added significance in the case of the Marat painting and drawings. For the moment it can be seen that in one painting the same figure plays the role of hysterical woman in a 'bourgeois' interior, in another the Mother of Christ.

It should now be clearer that the 'recasting' of this figure as Corday in the Marat painting has a particular semantic weight for Picasso, and does not merely reflect autobiographical concerns. A chain of connections is forged in the painter's mind between three hysterical women: the disturbed contemporary city-dweller; the Virgin Mary at the foot of the Cross,[35] and the vile murderous creature. In this respect, Kaufmann's observation that Picasso's subject in the *Crucifixion* is 'human irrationality in the form of hysteria, brutality and sadism' seems right, but her view that Picasso examined these themes according to an 'approach derived from Surrealist interests — that of the anthropologist and psychiatrist',[36] attributes an intellectual cool-headedness to these first images which may be both over-optimistic and misleading in the context of the slightly comic absurdity of the figures.

The Surrealist context for Picasso's lurid depiction of the hysterical woman in the late 1920s and early '30s was that of the debate on sexual liberation: in general, and for women in particular. As has now been recognized,[37] the general claim on the part of the early Surrealists to be on the side of sexual freedom was constantly tempered by the moralism and romanticism they attached to an ideal — if 'mad' — love. Whilst defending Charlie Chaplin's adultery,[38] some prominent members of the Surrealist group found Artaud's sexuality more awkward, and their almost entirely male panel assembled for 'Recherches sur la sexualité' was occasionally conservative when considering the breadth of human sexual possibilities.[39] On the subject of the sexuality of women, the tone of Surrealism in this early phase was consistently one of the obsessed male pursuant or investigator. 'L'amour' was sometimes romantically regarded as *the* revolutionary force.[40] Clearly, the toothy scream of the female figure in which we are interested does not relate to this side of early Surrealism.

Aside from the erotic goddess, there was one other type of woman who was awarded a central role in the Surrealist universe: the female assassin. The image of this type of woman is there from the very beginning of organized Surrealism: in issue one of *La Révolution Surréaliste* a collage of photographic portraits — including Picasso — surrounded a 'photo de criminel' of Germaine Berton (1902–1942) (plate 43). Berton was an anarchist who assassinated Maurice Plateau, secretary of the royalist organ *l'Action française*, in 1923. Philippe Daudet, editor-in-chief of the paper, fell in love with Berton and was drawn to anarchism, before committing suicide. Aragon contributed a short text in Berton's honour, whose opening remarks presage Bataille's 'Soleil pourri':

Absolute freedom offends, disconcerts. The sun has always injured the

43 Anon, *Photomontage of Surrealists and Germaine Berton, La Révolution Surréaliste*, no. 1, 1 December 1924, p. 17.

> eyes of its worshippers. Germaine Berton kills Plateau. Anarchists, and with them a very small number of men, myself, applaud. But then, she has, it would seem, served their cause. As soon as she is swept away by life — and who would follow her in what are called reckless detours — undoubtedly she will compromise her admirers. Then they will prefer to speak of sickness and demoralization. And certainly the anarchists exalt life and disapprove of suicide, which is a weakness, 'as we all know'. It is then that they make me feel shame: they leave me nothing else to do but to prostrate myself in complete and simple admiration before this woman who is the greatest defiance I know to slavery, the most beautiful protest raised on the face of the earth against the hideous lie of happiness.[41]

Aragon's article indicates the tone of much of the writing included in *La Révolution Surréaliste*: charged with earnest pessimism and affrontery. But the epigram from Baudelaire included with the photographs reveals the frisson of sexual interest which the image of the *femme-assassin* included: 'Woman is the being who casts the greatest shadow or the greatest light in our dreams.'[42]

Berton, as a political assassin, obviously bears comparison to Corday. Although, as Aragon points out, Berton's political position was attractive to *left*-wing activists, the political position of *femmes-assassins* was in general a matter of small importance. The real link between political motivation and the erotic charge of the *femme-assassin* was in her resistance to social mores. In this respect Surrealism forged a direct link between the idea of a release of psychic, often erotic energy and varieties of serious, usually violent crime. The principle of Surrealism's famous rejection of 'bourgeois' morality had, of course, been laid down in the 'First Surrealist Manifesto' of 1924, but in 1928 a visual development of the theme in relation to women appeared in the remarkable 'Le Cinquantenaire de l'Hysterie [The Fiftieth Anniversary of Hysteria] (1878–1928)'.[43] The text celebrated the 'greatest poetic discovery of the end of the nineteenth century' and opposed to a series of definitions of the phenomenon a Surrealist one.

> Hysteria is a more of less irreducible mental state characterized by subversion of the relationships which are established between the subject and the moral world, of which the subject believes herself fully a part, being free of all delirium. This mental state is based on the need for a *reciprocal* seduction, which explains the casual acknowledgement of the miracles provoked by the method of suggestion and response between patient *and* doctor. Hysteria is not a pathological phenomenon, and can, in all respects, be regarded as a supreme means of expression.[44]

This remarkably cavalier inversion of psychiatric moralism, emphasizing as it does the supposed creative and expressive dimensions of a pervasive, even collusive, hysteria, was brilliantly illustrated with six photographs of 'Les Attitudes Passionnelles en 1878' ('Passionate Poses in 1878') (plate 44). The ecstatic performance of this patient of Charcot at Salpétrière provides another foil to

LE CINQUANTENAIRE DE L'HYSTERIE

(1878-1928)

Nous, surréalistes, tenons à célébrer ici le cinquantenaire de l'hystérie, la plus grande découverte poétique de la fin du XIXe siècle, et cela au moment même où le démembrement du concept de l'hytérie paraît chose consommée. Nous qui n'aimons rien tant que ces jeunes hystériques, dont le type parfait nous est fourni par l'observation relative à la délicieuse X. L. (Augustine) entrée à la Salpêtrière dans le service du Dr Charcot le 21 octobre 1875, à l'âge de 15 ans 1/2, comment serions-nous touchés par la laborieuse réfutation de troubles organiques, dont le procès ne sera jamais qu'aux yeux des seuls médecins celui de l'hystérie ? Quelle pitié ! M. Babinski, l'homme le plus intelligent qui se soit attaqué à cette question, osait publier en 1913 : « Quand une émotion est sincère, profonde, secoue l'âme humaine, il n'y a plus de place pour l'hystérie ». Et voilà encore ce qu'on nous a donné à apprendre de mieux. Freud, qui doit tant à Charcot, se souvient-il du temps où, au témoignage des survivants, les internes de la Salpêtrière confondaient leur devoir professionnel et leur goût de l'amour, où, à la nuit tombante, les malades les rejoignaient au dehors ou les recevaient dans leur lit ? Ils énuméraient ensuite patiemment, pour les besoins de la cause médicale qui ne se défend pas, les attitudes passionnelles soi-disant pathologiques qui leur étaient, et nous sont encore humainement, si précieuses. Après cinquante ans, l'école de Nancy est-elle morte ? S'il vit toujours, le docteur Luys a-t-il oublié ? Mais où sont les observations de Néri sur le tremblement de terre de Messine ? Où sont les zouaves torpillés par le Raymond Roussel de la science, Clovis Vincent?

Aux diverses définitions de l'hystérie qui ont été données jusqu'à ce jour, de l'hystérie, divine dans l'Antiquité, infernale au Moyen-Age, des possédés de Loudun aux flagellants de N.-D. des Pleurs (Vive Madame Chantelouve!), définitions mythiques, érotiques ou simplement lyriques, définitions sociales, définitions savantes, il est trop facile d'opposer cette « maladie complexe et protéiforme appelée hystérie qui échappe à toute définition » (*Bernheim*). Les spectateurs du très beau film « La Sorcellerie à travers les âges » se rappellent certainement avoir trouvé sur l'écran ou dans la salle des enseignements plus vifs que ceux des livres d'Hippocrate, de Platon où l'utérus bondit comme une petite chèvre, de Galien qui immobilise la chèvre, de Fernel qui la remet en marche au XVIe siècle et la sent sous sa main remonter jusqu'à l'estomac; ils ont vu grandir, grandir les cornes de la

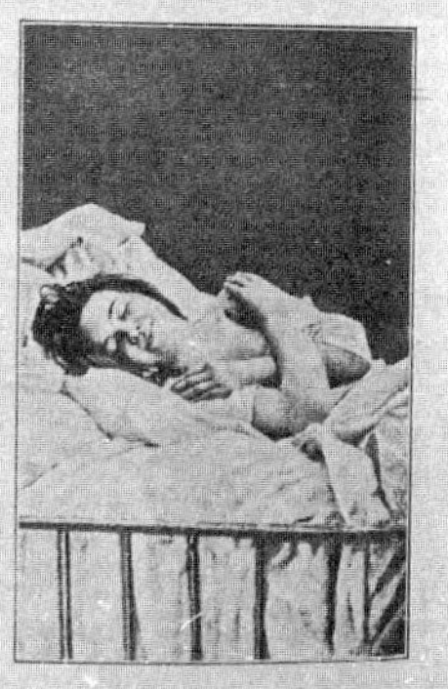

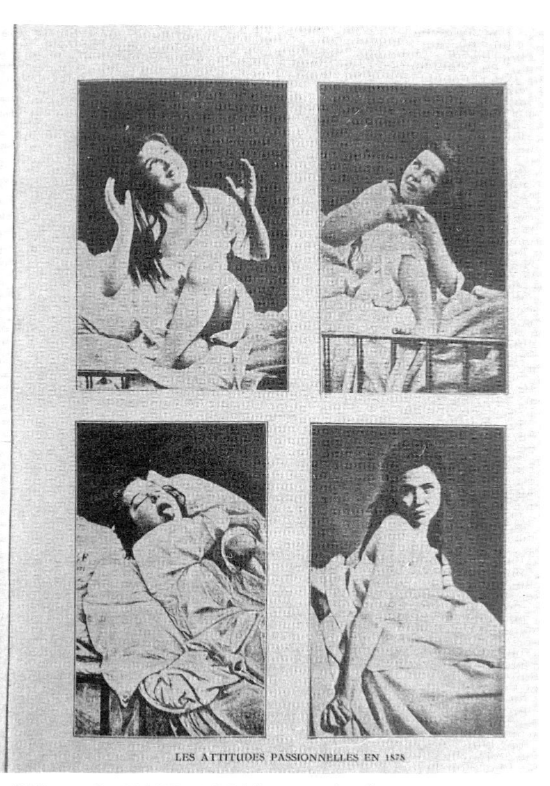

44 Aragon & Breton, 'Le Cinquantenaire de l'Hysterie (1878–1928)', *La Révolution Surréaliste*, no. 11, 15 March 1928, pp. 20–21.

Picasso's type of hysterical woman, and in particular the paroxysm evident in one image includes a violently protruding tongue, anticipating Picasso's later image of Corday. Turn two pages in this issue of the periodical and one finds Picasso's asexual *Harlequin* of 1927,[45] illustrating an appropriately entitled article by Benjamin Péret: 'La Maladie No. 9'. There is a subtle change in tone from the Berton article to the treatment of the Salpêtrière photographs which perhaps matches the change in imagery. Whereas Aragon's early piece sounds like an obituary in a revolutionary newspaper, the 1928 article is more academic and constructs its challenge to contemporary society out of the past. Discovering the creative potential of hysteria — an inner revolution — was both a retreat into poetic revolt and perhaps a humorous play upon glamorous images of the creative woman: diva, actress or dancer. As David Macey has noted, Breton later admitted that the images of the woman were the real object of interest: 'Hysteria becomes an iconography of femininity.'[46] Yet, as will be shown in the next section, contrasting images of the disturbed and violent woman appeared in Surrealist journals in 1933, calling into question the 'femininity' of this iconography.

The crucifixion images we have examined so far are probably based by Picasso on a variety of visual interpretations of that theme, many known to him in reproduction. A key connection between these variations and the Marat painting has emerged in the physical characteristics of the Virgin/Corday character. Certainly, the element of cruel humour in the *Crucifixion* has been little remarked. It can now be seen that this element derives in part from Surrealist treatments of the figure of the deranged woman, and especially from the creative hysteria of the Salpétrière patient.

Yet this section would not be complete without discussion of Marat. himself. The charge of Picasso's painting does not derive merely from the sedimented transformations of the Virgin figure mentioned so far, but also from the iconographic past of Picasso's Marat. The basic form of Marat in the 1931 painting derives from the Christ in Picasso's *Crucifixion*. David's identification of Marat with Christ was to emphasize his martyrdom, but in the *Woman with Stiletto* Picasso developed this in the direction of a kind of sexual martyrdom, through his preoccupation with the attendant hysterical women, and especially the woman at the foot of the Cross.[47]

After that first Marat painting was completed, Picasso made a series of thirteen pen and ink variations on the Grünewald *Crucifixion* in the *Isenheim Altarpiece* (1512–16, Musée der Unterlinden, Colmar), seven of which were published in the first number of *Minotaure*.[48] An argument for the special interest of the Grünewald can be advanced from the perspective of the David variations. We know that the David *Marat* was on show in Paris in 1928,[49] and that David's martyr is suggestively modelled on Renaissance Christs. In choosing Grünewald as his model, Picasso was, of course, picking the paradigm of a Christ whose *suffering* rather than whose divinity was expressed through the body. The *Isenheim Altarpiece*, known to Picasso only in reproduction,[50] was painted for a monastery which gave shelter to the sick, and there is no doubt that Grünewald's rendering of the body of Christ was meant to relate directly to the experience of these residents. The skin of the Grünewald Christ performed this task most strikingly of all, and undoubtedly this skin approached the condition of Marat's rather better than the skin of a Raphael Christ.

A fortuitous but amusing connection — which may have attracted Picasso — already existed between these two very different martyrs: Grünewald's Christ and Marat. The connection between Marat and Christ was first made by David, but perhaps Picasso realistically reforged that link by substituting a putrefying Christ for a perfect one?

III

It has been claimed that Picasso's *Woman with Stiletto* was indebted to Surrealism from a number of directions: anthropological (an interest in the iconography of sacrifice and religion), psychological (an interest in the image of the hysterical woman), and sexual (an interest in the erotic dimension of the *femme-assassin*). The tantalizing suggestion that Picasso's Marat pictures may have been prompted by an awareness of Sade's valedictory speech to Marat can now be developed, because it was against the background of these interests that serious publications on Sade began to appear in Surrealist journals in 1930. This can be seen in contrast to the scant interest shown in Marat himself: he was the subject of passing admiration as a revolutionary, but was barely featured in the main periodicals.

Paul Eluard had, in fact, published a two-page essay on Sade in 1926,[51] and the Marquis had been cited in the pages of preceding issues of *La Révolution Surréaliste*, but it was with the arrival of Maurice Heine (1884–1940) into the fold of Surrealism that study of Sade assumed scholarly proportions. Heine came from a medical background, and was a militant communist before being expelled from the party for extremism.[52] In the years after 1924 he founded the 'Société du roman philosophique' with the aim of publishing Sade's suppressed work.[53] As a result, he published an edition of *les Historiettes, contes et fabliaux et le Dialogue entre un prêtre et un moribond* in 1926, criticism of which may have provoked the Eluard article. In the same year Heine published a *Recueil de Confessions et Observations psycho-sexuelles tirées de la littérature médicale*,[54] including an introductory survey of major theories of psycho-sexuality. In 1930 *Les Infortunes de la vertu* appeared from a different publisher, and between 1931 and 1935 Heine's Société began the task of publishing a definitive text of the long-lost *Les cent-vingt journées de sodome*.

As far as I am aware Heine did not himself publish any short article during the period listing Sade's Marat speech. What can be said is that the speech was certainly known to him, because it was readily available in books which he cites in the 1930 introduction to *Les infortunes de la vertu*.[55] As for evidence of intellectual intimacy with Picasso, one can only point with certainty to a later period, that of the short-lived Contre-Attaque movement around 1935–36.[56] The idea that, prior to painting *Woman with Stiletto*, Picasso knew the speech from Heine must remain a supposition. The connections between this image and the speech can only be described as coincidental. Yet the circumstantial evidence of a stronger link is still more intriguing when we turn to a second Marat study.

Heine's Surrealist publications, begun as *La Révolution Surréaliste*, came to an end in December 1929.[57] In the second number of its successor *Le Surréalisme au service de la révolution*, Heine introduced the first 'Actualité de Sade': an unpublished letter written by Sade in 1779, and a letter of his own in defence of Sade as a literary figure. The third number featured Heine's open letter to Buñuel on the subject of the borrowings from Sade in *L'Age d'or*. The fourth and fifth numbers featured two more 'Actualité(s) de Sade'.[58] These results of diligent research were not particularly characteristic of the periodical: approaches to Sade at this stage in the development of the Surrealist movement are better expressed in Man Ray's photograph *Hommage à D.A.F. de Sade*,[59] or René Char's prose poem of the same title:

> Sade, love finally salvaged from the sludge of the heavens, hypocrisy overcome by weapons and eyes, this heritage will help men in times of famine, their beautiful stranglers' hands emerging from their pockets.[60]

These types of romanticism took root in Sade's prototypical combination of (apparent) political revolt and libertinism: the dangerous life which Sade had led *vis-à-vis* the authorities acted as a potent symbol for Surrealism's struggle with the PCF as well as the French censors.

Heine published more material, and on a more diverse range of topics, in *Minotaure*. He contributed an article to every issue bar number 2 and the double final number 12–13 of this marvellous periodical. Again the tone is generally scholarly, although Heine responds to the house style — an eclectic mix of anthropology and literary imagination — on a few occasions.

It is 1933, the first year of *Minotaure* and the last of *Le Surréalisme au service de la révolution*, which is supremely important in establishing a basis for Picasso's further interest in the theme of Marat's assassination.

Once again the focus of the interest is the figure of Corday the *femme-assassin*, but this is preceded, I will suggest, by a lyrical and transformative anatomy of Marat. Picasso's revival of the subject follows two notorious murder cases which were publicized, together with important images of the women involved in one case, in Surrealist journals in 1933. The first of these was the case of the Papin sisters, the second that of Violette Nozières. Both served to reinforce the linkage between the *femme-assassin* and trans-sexual or a-sexual identity; both break down the 'feminine' dimension of the Surrealist iconography of hysteria. Furthermore there were specific associations made with Sade on the level of sublime criminality. Once more, then, there exists a teasing promise of a genuine connection between the content of the Sade speech and Picasso's subject.

In what follows I will focus on the Papin sisters, whose case carried with it specific visual imagery which I believe was imported by Picasso into the Marat scenario.[61]

The Surrealist periodicals had long carried short notices reporting crimes and bizarre happenings, sometimes lifted verbatim from the popular local press of France. This idea seems to have been stolen from André Gide's *Nouvelle revue française*. Gide had been an elder supporter of many Surrealists, including Breton, during their Dada years immediately following the war, and had published with them in early issues of *Littérature*. Gide collected 'faits divers' or bizarre news items as a result of his interest in legal injustice and also in psychologically inexplicable acts. He published a collection of rather appalling examples in 1930.[62] In *Le Surréalisme au service de la révolution*, Eluard and Péret took this interest and turned it into a burlesque celebration of brutal murder, suicide and the supposed moral idiocy of the judiciary.

In thc case of the brief note on the Papin sisters, they readily linked the brutality of the murders committed to the repressions of religious upbringing and domestic service:

> The Papin sisters were pupils in the Convent of Le Mans. Then their mother placed them in service in a 'respectable' Le Mans household. For six years they endured with perfect obedience various duties, demands and injustices. Stupidity, fatigue, and humiliation slowly bred hatred in them, that sweet liquor which secretly consoles by promising physical strength to the violence which will join it sooner or later.
>
> The day came, Léa and Christine Papin rendered to evil its due, a payment in wrought-iron. They literally massacred their employers, tearing out their eyes, smashing in their heads. Then they carefully washed themselves, and, relieved, dispassionate, they slept in the same bed. The lightning had struck, the wood had burnt, the sun had been definitely extinguished.
>
> Emerging fully armed from Les chants de Maldoror . . . [63]

The text is followed by a popular illustration of a lewd winking nun. More significantly two extraordinary 'Avant–Aprés' photographs of the sisters were reproduced at the end of the issue (plate 45), subtitled by the last line of the above text. Aside from the obvious degeneration of the sisters from 'bourgeois' tidiness to 'déclassé' malevolence, there is a hint in the prison image of insanity in the rolling eye of the right-hand sister — probably Christine, the older of the pair. This loss of cleanliness, order and sanity has its counterpart in what may have been seen as an increase in *masculinity* in the appearance of the sisters. At this early stage in the reporting of the crime, gaining such an impression from the image would merely rest on prejudice and suspicion of a lesbian relationship between the two. That the sisters should have indulged in a transgressive sexual pact was undoubtedly of interest: the preceding pages of the periodical carried Man Ray's *Monument à D.A.F. de Sade*,[64] representing the archetypal pre-genital part of the body which Sade relentlessly celebrated, and Max Ernst's *Oedipe*,[65] symbolic victim of the deepest sexual guilt, and, of course, punishment by blinding.

These vague premonitions of confused sexuality in the fierce images of the incarcerated sisters received their confirmation in an article by Jacques Lacan published in *Minotaure*.[66] The Papin sisters committed their crime on 2 February 1933, and the details of the crime emerged from statements made mainly by Christine whilst in custody. Lacan relied on the extensive newspaper reports of the trial and may also have gained further information from the psychologist who acted as a major defence witness for the sisters in court, Dr Logre.[67] Lacan's article draws attention to the spontaneity of the apparently motiveless crime, and attempts to construct a psycho-biography for the sisters which would make it more comprehensible. Building on theoretical material in his doctoral thesis of 1932, Lacan argues that the sisters were victims of a 'délire à deux': a shared paranoia. The classic traits of paranoia are described, but Lacan also notes that psychologists have given different explanations of their origin. On the one hand, paranoia is located as a congenital defect of character. The alternative position argues that spontaneous perceptual difficulties are misinterpreted by the patient, and delirium sets in as a rational effort to explain these misinterpretations. On this view, the criminal act which often accompanies paranoia is an emotional reaction to the same delirious convictions. Lacan argues that both conceptions are inadequate to the complexity of the task. Of central interest to his Surrealist publishers was undoubtedly his assertion that the delirium evident in the paranoiac patient was merely an exaggerated form of that present in every subject. The commonality of this delirium is explained by its origin in 'tensions sociales'. For Lacan, all social life implies a 'camouflage de motifs' *vis-à-vis* the unconscious: a compromise is always necessary between unconscious desires and social exigency, and this compromise or camouflage is nothing other than basic delirium.

The second important aspect of the argument, however, is that the murderous aggressive drive of the paranoiac, again perhaps different only in degree from normalcy, bears a social imprint from the very beginning: it is built around ideas of punishment, revenge and the expiation of sin relating to fundamental social taboos. Unsurprisingly, the social taboos which Lacan identifies as particularly

AVANT

APRÈS

« Sorties tout armées d'un chant de Maldoror... » (Voir page 28).

45 Anon, *The Papin Sisters*, in *Le Surréalisme au Service de la Révolution*, no. 5, 15 May 1933, p.60.

potent, and frequently correlative with paranoiac delirium, are those relating to incest and 'perversion'. Following Freud, Lacan claims that whilst the basic hostility of siblings is reduced during the first stages of infantile sexual development, an occasional inversion can lead to incestuous desire. In fact this inversion appears to be universal in some degree, as Lacan argues that it is the primordial condition for the integration of instinctive tendencies with 'tensions sociales'. An element of tragedy attaches to this integration, however, because it marks the beginning of the personal sacrifice which sociality enforces.

Lacan somewhat unclearly sees in this experience of self-sacrifice a link with sadistic desires, presumably because inflicting suffering on another reverses the normal relation of the subject to social life, thereby effecting a release of psychic pressure. More importantly, the infantile establishment of this integration is painful because it is polluted. The integration of an idea of social life, of a life with the demands of others, is made via the line of least resistance: the infant selects as external loved one 'someone similar to the subject, giving rise to his or her homosexual tendencies'.[68] Crucially, this stage of idealizing a person close to the subject must be surpassed if the formation of an adult moral sense is not to be jeopardized. In the case of the sisters such an evolution had not occurred, probably obstructed, in Lacan's view, as a result of actual infantile incest. Lacan developed his argument by relating the case of the Papin sisters to that of Aimée, the major figure in his doctoral thesis. Aimée believed herself persecuted by various strangers who were all successful women: actresses, writers and the like. She invented the idea that these individuals plagiarized her own writings, and was eventually led to make a violent attack on one of them. According to Lacan, Aimée transferred from one woman to another a hateful image of her original self-ideal, her sister, for whom she had formed amorous desires as an infant. This image is hateful precisely because it evokes the guilt of incest.

So it was that in basing his account on Freud's view of the origin of paranoia as a defence against homosexuality, Lacan was able to render meaningful the acts of the Papin sisters. It was ultimately the 'auto-punitif' dimension of their paranoia which was significant. Paranoiacs of this sort develop murderous ambitions toward certain individuals because these individuals come to represent their ideal self, their infantile *semblable*. Yet in the case of the sisters, Lacan had to account for the fact that the filial object was of course actually present to each. Unlike Aimée, whose aggression toward images of her ideal self would ultimately lead to suicidal tendencies, the Papin sisters were so secure in their 'little island' of homosexual incest, that they could not easily distinguish ideal self from self. If they could not avoid importing with the desire 'social tensions', or feelings of guilt, neither could they resolve 'the enigma, the human enigma of sex' without the aid of an external image of their transgression. Rather than attack each other, rather than enter a suicidal pact, their 'true siamese souls' forced them to seek out two victims who might bear their guilt. Thus Lacan writes:

> That fateful evening, in the anxiety of imminent punishment, the sisters merged the image of their mistresses with the mirage of their own evil.

> It was their own distress which they detested in the two women whom they led in a ghastly quadrille.[69]

The Papin sisters murder their mistresses out of self-punitive desires. They thereby release their guilt: they act as their own executioners both metaphorically and literally, the latter as such an act cannot go unpunished. Their greatest punishment, however, if we are to believe Lacan, was the shock which Christine in particular experienced when physically, and then psychologically, she was separated from her double.

These are extraordinary arguments giving account of an extraordinary set of events: in them a world is presented which is subject to the immense transformative power of the mind. Nowhere does this power find greater expression than in the cases of identity and gender. A stranger can be the image of the self, or of an attribute of the self. Christine Papin can marry her sister: 'I am sure that in another life I would be my sister's husband.'[70] This power is also unmistakably shown to be uncontrollable and therefore mysterious. Lacan departs from his role as psychoanalyst, and approaches Bataille's anthropology, when he closes his text with an address to this dimension of the mind, penetrated as it has been by the 'innocent' Christine:

> The sacrilegious curiosity which has created anguish in humanity from the beginning of time; this was the thing which drove them when they tore their victims apart, when, in their gaping wounds, they hunted down what Christine was later, before the judge, to call in her innocence 'the mystery of life'.[71]

The effect of this text on Picasso, who must have known it, was in terms of an ecstatic linkage, through the imaginative substitution of roles, between murderous desire and self-punishment. This linkage is played out in the second major Marat picture. The prelude to it is a series of studies of a reclining female figure, which is perhaps a mixture of Corday and Marat: a mixture of assassin and victim. These ink drawings form a sequence of theatrical variations on the theme of a reclining figure in a claustrophobic interior, constructed out of a whole paraphernalia of domestic objects. The objects form the body parts, but the transparency of the figure carries with it the implication of a new 'anatomie' on the proverbial dissecting table. Why the interest in this bric-à-brac? Lacan's description of the Le Mans murders notably harps on the equipment employed by the Papin sisters, and the truly domestic procedure of their horrendous crime:

> . . . each set about an adversary, ripping their living eyes from their sockets — an unprecedented act, it is said, in the annals of crime — and suffocating them. Then, with the aid of whatever was to hand, mallet, pewter jug, kitchen knife, they unremittingly went to work on their victims, crushing their faces, and unveiling their genitals, making deep cuts into the thighs and buttocks of one in order to soil with blood those of the other. Then they washed the instruments of these horrifying rites, cleaning themselves and sleeping in the same bed. 'All

> neat and tidy'! That was the phrase they repeated to each other and which seemed to set the tone of sobering up, empty of all emotion, which followed after the bloody orgy.[72]

In addition to this account drawing attention to the apparatus of murder, we have earlier noted the significance of the still life in David's painting, and its reappearance in the Baudry. Thus Picasso renders his isolated disassembled woman amongst the jumble of her apartment in what is probably the first drawing, dated 2 February 1934 (plate 46). This paralysed individual has the protruding tongue of a Salpêtrière hysteric. It is not clear whether she is reclining on a bed or falling on a table. She is accompanied by a domestic cat, as is many a reclining nude, but this animal disappears in the later studies. More importantly, she wears a patterned tabard of the kind which Picasso would next bestow on Corday, and stares out of the window at a bird, usually identifiable as a swallow. The strange black streaks in the top right-hand corner reappear in this context in several other drawings in the series, as does the picture frame at bottom right. A number of drawings from 6 and 7 February develop the form of the woman in aggressive manner (plate 47; plate 48; and Z.VIII.172; 178; 179; 180; 182). In these the disjointed hysteria also carries faint echoes of the swooning mouths of Dali's *Phenomène de l'extase*,[73] which appeared in the same issue of *Minotaure* as Lacan's article on the Papin sisters. Of course, these vertical mouths also echo that of David's Marat. One drawing takes the transformation of the body into object parts to its extremity (plate 49); but the three remaining images **mix Picasso's female hysteric with the figure of the dying Marat**. In the first, dated 9 February 1934 (plate 50), the figure itself sprawls on a block emulating the famous packing-case, and Marat's pitifully limp arm is recalled, perhaps via that of Christ in the *Predella* of the Isenheim Altarpiece, in classical style. This arm is important in the two drawings of 10 February 1934 (plate 51 and Z.VIII.175), but here it holds up a compact mirror, capturing the image of a passing swallow and sending it onto the ceiling.[74] The greatest object in plate 51 is a giant quill, another fabulous recollection of David's painting.

Thus the complexities of Picasso's sources and themes bring about a surprising and fascinating turn in 1934. The second work which Picasso produced explicitly on the theme of Marat, sometimes entitled *The Murder* (plate 52), was drawn two and a half years later, and has led Roland Penrose to the view that Picasso's Corday represents a particular woman. More startling in view of the foregoing is his claim that the figure of Marat is now female:

> At the time that he was undergoing great emotional stress after his separation from his wife Olga and submitting to violent attacks from her due to her jealousy of his new love for Dora Maar, his whole production echoed his anger and passion. . . . The monster he could represent with such power was to continue to haunt him. . . . In a drawing of July 1934 . . . he seems to be laughing at his own obsession. A furious female figure has invaded the room like a whirlwind. Her face with small cruel eyes is dominated by a large open mouth with fangs bared and a swollen tongue thirsting for blood. With

46 Pablo Picasso, *Composition*, 6 February 1934, ink on paper, 23.5 × 31.5 cm. (Z.VIII,168)

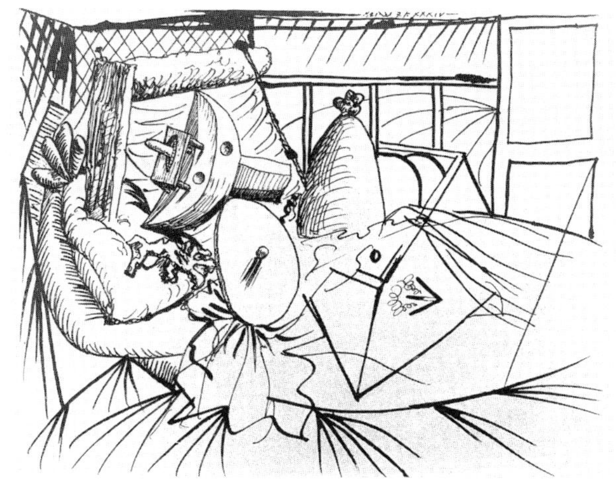

47 Pablo Picasso, *Composition*, 7 February 1934, ink on paper, 25 × 32 cm. (Z.VIII,171)

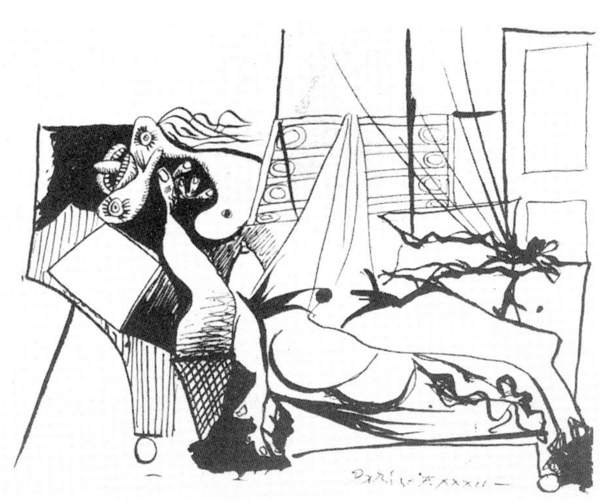

48 Pablo Picasso, *Composition*, 6 February 1934, ink on paper, 26 × 33 cm. (Z.VIII,177)

49 Pablo Picasso, *Composition*, 8 February 1934, ink on paper. (Z.VIII,176)

50 Pablo Picasso, *Composition*, 9 February 1934, ink on paper. (Z.VIII,174)

51 Pablo Picasso, *Hirondelles*, 10 February 1934, ink on paper, 25.7 × 30.7 cm. Musée Picasso (no. 1021), Paris. (Z.VIII,173)

52 Pablo Picasso, *Etude pour 'La femme au stylet d'après David "la mort de Marat"'*, [Boisgeloup], 7 July 1934, pencil on cardboard, 40 × 55 cm. Musée Picasso (no. 1135), Paris. (Z.VIII,216)

outstretched arm she plunges an enormous knife into the jugular vein of her victim seated like Marat in the bath-tub, but to our surprise it is not Marat who is being murdered. It is a girl with the profile of Marie-Thérèse Walter, the sensuous blonde model who appeared in so many of Picasso's paintings at the time. A few years later he made a coloured drawing in which Dora Maar while bathing finds herself confronted with a similar terrifying presence . . . There can be little doubt as to the origin in Picasso's mind of this particular monster.[75]

The hysterical construction of Corday's decorative body is clearly contrasted with that of the turbanned figure of Marat, but whether this Marat is in fact a woman is hard to decide. Certainly his/her features echo those angelic forms attributed consistently by Picasso at this time to a young woman of classical beauty in both painting and sculpture, and often identified with Marie-Thérèse.[76] Within such an area of permanent uncertainty it seems that Picasso has at least altered his sense of the clash between Corday and Marat. Whereas in the earlier painting the figure of Marat is feeble and bizarre, now he offers a graceful opposite to the horrific Corday. The theme on which Penrose was writing above, that of 'Beauty and the Monster', is thus very well expressed. But this theme can also include the confrontation of two self-images: an ideal one and a detestable one. The outcome of such an encounter, as with Aimée or the Papin sisters, can be very violent. Corday *may* have been a similarly unfortunate person, but the role of paranoiac fantasy is somewhat reduced in her case: one undoubtedly had a right to real fear of persecution by Marat, and Corday's willingness to be led to the scaffold afterwards is a *real* parallel of the self-punishment which the sisters craved.[77]

On 10 July 1934 Picasso produced his third version of the assassination of Marat.[78] Here, the sun streaming in onto his body, Marat faces the hideous Corday. The beautiful and monstrous beings confront each other at last.

One more teasing idea remains, and it relates to the rumour that Sade's own life was inadvertently saved by Corday's actions. We have already come across this claim in the Peter Weiss note with which we began. One biographer of Sade explains that Sade's life was actually saved twice in 1793.[79] The first occasion concerned Marat, who in his capacity as member of the 'Vigilance Committee' had read 'a most unflattering account of Sade's libertine career'. Marat mistakenly denounced the Marquis de *La Salle* in *L'Ami du peuple* on 2 June: the latter Marquis was guillotined. Incredibly, so the story goes, Marat then realized his mistake, and was on the point of rectifying it when he received his visit from Corday. If the story is true, then Sade's speech villified a woman to whom he owed his life.[80]

Neil Cox
University of Essex

Notes

The research for this paper was generously supported by the Baring Foundation and the Department of Art History and Theory, University of Essex. I would also like to thank: Orianna Baddeley for inviting me to present the material in its earliest form at Camberwell College of Art; Dawn Ades, Valerie Fraser and Margaret Iversen for their helpful comments; and Carole Lyons for assistance with the translations.

Throughout text and captions 'Z' refers to C. Zervos, *Picasso*, 33 vols, Paris, 1932–78.

1 The English version of the play was first performed at the Royal Court Theatre, London, in 1964, in a highly controversial production by Peter Brook. Its full title was *The Persecution and Assassination of Marat as performed by the inmates of the asylum of Charenton under the Direction of the Marquis de Sade*.

2 P. Weiss, 'Author's Note on the Historical Background to the Play', *Marat/Sade*, London, 1989, p.113.

3 As will become clear the speech could not, in fact, have been delivered at Marat's funeral, which it post-dated by several months.

4 See note 80 below.

5 The best example is Mary Matthews Gedo, *Picasso: Art and Autobiography*, London, 1980.

6 This was certainly the case with writing on Picasso's later paintings inspired by the 1988 exhibition, *Late Picasso* (Centre Pompidou; Tate Gallery). Powerful and perceptive critics

including John Richardson and David Sylvester saw a preoccupation with death in virtually every image. See, for example, J. Richardson, 'l'Époque Jacqueline', *Late Picasso*, London, 1988, pp. 17–47; and D. Sylvester, 'Endgame', ibid., pp. 137–46.

7 For example, Michel Leiris, 'Toiles récentes de Picasso', *Documents*, no. 3, deuxième année 1930 (*Hommage à Picasso*).

8 A. Brookner, *Jacques-Louis David*, London, 1980, pp. 112–13.

9 ibid., p.114.

10 Ch. Baudelaire, 'Le Musée classique du bazar bonne-nouvelle' [1846], *Oeuvres complètes*, II, Paris, 1976, pp. 408–414 (this reference p.409).

11 'On 12 September 1793, the Section de Molière et Lafontaine took the new name of the Section of Brutus, and on the 15th held a ceremony with speeches honoring Marat and Le Peletier. The Section du Panthéon had its similar rites on 22nd September, and installed busts of Marat, Le Peletier and Brutus. This triumvirate (with the most frequent addition of Chalier) entered into the ceremonies of most of the Sections.' R. L. Herbert, *David: Brutus*, London, 1972, pp. 100–101.

12 David's own speech to the Convention to commemorate his gift of the painting is equally rhetorically charged. See Brookner, op. cit., p.115.

13 'Sexe timide et doux, comment se peut-il que vos mains délicates ayent saisi le poignard que la séduction aiguisoit? . . . Ah! votre empressement à venir de jetter des fleurs sur le tombeau de ce véritable ami du peuple, nous fait oublier que le crime pût trouver un bras parmi vous. Le barbare assassin de *Marat*, semblable à ces êtres mixtes auxquels on ne peut assigner aucun sexe, vomi par les enfers pour le désespoir de tous deux, n'appartient directement à aucun. Il faut qu'un voile funèbre enveloppe à jamais sa mémoire; qu'on cesse surtout de nous présenter, comme on ose le faire, son effigie sous l'emblême enchanteur de la beauté. Artistes trop crédules, brisez, renversez, défigurez les traits de ce monstre, ou ne l'offrez à nos yeux indignées qu'au milieu des furies du Tartare.' Quoted in G. Lely, *Vie du marquis de Sade*, Paris 1989 [3rd edition], p.483.

14 Hilton notes that Picasso asked Brassai rather than Zervos, the latter then preparing his oeuvre catalogue, to photograph the picture. Brassai was the photographer who brought many of Picasso's works to the pages of Surrealist periodicals, again reinforcing the connection between the themes of the Marat pictures and Picasso's Surrealist phase. As was the case with a large number of now significant works — including the *Woman in a Red Armchair* and the *Crucifixion* — Picasso kept the Marat variations for himself. See T. Hilton, 'Introduction', *Picasso's Picassos*, London, Arts Council, 1981, pp. 31–88 (this reference pp. 66–7).

15 The subject of the assassination of Marat has attracted almost as many artists as that of his assassin. See Tanguy l'Aminot, 'Marat et Charlotte Corday vu par la droite', and Ch. Thomas, 'Portraits de Charlotte Corday', *La Mort de Marat*, Paris, 1986; A. Decauville Lachènée, *Charlotte Corday et ses portraits, et spécialement le pastel de Brard*, Caen, 1896; J. Delaporte, ' "Les métamorphoses" de Charlotte Corday', in *Charlotte Corday: Une normande dans la revolution*, Versailles, 1989; M. Marrinan, 'Images and Ideas of Charlotte Corday: texts and contexts of an assassination', *Arts Magazine*, April 1980, pp. 158–77.

16 This issue in Picasso studies is briefly discussed by Sam Hunter in his essay 'Picasso at War: Royan, 1940, Sketchbook No. 110, 1940', *Je Suis le Cahier: The Sketchbooks of Picasso*, London, 1986, pp. 141–50.

17 See also note 47.

18 Zervos dates the drawings between 1930 and 1931.

19 See R. Kaufmann, 'Picasso's Crucifixion of 1930', *The Burlington Magazine*, vol. 111, no. 798, Sept. 1969, pp. 553–61.

20 ibid., p.553.

21 ibid., p.554.

22 ibid.

23 Notably in Caravaggio, *Crucifixion of St Peter*, Rome; and Rogier van der Weyden, *Deposition*, Prado.

24 For example, Altichiero, *Oratory of St George*, Padua. Kaufmann claims that the horse's flank is pierced by the centurion's spear: this is *not* the case in any of the eight drawings. Loc. cit.

25 Matt. 27.45; Luke 23.44.

26 Bataille explicitly makes the connection in a later article 'Le sacré', where the caption to a photograph reads: 'Le torero Villalta devant le taureau qu'il vient de mettre à mort — Les courses de taureaux modernes représentent du fait de leur ordonnance rituelle et de leur caractère tragique une forme voisine des jeux sacrés anciens.' *Cahiers d'art*, 1939, 14e année, no. 1–4, pp. 47–50. The photograph is reproduced in the *Oeuvres complètes* I, Paris, 1970, plate 27.

27 *Documents*, no. 3, deuxième année, 1930 (*Hommage à Picasso*), pp. 173–4, reprinted in *Oeuvres complètes* I, op. cit., pp. 231–2.

28 Picasso made some whimsical drawings of such figures — a subject which is perhaps more identifiable with André Masson but not unheard of in Picasso's oeuvre — early in 1927. See D. Bozo et al., *Musée Picasso, Catalogue sommaire des collections*, Paris, 1987, plates 908; 909 [Accession Numbers

M.P. 1020; 1021.]

29 'Cette distinction entre deux soleils d'aprés l'attitude humaine a une importance particulière du fait que, dans ce cas, les mouvements psychologiques décrits ne sont pas des mouvements détournés et atténués dans leur impulsion par des éléments secondaires.' G. Bataille, 'Soleil pourri', op. cit., p.232.

30 'Toutefois, il est possible de dire que la peinture académique correspondait à peu près à une élévation d'esprit sans excès. Dans la peinture actuelle au contraire la recherche d'une rupture de l'élévation portée à son comble, et d'un éclat à prétention aveuglante a une part dans l'elaboration, ou dans la décomposition des formes, mais cela n'est sensible, à la rigueur, que dans la peinture de Picasso.' Loc. cit.

31 *Documents*, no. 2, May 1929, pp. 74–84, in *Oeuvres complètes* I, op. cit., pp. 164–70.

32 The manuscript contains an illustration of *Le songe de Nabuchodonosor*. The reproduction in *Documents* was accompanied by the Beatus version of the dream in Bataille's text: 'Une statue d'une hauteur extraordinaire se tenait devant toi et son regard était effroyable. La tête de cette statue était d'un or très pur; la poitrine et les bras étaient d'argent; le ventre et les cuisses étaient de bronze; les jambes étaient de fer; une partie des pieds était de fer et l'autre d'argile. Tu regardais cette statue lorsqu'une pierre se détacha d'elle-même d'une montagne et vint briser ses pieds de fer et d'argile. Alors le fer, l'argile, le bronze, l'argent et l'or se brisèrent ensemble et tout cela se dispersa au vent comme la paille de l'aire en été et il ne s'en trouva plus rien en aucun lieu: mais le pierre qui frappa la statue devint une grande montagne et emplit la terre entière.' Ibid., p.168.

33 The disturbing appearance and symbolism of 'La Mante réligieuse' were later the subject of an essay by Roger Caillois, published in *Minotaure*, no. 5, 1934, pp. 23–6.

34 See note 47.

35 Only one of the Gospels has the Virgin present at the crucifixion (St John 19.25), but all four attest to the presence of a number of women, including at different junctures two 'Marys'. St Luke 23.27 is pertinent to the drawings which have been discussed: 'And there followed him a great company of people, and of women, which also bewailed and lamented him.'

36 Kaufmann, op. cit., p.561.

37 See, for example, T. Stovall, 'Paris in the Age of Anxiety, 1919–1939', in S. Stich (ed.), *Anxious Visions: Surrealist Art*, Berkeley, 1990, pp.201–221, and especially pp. 210–15.

38 In the famous 'Hands Off Love!', *La Révolution Surréalist*, nos. 9–10, 1 October 1927, pp. 1–6.

39 'Recherches sur la sexualité', *La Révolution Surréaliste*, no. 11, 15 March 1928, pp. 32–40. The participants were Aragon, Baron, Boiffard, Breton, Duhamel, Morise Naville, Noll, Péret, Prévert, Queneau, Ray, Sadoul, Tanguy and Unik. The conversations have now been translated as J. Pierre (ed.), *Investigating Sex: Surrealist Discussions 1928–1932*, trans. M. Imrie, London, 1992. See the 'Afterword' by D. Ades for a more nuanced discussion of the vexed question of Surrealist moralism.

40 See 'Enquête' [on love], *La Révolution Surréaliste*, no. 12, 15 December 1929, pp. 65–76.

41 'L'absolue liberté offense, déconcerte. Le soleil a toujours blessé les yeux de ses adorateurs. Passe encore que Germaine Berton tue Plateau, les anarchistes, et avec eux un très petit nombre d'hommes, moi-même, applaudissent. Mais c'est qu'alors elle sert, paraît-il, leur cause. Dès que sa vie l'emporte, qui la suivrait dans ce qu'on nomme ses écarts, ses inconséquences, il y a trop à parier qu'elle *comprometttra* ses approbateurs. On préfère alors invoquer la maladie, la démoralisation. Et bien sûr que les anarchistes exaltent la vie, reprouvent le suicide qui est, comme on le sait, une lâcheté. C'est alors qu'ils me font connaître la honte: ils ne me laissent rien d'autre à faire qu'à me prosterner simplement devant cette femme *en tout admirable* qui est le plus grand défi que je connaisse à l'esclavage, la plus belle protestation élevée à la face du monde contre le mensonge hideux du bonheur.' Louis Aragon, 'Germaine Berton', *La Révolution Surréaliste*, no. 1, 1 December 1924, p.12.

42 'La femme est l'être qui projette la plus grande ombre ou la plus grande lumière dans nos rêves.'

43 L. Aragon and A. Breton, 'Le Cinquantenaire de l'hysterie (1878–1928)', *La Révolution Surréaliste*, no. 11, 15 March 1928, pp. 20–2.

44 'L'hystérie est un état mental plus ou moins irréductible se caractérisant par la subversion des rapports qui s'établissent entre le sujet et le monde moral duquel il croit pratiquement relever, en dehors de tout système délirant. Cet état mental est fondé sur le besoin d'une séduction réciproque, qui explique les miracles hativement acceptés de la suggestion (ou contre-suggestion) médicale. L'hystérie n'est pas un phénomène pathologique et peut, a tous égards, être considérée comme un moyen suprême d'expression.' Ibid., p.22.

45 Z.VII.73. ibid., p.25.

46 D. Macey, *Lacan in Contexts*, London, 1988, p.66.

47 As Kaufmann notes, 'An identification of this figure as the Virgin Mary can be obtained

from her similarity to another female figure in a crucifixion drawing of 1938 (Z.IX.193) who is linked to Christ by an umbilical cord.' Kaufmann, op. cit., p.557, n.8. She neglects to add that the same figure frantically grasps at Christ's genitals.

48 Of these seven, only five are reproduced in Zervos (Z.VIII.49, 50, 53, 55, 56). The figure seven includes as one drawing two tiny diagrams, one of a screw entering Christ's hand, and the other of a safety pin through a loop of cloth — presumably Christ's loincloth. Both diagrams are taken from a single sheet.

49 From January to March in *La Révolution Française* at the Bibliothèque Nationale, cat. no. 623. This large exhibition also included some Corday memorabilia amongst which were a record of the initial interview conducted with Corday in Marat's house after the assassination (no.115); the remarkable letter which she wrote to the Convention requesting that her portrait be made in prison (no.118); and her farewell letter to her father (no.119). Even more intriguing is the entry for exhibit no.117, a copy of *L'Ami du peuple* (no.678, 13 August 1792), purportedly stained with Marat's blood, and complete with provenance and attestations of authenticity. Note the path of that trail of blood in Picasso's 1931 painting.

50 On this and other issues relating to Picasso's response to Grünewald, see C. Heck, 'Entre le mythe et le modèle formel. Les Crucifixions de Grünewald et l'art du XXe siècle', in the exhibition catalogue (Musée Picasso), *Corps crucifiés*, Paris, 1993, pp. 84–107. Perhaps the most likely source for Picasso was L. Réau, *Mathias Grünewald et le retable de Colmar*, Nancy-Paris-Strasbourg, 1920, which is well illustrated with details of 'le Christ pourri de Grünewald' (p.170). It is also interesting to note that an article on Grünewald appeared in 1931: F.G. Pariset, 'Autour de Grünewald', *Gazette des beaux-arts*, 1931, pp. 275–83. Issues of nationalism in connection with the reinterpretation of the altarpiece and which may give another perspective on Picasso's work, are dealt with by A. Steiglitz, 'The reproduction of agony: toward a reception-history of Grünewald's Isenheim altarpiece after the first world war', *The Oxford Art Journal*, 12: 2, 1989, pp. 87–103.

51 P. Eluard, 'D.A.F. de Sade, écrivain fantastique et révolutionnaire', *La Révolution Surréaliste*, no. 8, 1 December 1926, pp. 8–9.

52 Breton's short biography of Heine claims that this expulsion was, remarkably, the work of Trotsky. A. Breton, 'Maurice Heine', *Cahiers de la Pléiade*, Summer 1948, pp. 115–16.

53 Under the provisions of a law of 1 July 1901, it was possible to publish these indexed books on the basis of subscription by society members. Volumes so published could not, of course, be sold on the open shelves. Predictably, the venture suffered from considerable financial insecurity.

54 Paris, 1926.

55 For example, Dr Jacobus X . . . , *Le Marquis de Sade et son oeuvre*, Paris, 1901, pp. 165–9. The speech is quoted in full, and may be the source for Apollinaire's remark that 'Le Marquis de Sade était un vrai républicain, admirateur de Marat . . . ', in G. Apollinaire (ed.), *L'oeuvre du Marquis de Sade*, Paris, 1909.

56 The evidence of relevant contact between my protagonists is typically tantalizing in the following, even down to the preoccupation with the French Revolution: 'Bataille personally took the initiative in 1935 to found a small political group which, under the name Counterattack, united some former members of the Communist Circle and, following a definite reconciliation with André Breton, the whole of the surrealist group. Some meetings of Counterattack took place in the 'Grenier des Augustins' (now Picasso's studio), with the last, on 21 January 1936, dedicated to the death of Louis XVI. Breton, Maurice Heine, and Bataille took the floor.' See G. Bataille, 'Autobiographical Note', [1958?], in *October*, 36, Spring 1986, pp. 107–110 (this reference p.109).

57 Heine was one of the respondants to the questionnaire on love in the final number, 'Enquête', *La Révolution Surréaliste*, no. 12, 15 December 1929, p.70.

58 The full references are: M. Heine, 'Actualité de Sade'; 'Lettre ouverte à M. Abel Hermant', *Le Surréalisme au Service de la Révolution*, no. 2, 2 October 1930, pp. 3–5. 'Lettre ouverte à Luis Buñuel', *Le Surréalisme au Service de la Révolution*, no. 3, December 1931, pp. 12–13; Anon. [Maurice Heine?] 'Actualité de Sade', *Le Surréalisme au Service de la Révolution*, no. 4, December 1931; 'Actualité de Sade (De Justine à la Nouvelle Justine à travers les petites feuilles inédites)', *Le Surréalisme au Service de la Révolution*, no. 5, 15 May 1933, pp. 4–10.

59 *Le Surréalisme au Service de la Révolution*, no. 2, October 1930, p.37.

60 'Sade, l'amour enfin sauvé de la boue du ciel, l'hypocrisie passée par les armes et par les yeux, cet héritage suffira aux hommes contre la famine, leurs belles maines d'étrangleur sorties des poches.' *Le Surréalisme au Service de la Révolution*, no. 2, op. cit., p.6.

61 The case of Violette Nozières was less nauseous but in many ways subject to more intense public scrutiny. Nozières was arrested at the age of eighteen on 28 August 1922, accused of, and admitting to, poisoning both

her parents on 21 August. The mother survived, but the death of her father prompted her to defend her actions by claiming that she had been the victim of sexual abuse by him since the age of twelve. The extremely high profile of the affair in the press prompted the Surrealists to produce a pamphlet in support of the parricide (A. Breton et al., *Violette Nozières*, Brussels, [1st December] 1933), published ten months after the full revelations of the trial in October 1934.

62 A. Gide, *Ne Jugez Pas*, Paris, 1930. Gide's introduction to 'L'Affaire Redureau', the paradoxically moving story of a young mass-murderer, gives a clue to the separation between his interest and that of the Surrealists: 'Nous donnerons, sur les affaires que nous exposerons, le plus de renseignements possible, sans crainte de lasser le lecteur. Notre désir n'est pas de l'amuser, mais de l'instruire.' p.98.

63 'Les soeurs Papin furent élévées au couvent du Mans. Puis leur mère les plaça dans une maison "bourgeoise" de cette ville. Six ans, elles endurèrent avec la plus parfaite soumission observations, exigences, injures. La crainte, la fatigue, l'humiliation, enfantaient lentement en elles la haine, cet alcool très doux qui console en secret car il promet à la violence de lui adjoindre, tôt ou tard, la force physique. Le jour venue. Léa et Christine Papin rendirent sa monnaie au mal, un monnaie de fer rouge. Elles massacrèrent littéralement leurs patronnes, leur arrachant les yeux, leur écrasent la tête. Puis elles se lavèrent soigneusement, et, délivrées, indifférentes, se couchèrent. La foudre était tombée, le bois brûlé, le soleil définitivement éteint. Sorties tout armées d'un chant de Maldoror . . . ', 'Revue de la presse', *Le Surréalisme au Service de la Révolution*, no. 5, pp. 27–8.

64 *Le Surréalisme au Service de la Révolution*, no. 5, 15 May 1933, p.60.

65 ibid., p.58.

66 J. Lacan, 'Motifs du Crime Paranoïaque: Le Crime des Soeurs Papin', *Minotaure*, no. 3, 12 December 1933, pp. 25–8.

67 The reports make extraordinary reading. They include the following pieces, all from *Paris-Soir*, some of which are referred to by Lacan, and which may also have been known to Picasso: J. Marèze, 'Christine et Léa Papin, qui assassinèrent au Mans leurs patronnes, étaient de délire de la persecution. "Je recommencerais s'il le faillait," a dit farouchement au juge l'ainée des deux soeurs.' 4/2/33, p.1 & 5; Anon, 'Les Victimes du Crime de Mans seront inhumées mardi', 5/2/33, p.1. (It was this report that carried the photographs of the sisters that were then reproduced in the Surrealist periodical); G. Imman, 'Le 29 septembre aux assises du Mans, les soeurs Papin répondront de leur double crime', 24/9/33, p.3; J. & J. Tharaud, 'A la veille des Assises du Mans les mobiles du crime des soeurs Papin restent obscurs', 29/9/33, pp. 1 & 3; 'Les soeurs Papin ont comparu cet après-midi devant les jurés de la Sarthe', 30/9/33, pp. 1 & 3; G. Oubert, 'Christine et Léa Papin ont décidé de se pourvoir en cassation', 1/10/33, p.1; J. & J. Tharaud, 'Jugées et condamnés, les soeurs Papin n'ont pas encore livré leur secret', 1/10/33, p.3; Anon, 'Christine Papin dans sa cellule tient des propos incohérents', 3/10/33, p.1; J. & J. Tharaud, 'L'affaire Papin et les experts', 8/10/33, p.2. *Paris-Soir* also provided saturation coverage of the Nozières trial throughout September 1933.

68 '. . . semblable au sujet: telle est la raison de son caractère homosexual.' Ibid., p.28.

69 'Au soir fatidique, dans l'anxiété d'une punition imminente, les soeurs mêlent à l'image de leurs maitresses le mirage de leur mal. C'est leur détresse qu'elles détestent dans le couple qu'elles entrainent dans une atroce quadrille.' Loc. cit.

70 'Je crois bien que dans une autre vie je devais être le mari de ma soeur.' Loc. cit.

71 'La curiosité sacrilège qui fait l'angoisse de l'homme depuis le fonds des âges, c'est elle qui les anime quant elles déchirent leurs victimes, quand elles traquent dans leurs blessures béantes ce que Christine plus tard devant le juge devait appeller dans son innocence "le mystère de la vie'." Loc. cit.

72 ' . . . chacune s'empare d'une adversaire, lui arrache vivante les yeux des orbites, fait inouï, a-t-on dit, dans les annales du crime, et l'assomme. Puis, à l'aide de ce qui se trouve à leur portée, marteau, pichet d'étain, couteau de cuisine, elles s'acharnent sur les corps de leurs victimes, leur écrasent la face, et, dévoilant leur sexe, tailladent profondément les cuisses et les fesses de l'une, pour souiller de ce sang celles de l'autre. Elles lavent ensuite les instruments de ces rites atroces, se purifient elles-mêmes et se couchent dans le même lit. "En voilà du propre!" Telle est la formule qu'elles échangent et qui semble donner le ton du dégrisement, vide de toute émotion, qui succède chez elles à l'orgie sanglante.' Ibid., p.25.

73 *Minotaure*, no. 3, 12 December 1933.

74 There is no obvious explanation for this bird, except perhaps to refer it back to the presence of a similarly unaccountable creature in the 1930 *Crucifixion*.

75 R. Penrose, 'Beauty and the Monster', *Pablo Picasso 1881–1973*, London, 1988, pp. 157–95 (this reference pp. 179–8).

76 On 21 July 1934 Picasso made a small — fourth — 'Assassination of Marat' etching in the corner of a large plate to illustrate

Benjamin Péret, *De Derrière des Fagots*, 1934. 'The image . . . may perhaps have been influenced . . . by Abel Gance's film, *Napoléon* (1926), in which Antonin Artaud had played the role of Marat.' See S. Goeppert et al., *Pablo Picasso. The Illustrated Books: Catalogue Raisonné*, Geneva, 1983, p.70. Gance's brilliant film, not in fact released until April 1927, won particular praise for the scene featuring Artaud, concluding as it did with a homage to David's painting. Perhaps the classical and intense androgyny of Artaud's visage in the film stayed with Picasso — and contributed more than the profile of Marie-Thérèse to the strange elisions of gender which are evident in the Marat series. The film also incidentally depicted the Marquis de Sade at another instance. Picasso's large copper plate, with the Marat image scored through but still visible, inverted in one corner, was used for plate 94 of the Vollard Suite, *Blind Minotaur guided by a Young Girl* I, (Georges Bloch, *Pablo Picasso, Catalogue of the Printed Graphic Work 1904–1967*, Bern, 1968, No.222.) Surely this was not a casual juxtaposition.

77 Picasso finally and whimsically addressed Corday's side of the story in 1950, when, with the young director Frédéric Rossif, he shot a short film provisionally entitled *La Mort de Charlotte Corday*. The film was never edited, but some stills and photographs taken during the filming are reproduced in the catalogue *Picasso à l'écran*, (Centre Georges Pompidou/Musée Picasso), Paris, 1992, pp. 32–7. In the photograph on p.32, in particular, one can see many of the key items in an improvised mise-en-scène: packing case; pot with brush representing the quill pen and inkwell; but this time Marat is a horned monster made of cardboard and fancy material, and Corday a classical portrait. Above the two figures another mysterious bird, a ceramic owl, watches over the event.

78 Z.VIII.222.

79 R. Hayman, *De Sade, A Critical Biography*, London, 1978, p. 190.

80 As Hayman acknowledges, the story derives from the famous nineteenth-century historian of the Revolution, Jules Michelet. For a sceptical discussion of Michelet's claim in the *Histoire de la Revolution française*, see G. Lely, *Vie du Marquis de Sade*, op. cit., pp. 485–6. Of the two recent scholarly biographies, M. Lever, *Donatien Alphonse François, marquis de Sade*, Paris, 1989, contains no discussion at all of these claims. J.-J. Pauvert, *Sade Vivant, Tome III: 'Cet écrivain à jamais célèbre . . .' 1793–1814*, Paris, 1990, includes the following: 'Dans le numero CXLIII de *l'Ami du peuple*, Marat s'en étant pris à M. de La Salle [tried in September 1789] comme "traître à la patrie", s'excuse ainsi le 24 juin 1790 dans son journal: "Je ne sais par quelle fatalité votre nom, que j'avais confondu avec celui de M. de Sade, qui a été impliqué dans tant d'affaires fâcheuses", p.69, n.1. Il est vrai que rencontrant un peu plus tard le gros militant des Piques, Marat n'eut pas été forcé de faire le rapprochement avec "le marquis scandaleuse". Il y avait d'ailleurs d'autres Sade en circulation, nous en parlerons.' It would seem that Michelet's story takes the Sade of Marat's journal entry (material undetected by Lely) to be unequivocally 'the divine Marquis'. The idea that these events occurred in *1793*, and that Corday's action saved the Marquis de Sade, must remain, after all, a seductive fiction.

Art History ISSN 0141-6790 Vol. 17 No. 3 September 1994 pp. 418–423

Danger and safety

Mark Cousins

The following text is a slightly modified transcript of a talk delivered at The Thursday Club, London, on 17 June 1993.

Although what I have to say is not immediately derived from psychoanalytic thought, many of the ideas that I put forward may well have arisen from that source. But the issues that I want to discuss are perhaps more urgent than an evening's debate about psychoanalysis. These issues immediately touch us all in respect of the politics of culture. So I have no wish to mortgage off what I have to say to your possible hostility to psychoanalysis. What I do want to do this evening is to raise a question about the relationship between safety and danger, and to ask how they might relate to politics and perhaps to something beneath the level of politics which, for reasons which will become clear, I would be very hesitant to call ethics.

The first question I would like to ask (for I do not know the answer) is why people are so little concerned with safety? If you were to mention safety to students at the Architectural Association where I teach, their eyes would glaze over. They would imagine you had turned up from a local authority. Indeed, it is an historical issue of interest as to why a developing capitalist economy was not really interested in safety. Why was it that the workers' movement was not more interested in safety? Why has it been that the trade unions in the post-war period have tended to raise the issue of safety as something that ought to be monetized, that is, ought to carry a financial bonus rather than demanding greater attention. So within both forces of the economy, both employers and trade unions, we see a curious lack of interest in safety.

Moreover, it would be difficult to imagine an issue so near the bottom of the artistic agenda. It would have been the kiss of death for any avant-garde movement to announce that the subversion of traditional categories was undertaken in the interest of safety. Yet the relative indifference to the question of safety needs some sort of historical and analytical explanation. For if you look at contemporary art, especially in the domain of conceptual art, and indeed in certain forms of popular culture, what is particularly at stake is the vivid issue of danger. Not danger in an abstract sense, but danger in respect to the human body. I am sure I do not have to persuade you that one of the central objects of investigation in both avant-garde culture and in forms of popular culture —

for example, in Hollywood or Japanese film — is the peculiar current of absorption in the question of damage to the body. How can damage to the body be represented? What possible mutations from the norm of the body can be thought? Neither in popular culture, nor indeed in architectural theory, is the body now represented as a classical idealized norm of perfection. Rather, it is something to be raided, mutated, deformed and hurt. Through this category of damage to the body many current fears are thought out. Fears of illness, fears of death, fears of impurity, themes of pollution, the experience of the uncanny and of the paranoid. It would seem, at the level of avant-garde conceptual and installation art, that far from being marginalized by the norms of non-representational art, the centrality of the body is in every gallery — the damage, the mutation, the record of destruction or threat which can be thought in respect of the body. Most Hollywood movies demonstrate much the same thing. The way these themes are advertised and justified is through claims that they are transgressive of certain norms, that they subvert certain classical idealism of the body, that they deal with certain fears. Notwithstanding the ways in which art historians have tried to periodize and characterize twentieth-century art, in fact we live in an artistic culture which insists on the body and this is true despite the rise of non-representational art. The issue of the body has insisted, not necessarily in representational forms, but in its imprint, in its fluids, and in the damage done to it as a record of catastrophe. We might even speculate that one of the curious effects of the demise of standard representational art is that in some sense the 'body' has triumphed, that is, the damaged body has triumphed. Escaping from the shackles of representation and escaping from the idealization of the human body as a model of harmony and proportion, this *thing* goes on imprinting, screaming, projecting itself across a whole swathe of contemporary culture.

I hoped that I would not be called upon to justify that observation, because I think in some ways it is there for all to see even if it is not always recognized or thought about. What I would rather do is to turn immediately to the question of politics. You do not need me to point out the present collapse of certain nineteenth-century schemes of politics. They are buried, if not dead. Those schemes which had grandiose expectations about the production of a new type of society are finished. Their goal of building a new type of society in which, amongst other things, there would be a determined relationship between art and politics now no longer even seems desirable. There seem to have been two parallel but quite opposed views of the relation between art and politics. There has been the left version, of course, which says that in some way politics and art will go together. They will either essentially express each other or they will sit in a kind of isomorphic harmony in which in some sense politics is in command but art reigns — a curious couple. Or, there has been a complete rejection of this in the form of a kind of aestheticism which refuses the link which it imagines makes art subservient to politics. It would be fair to claim that the history of aestheticism has not even yet taken measure of the way in which the extreme right has profited from that aestheticism in the domain of politics; we have only to think of Walter Benjamin's critique of fascism as its triumph.

These were models in which politics and art were set in a definite relation.

I suspect there is little support in this room for the view that they sit happily together, just as I suspect there are few who would say they are necessarily and completely disjunct. The question then is: 'What might be a new form of articulating the two?' I have talked already about an art which is concerned to investigate the extreme possibilities of experience including damage, mutation, pollution, death or whatever, as a serious aesthetic investigation of those conditions, but I now want to turn to apparently the opposite case. Have there emerged over the last twenty or thirty years any new forms of politics? I think it is not too early to claim that there is a disjunct but nevertheless articulated form of politics which takes as its central object the question of safety. What I am trying to suggest is that in contrast to the rise of an art of danger we find the emergence of a politics of safety.

I will just mention a few instances in which this arises. I think it arises centrally in respect of the political demands, forms of thought and organization that were developed from the early 1970s onwards in feminism. There has been in feminism from the beginning a desire for a political condition which might not eradicate, but would seek to oppose certain forms of violence. This may have been put in a highly exclusive way; many people would reject essentialist formulations to the effect that what is at stake is male violence against all women. But the point is that a whole deployment of issues and the capacity to articulate a set of that would, according to other political agendas, look like rather disparate issues, are put together by feminism in terms of safety. And I want to stress another point about feminism because I think it has constituted one of its most novel aspects. From the beginning feminism asserted the centrality of its concern for the integrity of the body and the safety of the body. It was in some sense the body that was in question. And here was some of the real novelty of feminism in terms of political theory. Although occasionally it borrowed the political language to which we are accustomed, namely the question of rights, that question was always saturated by a description of the endangered body and with the wish that it go undamaged.

The second area of concern which one might mention here is in respect to the child. Now nothing which I say wishes to undermine the importance of nineteenth-century philanthropy's concern for the welfare of the child. But there is a new edge dating from the 1970s to the issue of the integrity of the body of the child: not so much the child's rights in respect to this or that, but the body of the child and its protection from violence or abuse. A third aspect of the articulation of the politics of safety undoubtedly originates in the United States within the gay movement, where the response to the emergence of HIV infection at both an artistic and a detailed political level was a concern with the safety of the sexual body. In effect, this marks a beginning to the formulation of political demands and habits in that area which Foucault speaks of as the 'arts of life' around safety.

What I have tried to sketch so far is an apparently split and opposed situation. The rise of an art which investigates the issue of danger and, if I am right, the possible emergence of a politics which is profoundly concerned with safety. One could add to the latter side of the polarity the concern, like Amnesty International's, with the issue of torture. For it is not at all clear why anyone should be concerned with torture at the level of safety of the body. Nineteenth-century liberalism undoubtedly handled this issue by constraining police powers and by insisting upon constitutional rights. But what I am trying to suggest is that the symbolic claim of Amnesty International in opposing torture flows from the kind of excess surrounding the issue of torture, the symbolic excess that persuades you that there is something too dreadful about being held in a room, having your body rather than your rights assaulted.

I would like to spend the rest of the talk trying to suggest how the issues of danger and safety could be put together. I no longer think that an artistic strategy and a political strategy need in any sense to reflect each other. On the contrary, I am persuaded that it would be more productive if they went in opposite directions, and I will return to that in a moment. But before I do so, I want to try and say something very briefly about the place of ethics in this context. As I am trying to make a point which lies somewhere between politics and ethics, I do not have a language to do this. Now I do not think that it is just my failing. On the contrary, I believe it is a cultural failing whose roots have to be examined.

One of the reasons why I am suspicious of the language of ethics is because it deals with the soul and not the body. Whether we are talking about art which is concerned with damage to the body, or an emerging politics which might be concerned with the safety of the body, I want to stress that it is the body that is at question, the human body. It is not some version of the Christian soul. Perhaps it is a pity that we have lost the power of the doctrine of Habeas Corpus to influence us. Lawyers know that nowadays no judge will take seriously a claim of Habeas Corpus; they are all thrown out of court. While every school child is taught that Habeas Corpus is the foundation of the English law, no judge today will entertain its success.

The issue here, I think, is a problem about the category of the body. Habeas Corpus was formulated before the rise of the modern subject of rights in both constitutional and ethical thought. From Kant onwards the central issue of ethics and law has been rights. In jurisprudence, it is the subject of rights, an abstract subject of rights, which is central. And in that formulation, which has dominated European political jurisprudence and political objectives, the rights of the subject have come to dominate the entire discourse of conservatism, liberalism and socialism, much to the detriment of the way in which they formulate political projects.

There is one area in particular where this notion of the rights of subjects proves to be just such a poor friend to the human being; it is the question of tolerance. There are two great false friends to the idea of tolerance: Liberalism and Marxism. Conservatism is, of course, an open enemy, but I will come to that in a moment. Liberalism has a view that the problem about tolerance — tolerance of others — is a matter of that subject's rights which one should not abrogate. This seems an extraordinarily feeble thought, not least because it has never persuaded anyone. Once it starts to get difficult, one just unrights their rights. What Marxism adds to this is even more disastrous. Marxism has no theory of tolerance; it just has a theory of intolerance. That is to say, if you are intolerant of someone, or of some group, it is because you are suffering from prejudice. What you need is education. Your intolerance will vanish under the pressure of the truth. Here I will be psychoanalytic: anyone who thinks something vanishes under the pressure of the truth ought to have another think. There is only one basis on which anyone could be persuaded that tolerance is a good idea, which is that they think it is good for them or, to put it in pre-psychoanalytic terms, that it is a virtue, especially a virtue in the city, a virtue with a peculiarly urban genealogy. As Paul Hirst has recently suggested, if we are to rethink the issue of tolerance in the city, we will learn less from Athenian democracy than we will from Ottoman Damascus.[1] Athenian democracy was founded on a ruthless exclusion of those who did not share the truth. For a model of a pluralist society we would do well to look to Damascus. My suggestion is that perhaps we should move beyond the language of the eighteenth century to that of the seventeenth century. We would find there a language which has been suppressed for three centuries, concerned with the wish to have one's body left alone, unviolated.

One of the problems here is the emergence in the last two hundred years of a quite vile Christian and humanist conception of virtue in which we see the abstract discourse on ethics merging with a certain kind of Protestant virtue. I am supposed to have a hideous thing called a conscience. Remember the extraordinary way school teachers would talk about Martin Luther. They painted a picture of this weird guy standing up and saying 'Ich kann nicht anders' — 'I can do no other' — and everybody sighed in admiration, and I thought, 'Well, why couldn't you do something else. Surely there was something else you could do?' We have to re-examine the dreadful role played by that notion of conscience where conscience means, 'in the privacy of my heart I will decide and I will inflict untold damage in the pursuit of that because in the eye of God that doesn't count as a cost.' Well, somebody needs to start doing some adding up. We need accountants of damage. This cruel elevation of principle has been used by parents to give their children examples of correct moral conduct. It may turn out to have been quite disastrous.

By contrast, I am trying to suggest that in the seventeenth century there was a very real discourse on damage, a discourse of remorse on the damage that is caused. We need to recover some of the immediacy of that language. In fact, I dedicate these remarks to Montaigne. The safety of the body is an issue in which one could begin to find new allies in an otherwise sad political scene and to formulate quite strange and even quite popular objectives.

I want to end by returning to the apparent contradiction that I have set up. Is it a problem that there is an art of damage and a politics of safety? Should the one oppose the other? On the contrary, I think the two support each other. That is to say, we are not able to think of those issues of safety politically unless we can experiment using the full scope of the implementation of danger within art. If this seems a little perverse, I would like to quote here a small excerpt, not from Sigmund Freud, but from Immanuel Kant:

> On the other hand, consider bold, overhanging and, as it were threatening rocks, thunderclouds piling up in the sky and moving about accompanied by lightning and thunderclaps, volcanoes with all their destructive power, hurricanes with all the devastation they leave behind,

> the boundless ocean heaved up, the high waterfall of a mighty river, and so on. Compared to the might of any of these, our ability to resist becomes an insignificant trifle. Yet the sight of them becomes all the more attractive the more fearful it is, provided we are in a safe place. And we like to call these objects sublime because they raise the soul's fortitude above its usual middle range and allow us to discover in ourselves an ability to resist which is of a quite different kind, and which gives us the courage [to believe] that we could be a match for nature's seeming omnipotence.[2]

I think the course I am recommending — of an art of danger and a politics of safety — is captured very clearly in Kant's notion of the sublime, in which he gives the account of the brave soldier which is quite different from almost every account of bravery I have ever seen; the brave soldier is one whose sense of security lasts longer than that of others.[3] The intuitive possibility of linking an art of danger to a politics of safety finds its validation in another source — our enemies. For what else do the Jessie Helmses of this world advocate but an art of safety and a politics of danger? But that is another topic.

Mark Cousins
Architectural Association, London

Notes

1 Paul Hirst, lecture at the Architectural Association, March 1994.
2 Immanuel Kant, *Critique of Judgment*, Werner S. Pluhar (trans.), Indianapolis, 1987, p.120.
3 ibid., p.121.

Art History ISSN 0141-6790 Vol. 17 No. 3 September 1994 pp. 424–449

Bordering on Blank: Eva Hesse and Minimalism

Briony Fer

> The formal principles are understandable and understood. It is the unknown quantity from which and where I want to go. As a thing, an object, it accedes to its non-logical self. It is something, it is nothing. (Eva Hesse)[1]

> If we cannot see things clearly we will at least see clearly what the obscurities are. (Sigmund Freud)[2]

When Eva Hesse put *Metronomic Irregularity II* (plate 53) into the *Eccentric Abstraction* show at the Fischback Gallery in New York, Lucy Lippard, the exhibition organizer, was surprised by its precision. Hesse had made the work for the show which opened in October 1966, but it was not quite what Lippard was expecting. *Hang-Up* (plate 54), Hesse's work shown at the Graham Gallery in May of the same year, would have been fine, but this new piece was somehow less 'organic' and it was the 'organic' aspect of Hesse's work which Lippard had thought of when she conceived the show.[3] Though at the time Lippard admits to having been somewhat disappointed, her response also registered, I think, an important shift in Hesse's work. It did not quite fit with what she had done before, though its precision 'amounted in fact to the maze-like obsessiveness' which Lippard liked in her work.[4] In her text accompanying the exhibition, Lippard outlined what she understood by 'eccentric abstraction':

> In eccentric abstraction, evocative qualities or specific organic associations are kept at a subliminal level, without the benefit of Freudian clergy . . . Ideally a bag remains a bag and does not become a uterus, a tube is a tube and not a phallic symbol. Too much free association on the viewer's part is combatted by formal understatement . . .[5]

'Organic associations' are less important to *Metronomic Irregularity II* than to Hesse's other work, but, nevertheless, Lippard's comments remain astute, and central to any consideration of her work. Particularly from a psychoanalytic point of view, it is vital not to categorize the work in terms of a lexicon of symbols called 'Freudian'. What is more interesting is how Hesse's work may bear the

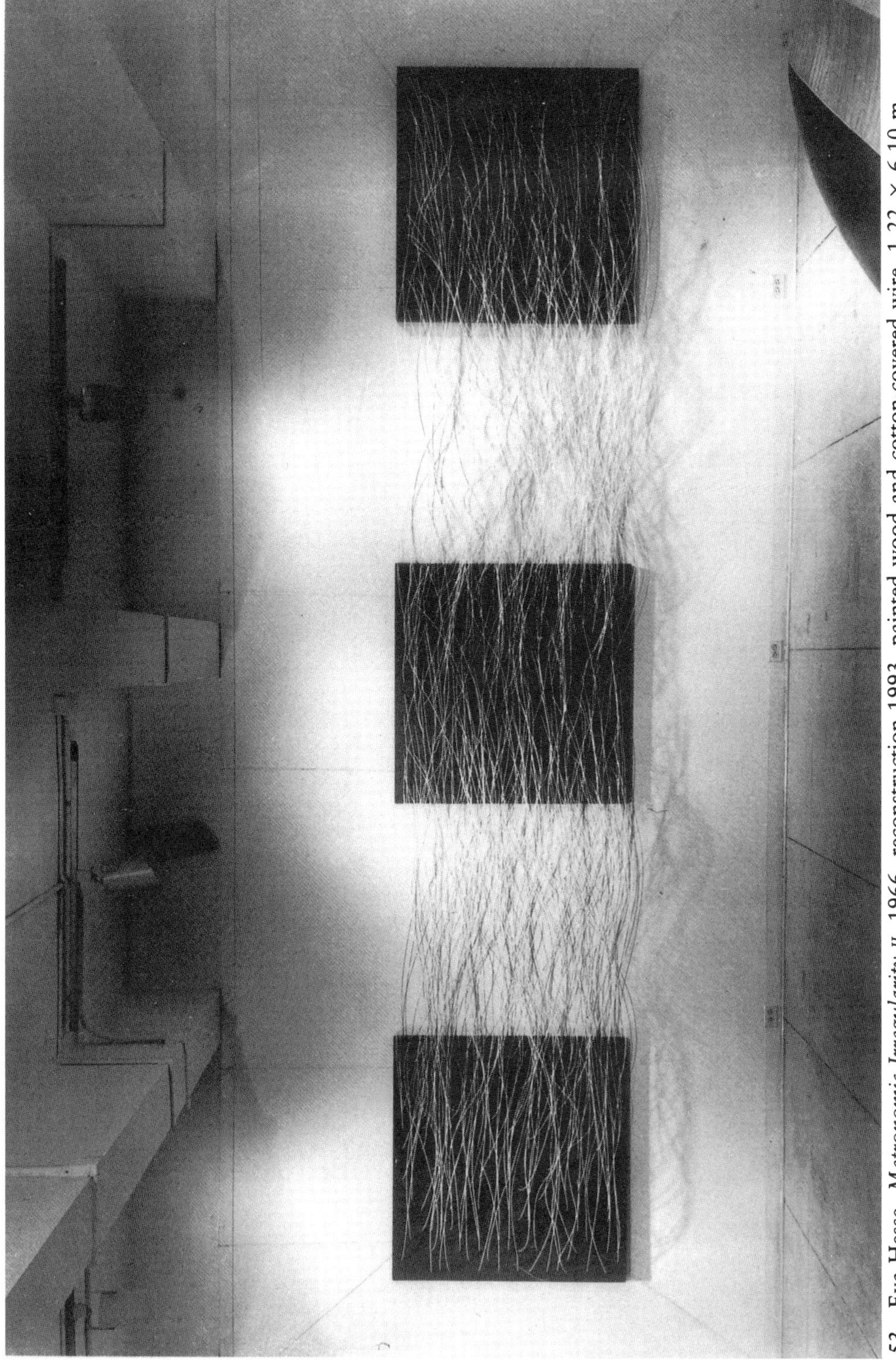

53 Eva Hesse, *Metronomic Irregularity II*, 1966, reconstruction 1993, painted wood and cotton-covered wire, 1.22 × 6.10 m (overall). The Estate of Eva Hesse and courtesy Robert Miller Gallery, New York.

54 Eva Hesse *Hang-Up*, 1966, acrylic on cloth, wood and steel, 1.83 × 2.13 × 1.98 m. The Art Institute of Chicago © The Estate of Eva Hesse. Photo: courtesy of Robert Miller Gallery, New York.

marks of the body, or have bodily connotations, without being *of* the body, and without being symbols in the sense of individual forms standing in for parts of the body.

In this exhibition, Lippard wanted to show artists whose work offered ' "eccentric" or erotic alternatives' to 'a solemn and deadset Minimalism'[6] — to that other kind of Minimalism which had clearly crystallized in the work of Judd, Morris and Andre. Their preoccupation with modern hard surfaces was thus challenged in a group show which included Louise Bourgeois, Alice Adams, Bruce Nauman and Don Potts. *Metronomic Irregularity II* turned out to confound such an opposition and, as I shall argue, Hesse's work, even when it looks more 'organic', has much more in common with those 'harder-edged' artists with whom she is often compared than is usually suggested. Certainly Hesse's work is individual; it does not form part of a 'school', but then neither does the work of the other Minimalists. As well as friendship with Lewitt and Andre, there is also a sustained dialogue between her work and theirs. Even taking into account its differences, Hesse's work dramatizes some tendency within Minimalism itself, not in terms of 'symbols' but in the realm of the 'symbolic' and the formal resistance to 'symbols' as such. This realm is, of course, not the exclusive preserve of psychoanalysis but it is the psychoanalytic construction of the symbolic which I wish to pursue. Rather than look at localized or particular forms as vehicles of meaning, I am interested in the symbolic procedure at work, which in Hesse's work, I shall argue, is based on an economy of loss.

There is little to be gained, from this point of view, from setting up Hesse as the 'feminine' to counter the 'masculine' hard surfaces to which Lewitt, Andre and others were drawn.[7] Hesse also was drawn to modern hard surfaces and not as symbols of virility. After all, it was the 'precision' of *Metronomic Irregularity II* which had so struck Lucy Lippard, and elsewhere Hesse used galvanized steel, aluminium and many other industrial materials. My point is that to see either forms or materials as iconic symbols simply introduces a subject matter where there is none. Hesse liked the way *Right After* (plate 55) 'looked like a big nothing.'[8] Bodily connotations may be there, more obviously in some works than in others, but specific connotations are also ruled out, rendered inappropriate, in works akin to Lewitt's constructions and Andre's floor pieces. But rather than understand these effects as pure negativity, Hesse's 'big nothing' points, I think, to something in the work which I would want to describe as a kind of blankness. Sometimes this is a literal blankness, as in *Hang-Up*, for instance, where all the incident is emptied out to the borders or frame of the work, as if the interest were all in the support. In *Metronomic Irregularity II*, on the other hand, the effects are less clear and more complex. It is built onwards on three panels of painted wood, with the remaining spaces between the panels acting as alternate sections. As if to cancel out the *tabula rasa* that was *Hang-Up*, she fills the space with a mass of cotton-covered wire which spans the work horizontally.

Hesse produced three pieces with the title *Metronomic Irregularity* in 1966. Although the second version was dismantled after the exhibition, it was recently reconstructed for the 'American Art in the Twentieth Century' show in Berlin.[9] The wires are finer here than in her first version (plate 56), which she gave to Robert Smithson, intertwining or lacing the three panels together as a kind of triptych, and leaving a kind of obscure tracery in the web of shadows on the wall. It is as if a screen of interference is superimposed over the regular geometric panels. Lippard notes that in some drawings from around the same time Hesse was thinking of working with wires in the vertical plane. These she never carried out, though in work before and after (such as plate 57) she developed that vertical axis.

Thinking in these terms, of horizontality and verticality, of spacing, of displacing attention to the support, is characteristic not only of Hesse but of other Minimalists too. The formal logic at work constitutes a way of thinking about the art work, and about what art could be made out of, precisely without resort to subject matter. In part, what Lippard was aiming at in her title 'Eccentric Abstraction' was a sense of what underlay this formal order. Beneath what Hesse called the 'formal principles' was another kind of structure, the object's 'non-logical self'.[10] In *Hang-Up* she contrived certain effects by putting the interest outside, onto the frame, and adding a rod that projects far too far into the

55 Eva Hesse, *Right After*, 1969, fibreglass over string, 1.98 × 3.05 m. Collection Milwaukee Art Center © The Estate of Eva Hesse. Photo: courtesy of Robert Miller Gallery, New York.

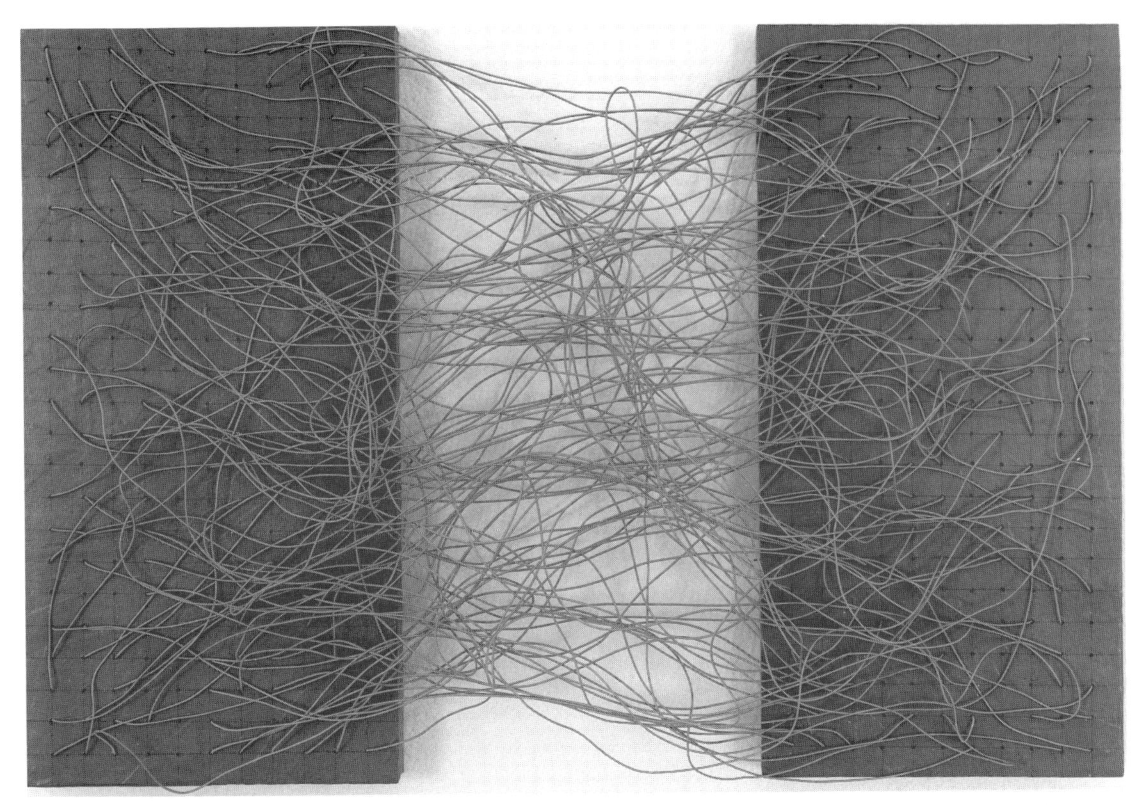

56 Eva Hesse, *Metronomic Irregularity I,* 1966, painted wood, sculpmetal, cotton-covered wire, 30.48 × 45.72 × 2.54 cm. Wiesbaden Museum © The Estate of Eva Hesse. Photo: courtesy of Robert Miller Gallery, New York.

spectator's space, exceeding its own logic; it looked to Hesse 'all tied up like a hospital bandage — as if someone broke an arm'.[11] The 'obsessive' character in Hesse's work has been discussed at length, and particularly well by Lucy Lippard. Yet one might want to ask what makes it appropriate to talk about the 'obsessive' character of Hesse's work such as the bandaged frame whereas it is described as a *rational* act to put together 126 firebricks as Carl Andre did in his *Equivalents* series, or to make a whole series of floor pieces out of the same shapes, but varying the metal, such as *Magnesium Floor* (plate 58). Far from Hesse representing the 'irrational' to Andre's 'rational', I want to suggest that this work embodies within itself both the formal ordering of modernism and its own arbitrary and obsessive underside. The sheer oddity of Lewitt's *Wall Structure White* and *Wall Structure Black* of 1962, with the protrusion at the centre of each, corresponds with similar effects in Hesse's work.[12] I certainly want to make some distinctions between the work of these artists, particularly between Hesse and Andre, but not on the basis of an opposition between the 'rational' or hard-edged character of Andre and Lewitt and the 'irrational' or organic character of Hesse. Least of all do I want to attach such differences to male and female artists. If, on the other hand, we take some account of an

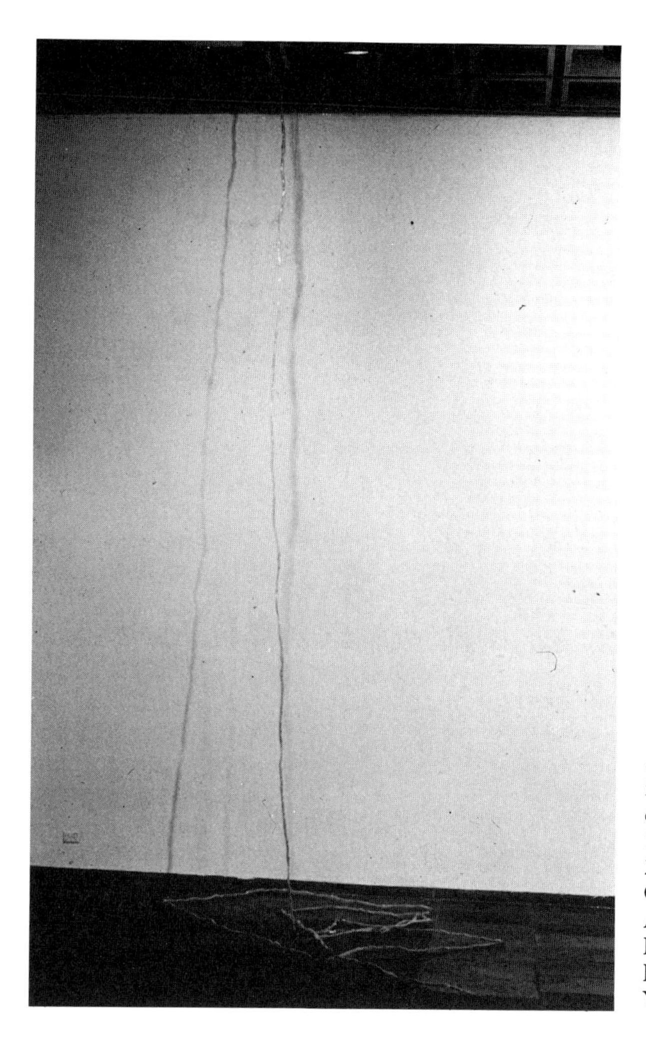

57 Eva Hesse, *Untitled*, 1969, fibreglass and polyester resin over cloth-covered wire, 18.59 m × 2.54 cm × 2.54 cm. The Art Institute of Chicago, through prior gift of Arthur Keating © The Estate of Eva Hesse. Photo: courtesy of Robert Miller Gallery, New York.

underlying irrationalism in Minimalism in general, then the whole question of Hesse's work in relation to femininity and her position as a woman artist becomes both more problematic and more productive.[13]

Blank Space

Like *Hang-Up*, Hesse's later Woodstock drawings play on the idea of emptying out a centre. They are loosely based on a window-frame motif, but characteristically the incident around the 'frame' frequently leaves a void, the paper left clean or drawn or washed over (plates 59 and 60). These are drawings on paper Hesse produced when she was too ill to make sculpture. In all of them, the more or less blank screens, whether they cover over traces or remain unmarked, are animated by the extraordinary activity in the border or frame.

58 Carl Andre, *Magnesium Floor*, 1969, magnesium, 1 × 366 × 366 cm, Tate Gallery London

There is a sense of limbo, or of meaning about to be declared. I do not mean by this that these works are only conceptual — though as has been remarked the fact that they are 'pictureless pictures' no doubt comes into play — but rather that the near blankness, the sheer lack of visual incident, is itself vivid. In the end, it was not only a kind of opacity but a kind of 'nothing' that Hesse, as she articulated it several times, was striving for — but one that could be meaningful and hold our interest in an art work. Though it is often rightly remarked that the term 'Minimalism' is a misnomer, for the work grouped under this heading is far from 'reductive', one characteristic feature of it is that works in which nothing much seems to be happening still have the capacity to hold a certain type of visual, and not only conceptual, interest. The interest in the merest incident on a surface can be seen in *Stratum* from 1967–8 (plate 61), a piece where the level of incident is not quite at a minimum, but where a little is dramatized to seem like a lot. This is the effect of the piece, not its actuality, for the working process is always complex in Hesse's work. Here a latex square is coated several times with rubber solution with bits of plastic tubing sticking through an irregular grid at odd angles; two grommets are inserted at the top

59 Eva Hesse, *Untitled*, 1969, gouache, watercolour, pencil and silver paint, 58.74 × 45.08 cm. Private collection © The Estate of Eva Hesse. Photo: courtesy of Robert Miller Gallery, New York.

60 Eva Hesse, *Untitled*, 1969, gouache and pencil, 55.56 × 43.81 cm. Sondra and Charles Gilman Jnr. Collection.

providing holes to fix the piece to the wall so that, unlike *Hang-Up*, this work does not have a frame at all. When lit in the gallery, it becomes a landscape of latex, with shadows falling across the irregular and slightly undulating surface.

In *Untitled* (plate 57), a wire coated in fibreglass is suspended from the ceiling and falls irregularly and slightly awkwardly to the floor. As Lucy Lippard commented 'it almost isn't there at all.'[14] And although 'blankness' is primarily a two-dimensional phenomenon, referring to what does not happen on a surface, it has resonance too in three dimensions. For crucial to the effect of this work is the sense of empty gallery space being altered, not 'filled', not 'occupied' but nevertheless transformed and changed. In 1930 Georges Bataille had used the term *altération* to describe what happened in the drawing process, and more broadly, in representation; each time a mark was made on a blank piece of paper, the surface was altered, in the sense of being spoilt or destroyed.[15] Here the sculpture, despite its spare elegance, is also a kind of disturbance, by virtue of its hardly being there. Of course, again, the effort involved in making it look 'hardly there' is a pains-taking procedure, which relies on Hesse's use and treatment of certain materials and their degree of transparency and opacity, a point to which I will come back later.

Modernist discourse has developed an elaborate framework for describing the formal properties of works of art which not only accommodates, but makes a positive value out of, such a low level of incident. The merest mark, for

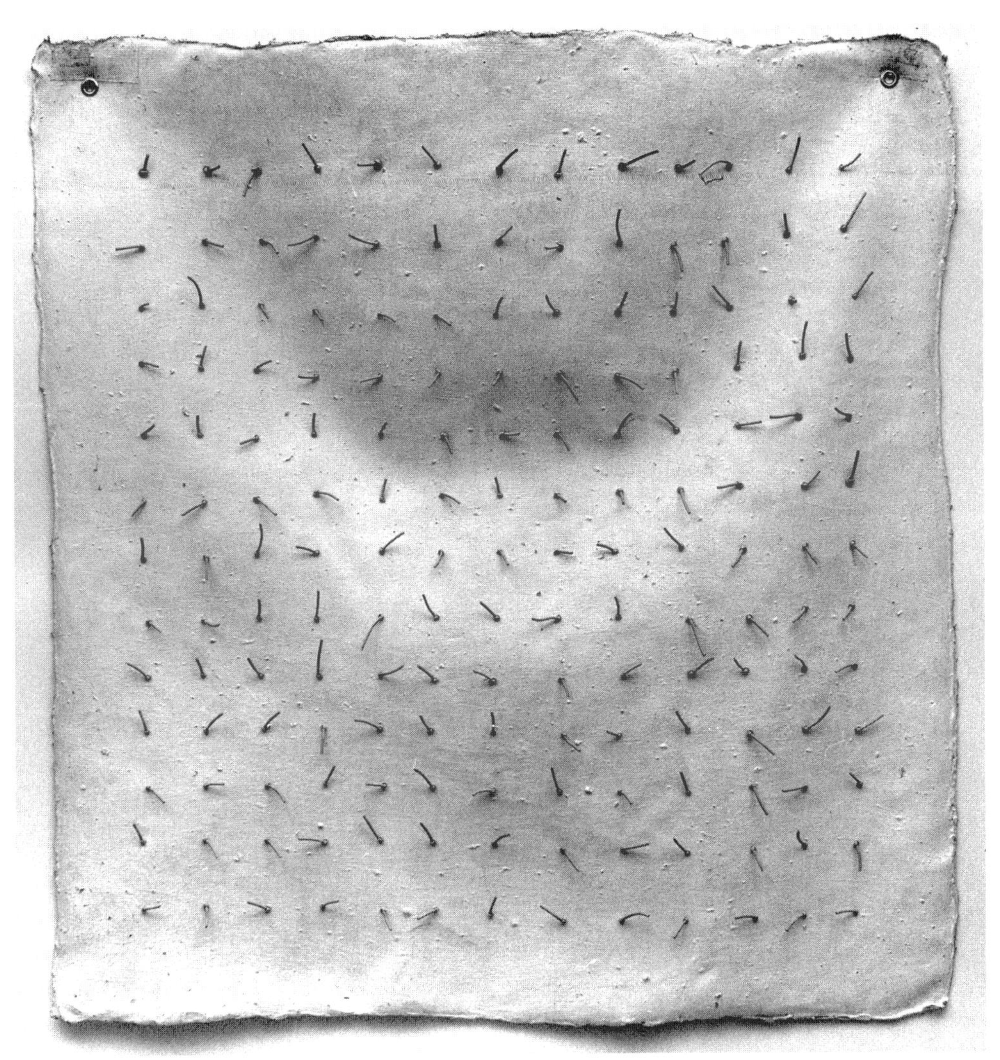

61 Eva Hesse, *Stratum*, 1967–68, latex, string and metal grommets, 1.07 × 1.07 m. Collection Mrs Sidney Gerber, Seattle (no longer exists) © The Estate of Eva Hesse. Photo: courtesy of Robert Miller Gallery, New York.

Greenberg, set up a spatial relationship on a canvas creating a dialectic between surface and depth, and Mondrian's work showed with what few means art could be made.[16] Ridding the work of art of what conventionally counted as visual incident had been an achievement of the early abstract painters in the first part of the twentieth century — artists such as Malevich and Mondrian — and was well established as part of a modern tradition by 1960. Malevich's *White on White* paintings were certainly not blank, but they played on the slightest variations of tone and texture to make these count for a lot. Barnett Newman's large areas of flat colour dramatize the edges of the strips or 'zips' which run down his canvases. His *The Name II* of 1950 is all white but leaves vertical strips of raw, cream canvas which divide the picture into three parts, again forming a kind of triptych. It is as if Newman has used the white paint to replicate the blank canvas, but only almost, because the modulations in the way the white paint is washed on actually provides, rather than negates, the visual interest. What had started off as a negative strategy to refuse the presence of figuration, had since even the late 1910s and early '20s become established in the repertoire of modern art as 'pure' painting. It was the treatment of the surface that Greenberg rationalized in terms of 'flatness and the delimitation of flatness'[17] which, far from negating the principles of picture-making, came to embody and assert the conventions of art. Indeed, Greenberg had argued that, far from modernist art being freed from convention, it was, with Mondrian, the epitome of convention-boundedness. The question of whether or not an object was art or not was, according to his argument, a blind alley; the point was whether a picture was any good — 'a stretched or tacked-up canvas already exists as a picture — though not necessarily a successful one.'[18] At stake, then, was quality, not the status of the art object. So when he discussed the whole question of the lack of visual incident in 'After Abstract Expressionism', the lack of what he calls 'prestigious handwriting à la de Kooning', it was certainly not as a 'non-art' factor. What interested him instead was the *exactness* of the choices the artist made — of medium, colour, shape and so on. Next to Newman's work, for example, 'most other contemporary painting begins to look fussy.'[19] To leave an area of canvas blank is far from neutral but a choice which the artist makes, just as in a Mondrian painting the decision to make the lines stop short half a centimetre from the edge *matters*.

Writing in 1960 from a very different perspective, Merleau-Ponty points to the paradox of such apparent choices. He relates how Matisse was shown a film in slow motion of himself at work, and was overwhelmed by it. What, to the spectator and maybe even to some extent to the artist himself, had seemed an uninterrupted flow, came to look like an extraordinary and often halting process of deliberation; but this was an illusion, for what occurs is not conscious choice but 'something else'.[20] It remains to Lacan, who seizes on Merleau-Ponty's example, to ask how to formulate the 'something else' that is involved in this process if it cannot be situated in consciousness.[21]

When Hesse drew a distinction between the formal principles in her work which were 'understandable and understood' and the work's 'non-logical self',[22] she was invoking the dimension of the 'something else', the unconscious. The 'formal principles' corresponded with an available set of descriptions and to that extent they were readable as art. But what interested her more was the possibility that they also bordered on some underlying inarticulateness. Her interest in those aspects of art which escape reason can be related back to the Surrealist desire to put the unconscious to work in representation. Of course, Greenberg saw Surrealism, with its overly literary and extraneous concerns, as a distraction or digression from the course of modernist art in the twentieth century.[23] And it is in relation to Greenberg's modernist logic that Hesse has recently been discussed by Rosalind Krauss; neither outside its laws nor totally within their grip, Hesse's work is seen as 'yet one more avatar of the optical unconscious',[24] vividly invoking the substratum of modernism's 'non-logical self'.

When Greenberg came to criticize Minimalism in his essay 'Recentness of Sculpture', he dismissed the relevance of the much-vaunted crisis of the art object, and made the point that 'minimal works are readable as art, as almost anything is today — including a door, a table, or a blank sheet of paper.'[25] In retrospect, now, the Minimalist object has come to look much more concerned with what you can make a sculpture out of rather than a negation of the category *tout court*. The monochrome painting without difficulty, and even automatically, 'declared itself to be a picture, to be art'[26] — but the question seems to have been 'what kind of a picture could be painted in the circumstances?' rather than 'is it or is it not an art object?' On this last point, Greenberg was surely correct. His argument was with the effects, not the status, of Minimalist works. He places those effects in a context of the recent development of art. He suggests a kind of orthodoxy by describing how, although he had not 'got' the sense of Rollin Crampton's show in 1951, Rauschenberg's exhibition of his all-white and all-black paintings at the Stable Gallery in 1953 already seemed old hat. He went on: 'The look of accident was not the only "wild" thing that Abstract Experssionism first acclimatized and then domesticated in painting; it did the same to emptiness, to the look of "void".'[27] For Greenberg, the look of void quickly became tame and even slick, even though this was persistently overlooked in the belief that 'both the accidental and the empty continued to be regarded as an art-denying look.' What originality they had once had was lost now in merely contrived effects and superficial appearance. But there is also a sense in which for Greenberg Minimalist works *were* 'art-denying', not because they were 'non-art', but because they denied him the kind of aesthetic experience furnished by modernist painting — at this time by such painters as Kenneth Noland, Morris Louis and Jules Olitski. The 'inert' look of the work somehow failed to deliver such experience and questioned the value of pure opticality. It disallowed the kind of discrimination modernist surfaces invited the spectator to engage in. It was quite different, therefore, from Newman's use of monochrome where the effects are subtle and nuanced, the surface anything but 'inert'. The 'look of void' was dismissed by Greenberg as a taming device, but his reaction to Minimalism is charged with the sense of an encounter with *lack*, with an art work which simply fails to return the look.

Symbolic Structures

So, to return to Hesse, what did the shift from *Hang-Up* to *Metronomic Irregularity II* involve? The series of moves that she made to get from one to the other seems to point to a crucial interval in her work. For the three versions of *Metronomic Irregularity*, and in particular the second and most successful, provided the prototype for the extraordinary suspended webs of *Right After* in 1969 (plate 55), which used fibreglass over threads to transform her earlier use of wires into three dimensions. There is a drawing from 1969 which Hesse also called *Right After* (plate 62). Lucy Lippard thinks they are unrelated[28] and, certainly, there seems little in common between the scant treatment of the drawing of horizontal lines and hatching, and the interlacings of fibreglass-covered thread

62 Eva Hesse, *Right After*, 1969, gouache, pencil, 55.88 × 37.78 cm. Constance C. Wittkoff, St. Louis.

of the hung sculpture. I want to argue, however, that there is some connection between these apparently dissimilar works, whether or not Hesse consciously intended it by naming them the same. My concern is with the 'other' side of the choices Hesse made; how the shifts in her work might be regarded 'in the perspective of the unconscious',[29] that is, seen from the point of view of an unconscious symbolic structure.

In an interview in 1970 Hesse said that *Hang-Up* was 'the most important early statement I made'.[30] She now thought it naïve, but she liked its extremity; she liked the fact that it was absurd and ludicrous. She now regretted the title, which had been suggested by a friend, but it had clearly marked a turning point for her. Although there are common themes in her work before and after — for instance, the way the drawings she produced in 1960–61 are echoed in the final Woodstock drawings — somehow the 'extreme' quality of *Hang-Up*, in retrospect at least, represented a new possibility. The moment of the transition was relatively short: having made *Hang-Up* in January 1966, she had finished *Metronomic Irregularity II* by the time of the *Eccentric Abstraction* show which opened on 20 September. In between, during that summer, her father died. Hesse worked intensely over these months and Lucy Lippard recounts how overwrought she was when, while she was hanging the work, it burst off the wall under the weight of all the wires.[31] Biographies of Hesse often see the tragic blow of her father's death as echoing the loss of her mother when she was three years old.

There is no doubt that the sense of loss experienced by Hesse was extreme at this point, as her diaries bear witness, but the problem remains how far the biographical account can explain the complex effects of the work. I am more interested in how the work embodies an economy of loss in its very procedures. This is first and foremost a question of effect, which may or may not correspond with Hesse's actual experience of loss and mourning — that we cannot know.[32]

In *Metronomic Irregularity II*, the blank wall which alternates with the panels is transformed and becomes a part of the work. The wall is activated and becomes a surface on which shadows play. It is this relation between blank space and the interlacing of line which produces the effect of symbolic exchange. That is to say, the work shows not a development or sequence from *a* to *b*, but rather a back and forth movement between the two poles. It thus forms a complementary axis to the vertical–horizontal work I have mentioned already, and to which I will return. It enacts a kind of give and take, repeated until the end of her career. So how can the kind of alternation or exchange at work here be thought of in terms of an unconscious structure?

In an essay entitled 'Infantile Anxiety Situations in a Work of Art and in the Creative Impulse',[33] Melanie Klein vividly described the way the infant's experience of loss is reactivated in adult life in depression through the metaphor of 'blank space'; and she did so with particular reference to the case of a woman artist. Although the story Klein relates is in no sense directly analogous to Hesse's, there is something in the symbolic structure she identifies which has resonance for Hesse's work, particularly in terms of establishing a relation between the work's 'non-logical self' and her position as a woman artist. Klein's essay allows us to speculate on the problems of femininity in this context.

Klein's essay was based not on a patient but on an article by Karin Michaelis called 'The Empty Space', about her friend the Swedish artist Ruth Kjär. Here was a woman of means 'who possessed remarkable artistic feeling, which she employed specially in the arrangement of her house, but she had no pronounced creative talent.'[34] She was subject, however, to bouts of depression and Klein quotes Karin Michaelis's description of her situation as follows:

> There was only one dark spot in her life. In the midst of the happiness which was natural to her, and seemed so untroubled, she would suddenly be plunged into the deepest melancholy. A melancholy that was suicidal. If she tried to account for this, she would say something to this effect: 'There is an empty space in me, which I can never fill.'[35]

Ruth Kjär's house was filled with the paintings of her brother-in-law, a successful modern artist; it was a veritable gallery of modern art, says Michaelis. When one of the paintings was removed and sold, 'this left an empty space on the wall, which in some inexplicable way seemed to coincide with the empty space within her.'[36] Ruth Kjär, at that time untrained and untutored, painted a picture in that space, making strokes at random with black chalk. When her husband returned 'she ran to meet him with a hectic brilliance in her eyes', which contrasted with the earlier description of her eyes as 'clouded with hopeless despair'.[37] The husband could not believe his eyes; he could not take his eyes from the sight, but he 'could not take it in, did not believe it, *could* not believe it.'[38] The artist brother-in-law insisted that she could not have painted the picture; it must have been painted by an experienced artist.

On the surface, this account seems to conform to a series of stereotypes: for example, woman's creativity directed to the home, the untutored woman artist and the spontaneity of the creative act. Klein's concern is with the way psychic states are 'reflected' in works of art, and not at all with the representational process or the ways in which expression may be mediated by convention. Moreover, whilst Lacan developed Freud's theory by finding in the unconscious 'the whole structure of a language', Klein's approach in general is marked by an absence of the signifier.[39] I want to suggest a reading of Klein's essay in the light of the extraordinary metaphors she deploys. For 'blank space' is a metaphor which suggests both invisibility and lack, which can usefully serve to dramatize the problems of art and its relation both to language and to femininity. Of course, the metaphor only comes about by being put into language. It is articulated *in* language, but also comes to refer to a psychic space prior to language; it is, therefore, both inside and outside the symbolic and therein lies its power. This contradictory situation is in part borne out by Klein's essay itself, which at one level claims to deal with the artistic impulse but, in fact, is less a discussion of the artist's work than an analysis of a set of descriptions of the work as it is interpreted by Michaelis. Klein even thinks of it as a 'another literary example', like the discussion of a review of Colette's libretto for Ravel's opera *L'Enfant et les Sortilèges* which it follows. The essay focuses attention on the constellation of unconscious conditions which underlie these narratives. Yet Klein's work also insisted on the power of the image, which served as a focus for analysis in her work on the drawings of her child patients. Violent feelings, as a spectator, were not foreign to her either. When, later, William Coldstream was commissioned to paint her portrait, she reacted so negatively to the image of herself that he painted that the project was abandoned; she even discussed with Adrian Stokes, who had initiated the commission, having the picture destroyed.[40]

For Klein, the question is how to explain the empty space within Ruth Kjär, or more precisely, the feeling that there was 'something lacking in her body'.[41] According to Klein, who makes a distinction between the early experiences of girls and boys, the sadistic desire experienced by the girl towards the mother's body is 'the equivalent of castration anxiety in boys'.[42] It is the sadistic desire to rob the mother's body of its contents, and to destroy the mother herself. This gives rise to anxiety that the little girl's body will in turn be mutilated in some way. Freud's emphasis on the girl's fear of loss of the loved object is, for Klein, a modification of this still earlier phase.[43] In Klein's essay, the metaphor of blank space works against structure, against language, as it refers to a stage prior to the acquisition of language. As the story unfolds, the blank space appears to coincide with the psychic space before the entry into language, and into the symbolic. Although the metaphor may conjure up a lack of structure, that space *is*, of course, structured, and Klein's argument is about how it is.

At the end of the account Klein comments on two portraits painted by Ruth Kjär. The first is of an old woman wrinkled with age, near death, and the most recent, a portrait of her mother as a magnificent woman of extraordinary strength and beauty — the one exploring the primary sadistic desire to destroy, the other making reparation. Although my concern is not with literally 'picturing' the mother, the ambivalent feelings towards the maternal object exemplified in these two portraits, as two sides of a coin, is absolutely crucial to Klein. Michaelis's comment on the last portrait is that 'the blank space has been filled', which Klein interprets as the making good of the injury done to the maternal object. Her British followers have emphasized this process of reparation, most notably in the writing on art and creativity of Hanna Segal and Adrian Stokes,[44] in contrast to the Continental stress on separation and loss. For example, Adrian Stokes claims, 'I believe that art tends to epitomize the process, the history, of the depressive achievement, to celebrate also thereby the blessings, more than the ills, of symbiotic relationship.'[45] The greatest power art has is the achievement of a state of unity which ultimately overcomes the trauma of loss and its sadistic repercussions. Reparation has the upper hand, even though it is inextricably linked with separation. His stress on the formal aspects of aesthetic experience owes much to Roger Fry, but, unlike Fry, he sees aesthetic experience structured by projection and introjection, and by our unconscious relationships to part and whole objects.[46]

Good/bad, part/whole, projected/introjected — such oppositions structure the Kleinian model. But if, returning to Klein's essay, we look at its language, we notice a rather different pattern. In the first description of Ruth Kjär's situation, for example, we encounter a cluster of metaphors in which the 'dark spot' threatens to take over and plunge her into depression; like some sort of stain, it clouds the picture of contentment; then there is the attempt to articulate the melancholy, which is put in language as 'empty space'. Initially her eyes are 'clouded with hopeless despair', later they radiate a 'hectic brilliance'. By turns shadowy obscurity, empty space and bright light organize the narrative, and it is this constellation of terms that return us to Hesse's work. There is no question here of an outpouring of an inner world, for Hesse's *Metronomic Irregularity II* is meticulously worked. If making the object is an attempt to master the situation and a form of reparation, then it is carried out with all the qualities of doing damage characteristic of a sadistic process; the panels are literally pierced, the wires punctuate the surface with acute precision.[47] They cover the already disjointed surface of the panels, but hardly fill it up with expressive content. Instead the effect is to blank out and obscure; the wires might appear to fill the space, but actually they obscure it, and so leave unrepaired the structure of the gap. And if it is this effect that we want to articulate, then by far the most important aspect of Klein's essay is her description of 'something lacking in the body', which she relates to loss and the mourning of the maternal object — a *tabula rasa* which is not pregnant with possibility, but incomplete and permanently wanting. Meaning is always just about to be declared and therein lies the possibility, rather than the fullness, of artistic expression. Hesse's work makes a drama out of that loss, as it is encountered by the viewer as a series of disconnections. What we encounter is fraught space in the discontinuous lines that seem to hover frenetically over *Metronomic Irregularity II*, achieving neither unity nor totality. The back and forth is between desire and loss, the twin poles of psychic life.[48] If we see blankness as a kind of *tabula rasa*, it is in the sense of the about-to-be, the pre-symbolic, which is only put in play through the symbolic order — without which the 'something prior' has no place.

Ruth Kjär's experience is treated by Klein as a problem of femininity, re-enacting the small girl's infantile experiences rather than merely replicating or negotiating the boy's experience of the castration complex in the Oedipal scenario. As an artist, the further problem she encountered was the disbelief of the male characters, the husband and brother-in-law, whom I take to stand for 'that arena where the world's power is at stake'.[49] They could not *see* the picture at all, because they could not see that it had been painted by a woman. The brother-in-law's insistence that her painting must have been the work of someone else could, in the context of the wider world, be translated into the familiar charge against the work of the woman artist — that her work is derivative (metaphorically speaking, done by someone else). This was precisely the criticism levelled at Hesse's *Metronomic Irregularity II* by Hilton Kramer when it was first exhibited. He wrote 'Second-hand . . . (it) simply adapts the image of Pollock's drip painting to a three-dimensional medium.'[50] Once it is made visible in the world, the figure of blankness is quickly transformed into a figure of not being seen or invisibility. These are the dynamics of looking and power which Klein's essay bring into focus.

The notion of the 'second-hand', of failing to deliver up the expressive surface associated with Pollock, but 'adapting' it to another medium, was seen by Kramer in terms of a kind of debasement, a corruption of original principles. Being merely derivative, a loss of Pollock's original feeling was incurred. Hesse is placed in Pollock's shadow, the fate of many artists certainly (Robert Morris and his felt pieces, for example); yet there is no doubt that being overshadowed by a master is the fate of the woman artist in particular. But what if the choices Hesse made had the effect of refusing the sublime, the transcendent surface? Perhaps she did not so much adapt as distort Pollock? After all, to look at *Metronomic Irregularity II*, with its distended and discontinuous threads, is almost to look at an anamorphic version of Pollock's webs and skeins — elongated and oblique, as if viewed askance.[51] It is just this stretching out of the threads that differentiates it from the first version where the tangled threads, moving from top to bottom and up again, more readily evoke an evenly worked, all-over surface. The second version, with its mass of horizontal lines, turns a series of removes, or separations, into the means of expression. Rather than merely being in the shadow of Pollock, Hesse made vivid use of her materials, the threads, the panels and the wall, as a kind of shadow play.[52]

Luminosity and lighting effects were as important in the repertoire of Minimalism generally as they were to Hesse. Don Flavin made light the animating force in his work with neon tubes, and in a more general way, as Robert Morris noted, Minimalist artists were interested in how the spectator 'apprehends the object from various positions and under varying conditions of light and spatial context.'[53] But Hesse's particular use of light and shadow is quite distinct, even though it no more evokes the sublime, nor the metaphysical, than does theirs. An undulating surface of latex, or threads doubled on a wall, act like a kind of chiaroscuro, where form is always already, as it were, cast as shadow. In her book on melancholia, Julia Kristeva took as her title Nerval's metaphor 'Black

Sun' which encapsulates this central paradox of intense light that obscures rather than illuminates, and which she relates to the psychic dimension of loss. This dimension of loss is intensified in three moments which interlink in the subject's experience: in Klein's infantile 'depressive position', predicated on loss through the imagined destruction of the mother in the formation of the ego; in depression in later life; and, finally, in death, which defies representation. Freud's essay 'Mourning and Melancholia' had shown a relationship between loss and melancholia or depression. He distinguished between mourning and memories of a lost external object and the complicated transactions of melancholia, in which a hostile attitude to a departed object is a crucial expression of infantile ambivalence. In Freud's terms, whilst mourning involves the loss of an actual object, melancholia involves some kind of loss of the self, or a part of one's self, which can result in a kind of narcissistic injury. Although distinct in important ways, then, both mourning and melancholia involve the loss of an object, and for Kristeva, in *Black Sun*, loss is the founding fact of psychic life.[54] Death cannot be represented in Freud's unconscious, but only imprinted, 'by spacings, blanks, discontinuities' which amount to the 'destruction of representation'.[55] In her discussion of Holbein's *Dead Christ*, which forms a key chapter in the book, the spatial relations within the picture correspond to a psychic space, by an act of severance, and by the picture's crushing horizontality — which refuses any prospect of redemption.[56] To fall, *cadere*, is the metaphorical movement of such 'dé-pression'.

The Fall From Grace

With the relation between a psychic and a literal space in mind, I want to return in the final part of this essay to the broader question of Minimalism, and in particular to the dialogue between Hesse's work and Andre's. First, though, we must ask whether the relation has only the status of an analogy — the kind of spatial analogy, for example, which is clearly problematic in Stokes, where spatial configurations in painting systematically mirror internal relationships within the subject, as if without mediation.[57] Although couched in the language of psychoanalysis, is it anything other than an extension of the pathetic fallacy, or, in an older rhetoric, the mirroring of the soul? If we are to justify some such relation in terms other than a similarity or coincidence of feeling, it needs grounding in the specific terms of Minimalism's resistance to a prevailing view of the expressive qualities of modernist art. In the 1960s much of the critical discussion of Minimalism and of Hesse's work focused on the problem of 'literalness' as that which denies the expressive. Hilton Kramer, for instance, in his review of the *Eccentric Abstraction* show, thought the work conformed to 'a general tendency to substitute the literal for the metaphorical'. In the first part of this essay I tried to show how Hesse's work might be seen as a part of a Minimalist project rather than running counter to it, but for Kramer it was this whole trend in recent art which was impoverished — 'what was formerly part of the metaphorical and expressive fabric of painting is now offered as a literal *thing*.'[58] If it is literal, in the terms offered here, then it cannot be metaphorical or expressive, which would seem to rule out the kind of 'unconscious perspective', a metaphorics if you like, that I have been discussing in this essay. On the other hand, if Minimalism can be seen to reformulate what the expressive might mean in relation to the work of art, precisely by looking at its limits, then such a straightforward opposition appears much less plausible as a way of accounting for the work's effects.

The problem of literalness was most persuasively brought into focus by Michael Fried in his much-discussed and fascinating critique of Minimalism in 'Art and Objecthood', first published in *Artforum* in June 1967. I want briefly to touch on two aspects of Fried's complex essay: his view that the works were overly 'literal' and 'theatrical'; and that Minimalism represented some undesirable departure from the absorptive properties of modernist painting at its best in which 'presentness is grace.'[59] For Fried, artists such as Stella, Noland and Olitski acknowledge literalness, but Judd and other Minimalists are 'literalist'. Although in some ways close to Greenberg's position, there are also some striking differences of emphasis. For Greenberg, Minimalism was too much 'a feat of ideation', whilst for Fried it was too literal; for Greenberg the look of the work was too inert, whilst for Fried it was too theatrical, it worked *too* hard at being there, rather than too little. Its presence — a term Fried drew from Greenberg — was mere 'stage presence', as if the object functioned for the spectator like another person in the room. On the other hand, the anti-theatrical work of the best recent art (Stella, Noland and so on) 'treated the spectator as if he were not there' and was able to 'defeat or suspend its own objecthood'. This suspension, the capacity to outdo the pull of literalness, enabled a state of grace, a state which is neither divine nor as simply 'transcendent' as it is often made out. The state of grace is regenerative and elevating in so far as it works *against the pull* of literalness, which, Fried insists, is everywhere ('We are all literalists most or all of our lives'[60]). What Fried had to say about theatricality and Minimalism was, as he made clear, 'all about a problematic of the spectator'. And he dealt centrally with the idea of the bodily experience of Minimalist work, the body's orientation, the points of view, which made it in his terms so 'incurably theatrical'. For the literalist object would not let the spectator alone, 'it refuses to stop confronting him, distancing him, isolating him.'[61] In reviewing Minimalism here, we might also reconsider another aspect of the bodily orientation involved, in the light not only of the external or lived body, but the 'internal body' as it had been understood by Klein and the unconscious processes described by psychoanalysis. To reintroduce the psychic split into the phenomenological body of Minimalism is to reintroduce also the idea of sexual difference and the thematic of desire and loss that I discussed in relation to Hesse. Yet a notion of bodily orientation remains crucial here, which is one of the reasons Fried's essay remains the most illuminating of all the contemporary critical writing on Minimalism.[62]

In the single fibreglass-coated wire which hangs from the ceiling in *Untitled* (plate 57), the accent is on the falling movement which rests in the awkward coil on the gallery floor. Likewise, in her work with nets and straggling threads, the clear geometry of the grid has been, as it were, digested and spat out. Whilst the fabric of her work is distinctive, the interest and effect of the pull downward is characteristic of much Minimalist work.[63] It is a movement which we can see

63 Eva Hesse, *Area*, 1968, latex on wire mesh, metal wire 6.1 × 0.91 m. Collection Wexner Center for the Arts, Ohio State University © The Estate of Eva Hesse. Photo: courtesy of Robert Miller Gallery, New York.

carried to extremes in Andre's floor pieces like *Magnesium Square* (plate 58), one of several works in the same format using different metals or different combinations of metal tiles. Hesse's *Area* (plate 63), which appeared in another show Lippard organized called *Soft and Apparently Soft Sculpture*, looks as if it has slipped down the wall to lie slumped and somewhat crumpled. It corresponds to Andre's pieces that extend down the wall and into the gallery space like some strange and abstract prosthetic extensions. Her *Schema* (plate 64), though not on the scale of Andre's large floor pieces, is placed flat on the floor like them.[64] It was made of rubber and cast by painting on several coats of latex with a brush. The rubber was translucent so originally the floor beneath could be seen through it, though now it is an opaque and syrupy yellow. Hesse only discovered latex rubber in the autumn of 1967 and this was one of the first pieces in which she used this technique. She used latex as an industrial material to create a modern kind of surface, but one which had in fact been 'painted' on. And as Hesse herself was aware, latex was a fragile material which in time decays. Many of her works have discoloured and disintegrated in this way. Susceptible to light and heat, it is hardly the kind of resilient material we

64 Eva Hesse, *Schema*, 1967, latex 1.07 × 1.07 m 144 units each 6.35 cm diameter. Philadelphia Museum of Art, Gift of Helen Hesse Charash © The Estate of Eva Hesse. Photo: courtesy of Robert Miller Gallery, New York.

associate with Andre or Judd. 'Eventually', Lippard writes, they 'will dry up, crack, and collapse into dust' unless a fixative is discovered.[65] Even at the time Lippard was writing, *Stratum* (plate 61) had already disintegrated, and now no longer exists. Fibreglass, the most durable of materials, is notable, in Hesse's work, for not looking as if it is. Hesse's strange, encrusted forms, particularly as they are subjected to decay through light — *light* of all things, the light which animates the shadow-life of her work — show solid form in the process of collapse, sculptural form laid waste.

The suggestion of a dialogue is borne out here. The possibility of material disintegrating, so evident in Hesse's work, acts reciprocally with (and on) the actual and imagined resilience of Andre's — actual because it can literally be walked on, bearing any amount of wear and tear, and imagined in the appearance of the surface as obdurate. As Minimalism has aged, such pristine durable surfaces seem somehow less important for their newness or their industrial origins than for the irrational ground that they inhabit. We might even imagine it gathering dust, like Man Ray's photograph of Duchamp's *Large Glass*, losing its precision in a continuous drift, a ground which is subject to decay. Such a link may seem far-fetched, but the point is to stress the unexpected, the 'happening upon' of the work, where the sculpture is allowed to bear the weight of the spectator's body. This quality, of a work that is not only in the space but in the 'way', can, Fried admitted, be disquieting.[66]

Sculptural form in Andre's floor pieces has been razed to the ground. There is an insistence on the lowest possible level of space which the work of art may occupy. The normal upright form a sculpture takes collapses to the ground. As opposed to his early work which owed much to Brancusi, where he hewed and worked the wood, here sculpture is literally cast down, forced to occupy the shallowest possible space. As Rosalind Krauss has put it, Andre's work 'presses illusionistic space out of sculpture' — there is no internal space here, no hollowing out.[67] By a series of expulsions, it has rid itself of the hollow space of a sculpture, to form a hard, encasing skin at floor level. Not even shadows can exist in a space of such extreme horizontality. We come across the work literally at our feet, forcing us to look down upon it, requiring an orientation which is, by the conventions of sculpture, *dis*orienting. It is displaced from where a sculpture 'should' be, in a move analogous with the kind of blanking out we saw earlier in Hesse's two-dimensional work. Although in *Schema* (plate 64) the material is semi-transparent and still encloses the space of a sculpture — if only just, in the small protruding hemispheres — the same disorientation occurs. Smithson called her work 'vertiginous' which suggests vividly just this type of effect.[68]

This way of looking at the work puts the emphasis on the processes of distortion and distancing that I discussed earlier. Fried refers to the distancing effect as the key to theatricality, for Minimalist art '*distances* the beholder not just physically, but psychically.'[69] Rather than see a continuity between a literal and a psychic space, there is a discontinuity, a series of displacements entailed in the 'perspective of the unconscious'. That is, the external bodily orientation and the 'internal body' do not work in neat unison, but are split. Rather than continuity, which suggests a kind of mirroring or empathetic identification, the emphasis here is on the something lacking, some lacuna in the body's schema. Crucial to this effect of distancing was, for Fried, the temporal dimension, its theatrical 'duration', where experience is 'incomplete' and inconclusive, as opposed to the instantaneous effect of the best art. He quotes Tony Smith on how there was 'something absurd' in going back over and over to look at a cube, which will not give itself up but offers only infinite duration. And he likens this aspect of Minimalism to a Surrealist sensibility, in terms of a deep affinity with its distancing and temporal effects — such as anxiety, expectation and memory. This is an odd connection to make, and one not often remarked, but absolutely to the point. By way of a coda to this discussion, it is to a Surrealist voice that I want finally to turn to suggest how Andre's work might be seen as a counterpoint to Hesse's.

If Fried could say of the best contemporary work 'presentness is grace', then the literal, theatrical endeavours of Minimalism represented a kind of fall. It is the idea of a fall which Georges Bataille had made a central motif in his theory of an avant garde. Writing in the late 1920s and early '30s, that is, contemporary with Klein's essay of 1929, Bataille defined representation as a process of destruction which operated at the level of sadistic desire.[70] In writing that is shot through with metaphors of verticality and horizontality, light and obscurity, he pits the elevation of the sun, and by implication the human spirit, against the notion of the fall, to 'baseness', which characterizes the human condition. 'The myth of Icarus', he wrote in 'Rotton Sun', 'is particularly expressive from this point of view: it clearly splits the sun in two — the one that was shining at the moment of Icarus's elevation, and the one that melted the wax, causing failure and a screaming fall when Icarus got too close.'[71] Flight is here equated with imminent fall, contrasting with Fried's image of 'hovering' in a mirage of suspended objecthood. For Bataille, the work of the avant garde was to search 'for that which most ruptures the highest elevation'.[72] In Bataille's preoccupation with the theme of castration, it is the vertical axis, and ultimately the fall from grace, on which the Oedipal origins of modern art play themselves out. The Oedipal moment is the privileged moment, animated by the fear of, and desire for, punishment at the hand of the father. Bataille's framework is based on the principle of insufficiency, not virility; if the paternal metaphor is invoked, so too, necessarily, is lack. From this perspective, it is possible to see the collapsing movement implied by Andre's floor pieces as 'abjected' in Bataille's sense, of being cast downward, whilst Hesse's are 'abjected' in Kristeva's sense, in which form and structure threatens to decompose and disintegrate.[73] Both senses revolve around some kind of expulsion, a casting out and down (*cadere*), and a loss of self-identity, a narcissistic injury.

This essay has been an attempt to look at Minimalism *through* the work of Eva Hesse. It has certainly not been my aim to suggest that Minimalism can be seen as a homogeneous movement into which Hesse fits more or less comfortably. Rather, her work and its particular compulsions prompt us to dislodge the rational frame in which the work of Minimalist artists is usually viewed. Her work does not replicate theirs, any more than Andre's replicates Lewitt's or Judd's. Nor would I want to claim that the particular economy of loss played out in her work, where 'blank space' and the 'dark spot' come to add up to pretty much the same, is replicated by Minimalism in general. What I do want to claim is the centrality of that constellation of metaphors that Klein's essay highlighted — metaphors which continue to pervade the discourses of modernism: between blank space and a stain, between light and obscurity, between the horizontal and the vertical, between visibility and invisibility, between elevation and a fall. And just as Klein's blank space evoked sadistic impulses, so apparently restrained surfaces can harbour violent fantasy.

Briony Fer
University College, London

Notes

I would like to thank Roszika Parker, Margaret Iversen, David Batchelor and Tamar Garb for their help and encouragement in the preparation of this article.

1 Quoted in Lucy Lippard, *Eva Hesse*, New York, 1976, p. 131.
2 Freud 'Inhibitions, Symptoms and Anxiety' (1926), vol. 10, *On Psychopathology*, The Penguin Freud Library, Harmondworth, 1993, p. 280.

3 *Hang-Up* was exhibited along with *Ishtar* and *Long Life* in 'Abstract Inflationism and Stuffed Expressionism', May 1966. Lippard explains her responses op. cit., p. 83.
4 ibid.
5 ibid.
6 ibid.
7 See, for example, Anna C. Chave's 'Eva Hesse: A "Girl Being a Sculpture" ' in *Eva Hesse: A Retrospective*, New Haven and London, 1992. Here Hesse's work is set against that of Judd and Morris 'who flaunted a rhetoric of virility and power in promoting a visual mode as deindividualized as possible' (p. 110). Hesse, by contrast is seen as creating a kind of 'écriture feminine'. For Chave's view of Minimalism, see her article 'Minimalism and the Rhetoric of Power', in which she argued that 'The blank face of Minimalism may come into focus as the face of capital, the face of authority, the face of the father.' *Arts Magazine*, no. 64, Jan. 1990, pp. 44–63. Clave's view is discussed by David Batchelor in 'Abstraction, Modernism, Representation' in Andrew Benjamin and Peter Osborne (eds.), *Thinking Art: Beyond Traditional Aesthetics*, London, 1991, p. 49.
8 Lippard, op. cit., p. 182.
9 Though not in the London installation of the show, Royal Academy of Arts, 1993.
10 Lippard, op. cit., p. 131.
11 ibid., p. 56.
12 David Batchelor has discussed the irrational and arbitrary qualities of Sol Lewitt's work in 'Within and Between', *Sol Lewitt — Structures 1962–1993*, The Museum of Modern Art, Oxford, 1993. See also in this catalogue Rosalind Krauss's essay 'The Lewitt Matrix' and her earlier essay 'Lewitt in Progress' in *The Originality of the Avant-Garde and Other Modernist Myths*, Cambridge Massachussets and London, 1986.
13 Roszika Parker and Griselda Pollock wrote of *Hang-Up*: 'Woman is absent as an image, but present as the maker'. They raise problems about Hesse's work from the point of view of identity and the position of the woman artist that I have pursued in this essay. See *Old Mistresses: Women Art and Ideology*, London, 1981.
14 Lippard, op. cit., p. 152.
15 Georges Bataille, 'L'Art Primitif', *Documents*, 1930. See also my discussion of Bataille's view of representation in 'Poussière/Peinture; Bataille on Painting' to be published in Carolyn Gill (ed.), *George Bataille: Writing the Sacred*, London, 1994.
16 Clement Greenberg, 'Modernist Painting' in John O'Brian (ed.), *Clement Greenberg: The Collected Essays and Criticism*, vol. 4, Chicago and London, 1993, p. 90.
17 Clement Greenberg, 'After Abstract Expressionism', originally published in 1962, ibid., p. 131.
18 ibid.
19 ibid., p. 133.
20 M. Merleau-Ponty, *Signs* (first published in French, Paris, 1960), Evanston, 1964, pp. 45–6.
21 J. Lacan, 'What is a Picture?', *The Four Fundamental Concepts of Psycho-Analysis*, Harmondsworth, 1979, p. 114.
22 Hesse quoted in Lippard, op. cit., p. 131.
23 Hesse's relationship to Surrealism has been widely commented on, for example, by Lippard, ibid., p. 185.
24 R. Krauss, *The Optical Unconscious*, Cambridge, Mass. and London, 1993, chapter 6 Bis. Krauss's discussion of Hesse draws on Deleuze and Guattari's *Anti-Oedipus*, which in turn draws on the work of Melanie Klein, particularly in the idea of the 'paranoid body'.
25 Clement Greenberg, 'Recentness of sculpture' in John O'Brian (ed.), op. cit., p. 253.
26 ibid. p. 251. Greenberg's responses to the monochrome in the early 1960s as a complex series of defensive strategies are interestingly discussed by Thierry de Duve in 'The Monochromatic and the Blank Canvas' in S. Guilbaut (ed.), *Reconstructuring Modernism: Art in New York, Paris and Montreal 1945–1964*, Cambridge, Mass. and London, 1990, pp. 244–310.
27 Greenberg, op. cit., p. 251.
28 Lippard, op. cit., p. 169.
29 J. Lacan, op. cit., p. 79. I should make clear that the 'other' side of the choices is evident only in the work's effects, and does not in my view reside in intentionality.
30 Lippard, op. cit., p. 56.
31 ibid., p. 78.
32 Hesse's diaries have been used extensively as a means of explaining her work, as if they unlock its meaning. See also Lippard on the possible role of infantile sexuality: 'In Hesse's case, she might be seen as thrown back into herself because the first object of her love — her mother — had "rejected her" by dying', ibid., p. 188. This kind of retrospective psychobiography seems inherently problematic. Relevant here is Kristeva's treatment of Holbein and the 'melancholy moment', which may or may not correspond with Holbein's own melancholy *Black Sun: Depression and Melancholia*, New York, 1989, pp. 107–138.
33 'Infantile Anxiety Situations in a Work of Art and in the Creative Impulse' was published in the *International Journal of Psychoanalytic Studies* in October 1929. Reprinted also in Juliet Mitchell (ed.), *The Selected Melanie Klein*, Harmondsworth, 1986.
34 ibid., p. 90.
35 ibid.
36 Karin Michaelis, 'The Empty Space', quoted

by Klein, ibid., p. 91.

37 Michaelis, ibid. The 'hectic brilliance' of the eyes of the hysteric contrast here with the melancholic. Both melancholy and hysteria can be seen to be in a relation to narcissism (figured here in terms of the adornment of the home). The relation of depression and narcissism is discussed by Julia Kristeva in *Black Sun*, op. cit., p. 5.

38 Michaelis in Klein, op. cit., p. 91.

39 According to Lacan, the Kleinian School was 'incapable of even so much as suspecting the existence of the signifier', *Ecrits: A Selection*, London, 1977, p. 272. As Christian Metz has discussed, Lacan's criticism of Klein was that she dealt with the Imaginary and not at all with the Symbolic, *Psychoanalysis and Cinema*, London and Basingstoke, p. 6.

40 Letters to Stokes from Klein, dated 4 Sept. 1952 and 11 Dec. 1952, Adrian Stokes Papers, Tate Gallery Archive, TGA 8816. In the recent Tate Gallery catalogue, this portrait, dated 1952, is said to be 'unfinished'. See *The Paintings of William Coldstream*, Tate Gallery, London, 1990.

41 Klein, op. cit., p. 92.

42 ibid., p. 92. For Klein, castration anxiety in boys relates back to earlier anxiety situations, and the 'Oedipus conflict begins under the complete dominance of sadism', see her discussion, ibid., p. 87.

43 Klein mapped out the stages that she thought preceded Freud's pivotal Oedipal moment. She developed the idea, proposed by Freud, that 'the ego has been prepared to expect castration by having undergone repeated object-losses' by examining what those prior stages entailed. For Freud, anxiety is a reaction to a loss or separation; in boys it is a signal of danger, a danger most often associated with the threat of castration; in girls with the loss of the love object. See Freud 'Inhibitions, Symptoms and Anxiety', op. cit., p. 286. Following the later Freud, she believed the aggressive instincts played as much a part as the libidinal ones, but she thought the stages which preoccupied Freud were anticipated by still earlier ones, in which the most crucial relationship was with the mother. Later this became theorized as the 'depressive position', first introduced in 1934 in her essay 'A contribution to the Psychogenesis of Manic-Depressive States', Klein, op. cit.

44 Hanna Segal discusses this particular paper in *Dream, Phantasy and Art*, London, 1991, pp. 81–6. See also her 1952 paper 'A Psycho-analytic Approach to Aesthetics', which deals with the relation of the artistic impulse to the depressive position. For the influence of Klein on aesthetics see also the work of the Imago Society of the 1950s, a group influenced by Klein's writing, including Stokes, Meltzer, Bion and Wollheim.

45 A. Stokes, 'Landscape, Art and Ritual', *The Invitation in Art*, London, 1965, p. 54.

46 Segal's work is much more explicitly dependent on Fry's approach, even though Fry had objected to Freud's concern with content over form in R. Fry, *The Artist and Psychoanalysis*, London 1924. See also Richard Wollheim's succinct and illuminating discussion of Stokes in his preface to Stokes, op. cit.

47 It was when Hesse had almost completed the process of placing the wires in the holes that the piece burst off the wall, Lippard recounts, and Hesse was 'hysterical', Lippard, op. cit., p. 78.

48 Rosalind Krauss has discussed the push and pull of the 'pulsatile' as the beat of the unconscious. See, in particular, her discussion of Duchamp's *Rotoreliefs*, chapter 3, and Picasso's sketchbooks, chapter 5, *The Optical Unconscious*, op. cit.

49 Kristeva, *Black Sun*, op. cit., p. 30.

50 *New York Times*, 1966, quoted in Lippard, op. cit., p. 83. Kramer later changed his view of Hesse, see ibid., p. 132.

51 See Lacan on anamorphosis in Holbein's *The Ambassadors*, op. cit., pp. 86–9. Krauss has discussed in detail the problem of anamorphosis as it relates to Hesse's work in her essay for *Eva Hesse; A Retrospective*, Whitechapel Gallery, London, 1979.

52 Rather than a contrast with Pollock, this suggests a re-reading of Pollock, where the cut-outs are exemplary, which is to say that Hesse read Pollock correctly in some sense.

53 Quoted in Colpitt, *Minimal Art: The Critical Perspective*, Seattle, 1990, p. 88.

54 She deploys this idea in her analysis of Holbein's *Dead Christ*, Kristeva, op. cit., pp. 107–138.

55 ibid., p. 265.

56 The reading of Holbein is highly specific and I am not advocating applying it to the quite different circumstances of Minimalism, but in the mechanisms she describes. In the context of the book as a whole, there is an interesting discussion of modernism in terms of melancholia, ibid.

57 See Wollheim's discussion of this in his Preface to *The Invitation in Art*, op. cit., p. xvi.

58 *New York Times*, 25 Sept. 1966, quoted by Lippard, op. cit., p. 188.

59 Michael Fried, 'Art and Objecthood', *Artforum*, vol. 5, no. 11, June 1967. Revised version in Gregory Battcock (ed.), *Minimal Art: A Critical Anthology*, New York, 1968, pp. 116–47.

60 ibid., p. 147.

61 ibid., p. 140.

62 Merleau-Ponty's ideas had influenced Michael Fried in his view of the bodily experience in art. *The Phenomenology of Perception*,

translated into English in the 1960s, also influenced this generation of Minimalist artists. On Merleau-Ponty's view, the body and its dimensions of time and space was central to consciousness. On the other hand, when Lacan took up Merleau-Ponty he engaged with the posthumous *The Visible and the Invisible* in order to insist on the split between the eye and the gaze, between the scopic field and the drive manifested at the level of the scopic field, i.e., the strange contingency, the lack that constitutes the castration anxiety. In this last work, Merleau-Ponty links the visible–invisible axis to metaphors of intertwining, verticality, ground and depth in a way which further complicates the relation of internal to external, of literal to metaphorical.

63 This aspect of Minimalism is discussed by Margaret Iversen in 'The Deflationary Impulse: Postmodernism, Feminism and the Anti-Aesthetic' in Andrew Benjamin and Peter Osborne (eds.), op. cit., pp. 81–93.

64 Lippard notes that the hemispheres were not fixed on the mat, giving it a certain fragility, and that this, plus its position on the floor, 'may have been partially due to Hesse's friendship with and admiration of Carl Andre and his unfixed "rugs" of different metal plaques in a grid, but the idea itself is fundamentally a pictorial one, and another source is her own earlier work — the circle drawings, or reliefs like *Ditto*', op. cit., p. 112. Of Hesse, Andre has said, 'No one seems able to answer the questions that Eva Hesse asked. She is more alive than most of the living are now', in '3000 Years: Carl Andre Interviewed by David Batchelor', *Artscribe*, no. 76, Summer 1989, p. 63.

65 Lippard, op. cit., p. 115. These effects of temporality were extended in Serra's treatment of materials, in which the effects of rusting come to be a part of the works.

66 Fried, op. cit., p. 127. Though Fried was referring here to the much larger pieces, the introduction of the object into the spectator's path is, I think, still relevant.

67 Rosalind Krauss, *Passages in Modern Sculpture*, Cambridge Mass. and London, 1981, p. 272.

68 Smithson quoted in Lippard, op. cit., p. 192.

69 Fried, op. cit., p. 126.

70 *Documents*, no. 7, 1930, reviewing G.H. Luquet's *L'Art Primitif*, Paris, 1930.

71 Bataille, 'The Rotten Sun' in Allan Stoekl (ed.), *Visions of Excess; Selected Writings 1927–1939*, Minnesota, 1985, p. 58.

72 ibid., p. 58. Although this was only noticeable, Bataille claimed, in the work of Picasso. Academic painting corresponded with elevation.

73 In his sociological essay, 'L'Abjection et les formes misérables', Bataille discussed how subversion entailed the abolition of the rules which govern a spatial relationship between 'haut et bas', and the symbolic spacing of social classes in relation to one another; social abjection was linked to infantile experience 'étant subie par impuissance en raison de conditions sociales données', *Georges Bataille: Oeuvres Complètes II Ecrits Posthumes 1922–40*, Paris, 1970, pp. 216–21. In Kristeva's reworking of the term abjection, she reinscribes the maternal metaphor in the Oedipal triangle, just as Klein had insisted earlier on the centrality of infantile ambivalence to the maternal body. See Kristeva's *Powers of Horror*, op. cit.

Art History ISSN 0141-6790 Vol. 17 No. 3 September 1994 pp. 450–464

What is a photograph?

Margaret Iversen

Roland Barthes's last book, *Camera Lucida* (1980), begins with the words, 'One day, quite some time ago . . .', clearly announcing its status as a fiction, as art.[1] The central character is a scholar who, throwing off his academic robes, his whole culture even, retires to his study rather like Descartes, and meditates in the first person on photography. Or, more precisely, he meditates on his desire in relation to those photographs which somehow move him. These few instances then furnish a bedrock of personal but irrefutable evidence from which he hopes to extrapolate the essence of photography in general. It is a lovely, alluring story in which we want to believe, but by which we ought not to be taken in completely. Rather we should inquire as to why the book is written in this form. There are, no doubt, many answers to this question, chief among them being Barthes's avowed desire to write fiction. My proposal is that the book is a kind of fable about photography which also serves as a commentary on a difficult, frequently impenetrable seminar given by Jacques Lacan in 1964 and published in English as *The Four Fundamental Concepts of Psycho-analysis*.[2] Lacan's writing seems to inspire this oblique form of commentary. I am thinking particularly of Slavoj Žižek's readings of Hitchcock's films as elucidations of Lacanian theory, of Malcolm Bowie's Lacanian reading of Proust, and of Mary Kelly's image–text installations, which are inquiries into gender and identity informed by Lacan.[3] Perhaps the psychoanalyst's fertile ellipticality even demands this approach.

The dramatic opening gesture of eschewing all technical, semiological, sociological and historical approaches to photography has the consequence of drawing Barthes closer to the tradition of phenomenological description of lived experience: in fact, the book is dedicated to Sartre and his *L'imaginaire*.[4] But Barthes adds something conspicuously lacking in that tradition — affect. His kind of phenomenology would be 'steeped in desire' (p. 21) and, I will argue, psychoanalytical through and through. *Camera Lucida* is in many ways a sombre book, haunted as it is by the recent death of the author's mother and, for us, in retrospect, by his own. It circles around the thought that the essence or specific character of photography is a 'that-has-been' — a certificate of the presence of something that is past. The nature of the medium as an indexical imprint of the object means that any photographed object or person has a ghostly presence, an uncanniness that might be likened to the return of the dead. Yet the title of the book is anything but sombre. *La Chambre claire* literally means the light or bright room. It also refers, we are told, to a draughtsman's technical aid, quite different from the dark chamber of the *camera obscura*, which projects an image onto paper by means of a prism (p. 106). For those who have read the book, it might also invoke its key, though unreproduced, photograph, which shows Barthes's mother as a child in a conservatory or winter garden.

The Real

The occasion for writing the book, according to the fiction, was given by the death of the mother and the son's melancholy search for her in a pile of old photographs. But its underlying theme is taken from Lacan's account of the encounter with the Real which is ultimately an encounter with the persistently denied fact of one's own mortality. Barthes declares that every photograph contains an 'imperious sign of my future death' (p. 97). Looking at old photographs one thinks simultaneously of a future — 'he is going to die' — and of an absolute past — 'he has died' (p. 96) — a collapse of time that seals one's own fate. But Barthes, so to speak, develops this painful recognition from a negative into a positive, from dark to light, through Freud's conception of the death instinct as mediated by Lacan.

The death drive, as it is better translated, is not something that had previously much concerned Barthes, although it might well be argued that his earlier aesthetics of *jouissance* or bliss (also a Lacanian conception, but owing much to Bataille's theories of eroticism) in *The Pleasure of the Text*[5] already carried something of that which is 'Beyond the Pleasure Principle'.[6] The topography of instinctual drives developed by Freud in that article (1920) set the pleasure principle in opposition to the death drive. The first principle relates to the theory of constancy whereby the psychical apparatus tries to keep levels of excitation low or constant through the discharge of unpleasurable tension. It has to do therefore with the maintenance of a homeostatic system, the preservation of life, libidinal satisfaction and the stability of the ego — in short, everything Freud groups under the rubric of life instincts.[7] Barthes's constant association of pleasure with what is coded, cultural and collective fits in with Freud's conception of the pleasure principle as integrative. And Barthes follows Lacan's rather low estimation of pleasure, evident in statements such as, 'Pleasure limits the scope of human possibility — the pleasure principle is a principle of homeostasis.' (p. 31) 'Bliss' must then participate in the disintegrative energies of the death drive which would include pain, loss, death and the shudder of annihilation. According to Freud, the death drive 'seems more primitive, more elementary, more instinctual than the pleasure principle which it overrides.'[8] However, the sexual frisson of *jouissance* (which also means orgasm) is very muted in *Camera Lucida*.

The Lacan text which I am suggesting set Barthes's agenda here concerns the third, rather elusive term in his tripartite topography, in which the relation between the Imaginary and Symbolic Orders is complicated by the Real. *The Four Fundamental Concepts* contains several chapters exploring the Real as it is manifested in the visual field, that is, as the Gaze. There is, admittedly, little overt evidence in *Camera Lucida* to support my case for the central importance of Lacan's Séminaire XI, except in the French version, which contains a brief bibliography that cites it. Also, right at the beginning of the book, Barthes observes that the defining characteristic of photography is its attachment to 'the absolute particular, the sovereign Contingeny, matte and somehow stupid, the *This* . . . in short, what Lacan calls Tuché, the Occasion, the Encounter, the Real, in its indefatigable expression' (p. 4). The fifth chapter of *The Four Fundamental Concepts* is called 'Tuché and Automaton'. (Tuché might have been more readily recognizable as the Greek principle of Fate in its usual English transliteration as Tyche.) The terms are borrowed from the second book of Aristotle's *Physics* in a discussion of causality, but Lacan redefines them as 'the encounter with the real' and 'the network of signifiers' respectively. While the automaton or network of signifiers involves the subject in his or her relation machinery of the symbolic register, the tuché or Real is a relation outside that system. The subject, then, is not exhausted by or subsumed into the symbolic, linguistic, conceptual apparatus of culture. Interestingly, Lacan explicitly connects the automaton to 'the insistence of the signs by which we see ourselves governed by the pleasure principle' (pp. 53–4). Tuché, on the contrary, is experienced by the subject as a painful intrusion, as a trauma.

Lacan is adamant that this painful encounter with a Real beyond the pleasure principle was the constant object of Freud's research. In 'The Subversion of the Subject', for example, he writes, 'for to ignore the death instinct in his doctrine is to misunderstand that doctrine entirely.'[9] Lacan's reading of Freud no doubt privileges the post-1920 topography, but it does at least have the virtue of directing our attention to those moments in Freud's thought where the unconscious is given a fateful, accidental character as, for example, in his paper on the uncanny.[10] But in *The Four Fundamental Concepts*, Lacan delves into the early *Interpretation of Dreams* (1900) and comes up with a dream that is riven by trauma and does not at all conform to the general thesis of the book that dreams are disguised, hallucinated wish-fulfilments.[11] The dreamer is a man whose young son has just succumbed to a fatal illness and who, weary from his long vigil, leaves an old man to watch over the body. The old man falls asleep, a candle falls on the bedding and it ignites. The father in an adjoining room dreams that his son comes to wake him, takes hold of his arm and whispers reproachfully, 'Father, can't you see I'm burning?' The accident which finds its way into the dream has an awful necessity about it as it repeats the death, perhaps by fever, of the boy. Like Freud's shell-shocked soldiers who repeatedly dreamed of their horrific experiences, this dream is a (missed) encounter with the Real, that is, with the irredeemable loss of the child. 'How can the dream,' inquires Lacan, 'the bearer of the subject's desire produce that which makes the trauma emerge repeatedly — if not its very face, at least the screen that shows that it is still there behind.' (p. 55)

The Real would seem, then, to be a hitch in the circuit of life-preserving, pleasure-seeking drives which cannot be smoothed over and which insistently repeats. The 'compulsion to repeat' is, for Freud, the hallmark of that which cannot be assimilated and subdued. An example of such repetition discussed by Freud in 'Beyond the Pleasure Principle' is the '*fort-da*' game invented by his one-and-a-half-year-old grandson.[12] The little boy repeatedly threw a cotton reel attached to a piece of thread into his cot where it disappeared from view, and then reeled it back, accompanying these alternating actions with sounds meaning 'gone' and 'there'. For Freud, the game is a re-enactment and a working through of the original trauma of the boy's separation from his mother. For Lacan, the cotton reel is a small piece of the subject with which he attempts to span the 'ditch', the 'ever-open gap' around his cot created by the mother's absence (p. 62).

The most obvious connection between this 'repetition compulsion' and photography is the fact of mechanical reproduction and Barthes picks up on this link: 'the photograph mechanically repeats what could never be repeated existentially.' (p. 41) It has, therefore, some of the uncanny, fateful character of the compulsive repetition discussed by Freud. But Barthes tends to locate the photography's uncanniness more in its insistence on the referent. The object is not just represented as in a drawing or a painting — rather, it clings to the photograph in a disconcerting way. One way of reading *Camera Lucida* is as a reassessment of realism by an ardent modernist. But realism, in this context, must be detached from the collection of threadbare academic conventions and aligned with the Lacanian Real. Not all photographs, however, are susceptible to this realignment. In Lacan's terms the photograph can either be fully integrated in the network of signifiers or it can be tychic. Or, as Barthes observes, it can either be experienced as tame, that is, 'tempered by aesthetic and empirical habits', or as mad (p. 119). Barthes's 'mad' realism is related to Surrealism in which a disruptive reality unsettles the 'civilized codes' (p. 119).

Shock

Although my aim is to read *Camera Lucida* through *The Four Fundamental Concepts*, I want to pause here to consider what I take to be another important, though unacknowledged, inspiration for the book — a text by a writer deeply marked by Surrealism, Walter Benjamin, called 'A Small History of Photography' (1931).[13] Part of that essay concerns photographic studies of anonymous subjects made by the painter David Octavius Hill. With paintings of such subjects, Benjamin notes, interest in the identity of the sitters soon fades. But confronted, for example, by Hill's Newhaven fishwife there remains

> something that cannot be silenced, that fills you with an unruly desire to know what her name was, the woman who was alive there, who even now is still real and will never consent to be wholly absorbed in art.[14]

Barthes's sense of the photograph as an insistent presence of the real emanating from the past is clear enough here, but with his next example Benjamin adds another dimension important for Barthes, that of trauma. Hill took a photograph of Dauthendey and the fiancée he was to find, shortly after the birth of their sixth child, lying in the bedroom with her arteries severed. Benjamin reflects:

> No matter how artful the photograph, no matter how carefully posed his subject, the beholder feels an irresistible urge to search such a picture for the tiny spark of contingency, of the Here and Now, with which reality has so to speak seared the subject, to find the inconspicuous spot where in the immediacy of that long-forgotten moment the future subsists so eloquently that we, looking back, may rediscover it.[15]

This clearly refers to Freud's theory of the trauma. But why should the camera be able to spot the trace left by the original trauma making it possible for us to predict retrospectively the future disaster? Benjamin seems to indicate that it may be the camera's inability to censor the 'inconspicuous spot': 'For it is another nature that speaks to the camera than to the eye: other in the sense that a space informed by human consciousness gives way to a space informed by the unconscious.'[16] Unfortunately, this promising suggestion then quickly deteriorates into Benjamin's familiar and disappointing parallel between the technical devices of photography (the fraction of a second, enlargement and so on) which 'reveal secrets' opening up an 'optical unconscious', just as the techniques of psychoanalysis reveal the instinctual unconscious.[17] But do the photographs of Muybridge and Marey give us insight into an unconscious in anything like a Freudian sense? I doubt it. Rosalind Krauss, in her recent book *The Optical Unconscious* points out the difficulty of thinking of the visual field as having an unconscious.[18] Yet, as I will try to show, when we understand, with Lacan, how the Real appears in the visual field as the Gaze, the difficulty unravels. In my view, this is what Barthes proposes in *Camera Lucida*.

Before moving on to consider the Lacanian conception of the Gaze, we need to address the psychoanalytic understanding of trauma and Barthes's appropriation of it. There is little point in pausing too long here, however, because the job has already been thoroughly done by Andrew Brown in his monograph called *Roland Barthes: the Figures of Writing* which closes with a chapter simply called 'The Trauma'.[19] For Freud, the trauma is linked to what he termed the primal scene: the child witnesses or experiences something at an age too young to comprehend its meaning. This unassimilable memory is preserved until at a later date another, perhaps innocuous, event occurs which recalls the first and floods it with sexual meaning. By a process of 'deferred action', then, the childhood experience becomes traumatic. A good example of this process is given in Freud's case study known as 'The Wolf Man' (1918 [1914]).[20] The adult patient reports to Freud a frightening dream he had at five years old: wolves were sitting motionless in the branches of a tree outside his bedroom window staring at him. Freud suggests that the impact of the dream derives from a much earlier impression although key aspects of that event are reversed and filtered through fairy tales. As an infant, he had woken and stared transfixed at a scene of violent motion — his parents copulating 'in the manner of animals'. The unconscious recollection of such a scene would have confirmed the reality of castration once that eventuality had become a burning issue for the boy. The traumatic primal scene can hardly be said to have taken place as the trauma lags so far behind the event. Lacan adds to this that the trauma is Real in so far as it remains unsymbolizable — a kernel of nonsense at the heart of the subject.

Camera Lucida is structured around the idea of the trauma. The recent death of his mother, we may suppose, had reactivated in Barthes the original wound of separation. In one of the fragments of *A Lover's Discourse*, he recalls his intense suffering as a child: 'interminable days, abandoned days, when the mother was working away'.[21] His search for her authentic image, then, is less a matter of solace than of repetition compulsion.

As Brown rightly points out, there is a close connection between the theory of the trauma and the aesthetics of shock.[22] For Benjamin, traditional art was for the most part ego-sustaining; it kept its distance and this constituted its aura. But now that we are bombarded from all sides by the unassimilable shocks of modern life, our psyches require something beyond the pleasure principle. We subject ourselves to the shock effects of violent cinema images, for example, as a way of 'binding' threatening stimuli and of building up a protective 'crust' (Freud's terms). The short strip of amateur film which recorded Kennedy's death is endlessly replayed to a nation which cannot overcome its trauma. Yet it would be very misleading to assimilate the shock effects of Benjamin's anti-auratic art to Barthes's traumatic photographs. The sections of *A Short History of Photography* which clearly interested Barthes were those that dealt with our response to auratic, early photography with its atmospheric effect of 'light struggling out of darkness'.[23] Barthes seems interested in restoring the shock of precisely those photographs and ironically he uses Benjamin to do it. Photography is particularly susceptible to this treatment because, as Barthes points out, it has an inherently 'traumatic' structure: I witness something in the past by 'deferred action' (p. 10). Brown draws attention to an interesting passage from Freud's *Moses and Monotheism* where an analogy is drawn between photographic and psychic deferred action: the latter may be made 'more comprehensible by comparing it with a photographic exposure which can be developed after any interval of time and transformed into a picture'.[24] In order to assess what is distinctive about Barthes's notion of the traumatic photograph we have to understand his theory of the punctum.

A fair portion of *Camera Lucida* is taken up with a discussion of the distinction Barthes makes between two fundamentally different types of interest we take in photography. The 'studium' is a generalized interest, pleasure or concern we might take in a photo. Photographs with a studium we judge 'good'. But in some photographs there also lurks a detail, a punctum, which takes the viewer by surprise, 'pricks' him or her, and alters the sense of the image. The detail does not promote a re-interpretation which would subsume it dialectically and integrate it into the whole; it shares with the trauma and Lacan's Real an uncoded, unassimilable quality. It is unnamable and, writes Barthes, 'what I can name cannot really prick me. The incapacity to name is a good symptom of disturbance.' (p. 51) In the discussion of one photograph which has this lacerating detail for Barthes, he first lights on a woman's strapped shoes (p. 39) and then, like an analysand working through screen memories toward the original trauma, shifts to her necklace, which reminds him of one worn by his maiden Aunt but since her death kept shut up in a jewellery box (p. 53). Jane Gallup's interesting discussion of Barthes's distinction in her *Thinking Through the Body* emphasizes the way a photograph with only a studium stays put within the confines of the picture — its coherence is entirely internal. In contrast, the punctum breaks up that coherence bursting through the frame and plane. As a consequence the photograph endowed with a punctum has a 'blind field', something equivalent to what is masked on the edges of the cinema image (p. 59). There is, then, a kind of symmetry between the photograph's and the subject's openness to alterity.[25]

Barthes's studium/punctum distinction recalls aspects of his earlier essay on stills from Eisenstein's films. In 'The Third Meaning' (1970) he pointed to the presence in these stills of an 'obtuse' meaning which exceeds the 'obvious' signification of symbolism and narrative. Certain details 'hold' or touch him, but without his being able to say why.[26] They remain mute signifiers and open on to the field of *signifiance* as understood by Kristeva.[27] Although there may be some overlap between the obtuse meaning and the punctum, we should also be alerted to the difference between them by the fact that the concepts have exactly opposite connotations of blunt and sharp. The saving bluntness of the third meaning, its ungraspable resistance to conceptual consumption, preserves the image–text from any fixity of interpretation. The sharpness of the punctum, on the other hand, cuts through the deliberate decorum of the pose and the prop and reactivates a trauma. While one implies an acknowledgement of subjective loss, the other actually awakens the Real of that loss. It is perhaps pertinent that *Camera Lucida* is dominated by the genre of portrait photography in which the question of the presence/absence of the represented subject is most insistent.

The Gaze

Barthes's opposition between the studium and the punctum of photographs can be further elucidated by reference to Lacan's critique in *The Four Fundamental Concepts* of classical optics and perspective construction. The point of carrying out the critique is to explode the idealist illusion of 'seeing oneself seeing oneself' (p. 83), that is, the optical equivalent of the illusion of self-reflective consciousness. More than once Lacan here acknowledges his indebtedness to Merleau-Ponty, and particularly to a posthumous work which had just appeared: *The Visible and the Invisible* (1964). He makes specific reference to a chapter of that book called 'The Intertwining — the Chiasm' where the philosopher is trying to show that our own corporeality, making us objects of sight in the world, is the necessary condition of our being subjects of sight.[28] While I look at things, I am looked at. My activity, then, is equally a passivity. Visual perception, tied to the body, is perspectival and partial. As Lacan observes, 'I see only from one point, but in my existence I am looked at from all sides' (p. 72). Merleau-Ponty's reflections on vision helped Lacan to formulate his sense of the necessary pre-existence of the Gaze which, in a visual register, shows the subject as constituted by the desire of the Other. The subject is thus decentred in relation to any originary point of sight. It should be noted in this context that the traffic between the two thinkers was two-way: Merleau-Ponty used Lacan's 1949 essay 'The Mirror Stage' in formulating his conception of the 'visible seer'.

A key characteristic of our relation to the studium of a photograph is our confident self-possession: we are conscious and in control of our interest. Or, as Barthes puts it, 'I invest the field of the Studium with my sovereign consciousness.' (p. 26). This sort of perception has similarities with geometral perspective in which a single point of sight inaugurates and organizes the field. For Lacan, this system is the optical equivalent of the classical concept of consciousness as formulated by Descartes; the Cartesian subject, he notes, 'is itself a sort of geometral point.' (p. 86) And this conception of self-reflective consciousness is founded on a misrecognition which in the visual register would be called a 'scotoma', that is, a blanking out of something that is traumatic. What is blanked out, in either case, is the fact that the subject is not just a subject of consciousness, but also a subject of desire. This subject, which can only be heard in the lacunae of discourse, can only be glimpsed in the gaze. My suggestion is that Barthes's punctum is equivalent to Lacan's gaze or, in other words, to that which is elided in classical optics. Because, as Lacan argues, desire is constituted by a lack (separation from the mother, symbolic castration), that lack as gaze inevitably looms up in the visual field and disorganizes it (p. 89). The punctum, as we have seen, also reverses the direction of the lines of sight and disorganizes the visual field, erupting into the network of signifiers that constitute 'reality'. 'This time it is not I who seek it out, it is this element which rises from the scene, shoots out of it like an arrow, and pierces me.' (p. 26) The terms Barthes uses to describe this experience (prick, wound, hole) clearly suggest their relation to lack.

Lacan's discussion of anamorphosis serves to illustrate the disparity between one's position as sovereign subject of sight (studium) and as object of the gaze (or the punctum). From an orthodox position, the viewer of Holbein's *Ambassadors* shares their confidence and vanity; he is master of all he surveys. But something incomprehensible, a shadowy phallic shape, floats in the foreground. Only when one starts to leave the room and casts an oblique glance back does the shape resolve itself into a human skull. 'It reflects our own nothingness, in the figure of the death's head.' (p. 92) In other words, only when the position of illusory mastery is vacated does the gaze come into full view. The two positions are mutually exclusive: the world of representation is given only if the immediacy of the Real is sacrificed, and the Real is glimpsed only when the vanity of the world conceived as my representation is renounced. There is, then, a blind spot in the orthodox perceptual field which Lacan calls the stain (*la tache*), defined, like the gaze, as 'that which always escapes from the grasp of that form of vision that is satisfied with itself in imagining itself as consciousness' (p. 75). This term is taken up by Barthes in one of his definitions of the punctum: 'For punctum is also a sting, speck (*petite tache*), cut, little hole — and also a cast of the die. A photograph's punctum is the accident which pricks me.' (p. 27, french p. 49) This same 'spot', it seems, also makes an appearance in a passage from the book *Working Space* (1986) by the American artist Frank Stella, helpfully cited by Malcolm Bowie: the painter 'worries that there is something that he cannot see, something that is eluding him . . . a dark spot.'[29] It would seem that this stain or spot must be approached indirectly, viewed awry, glancingly, without conscious deliberation. One requires visual equivalents of the strategies of indirection invented by Freud to approach the unconscious — dreams, free association, transference. As Lacan notes, 'It is not, after all, for nothing that analysis is not carried out face to face.' (p. 78)

The gaze as stain stresses the opacity and negativity of that which is both object and cause of the scopic drive. This contrasts with the transparency and fullness of vision associated with the Imaginary register's specular mirroring of the ego. The difference is attributable to the fact the gaze or stain does not represent the ego, but rather gestures toward the unrepresentable subject. It reflects not the body-image as idealized, coherent and coordinated, but the subject as castrated and in the grip of desire.[30] In order better to understand the way in which this subject can be shown, it is necessary to consider Lacan's formulation of the '*objet petit a*'. His account of the constitution of the subject involves a series of painful self-alienations which are described almost as bodily auto-mutilations. One's very birth involves the casting off of a vital part of the organism, the placenta. Then one is weaned from the breast, understood by the infant as co-extensive with the body. One 'gives up' urine and faeces. Finally, symbolic castration seals one's fate as a desiring subject haunted by lack and retrospectively turns all the other infantile experiences of loss into forms of castration. In each case a cut is made which initiates both an erotogenic zone (lips, rim of anus, tip of penis, slit of eyelids) and an object (nipple, faeces, urinary flow, phallus as imaginary object, 'the phoneme, the gaze, the voice — the nothing').[31] The 'part objects' formed by the cut are the *objets petits a*. '*The objet a* is something from which the subject, in order to constitute itself, has separated itself off as organ. This serves as a symbol of lack, that is to say, of the phallus, not as such, but in so far as it is lacking.' (p. 103) The gaze as *objet petit a* must refer to the lost parental gaze from which the infant so ardently sought recognition. These lost morsels of flesh, hollowed out bits of one's being, play a critical role in Lacan's understanding of the subject's relation to the world. Were it not for them, we would be caught between the specular idealizations of the Imaginary and the impersonal law of the Symbolic.

Light

Lacan's references to visual art in *The Four Fundamental Concepts* are mostly taken from the history of painting. He does mention photography once, however, though admittedly in a context which indicates that we are not supposed to take it literally. He is insisting on the externality of the gaze which has the effect of turning me into a picture.

> What determines me, at the most profound level, in the visible, is the gaze that is outside. It is through the gaze that I enter light and it is from the gaze that I receive its effects. Hence it comes about that the gaze is the instrument through which light is embodied and through which — if you will allow me to use the word, as I often do, in a fragmented form — I am photo-graphed. (p. 106)

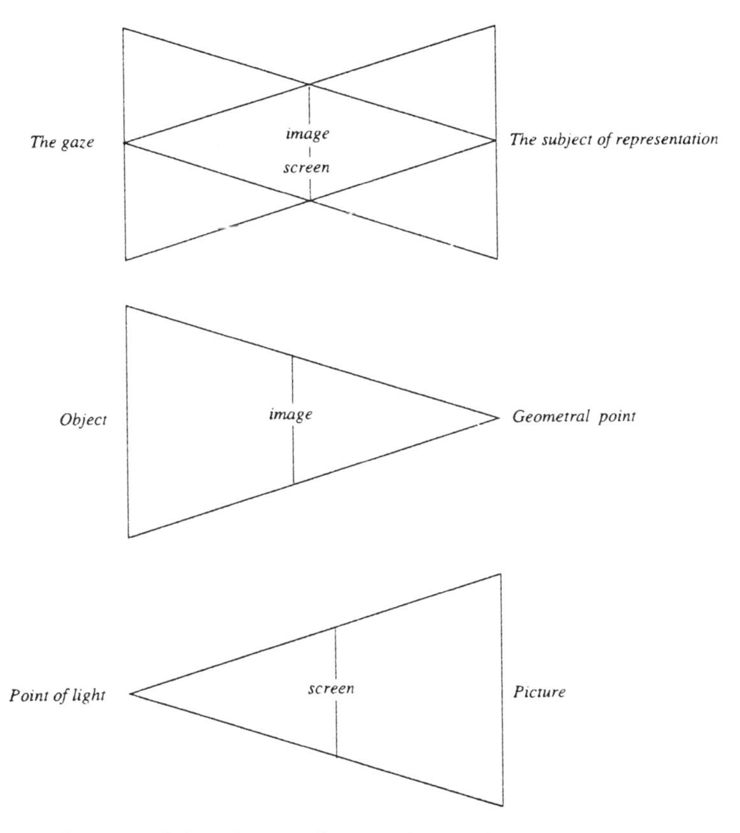

65 Lacan's diagram of the Chiasm of Vision from *The Four Fundamental Concepts of Psycho-analysis*

If traditional optics can be represented by a triangular diagram showing an eye at the geometral point which views an image correlated to an object, then the geometral point is where the ego's eye is installed (plate 65). It is essentially an Albertian model of representation, transposed into a Kantian model of experience in which phenomena are correlated with (unknowable) noumena. This is the story consciousness tells itself about vision. But the unconscious also sees, throwing onto a screen its projected desires, fantasies and fears. The diagram of geometral perspective must accordingly be intersected by an inverted triangle showing a point of light projecting a picture onto a screen. While the subject of representation is figured as a neat point, from the perspective of the gaze (point of light) the subject is represented as the base of a triangle — anamorphically distorted and blurred. If the subject is to appear in the picture, it must be as a screen casting a shadow — like a prisoner in Plato's cave, creating a blind spot in the passing spectacle.

Lacan insists that the point of light is outside: 'In the scopic field, the gaze is outside, I am looked at, that is to say, I am a picture.' (p. 106) This insistence is consistent with Lacan's conception of the unconscious as an intersubjective relation (desire is the desire of the Other) and his view of the subject as radically split by the castrating intervention of the register of the Symbolic. Lacan suggests that we can observe this fracturing even in the animal kingdom in the phenomenon of display when an animal swells or grimaces, makes itself into a semblance, to ward off its predator (p. 107). But this split can be observed, not just in the mimicry of intimidation, but also in camouflage. An insect, for example, can accommodate itself so well in its environment that it becomes invisible. Roger Caillois's essay on mimicry in the Surrealist magazine *Minotaure* (much admired by Lacan), proposed that this activity amounts to a kind of death drive in which the organism loses its integrity and is swallowed up by space.[32]

The composite diagram of visuality also makes clear the reversibility of the positions of object and subject produced by this intersubjectivity and splitting. Lacan illustrates this point with an amusing anecdote about his student days when he joined working fishermen for the summer. One of the fishermen had pointed to a floating sardine can glinting in the sun and joked, 'See that sardine can? Well, it doesn't see you!' But it did; Lacan has been photo-graphed and suddenly feels very ill at ease in the picture (p. 95). This reversal of subject and object is facilitated by the phenomenological fact that 'I see *outside*' or, to put it another way, 'perception is on the objects that it apprehends.' (p. 88)

Barthes often acknowledges this externality and passivity in relation to the punctum. We have already seen how, for him, 'it fills the sight by force.' (p. 91) There is also a discussion, useful in this context, about posing in front of the camera. Posing involves putting on a look drawn from the image repertoire: 'I transform myself in advance into an image.' (p. 10) But then, suddenly, something intervenes which shatters this ego-protecting shield. The shutter clicks and 'I then experience a micro-version of death,' the sound 'breaking through the mortiferous layer of the pose' (pp. 14–15). Here is perhaps an example of an aural punctum finding a chink in the armour of the Imaginary.

Another discussion which bears on Lacan's sense of being photo-graphed comes when Barthes is stressing the greater importance of chemistry for photography over that of its relation to the camera obscura. The optical device does not fix the image and it is the magic of light-sensitive paper that gives the photograph its essential nature as a 'that-has-been':

> The photograph is literally an emanation of the referent. From a real body which was there, proceed radiations which ultimately touch me, who am here . . . A sort of umbilical cord links the body of the photographed thing to my gaze: light, though impalpable, is here a carnal medium, a skin I share with anyone who has been photographed. (p. 81)

This passage also connects with the chapter in Lacan's book called 'Line and Light'. Here again geometral optics is the target of criticism, but now its inadequacy as a theory of vision is attributed to the fact that what it calls rays of light can easily be figured as threads or sticks. It is really a spatial mapping which even a blind man could comprehend and so it would seem to miss entirely what is essential about vision. As Rosalind Krauss points out, the contrast Lacan is making is that between a tactile visuality that is palpably obvious and easily mastered and an optical visuality or 'atmospheric surround' in which the viewer, no longer a surveyor, is 'caught within the onrush of light'.[33] As Lacan observes: 'Light may travel in a straight line, but it is refracted, diffused, it floods, it fills — the eye is a sort of bowl — it flows over, too.' (p. 94) What both Lacan and Barthes wish to express is the chiasm of vision: I may see objects, but I am also enveloped by a light or gaze which unsettles the position I want to occupy as source of the coordinates of sight.

Tame or Mad?

Barthes's essay closes with a sad reflection on the inevitable banalization of the photograph in a society where they come so thick and fast that none can have the special force that Barthes describes. With an apparent glance sideways at Baudrillard,[34] he describes the United States as a society so dominated by images that the relation of image to subject is reversed and people tailor themselves to the stereotypical image repertoire. Lacan is equally concerned about what he called 'imaginary capture', but remarks that only the human subject is not completely caught up in it. Rather, 'he maps himself in it. How? He isolates the function of the screen and plays with it.' (p. 107) The screen which, as we saw, is interposed between the gaze and the picture of the subject, might be interpreted as the cultural image repertoire. As Kaja Silverman points out, the possibility of playing with the screen or mask has political implications for those 'attempts at a collective self-redefinition which rely upon masquerade, parody, inversion and bricolage . . .'.[35]

In the chapters called 'The Line and Light' and 'What is a Picture?' Lacan broaches the question of the function of art from the point of view of psychoanalysis. The artist, he says, wants to present himself as subject, as gaze, and the gaze is there, even in paintings with no pair of eyes, in what we call style: there is 'something so specific to each of the painters that you will feel the presence of the gaze'. (p. 101) If, as I have suggested, the *objet petit a* is that (missing) morsel of one's being outside symbolic matrixes and public images, then it follows that the *objet petit a* as gaze would inhere in that individuality of style. Lacan also considers the function of art from the spectator's side. Painting, he says, is an opportunity 'to lay down one's gaze' and he calls this effect the '*dompte-regard*', the tamed gaze and adds, 'This is the pacifying, Apollonian, effect of painting.' (p. 101) Art offers something for the eye and gives the spectator a sense of mastery in relation to the visual field and a sublimated pleasure that compensates for instinctual renunciation (p. 111). Yet, he continues, there is a whole field of painting, Expressionist for example, which answers the scopic drive — it offers something for the gaze. The difference between these two functions is illustrated by the retelling of the classical tale of the competition between Zeuxis and Parrhasios. Zeuxis deceived the eye of a bird who flew down to peck on his painted grapes, but Parrhasios, in reply, painted a veil which incited Zeuxis to ask, 'What have you painted behind it?'

For Lacan, the latter is the true case of trompe l'oeil — a triumph of the gaze over the eye (pp. 103, 111–112). The veil animates the desire of the viewer and its full effect is only felt when one realizes that nothing lies behind it.

Do *dompte-regard* and *trompe l'oeil* correspond to what Barthes calls tame and mad receptions of photography? I think so, but with the difference that Lacan seems to accept the legitimacy or psychic value of both functions, whereas Barthes challenges us to choose one stance or the other, tame or mad:

> Such are the two ways of the Photograph. The choice is mine: to subject its spectacle to the civilized code of perfect illusions, or to confront in it the wakening of intractable reality. (p. 119)

These are the last lines of the book. A retrospective glance through the plates reminds one that the frontispiece reproduces a strange colour photograph of an interior showing only thin curtains drawn against a brilliant light.

Margaret Iversen
University of Essex

Notes

1 Roland Barthes, *Camera Lucida: Reflections on Photography*, New York, 1981; trans. of *La chambre claire: Note sur la photographie*, Paris, 1980. All subsequent page references to this book will appear in parenthesis in the text.

2 Jacques Lacan, *The Four Fundamental Concepts of Psycho-Analysis*, ed. Jacques-Alain Miller, trans. Alan Sheridan, Harmondsworth; trans. of *le Séminaire de Jacques Lacan, Livre XI, 'Les quatre concepts fondamentaux de la psychanalyse'*, Paris, 1973. All subsequent page references to this book will appear in parenthesis in the text.

3 Slovoj Žižek, *Looking Awry: An Introduction to Jacques Lacan through Popular Culture*, Cambridge and London, 1991; Malcolm Bowie, *Freud, Proust and Lacan: Theory as Fiction*, Cambridge, 1987; Mary Kelly, *Post-partum Document*, London and Boston, 1983 and *Interim*, The New Museum of Contemporary Art, New York, 1990. See also Parveen Adams, 'Mary Kelly's *Interim* and the Discourse of the Analyst', *October*, no. 58, Fall 1991, pp. 81–96. The whole issue of *October* edited by Adams is devoted to 'Rendering the Real'.

4 J.-P. Sartre, *L'Imaginaire: Psychologie phénoménologique de l'imagination*, Paris, 1940; trans., *The Psychology of Imagination*, New York, 1991.

5 R. Barthes, *The Pleasure of the Text*, New York, trans. Richard Miller, 1975 (1973). See also G. Bataille, *Eroticism*, trans. Mary Dalwood, London, 1987; and J. Mitchell and J. Rose (eds.), *Feminine Sexuality: Jacques Lacan and the école freudienne*, London, 1982.

6 S. Freud, 'Beyond the Pleasure Principle', *Pelican Freud Library*, vol. 11: *On Metapsychology: The Theory of Psychoanalysis*, pp. 269–338; *Standard Edition*, vol. 14, pp. 237–58. See also helpful discussions of the pleasure principle, the death drive and related concepts in J. Laplanche and J.-B. Pontalis, *The Language of Psycho-analysis*, London, 1980.

7 ibid., pp. 275 ff.

8 ibid., p. 294.

9 J. Lacan, 'Subversion of the Subject', *Écrits: A Selection*, trans. Alan Sheridan, London, 1977.

10 S. Freud, 'The Uncanny' (1919), *Pelican Freud Library*, vol. 14: *Art and Literature*, pp. 335–76; *Standard Edition*, vol. 17, pp. 217–52.

11 S. Freud, *The Interpretation of Dreams*, *Pelican Freud Library*, vol. 4, pp. 652 ff, and Lacan, op. cit., 1979, pp. 34 ff and 56 ff.

12 S. Freud, 'Beyond the Pleasure Principle', op. cit., pp. 283–7.

13 W. Benjamin, 'A Small History of Photography', *One-Way Street and Other Writings*, trans. E. Jephott and K. Shorter, London, 1979, pp. 240–57. Another text important for Barthes, but not discussed here, was Susan Sontag, *On Photography*, New

York, 1973.
14 ibid., pp. 242–3.
15 ibid.
16 ibid.
17 ibid.
18 Rosalind Krauss, *The Optical Unconscious*, Cambridge, Mass., 1993, p. 178.
19 Andrew Brown, *Roland Barthes: The Figures of Writing*, Oxford, 1992, pp. 236–84. There are many monographs devoted to Barthes. I will mention only A. Lavers, *Roland Barthes: Structuralism and After*, London, 1982; M. Moriarty, *Roland Barthes*, Oxford, 1991; S. Ungar, *Roland Barthes: The Professor of Desire*, Lincoln, Nebraska, 1983. Unfortunately, Martin Jay's book *Downcast Eyes: The Denigration of Vision in Twentieth-Century French Thought*, Berkeley, 1993, which has chapters devoted to Lacan and Barthes, did not reach these shores in time to be taken into account here.
20 S. Freud, 'From the History of an Infantile Neurosis' (the 'Wolf Man') (1918 [1914]), *Pelican Freud Library*, vol. 9: *Case Histories II*, pp. 259 ff; *Standard Edition*, vol. 17, pp. 1–122.
21 R. Barthes, *A Lover's Discourse: Fragments*, trans. Richard Howard, New York, 1978.
22 A. Brown, *Roland Barthes*, op. cit., p. 275 ff.
23 W. Benjamin, 'A Small History of Photography', op. cit., p. 248.
24 ibid., p. 270; S. Freud, 'Moses and Monotheisim', *Pelican Freud Library*, vol. 13: *The Origins of Religion*, p.374.
25 Jane Gallup, *Thinking Through the Body*, New York, 1980, pp. 151–5. Norman Bryson's distinction in the chapter called 'The Gaze and the Glance' of his *Vision and Painting: The Logic of the Gaze*, New Haven and London, 1983, has affinities with Barthes's Studium/Punctum.
26 R. Barthes, 'The Third Meaning: Research Notes on Some Eisenstein Stills', *Image/Music/Text*, trans. S. Heath, New York, 1977, pp. 52–68. The theory of the punctum is more nearly approximated in a still earlier essay on photography, 'The Photographic Message' (1961), where Barthes considers the possibility of a photograph without connotation: 'If such a [pure] denotation exists, it is perhaps not at the level of what ordinary language calls the insignificant, the neutral, the objective, but, on the contrary, at the level of absolutely traumatic images', in *Image/Music/Text*, p. 30.
27 J. Kristeva, *Revolution in Poetic Language*, trans. Margaret Waller, New York, 1984 (1974), p. 17. See Victor Burgin, 'Re-reading *Camera Lucida*' and his discussion of photography and *significance*, in *The End of Art Theory: Criticism and Postmodernity*, London, 1986, pp. 71–95.
28 M. Merleau-Ponty, *The Visible and the Invisible*, ed. Claude Lefort, trans. Alphonso Lingis, Evanston, 1968, pp. 130–55.
29 Malcolm Bowie, *Lacan*, London, 1991, p.169; Frank Stella, *Working Space*, Cambridge, Mass. and London, 1986, pp. 6–9. Bataille's notion of '*la tache aveugle*' is also relevant here. See Denis Hollier's illuminating discussion of it in *Against Architecture*, Cambridge and London, 1989, pp. 94–8.
30 Joan Copjec reads the analysis of vision (and particularly the 'sardine can' anecdote) in *The Four Fundamental Concepts* as a revised version of the mirror stage, which in some ways it clearly is. I am concerned, however, to preserve as distinct moments the mirror stage and the subject's relation to the Real in the visible even if there are overlaps. Copjec, 'The Orthopsychic Subject: Film Theory and the Reception of Lacan', *October*, no. 49, Summer 1989, pp. 53–71. The anecdote is an interesting variation on the famous one told by Sartre in *Being and Nothingness*, to which Lacan refers, where a voyeur bent over a keyhole thinks he hears footsteps and is covered in shame. Sartre writes that 'this changes all the perspective, the lines of force, of my world' in J.-P. Sartre, *Being and Nothingness: An Essay on Phenomenological Ontology*, trans. Hazel Barnes, London, 1969, p. 277.
31 J. Lacan, *Écrits*, op. cit., p. 315.
32 R. Caillois, 'Mimicry and Legendary Psychasthenia', trans. John Shepley, *October*, no. 31, Winter 1984, pp. 17–32. Originally published as 'Mimétisme et psychasthénie légendaire', *Minotaure*, no. 7, June 1935.
33 R. Krauss, op. cit., p. 33.
34 See, for example, Jean Baudrillard, *Simulations*, trans. P. Foss, P. Patton and P. Beitchman, 1983.
35 Kaja Silverman, 'Male Subjectivity at the Margins', New York and London, 1992, pp. 149–50.
36 For a quite different interpretation of Lacan on painting, see Jonathan Scott Lee, *Jacques Lacan*, Amherst, 1990, pp. 159–61.

Art History ISSN 0141-6790 Vol. 17 No. 3 September 1994 pp. 464–504

REVIEW ARTICLES

'Polly Put the Kettle On'

Lindsay Smith

Painting Women: Victorian Women Artists by *Deborah Cherry*, London: Routledge, 1993, 275 pp., 47 b. & w. illus., £40.00 hdbk, £12.99 pbk

The potentials afforded by rituals of tea-drinking were not lost on Victorian women. As Isabella Beeton's *Book of Household Management* (1861) testified, the national beverage required 'very little art' providing the water was 'actually *boiling*'.[1] In Mary Elizabeth Braddon's novel *Lady Audley's Secret* (serialized in 1861–2) the bigamous heroine Lucy Audley is described as bewitchingly controlled in her madness as she pours tea for herself and two other women in her boudoir. In a novel concerning the categorizations of female 'madness' as either inherited or socially produced, Braddon makes ironic the control of tea-pouring as a 'feminine' magic indicative of a wider control on the part of a woman. Lady Audley does more than merely 'wet her whistle', and making the infusion is quite a business, according to the narrator's disquisition upon tea, which we are certainly not meant to take straight:

> She looked very pretty and innocent, seated behind the graceful group of delicate opal china and glittering silver. Surely a pretty women never looks prettier than when making tea. The most feminine and most domestic of all occupations imparts a magic harmony to her every movement, a witchery to her every glance. The floating mists from the boiling liquid in which she infuses the soothing herbs, whose secrets are known to her alone, envelop her in a cloud of scented vapour, through which she seems a social fairy, weaving potent spells with Gunpowder and Bohea. At the tea-table she reigns omnipotent, unapproachable. What do men know of the mysterious beverage? Read how poor Hazlitt made his tea, and shudder at the dreadful barbarism. How clumsily the wretched creatures attempt to assist the witch president of the tea-tray; how hopelessly they hold the kettle, how continually they imperil the frail cups and saucers, or the taper hands of the priestess. To do away with the tea-table is to rob woman of her legitimate empire.[2]

The Victorian artist sisters Sophia and Ellen Beale who, during the late 1850s and early 1860s, enjoyed considerable freedom walking unchaperoned in London, visiting museums and art schools, and having use of their own recreation room separate from the regular domestic space of the household, also recorded the significance of a singing kettle:

> After painting at the studio, or the Galleries, we return here and bring our friends to partake of a dish of tea . . . We are not beholden to the domestic

> authorities as we make our own tea in our own pot, boiling our own kettle on our own hearth, and we toast our own muffins at our own fire.[3]

For the Beales, the dependency generally assigned to the domestic realm can be turned around, to provide autonomy. The notion of simple polarized spheres (man belonging to the public, woman to the private) is challenged, for the painters put an investment in the control of the domestic such that boiling one's own kettle on one's own hearth is of quite a different order from having someone boil it. Freedom from the regime of the bourgeois household can be achieved within that very space; it is all a question of who puts the kettle on, and of who plays Sukey.

Along the same lines, Jane Bowkett's painting *Preparing Tea* (1860s) juxtaposes a newly industrialized space outside a window (belching chimney and train snaking through the landscape) with the cosy interior glow of the hearth. A mother looks out of the window onto an urban scene as she and her young daughter are engaged in toasting and buttering bread; a second daughter appears in the doorway with a pair of gentleman's slippers. As is frequently the case in paintings (and indeed combination photographs) of the period of domestic interiors, the hearth itself is barely visible in the composition. Here, it is present only in a reflected glow upon the lounging girl holding a toasting fork and in the smug demeanour of the family cat. We do not need to see the kettle to know that it hums off-centre-stage, but at first glance we have a far cry from Sophia and Ellen Beale's scenario; for even though there is no domestic authority present, the slippers wrest our attention from the females themselves to their anticipation of an absent man.

Deborah Cherry's *Painting Women*, which develops from the catalogue of the exhibition of the same title at Rochdale Art Gallery (1987), takes representations of domesticity as its seventh chapter and locates Bowkett's painting within the terms of an absent masculinity defined by its domestically occupied opposite, as bringing together 'discourses on domestic femininity and the moral topography of the city'. (p.134) Meaning is constructed, for Cherry, around the expectation of the father returning home from the world of commerce to the comfort of home. She identifies 'the tea-table and the fireside [as] two of the most prevalent signs of domestic felicity in the 1860s' and, by extension, the image as a whole as suggesting a 'consolidation of the differences between outside/inside, commerce/domesticity, masculinity/femininity' (p.135). Her reading regards all activity depicted as geared to, and explained by, the imminent arrival of the patriarch, or in the words of her earlier catalogue, as showing that 'femininity exists for masculinity.' But while the mother might well be poised looking out of the window at the approaching train, the daughter in the foreground is engrossed in toasting and, for all we know, her ardent watching is preventing a kettle from boiling. With pinafore slipping from her left shoulder, she appears oblivious to the rest, and we attend to her deliberation just as much as we do to the distraction of the mother. The representation of a child's pleasure is not subordinate in the picture to other 'weightier' topics, nor can that pleasure be said primarily to serve the purpose of consolidating a determinate concept of masculinity.

This spell of hearth calls into question Cherry's assertion that 'the composition organizes clearly demarcated spaces and identities for masculinity and femininity: femininity is pictorialized as domesticity, dependence and familial service whereas masculinity is outside the home and at the same time the pivot for its social activities and kinship relations.' (p.135) Cherry, of course, is partially right. Yet while the painting brings together an inside and an outside, within the inside things are going on that are not entirely reducible to categories of masculinity and femininity as discrete and entirely knowable. The private is not presented unquestionably as defined by the public. There is a celebration of hearth here, not so far removed from that of Sophia and Ellen Beale, that cannot be read as complicitous with a patriarchal division of spheres, with a polarity in which one term is invariably and unproblematically privileged over the other.

As this example suggests, the ideology of separate spheres that underpins the whole of Cherry's argument is not perhaps the most useful model by which to approach the work of nineteenth-century women painters. In itself, their identification of subtle permeations within the domestic realm (such as the Beales' appropriation of hearth) indicates that a discussion of women's painting in the context of its production should not simply begin from the premise of a desire to overthrow the tyranny of the domestic by appearance in public life, or by the aspiration to a civic identity. Instead, it should also re-address the cardinal function of the hearth (as linchpin of separate spheres) in gender politics of the period. While the first part of *Painting Women* provides invaluable historical material on the inter-relations between and working habits of a large number of women artists, attending in particular to the dynamics of daughters, wives and sisters in artists' families, to spinsterhood and women's partnerships, to constructions of sexual difference in art training for women and in art institutions and, briefly, to the participation of women artists in the women's movements, discussions of paintings in the second part show to what extent representations of domesticity (and there are many of them) are regarded as ultimately less complex than, say, historical subjects, because they fail to transgress their position as subordinate term in the public/private binary. That woman is required to occupy the position of guardian of the province of hearth testifies to its importance in social life in constructions of masculinity; but it does not mean that there is nothing in the hearth for women themselves. That women painters, writers, photographers take up the hearth as a point of political re-definition demonstrates its centrality to discourses of the period in its multi-valent meanings.

Strict dualities are subject to recurrent questionings in Cherry's book, but nonetheless they are inflected strongly throughout in the fundamental aim of the project to show the *difference* of women's painting, to determine the ways in which nineteenth-century women's paintings are distinct from those of nineteenth-century men. *Painting Women* begins and ends with two questions: 'What are the differences, then, of women's works? And how have they been differently perceived, treated and located in the institutions of culture and the histories of art?' Potentially, these are interesting considerations. The problem is, however, that they should be one question if we are to take up the primary theoretical models the author proposes (an uneven pairing of big books by Foucault, with a single review essay by Elizabeth Cowie).[4] How, without recourse to a humanist narrative (which the book seeks to deny), can there be a distinction between a concept of the differences of women's works and of how they have been differently perceived? For the second question attributes to the first an absolute and stable point of reference. The suggestion, in spite of claims to the contrary, is one of essential retrievable difference from paintings by men, along with a second category of subjective perceptions of that difference.

Cherry's interest is in wholesale subversion; the book has little time for that unsettling that can be brought to bear within a binary when a strict overturning of it might not be on the cards. Although she acknowledges the contradiction of women painting scenes of dependency from the empowered position of artist, Cherry seems not to want us to indulge ourselves as consumers of paintings of afternoon tea because she considers works such as Edith Hayllar's *Feeding the Swans* (1889) first and foremost as 'participat[ing] in the containment of the perceived crisis in the social organization of alterity brought about by women's paid employment, feminist "speaking out" against masculine sexuality and marriage . . . ' (p.140) (Who is fixing meaning here?) For me, the fact that paintings by women show women drinking tea means that the artists were not presenting a simple model of a consumer of Braddon's mysterious beverage. Paintings of women innocuously doing nothing in the home offer rich possibilities for re-conceptualizing their stake (and the stake attributed to them by patriarchal society) in the domestic. To be shown in the process of being a dutiful wife and mother is to be at a far removal from the actual practice of the woman painter as cultural producer; the going against type necessary in order to produce the painting is patently evident in the women rendered as cultural consumer. The position of women as producers is both revealed and obscured in their depiction of themselves primarily as consumers, whether it be of French novels or crumpets.

By extension, and precisely because of an assumed harmless compatibility with tea-drinking, still life would seem a consummate genre by which women could contest ascribed social roles, and it affords a viewer space to re-conceptualize the place of the genre within the wider terms of hierarchies of representation. *Painting Women*, however, pays scant attention to this genre (in spite of the tempting second plate of Eloise Stannard's *Strawberries on a Cabbage Leaf with a Flower Pot Behind*, 1881, with its wasp-ravaged fruit) because of its historical position as an acceptable and safe domain for women artists. It would seem important, if only initially because less predictable, to reclaim the domain of still life as a genre traditionally ascribed to women. While the book does marginally more than the original catalogue which saw still life as simply a visual manifestation of coercion ('in the middle-class home bowls of flowers were part of the ordering of respectable womanhood') and of flagrant 'exploitation by a prosperous middle class of rural labour', it primarily regards the genre as a sanctioned one for women; one that could be aligned with feminine accomplishment and regarded as an excuse to prevent women from painting landscape and from seeking subject matter outside the home. Yet still life cannot be unproblematically ascribed to the invalid or the constitutionally less robust, as negating its potentialities as medium.

The painting of still life, as Stephen Bann has inimitably shown, is a genre that brings to the fore a fundamental relationship of matter to spirit, invariably raising the question (a not inconsiderable one in the nineteenth century) of a matter divest of spirit.[5] And although throughout the book, Cherry's project is to show how sexual difference is worked out by women painters in different generic spaces, she does not locate the genre of still life within larger questions of a Western tradition of 'presentational realism' and a historicization of different representational conventions. Nor does she appear to be saying that women use the conventions of this genre to particular ends, but rather that by definition still life is one of the least fruitful options for women.

If still life can conjure matter without spirit, its analogue in the genre of portraiture would be body without soul. But Victorian women artists, we learn, were especially partial to a concept of soul. I find this highly problematic as I do the recourse made throughout to Elizabeth Cowie's article 'Woman as Sign', from the first number of the journal *m/f* of 1978. Why, the reader asks, this semiological analysis in particular, other than for the fact that the author has used it previously in a collaborative essay with Griselda Pollock, 'Woman as Sign in Pre-Raphaelite Literature: a Study of the Representation of Elizabeth Siddall'?[6] Cherry uses the formulation 'woman as sign' widely throughout the book (which rather than 'advanc[ing] debates on spectatorship' creates the effect of running on the spot) in order to claim that women painting women do not produce woman as sign, rather that:

> In high culture as in the modest practices of civil society women produced and exchanged the visual sign woman, and in so doing they re-signified this sign to generate meanings about women's cultural exchanges and feminine/feminist pleasures. (p.119)

'Differencing the Gaze', the chapter from which this quote comes, marks the beginning of Part II, in which the presence of conspicuous 'theory' is flagged by such infelicitous transformation of nouns to verbs. Not only is it questionable whether a person can 're-signify' a sign, but a problematic shift has occurred in the use being made of Cowie's article since Cherry's essay written with Pollock. In that earlier piece the name 'Siddal', as purposely and persistently misspelt by Rossetti and members of the Brotherhood, was analysed in its function as the *sign* of creative genius and male desire in the literature on paintings in which Elizabeth Siddall is depicted. In *Painting Women*, as in Pollock's 'Woman as Sign: Psychoanalytic Readings' in *Vision and Difference*, the use of the woman as sign model has moved from the linguistic to the visual, from the word 'Siddal' to a concept of a 'face-sign' in Rossetti's paintings of women, in order to enable extrapolation of their difference from portraits of women by Victorian women. It is one thing to write about the sign 'Siddal' in discourses of Art History and altogether another thing merely to apply this use of the concept to visual images.

Just as the original essay prescribed a monolithic way of reading Rossetti's paintings, which situated them historically only within the context of one line of response to his work, in *Painting Women* once again implicit is the argument that male painters (D.G. Rossetti is fall-guy once more) produce non-portraits of women as 'sign' of masculine desire, creativity or genius, while by contrast women painting friends or lovers draw attention to the face of the sitter in particular as embodying 'the actual appearance of the woman while indexing' the spiritual. (p.51) Cherry invites us to read Annie Swynnerton's portrait *Susan Isabel Dacre* (1880) as registering a crucial difference along the lines of an absence of 'conventional standards of elegance or fashionability' and the presence of an 'inner beauty of the beloved and that of moral purity which was believed to set women's friendships apart and raise them above other relationships':

> The face of the beloved thus became the locus of pleasure, and its visual representation was the site and sight of desire which registered the special values of women's friendships. (p.51)

To write about the portrait as bodying forth a particular type of female friendship is to draw upon a humanistic model which relies for its definition upon a fundamental elevation of soul over body, pure soul over sexualized body. A further difficulty with this 'surpassing the love of men' line of argument is that it comes very close to the way in which Rossetti was criticized by his male contemporaries, as manifest in the attack by Robert Buchanan in the *Contemporary Review*, 1871, for example, which levelled the charge against the painter of extolling fleshliness at the expense of soul.[7] What does it mean for us as feminists to dismiss Rossetti's work within the very terms in which it was denounced by Buchanan and to recuperate the work of Elizabeth Siddall or other women artists for doing precisely the opposite, for diverting attention from the body or its contours as revealed through a focus upon clothing? If we accept, as the author wants us to, that such a privileging of soul over body is an implicitly 'good' thing for a Victorian woman painter to be doing, are we not simply replicating objections to the violation of the body/soul duality as raised by Buchanan in the nineteenth century? This seems to be a very serious question and one which requires us to situate Siddall and Rossetti within wider debates on sexuality in the period. For in nineteenth-century critical opinion Rossetti's 'extolling of fleshliness' along with that of Swinburne, Morris and parts of Tennyson represented an unmanliness, an effeminacy threatening to contemporary concepts of masculinity.

Cherry's choice of Cowie is possibly sound; Cowie analyses Levi-Strauss's discussion of 'value' in kinship structures and Cherry's own identification of the difference of

Victorian women's paintings is about cultural value. But her writing is at its best when she is not trying to fit a quart into a pint pot. The wealth of material under discussion is not well served by an article which itself has problems with Saussure. Cherry might have turned up more had she gone back to Levi-Strauss himself (and his discussion of a particular set of premises about a state of nature) in order to acknowledge more fully the particular context of his use of woman as sign as the pinnacle of exchange in general.[8] Yet, there is a contradiction in Cherry's controlling argument that her use of the Cowie article exacerbates: on the one hand Cherry claims that we, as informed readers after 'poststructuralism', cannot map representations of women onto the contours of 'real women', that painting (like film in Cowie's essay) does not reproduce an already stable meaning 'woman' from out there in 'real life'. On the other, she criticizes Rossetti for failing to convey images of women of which women viewers would approve, unlike Marie Spartali, for example, or Lucy Madox Brown whose women have 'none of the tousled hair, exotic jewellery, opulent dress, stylised facial features used by Dante Gabriel Rossetti and others'; and for painting instead images in which woman, 'limited to a signifier of masculine desire', functions simply as a 'sign' of a thing called male fantasy (as knowable, unified and already constituted category). Cherry concurs with Pollock's line on Rossetti's portraits: 'these are not faces, not portraits but fantasy.'

There is clearly a danger in saying that where Rossetti predictably eroticizes female figures, Siddall obscures the contours of the body, has little interest in 'fleshly' concerns, such that the woman in *Lady Affixing a Pennant to a Knight's Spear* 'wears a plain, unadorned dress [which] shrouds rather than displays the figural form, displacing it from a desiring gaze.' (p. 191) The subversive nature of Rossetti's painting for Buchanan lay in its failure to represent a duality in its wresting of body from soul. Therefore, although many readers will welcome Cherry's valuable reclamation of the work of nineteenth-century women artists, they may, as I have suggested, also have reason to question whether such a reclamation should necessitate an implicit denial of the body; or preclude the enjoyment of what is invariably going to be a 'nice cup of tea'.

Lindsay Smith
University of Sussex

Notes

1 I. Beeton, *Book of Household Management*, London, 1861, p. 879.
2 M.E. Braddon, *Lady Audley's Secret*, Oxford, 1987, p. 222.
3 S.S. Beale, *Recollections of a Spinster Aunt*, London, 1908, p. 134.
4 M. Foucault, *The History of Sexuality. Volume 1: An Introduction*, Harmondsworth, 1981; *Discipline and Punish, the Birth of the Prison*, Harmondsworth, 1982; E. Cowie, 'Woman as Sign', *m/f* 1, 1978.
5 S. Bann, *The True Vine: On Visual Representation and the Western Tradition*, Cambridge, 1989, pp. 68–101.
6 D. Cherry and G. Pollock, 'Woman as Sign in Pre-Raphaelite Literature: a Study of the Representation of Elizabeth Siddall', *Art History*, vol. 7, no.2, 1984.
7 R. Buchanan, 'The Fleshly School of Poetry', *Contemporary Review*, 1871, reprinted in J. Bristow (ed.), *The Victorian Poet: Poetics and Persona*, London, 1987, pp. 140–5.
8 C. Levi-Strauss, *The Elementary Structures of Kinship*, London, 1969.

Politeness and Profit

Diana Donald

Painting for Money: The Visual Arts and the Public Sphere in Eighteenth-Century England by *David H. Solkin*, New Haven and London: Yale University Press, 1993, 312 pp., 88 col. and b. & w. illus., £40.00

These are heady times for students of eighteenth-century England. Firstly, the revisionism of J.C.D. Clark in the mid-1980s has set off a lively historiographic debate: to what extent were aristocratic power structures actually modified by the burgeoning commercial and professional classes?[1] Then, in the field of material culture, the role of the middling ranks has again come under scrutiny. Here Neil McKendrick's hypothesis that Adam Smith's Britain witnessed the birth of a consumer society contrasts with other more cautious or speculative assessments of customer behaviour.[2] Finally, the study of eighteenth-century art itself has in the last ten years broken free of the connoisseurship and biography that used to restrict it, offering interpretations based on the cultural values, especially the social consciousness, of the time.[3]

A book on 'painting for money' bids fair to unite many of these fields of inquiry, particularly as its author, David Solkin, was in the early 1980s one of the pioneers of the 'politicization' of British eighteenth-century painting. His *Richard Wilson*, boldly subtitled *The Landscape of Reaction*, claimed that Wilson transformed 'patrician mythology into persuasive landscape form'.[4] It was a thesis based on exhaustive analysis of particular paintings, which Solkin referred to political contingencies and to a wide range of contemporary literature. This was not simply to 'contextualize', but to treat the formal language of Wilson's art as itself a record of history, as expressive of the preoccupations of the gentry classes in the mid-eighteenth century. Readers of *Richard Wilson* will recognize the same approach in *Painting for Money*, which often yields fascinating conclusions. But there are important differences. The most obvious is that, while Wilson's landscapes were interpreted as the embodiment of patrician values, in retreat from the thrusting vulgarity of the nouveaux-riches, *Painting for Money* analyses the art of the early to mid-eighteenth century as an aspect of the culture of commercial society itself: as an important part of a strategy to legitimize the operations of capitalism.

This shift relates to another key difference from *Richard Wilson*, namely Solkin's ambition to coordinate the direct analysis of paintings with a larger discursive scheme; the origins of which lie in the influential theories of J.G.A. Pocock.[5] Pocock's famous study of the discourse of 'civic humanism' in the history of political theory showed how the Renaissance ideal of a virtuous society, which eighteenth-century England inherited (notably in Shaftesbury's philosophy), elevated the concept of political man as a landowner: free, autonomous, and therefore capable of nobly disinterested participation in decision-making in the public sphere. However, the holding of property in moveable goods rather than in land; the pursuit of private rather than public, communal interest; the specialization of economic functions and division of labour; the dangers of debilitating luxury; most of all, the power of money to corrupt the political process: all threatened the purity and stability of the ideal state and stood in need of ethical justification. In John Barrell's *The Political Theory of Painting from Reynolds to Hazlitt: 'The Body of the Public'* (1986), which Solkin cites on p.1 of *Painting for Money*, Pocock provided the inspiration for a tendentious interpretation of the discursive language employed by writers on art at this period.[6] Solkin's project is more complicated, in that Pocock's study of civic humanism is correlated with the work of several other cultural theorists, and applied to a varied body of artistic practice.

Solkin's study of 'commercial politeness' — seemingly a paradoxical formulation — can thus only be understood within his theoretical frame of reference. Pocock's view was that the eighteenth-century cult of politeness constituted a means by which an increasingly commercialized society could sanctify the transactional basis of social relations, seeking to present 'an indefinite and perhaps infinite enrichment of . . . personality', the progress of the arts and even of civilization itself as direct results of the growth of capitalism.[7] Lawrence Klein's related studies of the concept of politeness in the writings of Shaftesbury and his contemporaries also make an important contribution to Solkin's thought at various points,[8] as do the literary theories of Terry Eagleton. However, the most significant aspect of Solkin's argument depends on the junction which he effects between Pocock's construct of 'commercial humanism', and Jürgen Habermas's theory of a bourgeois 'public sphere', which developed in eighteenth-century England as an expression of the rational and enlightened public discourse of private citizens: the voice of 'public opinion' stimulated and conducted through the press, and consciously opposed to the arbitrary exercise of state power of the traditional kind.[9] Despite the common ground between these ideas, it will be seen that they hold the potential for evaluative conflict. In the context of 'civic humanism', efforts to dignify capitalist competition and exploitation through an evocation of cultural consensus could only appear disingenuous and doomed to failure; whereas Habermas conceived the 'bourgeois public sphere' as vital to political and cultural advance in the early industrial period. These differences correspond to the apparent ambivalence of Solkin himself, which the book does not resolve. Indeed, the opposition it implies between a (hypothetical) public art dependent on communal forms of patronage, in Barrell's words 'at once, based on the "universal" principles of human nature, and capable of being understood only by a liberal élite'[10] — and the commodification of culture, its 'privatization' by commercial interests on popular lines, sometimes seems to have more to do with the cultural politics of the 1980s that those of eighteenth-century England.

Solkin tells a story of the gradual formation of a new kind of 'polite' art, which reflected the sociable and sentimental ideals of commercial society, and was distinctive both in subject matter and style. The historical materials this story brings into play are themselves mostly familiar to students of the eighteenth century, ranging from conversation pieces to the popular pictures of everyday life at Vauxhall Gardens, paintings of modern history by Hayman and West, and Joseph Wright of Derby's 'candlelights' of the 1760s. It is thus firmly grounded in traditional art history, and makes less reference than *Richard Wilson* to political and social developments: surprisingly, there is no mention of the spate of recent work on the connections between urban middle-class consumer society and the fashion for 'genteel' arts, which is highly pertinent to Solkin's argument.[11] The shifting focus of the book, which concerns itself partly with the development of institutional patronage and public art exhibitions, partly with the formation of genres or the work of individual painters, risks a certain discontinuity, particularly in view of Solkin's theoretical eclecticism. However, the close reading of particular images and their articulation to the broad theme of the book, a process which is sometimes extended and arduous, is productive of many new insights. It overwhelmingly confirms the importance of philosophical inspiration in English eighteenth-century painting and the symbolic nature of its language — a further corrective to the style–history approach or literalism of older studies.

Pursuing the notion of polite social intercourse as the key to the new character of

English art, Solkin is able to use Habermas's theory that the coffee house and club society of early eighteenth-century London contributed to the creation of a 'bourgeois public sphere' and Pocock's view that the Whig hegemony, partly through the voice of the *Spectator*, 'began building a broad ideological consensus based on "social, cultural and commercial values" ', the aesthetics of graceful manners being 'the very stuff of their politics'.[12] This combination of ideas informs a telling analysis of Kneller's Kit Kat Club portraits, in which Solkin distils their peculiar blend of formal gesture and self-consciousness, of conformity and individualism. The sociable tendencies of the Kit Kats lead Solkin on to an original account of the evolution of the polite conversation piece. He suggests that the frequently voiced fear of 'luxury', as a cause of national degeneration, inhibited and conditioned the display of fashionable commodities which formed an indispensable feature of this genre. The belief that the social dominance of women was implicated in the spread of luxury, indeed the discursive characterization of credit and consumption as female, which Pocock remarked, were further problematic factors in the depiction of familial relations.[13] However, the conversation piece in its mature form was designed to evoke the companionate marriage; the civilizing influence of women within the domestic sphere; consumption as an hospitable, mutually enjoyable, and therefore virtuous social act; even that network of voluntary social interactions between supposedly autonomous private individuals which, in Habermas's view, provided a pattern for the public sphere. The unexpected hero of this story is Hogarth: even his technique, building up from rough underpainting to delicate Rococo detailing of faces and dresses, but letting both stages remain visible, constituted a visual metaphor for the progress from unimproved English plainness to 'commercial politeness'.[14] This is an instance of Solkin's willingness to read the language of art as an aspect of historical meaning, which, if sometimes pushed too far or misdirected by theory, is never less than interesting and suggestive.

The 'improvement' of social behaviour as a key aspiration of commercial society was, Solkin believes, projected at Vauxhall Gardens, one of the first sites for the display of the arts to paying customers, and hence an actual, physical 'public sphere' of a new kind. In adopting the thesis of Peter Stallybrass and Allon White[15] that the 'will to refinement' involved the shunning of the carnivalesque (which could nonetheless be readmitted into the polite sphere as safely controlled 'negative examples'), Solkin proposes an interpretation of Vauxhall imagery which I find partial and misleading. It misses the humour and zest for human variety in the supper-box pictures and popular prints, and significantly omits Hogarth's *Four Times of Day*, of which there were painted copies at Vauxhall: images bursting with the crude vitality of city life, its rowdyism and sexual transgressions.[16] Solkin suggests a progress in refinement over the years, perceptible in literary allusions to Vauxhall and in a comparison of earlier and later prints depicting it: but this is to leave out of account one of the most famous representations of the Gardens, Rowlandson's large watercolour shown at the Royal Academy in 1784, in which the Prince of Wales and people of fashion consort unceremoniously with the plebs, and vulgar city wives mingle with whores.[17]

The point here is not to argue with Solkin over the ratio of 'undesirables' in the Vauxhall clientele, although he may have exaggerated its social exclusiveness; it is to suggest that his interpretation of eighteenth-century attitudes to 'politeness' is too restrictive. Given the centrality of the concept to the whole argument of *Painting for Money*, it is a weakness of the book that 'politeness' is not more closely defined: the reader must infer the meaning Solkin attaches to it from the context of writings by Pocock, Klein et al. But Pocock's broad opposition of the (socially and politically) enfranchized and unenfranchized, which Solkin by and large adopts, hinders a more nuanced discrimination of class-based, patriotic and religious views; reducing all to the alleged desire for cultural consensus. Yet a myth just as old as 'civic humanism' in England celebrated the very heterogeneity of English society as a sign of its political freedoms, which allowed every citizen to be himself without fear of persecution.[18] This celebration of intransigent John-Bullism was easily coordinated with a conscious *opposition* to polite culture, seen as the concomitant of court politics, and even of French tyranny. Although Solkin refers to the English dread of luxury, with its associated francophobia, he is not always sensitive to the ironies and contradictions which are apparent in images of the fashionable world. It was not only Rowlandson, in *Vauxhall Gardens*, who relished the resolutely uncouth: in Brandoin's *The Exhibition of the Royal Academy in 1771*, where the comic disparity and distraction of the visitors suggest to Solkin the breakdown of any attempt to achieve 'a truly public visual culture',[19] one might, on the contrary, construe a delight in idiosyncrasy as almost the defining characteristic of 'Englishness'. Moreover, it was not only on political and patriotic grounds that the people of eighteenth-century England might resist, or seek to redefine, the traditional notion of fine manners: Protestant scruples equally played their part. From Wesley to Hannah More it was suggested that the Bible was a better guide to social behaviour than books of etiquette,[20] and one of the many hostile critics of Lord Chesterfield's *Letters to his Son* (published in 1774 and intended as a course in politeness) set the type of the courtier in explicit opposition to the Christian.[21] Thus the candour, sobriety and high seriousness which Solkin so ably brings out in Wright of Derby's scenes of middle-class life may have suggested to viewers 'their world's "better part" — people "of quality", both materially and morally';[22] but it is a 'quality' increasingly defined in contradistinction to aristocratic decadence and artifice.

In the last chapters of *Painting for Money*, Solkin extends his account of the emergence of 'public' art as an expression of 'private' sensibilities into the actual public spaces of the Foundling Hospital, the gallery of large historical pictures by Hayman at Vauxhall, the Society of Artists' exhibitions in the 1760s, and the first years of the Royal Academy; culminating in West's *Death of Wolfe* (RA 1771), an ostensibly high-minded patriotic symbol which appears on the dust-jacket of the book in challenging confrontation with its title. Solkin is, in fact, inclined to be dismissive of the moral and religious motives which may have prompted such works, or their contribution to the formation of national identity: suspecting that 'art and literature had now taken it upon themselves to provide an ethical excuse for those who profited from the "free" and "rational" working of the marketplace.'[23] This negative judgement does not prevent a very interesting discussion of the depictions of modern history, linked to mid-century aesthetic theory and to the rise of art journalism. The new emphasis on 'authentic' detail, at variance with the generalization of form recommended by Reynolds in the *Discourses*, is referred back to a fascinating fictional debate on art appended to Mandeville's *Fable of the Bees*, that notorious defence of 'luxurious' consumption which Solkin discusses in his introduction. Mandeville has a Shaftesburian believer in civic humanism argue for grand universality in painting, against a Mandevillian admirer of Dutch naturalism.[24] The opposition thus established allows Solkin to represent the hybridization of 'high' and 'low' styles in history paintings of the 1760s as indicative, not simply of the artistic ignorance of the enlarged public (more concerned with matter than manner), but of the individualism and splintering of the unitary ideals of public man inseparable from the growth of capitalism.[25]

The popularization of history painting had an equally significant effect on subject matter. Solkin points out the curious fact that, in paintings like Hayman's *The Surrender of Montreal to General Amherst* (1760–1) or Penny's *The Marquis of Granby Relieving a Sick Soldier* (1764), victorious military commanders, embodiments of 'courageous and public masculinity', were consistently represented in actions which celebrated the 'humane and pacific'; or, as in the various versions of the *Death of Wolfe*, as objects of compassionate sympathy.[26] The leaning to pathos rather than heroics must surely be partly due to the political controversy surrounding the Seven Years' War, and indeed the American War of Independence. However, Solkin argues persuasively that this quality corresponds to the view of Alexander Gerard, David Hume and others that art could inspire 'refined and sympathetic virtues', as 'the crowning glory of a prosperous commercial state': it was likely to gratify a bourgeois public which prided itself above all on the possession of such virtues.[27] If this approach seems unduly cynical, it is redeemed by Solkin's splendid exegesis of the early subject pictures of Wright of Derby, especially *Three Persons Viewing the Gladiator by Candlelight* (Society of Artists, 1765). Through extensive reference to eighteenth-century sources and fine-textured analysis of the paintings, Solkin reveals layer upon layer of meaning in the symbolism of light and vision, perception of the mysteries of nature and its transmutation into art, even analogies between the cosmos and the ordering of human society. Although still associable with the tradition of the private conversation group and its emphasis on material goods ('any . . . English collector could order a reduced cast of the Borghese Gladiator . . . for £1 11s. 6d.'), such paintings transcend this tradition to evoke the refined pleasures of knowledge, gained through the shared exercise of judgement and reason: 'we are seeing an aesthetic principle at work in the production of community', and the creation of a new kind of public art.[28]

After this, the reader may be dismayed by Solkin's conclusion that 'if ours has been the account of an ideology made visible, we have also been revealing a history of wilful blindness — of the public sphere's constant struggle to deny its instrumental role in promoting the private interests of a propertied minority, and in greasing the wheels of capital.' The delusiveness of claims that there was any kind of 'cultural consensus' emerged, in Solkin's view, from the events of 1768: the secession of the Royal Academicians from the Society of Artists and the bitterness between them, in which the cultural elitism of the Academy played a part. The Academy had, however, 'arrived too late' to prevent the fatal inroads of commerce into the art world, or to instate a truly public art; and the book ends at this moment of 'crisis'.[29]

The conclusion seems unsatisfactory from several points of view. By leaving the story at this point, Solkin declines to engage with the rich, complex and original developments of English art after 1770, made possible by the trends he has defined; the hybridization of genres, the partial rejection of hierarchy, the multiplying opportunities for artists, and the diversity and enthusiasm of the public for art. It is difficult to reconcile Solkin's dying fall with the sanguine view of a writer like the Rev. Robert Bromley, West's apologist, writing in the 1790s. In the early years of the century, Bromley reminded his readers, the fine arts were 'at a low ebb indeed . . . nothing that deserved the name of superior art'; but through national improvements in manners 'the arts have taken a most deep and comprehensive root, and in the space of the last thirty years have thriven . . . to a strength and vigour which is absolutely unexampled, within an equal period of time, in any age of the world.'[30] Bromley was clear that commerce had facilitated this process of refinement, as much as it had benefited from it. How, indeed, could a history of English art be conceived in any other terms? The 'public sphere' which Shaftesbury had envisaged at the beginning of the century existed only at the level of philosophical discourse: that is, if one excludes, as Shaftesbury would have wished to exclude, works conducted under royalist or 'papist' auspices. It is worth remembering that the *Judgement of Hercules* (1713) which he commissioned from Paolo de Mattheis — referred to several times by Solkin as a paradigm of 'civic humanist' ideals — was in fact a collector's painting, the direct, particular expression of one nobleman's taste, and in its engraved form served to illustrate a text.[31] The creation of an *actual* public sphere could, in the conditions of eighteenth-century England, have occurred only through the kinds of entrepreneurial enterprise which Solkin describes; and here the print-publishers played an increasingly significant role as patrons. It is puzzling that, although Solkin refers several times to the importance of the print trade in extending the public for art, this crucial aspect of commercialization is never given the prominence it deserves: in a work on *Painting for Money* the print publisher Boydell, who is said to have made fifteen thousand pounds from the engraving of West's *Death of Wolfe* alone, is not even mentioned.[32] Yet, just as Habermas identified the printed word as the key agent through which, in eighteenth-century England, 'private people came together as a public', so printed pictures — reproductive engravings and later book illustrations — were an art form at once intimately domestic and universal.[33] In the last thirty years of the century, such imagery began to contribute at many levels to the formation of national consciousness: but this is a story which has yet to be written.

Diana Donald
Manchester Metropolitan University

Notes

1 Jonathan C.D. Clark, *English Society 1688–1832: Ideology, Social Structure and Political Practice during the Ancien Regime*, Cambridge, 1985. Paul Langford, *A Polite and Commercial People: England 1727–1783*, Oxford, 1989, and *Public Life and the Propertied Englishman 1689–1798*, Oxford, 1991. Seminar papers by Clark, Roy Porter and Jeremy Black were published with an overview by William A. Speck, *British Journal for Eighteenth-century Studies*, vol. 15, no. 2, Autumn 1992, pp. 131–49.

2 Neil McKendrick, John Brewer, J.H. Plumb, *The Birth of a Consumer Society: the Commercialization of Eighteenth-century England*, London, 1983. Colin Campbell, *The Romantic Ethic and the Spirit of Modern Consumerism*, Oxford and New York, 1987. Lorna Weatherill, *Consumer Behaviour and Material Culture in Britain 1660–1760*, London and New York, 1988. John Brewer and Roy Porter (eds.), *Consumption and the World of Goods*, London and New York, 1993.

3 For example, on portraiture, Desmond Shawe-Taylor, *The Georgians: Eighteenth-century Portraiture and Society*, London, 1990; Marcia Pointon, *Hanging the Head: Portraiture and Social Formation in Eighteenth-century England*, New Haven and London, 1993.

4 David H. Solkin, *Richard Wilson, The Landscape of Reaction*, Tate Gallery, London, 1982, p. 133.

5 J.G.A. Pocock, *The Machiavellian Moment: Florentine Political Thought and the Atlantic Republican Tradition*, Princeton and London, 1975; and *Virtue, Commerce and History: Essays on Political Thought and History, Chiefly in the Eighteenth Century*, Cambridge, 1985.

6 Fundamental criticisms of Barrell's book are made in a review article by Andrew Hemingway, 'The Political Theory of Painting Without the Politics', *Art History*, vol. 10, no. 3, September 1987, pp. 381–95.

7 Pocock, op. cit., 1985, p. 49. Solkin in *Painting For Money*, p. 157, relates this notion to the views of David Hume. A further contribution to discussion of civic humanist ideals and the cult of politeness is Stephen Copley's 'The Fine Arts in Eighteenth-Century Polite Culture' in John Barrell (ed.), *Painting and the Politics of Culture: New Essays on British Art 1700–1850*, Oxford and New York, 1992.

8 Lawrence E. Klein, *Shaftesbury and the Culture of Politeness: Moral Discourse and Cultural Politics in early Eighteenth-century England*, Cambridge and New York, 1994.

9 Jürgen Habermas, *The Structural Transformation of the Public Sphere: An Inquiry into a Category of Bourgeois Society*, Cambridge, 1992 (first published 1962).

10 John Barrell, *The Political Theory of Painting from Reynolds to Hazlitt: 'The Body of the Public'*, New Haven and London, 1986, p. 341.

11 Notably Peter Borsay, *The English Urban Renaissance: Culture and Society in the Provincial Town 1660–1770*, Oxford, 1989. See also note 2.

12 Solkin, op. cit., p. 29.

13 ibid., p. 48.

14 ibid., pp. 94–5.

15 Peter Stallybrass and Allon White, *The Politics and Poetics of Transgression*, London, 1986.

16 Among a huge literature: Ronald Paulson, *Hogarth: His Life, Art, and Times*, New Haven and London, 1971, vol. 1, pp. 398f; Sean Shesgreen, *Hogarth and the Times-of-the-Day Tradition*, Ithaca and London, 1983.
17 *Vauxhall Gardens* in the Victoria and Albert Museum, London. John Hayes, *The Art of Thomas Rowlandson*, Alexandria, Virginia, 1990, pp. 66f. An engraving of 1785 by Pollard and Jukes, published by J.R. Smith, is reproduced in M. Dorothy George, *Hogarth to Cruikshank: Social Change in Graphic Satire*, London and Harmondsworth, 1967, col. pl. IV. Another, probably earlier, version of the design is in the Mellon collection: John Riely, *Rowlandson Drawings from the Paul Mellon Collection*, New Haven, 1977, pp. 4–6, col. pl.1.
18 The *locus classicus* is Sir William Temple's 'Of Poetry' in *Miscellanea*, 1690, reprinted in J.E. Spingarn (ed.), *Sir William Temple's Essays on Ancient and Modern Learning and on Poetry*, Oxford, 1909, p. 74. The idea was endlessly reiterated during the eighteenth century.
19 Solkin, op. cit., pp. 274–6.
20 John Wesley, *Sermons on Several Occasions*, vol. 2, 1748, p. 100. [Hannah More], *An Estimate of the Religion of the Fashionable World, by One of the Laity*, 2nd ed., London, 1791, p. 78.
21 Rev. Thomas Hunter, *Reflections Critical and Moral on the Letters of the Late Earl of Chesterfield*, London, 1776, pp. 93, 151–2 and *passim*.
22 Solkin, op. cit., p. 236.
23 ibid., p. 158.
24 ibid., pp. 14–18.
25 ibid., pp. 171, 232 (a propos of Wright of Derby), 255–9.
26 ibid., p. 206.
27 ibid., pp. 188, 197.
28 ibid., pp. 221, 225.
29 ibid., pp. 274–6.
30 Rev. Robert A. Bromley, *A Philosophical and Critical History of the Fine Arts . . . With Occasional Observations on the Progress of Engraving . . . Deduced from the Earliest Records . . . to Their Present Establishment in Great Britain under . . . George III*, London, vol. 1, 1793, pp. 98, 101.
31 Anthony Ashley Cooper, Earl of Shaftesbury, *A Notion of the Historical Draught or Tablature of the Judgement of Hercules*, first published 1713. Solkin reproduces Gribelin's engraving after de Mattheis on p. 63.
32 David Alexander and Richard Godfrey, *Painters and Engraving: the Reproductive Print from Hogarth to Wilkie*, New Haven, 1980, p. 58. Yet in *Richard Wilson* Solkin demonstrated the key importance of print publication even for this artist (pp. 20, 59, 200, 228–9).
33 By the early nineteenth century, an illustrator like George Cruikshank could seem to typify the values of the English public. Cf. the anonymously published 'Lectures on the Fine Arts No. 1 On George Cruikshank', *Blackwood's Edinburgh Magazine*, vol. 14, no. 78, July 1823, p. 18; 'GENIUS in its truest sense — strong, original, English genius'.

Faint Praise?

Colin Roth

Psychoanalysis, Mind and Art: Perspectives on Richard Wollheim edited by *Jim Hopkins and Anthony Saville*, Oxford: Basil Blackwell Ltd, 1992, 383pp., £40.00

Richard Wollheim's contribution to our way of thinking about the experience of art has been considerable, largely because his small book, *Art and its Objects*, has, since its first publication in 1968, seemed to provide a coherent explanation for and solution to many of the difficulties of understanding and belief which our modern culture has had in relation to cultural artefacts, their use and value. In his subsequent contributions to the field, though, the different traditions and outlooks of the cultures Wollheim bridges, psychology, philosophy and art history, jostle uncomfortably against each other, and condition his perceptions and methodology in a way which diminishes their implied universal truth.

For the philosopher, there is a reasonable belief that long contemplation, the application of careful rationalization to perception, is the right way to tackle most problems. Even in the first flush of empiricism, during the eighteenth century, the strength and significance of experiential perception was a matter to be understood rather than a vehicle of understanding in itself. For the psychologist, whose practices depend on the scientific and creative strategies of the late nineteenth and early twentieth centuries, truth emerges from the same kind of rational contemplation, now applied to experiential perceptions and their behavioural consequences, but still essentially a matter of thinking and understanding relating to pre-existing knowledge and experience. For the art historian, too, the urge to understand cultural processes and their development within a managed structure of beliefs throws emphasis on to careful thought after careful research, rather than on to insight into experience itself, which is devalued as a matter of mere connoisseurship.

Wollheim's subject is essentially the understanding of our experience of life, and of particular interest here, the understanding of our experience of art. The problem with his work is that he applies a way of thinking about his subject that is the product of the academic cultures he has been trained in, dependent upon rational thinking about the meaning of experience, which excludes the possibility that some art might work in a way for which long thought is an inappropriate means of understanding.

The working artist, on the other hand, is in the business of communicating, and uses different strategies at different times to achieve an effective address to their audience. In Poussin's time, paintings were meant to work slowly, to be thought about and talked about. Their value arose from the depth of debate they could stimulate over time, rather than from an immediate visceral impact. In the later nineteenth century, the vituperative exchanges between Ruskin and Whistler about how best to communicate morally meaningful narrative content in art, whether through iconographically legible representation or aesthetic impact, revealed that painting might communicate much more immediately. Cubism's wrestling with the problem of perception through time, by incorporating multiple perceptions within a compound image, depends as Poussin did on the length of time we are prepared to spend with an image, but some of the most interesting work of recent time works in a quite different way, demanding only the most limited direct exposure to the artefact itself, and a value which arises from power and depth of strike rather than from complexity or the long pleasures of intellectual onanism.

In *Psychoanalysis, Mind and Art, Perspectives on Richard Wollheim*, the focus is quite properly on the positive contribution his followers believe Wollheim has made to our understanding. The avenues they explore, each taking a facet of the master's own work from which to travel, expose the limitations of Wollheim's outlook as much as they illuminate its merits.

In 'Painting as an Art: Persons, Artists, Spectators and Roles', Alexander Nehemas, writing in a startlingly baroque manner, exposits an outline of Wollheim's arguments in *The Thread of Life* (1984). The book, he says, 'begins with the idea that in order to understand what it is to be a person, we must first distinguish between the person, the person's life, and the living of that life — a thing, a product, and a process that culminates in the product.' (p. 239) He asserts 'the primacy of the process of leading a life over both lives and persons' as a means of recognizing and understanding identity, and explains Wollheim's version of Heidegger's placing of present action and experience in terms of time. We are asked to accept that we use the past in 'iconic mental states':

> Essential to our ability to have and understand these states and to use them

> . . . is the fact that we assume different roles within them . . . We construct mental narratives in which there are characters, among whom we often include ourselves, and we are affected in particular ways by what these characters undergo. (p. 241)

As so often in writing which aims to model mental process, what we have is not an objective description of process in general so much as an objectified account of the author's — in this case Wollheim's — personal experience of thinking and feeling.

This explanation of Wollheim's views goes some way to explaining the peculiarities and inadequacies of *Painting as an Art*, which Wollheim wrote as a record of his 1984 Mellon Lectures. In the preface to his book of that title, published in 1987, Wollheim explains: 'I came to recognise that it often took the first hour or so in front of a painting for stray associations or motivated misperceptions to settle down, and it was only then, with the same amount of time or more to spend looking at it, that the picture could be relied upon to disclose itself as it was.' Though the contemplation is carried on in terms of a past filled with knowledge and ideas, the product of such contemplation is inevitably more to do with Wollheim's process of seeing than with its professed object, the process of painting being gazed at. As with so many theories of what Wollheim calls 'general aesthetics' since Addison and Richardson in the early eighteenth century, they firmly resist application to real experience, and real experience has to be tortured to fit them. We learn more about 'painting as an art' from what artists have to say about their objectives and craft — in Hogarth and Ramsay, for example — than from this kind of self-centred and indulgent theorizing.

Wollheim's view that 'we can speak in terms of standards for a spectator's seeing what is in the painting correctly or incorrectly' (p. 248) is based on his notion of 'twofoldedness': that artists are spectators as well as creators of their works, whose meaning they *must* manipulate as spectators so that our 'projection' is effectively controlled. Dressed in the complexities of language of this article and of Wollheim's own book, this sounds like it might be 'one of Wollheim's most important (if controversial) contributions to our understanding of representation in general'. (p. 248) But seen for the imperial fashion it is, does not the observation simply assert that any artist worth the name will manage their image to stimulate and convey meaning as well as they can, not simply engage in unthinking activity? The long description and discussion of Duchamp's last work (p. 251) elevates commonplace observation to the status of grand insight in a way that would have delighted Duchamp. Asking, as we must, whether we learn anything from the passage that we did not already know is exactly the challenge to certainty Duchamp espoused, a praiseworthy quality but not, perhaps, that which the article's author was aiming to achieve. Paradoxically, then, the article stands as an exemplar of the difficulty of convincingly stating the position it expresses.

Malcolm Budd's 'On Looking at a Picture', lucid by contrast with some of its companions in this volume, praises Wollheim by the practice of 'systematic irreverence': Budd dismantles 'seeing-in' as a legitimate explanation of our experience of pictures, and finds it wanting. The weakness of his argument, both in its finding of flaws in Wollheim's logic and his criticisms of Gombrich's ideas, is that his approach is rooted in an assumption that if words are used rationally, truth will emerge. The way language works is not a necessary analogue of the way our minds and feelings work: as Hume argued, our experience leads us to expect a relationship — in this instance the philosopher expects the structure and use of language to reflect mental process and feeling — but their frequent correlation is not in itself proof of a causal relationship's existence. Budd, by not allowing that experience of the visual might have a different nature to structures in language (a central proposition of Wollheim's), misses the essence of Wollheim's and

Gombrich's stance as psychologists as much as philosophers: that experience described is a proper source of knowledge, even when the way we use language cannot, or does not seem to, provide rationally valid explanations of that knowledge. The delightful paradox is that, relatively speaking, Wollheim and Gombrich personify the English philosophical tradition of empiricism to which Budd applies an apparently Continental deductive logic.

In the opening essay of this volume, Jim Hopkins, the book's co-editor with Anthony Saville, seeks to demonstrate that psychoanalysis' status as 'science' is impenetrable to outsiders because it is 'slowed down'. It uses, he explains, 'scattered data' which require great experience in their interpretation. Hopkins advances two principles representing ideals of scientific objectivity, communication and rational criticism: that explanations of 'truth' are only 'objective' if their cogency, and the material and arguments used in forming them, are comprehensible to 'any rational person who fully understands them'; and that cogency 'can be properly evaluated only by someone who knows how that hypothesis or theory is used; that is who understands it, the data it is supposed to explain, and how it does so.' (p. 23) These principles seem to have been formulated to provide ammunition against anti-psychoanalytic arguments by Popper and Grunbaum, but because they are presented as 'ideals of scientific objectivity' rather than as legitimate elements in a broad discussion of 'scientificity', the motivation for their form seems more obvious than their inherent value as interpretive explanations of scientific doctrine. That their motivation should seem more significant than their function is inevitable in an essay whose greater part is spent developing an analogy between the processes of linguistic expression and the motivation of human behaviour. The central argument is that the grammar of our sentences gives substance to our intuitive belief in causal relationships. Hopkins analogizes to argue that such causal links underpin behavioural motivation too, as though behaviour can be explained in terms of desires satisfied or not.

Writing of an inductive fallacy, Hopkins argues that behaviour, like language, cannot be interpreted in terms of simple inductive logic. He does not address, though, the variety of causal triggers that can stimulate behaviour, or their correlation with the laterally connected chains possible in our handling of and responses to language. The complexity of behavioural motivation is an important stick to grasp, but it seems to have been grabbed at the wrong end here: using grammatical structure to pinpoint one way in which behaviour can be interpreted in terms of causal links sheds more light on the nature of our interpretive effort than on the substance of behaviour's motives.

Hopkins presents a model of our mind as 'a semantic engine; that is, a device which draws on information from the environment and transforms this into motive with environment-directed conditions of satisfaction'. (p. 22) But this model of mental process only describes what Heidegger called 'intentional activity'; it fails to acknowledge or describe 'coping with' and the characteristic subconscious mechanisms that modify and re-model behaviour irrationally in a balance between 'timeless' motives and continually developing behavioural skills and resources. *How* we achieve an end is open to change and subject to subconscious thought; *what* we aim to do seems much less open to learning.

In seeking to assert that psychoanalysis is legitimately described as science (is it really necessary to do this any more?), Hopkins focuses on a narrow strand of its interpretive mechanism. To the extent that his paper reads as a description of psychoanalysis' whole effort and intent, this narrowness is misleading. An historical, as opposed to analytical, critique might have been more helpful if an assertion of psychoanalysis' scientific status was the objective — though consideration of the existential elements which Freud's own arguments unwittingly share with those of his contemporaries, Heidegger and Otto, and of Freud's emphasis on the primacy of cathartic change (that is, therapeutic functionality) over theoretical modelling, might even then have problematized the narrow focus of this argument.

If, however, the real motivation of the essay is to defend psychoanalysis from the assaults of Popper and Grunbaum, specifically their assertions that its methodologies disqualify it from scientific status, then a more fruitful approach might have been to tackle the validity of our constructs of scientificity and causality, themselves a curious product of Romantic individualism, which glorifies the subjective by inventing a contrary, 'objective' reality for the poetic and spiritual to polarize against.

'The Nature and Source of Emotion' by Sebastian Gardner seeks to show that emotion is 'a kind of mental state which cannot be understood apart from — for the reason that it is derived from — the kind of mental state that psychoanalytic theory refers to as phantasy'. (p. 35) By describing ways in which rational and empirical perceptions interlock and disconnect, Gardner builds up a structure of agreed 'knowledge' about emotions on which he believes his case will stand. For example, on p. 37 he asserts that 'someone who is blind to [the way emotions characteristically operate in inescapably interlinked clusters] lacks a substantial piece of basic psychological knowledge.' He says, 'the relation of anger to malice is paralleled by the relations of guilt to reparation, melancholy to loss of interest in life, envy to destructiveness and so on.' It is an effective emulsion of rationality and empiricism, because it generates a strong sense of substance through its blending of otherwise incompatible elements. What binds the emulsion, though, and gives it longevity, turns out to be the arcana of post-Freudian psychoanalytic theory, which posits quasi-scientific descriptions of rationally deduced states of mind. The 'solutions' which logically flow from these constructed 'difficulties' actually combine rational deduction and empirical observation: the binding agent is the chimera of scientific authority. The premise which is embedded in the discussion of emotion's source is that an historic explanation of its structure is proof that its structure, and its existence, have historic roots rather than simply historically conditioned pattern. The language of the article confines its intelligibility to a narrow group of psychoanalytically trained individuals; there is none of Freud's own determination that knowledge and understanding should be accessible, transparent and elegant.

In 'Acting on Phantasy and Acting on Desire', Hanna Segal takes up an idea expressed in Richard Wollheim's *The Thread of Life* (1984), in which he distinguishes between 'acting and phantasy' where 'phantasy' constitutes the power of the past over our present, and 'acting on desire', a more directly active behaviour. Hanna Segal shows that 'phantasy' has great power over present action through a mechanism of 'projective identification'. Renaming 'acting on phantasy', 'acting on delusion', Segal gives a sequence of illustrations which illuminate her argument in fluent and lucid prose. There are some odd unchallenged survivals of Freudian orthodoxy, as in the bizarre reading of homosexuality as a part of personal development rather than, as more recent work suggests, as a genetically based element of the personality, but Segal is admirably careful to treat Freud as an historical source, recording the shifts in his ideas and interpretations with an historian's care — a considerable rarity in this volume.

Unfortunately, as the article nears its end, the initial avoidance of impenetrable jargon is forgotten, and the ugly systematic structures of post-Freudian theory cloud what began as clear and cogent presentation. 'Dispositional' and 'occurrent' fantasies appear on the article's last page, without even passing definitions. Granted that it is a reasonable function of a festschrift to turn your attention to the work of the author praised, it seems hard that here one needs to read Wollheim to understand even basic meanings.

Anthony Saville's piece, 'Painting, Beholder and the Self', shows how alarmingly far from art and our understanding of our responses to it we can travel. With the exception of some references to Vernet's perspective, there is no detailed contact with any picture — at least Wollheim's own philosophical reveries have that virtue — and instead we are led through a contemplation of different varieties and degrees of self-consciousness in the face of art, a philosophical fantasy with no ground beneath it. No historical evidence is allowed to intrude, so the writer blithely assumes that eighteenth-century beholders looked at pictures in solitary contemplation of their experiential address to the individual, as they might address us as individuals today. In the period Saville treats, the second half of the eighteenth century, in terms of Diderot's *Salons* seen through the eyes of Michael Fried,[1] art was a focus for discussion between people: it was disseminated in engravings littered with commentary designed to prompt engagement with the images' discursive content in a way that tells us how the oil originals of these images must have been tackled by contemporaries. Saville's argument, that there is a complex shift in the nature of the beholder's self-conscious engagement with the picture, does have some basis in painting of the period: Watteau had been fond of a girl's figure that looks out at the beholder from *Les Champs Elysées* in the Wallace Collection amongst others. She 'invites' us to join her in the picture space, clearly invoking a fantasy that depends on the beholder imagining themselves stepping into the picture's world.[2] This was the period during which painting and the other arts developed as an address to the sensuous capacities of their audience (Fragonard's *Swing*, Goethe's *The Sorrows of Young Werther* and Haydn's '*Sturm und Drang*' symphonies are all contemporary with Diderot's forays into art criticism), and in which the expectations of the audience were still emphatically rooted in discursive communication through signing. As Norman Bryson has explained,[3] art in this period coheres in a perfectly explicable pattern of development if only the historian drops the old obsession with stylistic change, and recognizes the significance of patterns of varying intensity in narrative discourse which characterize these works. This article proposes a new kind of misreading of the art, which transports a psychologically self-conscious viewer back to the eighteenth century, and asks them to see post-existential patterns of contact where they cannot possibly have been intended. Not to be found in Hume's experimental process, Diderot's distinction between objective and subjective experience[4] is a primary conceptual construct in Romanticism, and ultimately the source of the obsession with personal experience which cobbles this article's validity as an address to its subject, if French eighteenth-century art is that.

Much of the argument of the article is built around a set of examples of notional paintings, designed to challenge and to allow the elucidation of Saville's theories. None is any more paintable than the *Portrait of Dorian Gray* — which book tells us more about the way we experience art than does this article.

Antonia Phillips's article, 'Drawing from Life', is a development of an idea in another Wollheim essay, his 'On Drawing an Object' of 1965. Discussing the 'highly problematic . . . notion of likeness', Phillips notes,

> The intuitive notion I have in mind is one of likeness holding between picture and object relativized to a perceiver, so that when I talk of a picture x being a likeness of an object y, I mean that x seems to a perceiver A like y (x strikes A like y). (p. 317)

The article seems to me to torture sense as much as it tortures language, with false analogies jostling with illogical concatenations of experience against deductive logic. In its determination to make words mean something exact and fixed, it continually passes obvious common sense on the road to intellectual ruin. 'No one would claim that the Bayeux Tapestry shows us how any battle looked, let alone the Battle of Hastings' (p. 326), doesn't make any sense in an essay which carefully begins by explaining that drawing shows not objects, but what artists see in them. The Bayeux Tapestry surely shows us very well what was seen at the time: an incident whose totemic value as propaganda was far more important than its mere physical appearance. The essay concludes, 'it is essential . . . to take into account the variety of processes by which pictures can be produced. Notions of likeness and intention, even when reinforced by reference to causal connections, cannot by themselves provide for a fine-grained enough account of what it is for pictures to be *of* objects.' (p. 334) That, it seems to me, makes clearer sense than the substance of the essay.

The festschrift contains four groups of essays, on 'Psychoanalysis, Values and Politics'; 'Bradley and Green'; 'Art and Vision'; and 'Memory and Motive'. It may be that the sections which celebrate Wollheim's contributions to philosophy and psychoanalysis do him greater credit than that relating to his writing on art, but for art historians, the main virtue of this volume is that it shows how limited some of Wollheim's apparently universal insights are, and shows (by forcing us to disagree) how fruitless and arcane their consequences can be. If that reduces the high regard in which *Art and its Objects* is held by art historians, or diminishes its perceived value as a contribution to the debate of aesthetics, this volume will have had a sad effect. For whatever the limitations of some of Wollheim's work, *Art and its Objects* deserves to stand as one of the great contributions to aesthetics, for its clarity, its potency and because it probably comes nearer to offering a universally defensible explanation of the way art works than any other book of our time.

Colin Roth
Sheffield

Notes

1 Saville's reference to *Absorption and Theatricality; Painting and the Beholder in the Age of Diderot*, Michael Fried, Chicago, 1980.
2 Donald Posner, *Watteau*, London, 1984.
3 Norman Bryson, *Word and Image*, Cambridge, 1981.
4 'Rococo as a paradigm of mid-eighteenth century culture', Colin Roth, in *Journal 1*, Derby Porcelain International Society, 1989.

More Than Ornament: The Significance of Riegl

Paul Crowther

Problems of Style: Foundations for a History of Ornament by *Alois Riegl* (translated by Evelyn Kain), Princeton: Princeton University Press, 1992, 439 pp., 197 b. & w. illus., £30.00

Alois Riegl: Art History and Theory by *Margaret Iversen*, Cambridge, Mass., and London: The MIT Press, 1993, 232 pp., 19 b. & w. illus., £22.50

Given the renewed interest in art historiography in recent years, it was only to be expected that the work of Alois Riegl would eventually be given its due in the English-speaking world. *The Late Roman Art Industry* (1901) appeared in English translation in 1985 (in an edition that leaves much to be desired in several respects), and now *Problems of Style* (1893) has been published in a format that is eminently acceptable. Not least of its editorial achievements is the set of annotations by David Castriota, which relates

Riegl's original analyses and speculations to more recent scholarship in the field. In this respect, Riegl's book shows itself to have withstood the test of time to an impressive degree.

Riegl's general strategy is to provide the *foundations* of a history of ornament. In his terms this means 'to secure a few positions, a connected series of strongholds from which a comprehensive, systematic, and complete offensive can later be launched'.[1] Hence, much of Riegl's argument is negative in character. On the one hand, he marshals empirical evidence and conceptual points to refute the materialist–technological reductionism of Semper's followers (a view which I shall return to, a little further on); and, on the other hand, he similarly endeavours to refute William Goodyear's attempts to link continuity in the history of ornament to an underlying and continuing influence of sun cults. Against these views Riegl's own substantive claim is that the history of ornament is that of a continuous series of stylistic transformations whose basic impetus is internal to the formal and stylizing interests of art itself. He traces this specifically in relation to the development of vegetal ornament from ancient Egyptian times, to that of Byzantium and its legacy in the 'arabesque' of Islamic culture.

Riegl's starting point, however, is, in both chronological and conceptual terms, prior to this. It is to be found in his decisive chapter on the 'Geometric Style'. I say 'decisive' here, because it is in this portion of his narrative that Riegl establishes his main methodological points and strategies. I shall now address these in detail.

First, Riegl suggests that

> All art, and that includes decorative art as well, is inextricably tied to nature. All art forms are based on models in nature. This is true not only when they actually resemble their natural prototypes but even when they have been drastically altered by the human beings who created them. . . .[2]

The stylization to which Riegl alludes in the latter part of this quotation, is further held to be especially pronounced when an image is adapted and modified for representation on a flat surface. This leads Riegl to what he himself describes as an a priori assumption. It consists in the claim that sculpture is the earlier, more primitive, art medium. There is, for example, no great complexity involved for early humans in modelling an animal in wet clay — because the model is given in nature.

> When, however, they first attempted to draw, engrave, or paint the same animal on a flat surface, they were involving themselves in a truly creative act. In this case they could no longer copy the three-dimensional physical model, instead, they had to invent the silhouette or contour line freely, since it does not exist in reality. Only after this creative act did art begin to acquire its endless representational possibilities.[3]

The invention of the line as a pictorial device, in other words, freed the imagination so as to allow deviation from nature and the greater exploitation of formal possibilities. This outburst of linear creativity, however, was always guided by 'fundamental artistic laws of symmetry and rhythm'.[4] Indeed, it is the influence of these laws which enabled the straight line to be articulated in terms of such forms as triangles, squares and zig-zag patterns etc.; and curved lines in terms of circles, spirals and the like. These plane-geometric shapes are not wholly apart from the forms of nature. Rather they enable the creative articulation of line to allude to formal structures which are latent in nature.

Now it is at this point that Riegl stages his first major confrontation with the followers of Semper. This hinges on two related points. The first is the fact that the

Geometric Style is universal. This suggests that it is not a result of geographical contacts between cultures, but is, rather, spontaneously generated. We are thus led to the second point. If we are to account for spontaneous generation, we must be able to link the Geometric Style to fundamental aspects of the relation between human beings and their environment. The neo-Semperians look for this link in the need to find protection from hostile forces and the elements, through the creation of wickerwork fences and woven textiles. On the basis of this, it is assumed that the interweaving of lines and fibres in such artefacts would have suggested geometric configurations such as the zig-zag pattern. The Geometric Style of ornament, in other words, is *derived* from the appearance of utilitarian artefacts — from the domain of materials and techniques.

Now whilst Riegl is prepared to countenance the fact that the Geometric Style is spontaneously generated, he does not accept the claim that it is a fortuitous derivation from mere items of utility. This, for example, leaves unexplained the question of *why* the interweaving of lines and fibres should be found so delightful as to be adopted into ornament. Riegl's further reservations run deeper still, and constellate around a major counter-example to the neo-Semperian reductionist strategy. This is provided by the cave dwellers of the Dordogne, who possessed artistic abilities, but without any culture of textiles over and above sewn animal skins. Indeed, the visual artefacts produced by them exceed in complexity any mere variation on the sewn-seam.

The Dordogne artists carved or engraved bone in the round

> Then comes a whole series of developmental phases during which the sculptural characteristics gradually disappear: at first, three-dimensional sculpture becomes flattened, then various degrees of high relief are followed by low relief, finally resulting in pure engraving.[5]

As one might expect, Riegl regards the appearance of the outline as the crucial element in this transition, since it is the key component in drawing, painting, and, indeed, two-dimensional art in general. In relation to this transition to line, Riegl further claims that

> The impetus did not arise from the technique, but on the contrary, from the particular artistic impulse. First came the desire to create the likeness of a creature from nature in lifeless material, and then came the invention of whatever technique was appropriate. A carved reindeer on the hilt of a dagger certainly does not make it any easier to handle. Therefore, it must have been an immanent artistic drive, alert and restless for action, that human beings possessed long before they invented woven protective coverings for their bodies . . .[6]

The further effects of this impetus are found in the Dordogne artists' development of the Geometric Style in terms of crossed lines and more regular crosses. As Riegl puts it

> They have obviously not been copied from nature but are purely decorative patterns intended to adorn a given surface. Their creation was guided by the same desire to decorate, that informed the animal images.[7]

The ubiquity of the Geometric Style, however, is not just a function of this urge to adorn. Its systematic development can also be explained by the fact that (once originated) geometric forms are easier to create and distribute on a surface, than are animal forms and the like. We are thus led to Riegl's first major generalization of his theoretical position.

All of art history presents itself as a continuous struggle with material, it is not the tool — which is determined by the technique — but the artistically creative idea that strives to expand its creative realm and increase its formal potential.[8]

Given all these points, it is clear that Riegl has already assembled most of the elements central to his notion of the *kunstwollen* (or 'art drive', as I shall term it) which is more fully developed in his later works.

We are thus in a position to consider the remaining central trajectory of Riegl's arguments and analyses. This really begins with his third chapter on Vegetal Ornament, and, in particular, the ancient Egyptians' use of it. The art of the Egyptians is not, in its origins, a purely artistic one determined by the need to adorn or decorate *per se*. Rather, it is animated by religious symbolism and significance. However, as Riegl observes:

Any religious symbol can become a predominantly or purely decorative motif in the course of time if it has artistic potential. When a motif is frequently and continuously executed in a variety of materials because of its religious associations, a stereotype is created, which can then become so familiar as to seem to a certain extent ingrained.[9]

For Riegl the *lotus* is the fundamental stereotype of the Egyptians — one whose artistic potential is as rich as its religious significance. Of especial importance in this respect, are frontal and profile views of the lotus blossom, and combinations thereof. Riegl distinguishes these and other permutations at great length, and traces their use and stylistic development in a variety of decorative contexts. His evaluation of the Egyptians' achievement is a mixed one. For whilst the value of Egyptian ornamentation is high, the decorative task was more successfully elaborated by their successors. In particular, the Egyptians' limitations are illustrated by their treatment of borders 'which seldom relate harmoniously to the fields that they frame. The solutions used for corners are even less successful and often strike the eye as downright unpleasant.'[10]

At the heart of the Egyptians' limitations, according to Riegl, is the fact that

This culture was no doubt already trying to strike a balance between the two poles of artistic concern — at the one a decorative urge demanding a feast for the eyes and at the other a desire to give concrete expression to the most significant ideas and feelings of humanity. The Egyptians were the first to be keenly aware of this polarity. They can hardly be blamed for not having found an ultimately satisfying solution.[11]

Riegl suggests that just as individuals are limited in what they can achieve, so are cultures. It is only with Greek civilization that the 'goal' intimated in the above passage is achieved, i.e. 'the harmonious fusion of formal beauty and profound content'.[12]

After having addressed the fundamental role of variations on the lotus in other near- and middle-eastern cultures, Riegl turns his attention to the Greeks. Again the central trajectory of his argument is one which affirms an essentially internal continuity of stylistic variation and transformations of motifs ultimately derived from the lotus. There is, however, one utterly crucial formal innovation — found in Mycenean art — which cannot be traced to the articulation of lotus prototypes. As Riegl puts it:

Just as the Greeks restyled age-old Egyptian blossom motifs in the most delightful way imaginable to accord with their own standards of formal

> beauty, they also discovered the most perfect way of linking them together, namely with the tendril, moving to and fro in a mellifluous rhythm. Obviously nothing in nature could have had a direct influence on the appearance of the undulating tendril, since both of its characteristic forms, especially the intermittent type, imitate no known plants: it is a product of the imagination, freely created by the Greek artistic spirit.[13]

Riegl goes on to trace the many refinements and variations of this and other motifs (notably the acanthus) placing, as always, the emphasis of such derivations on stylistic response to existing formats, rather than a return (or turn) to natural sources. Indeed, the progressively less naturalistic articulation of the undulating tendril was so developed in the classical world that, by the time of the collapse of Rome's political domination (around AD 400) it served as an important basis of independent development.

The most radical articulation of this, is found in the influence of Byzantium upon Islamic culture, and, specifically, in the creation of the arabesque. The most distinctive phase of this development consists in an organizational principle which Riegl terms 'infinite rapport'. He characterizes it as follows:

> As a rule, a simple element — even if it is a composite one — provides the basis of the entire decorative conception: either by duplication or division, so as to establish a continuous pattern of interrelation.[14]

This formal device is familiar from the Geometric Style where it is usually articulated in terms of networks of squares and diamonds. However, for Riegl, the principle only becomes really interesting when it advances beyond these 'rudimentary banded registers' through assimilating the more (but, of course, not absolutely) naturalistic tendencies of Greek vegetal ornament.

We are now in a position to summarize Riegl's overall position. In his own words:

> At no time did the creation of ornament involve an arbitrary dependence upon the natural plant world to the extent usually assumed. When this did occasionally occur, it never produced any lasting results. In contrast, the stylized palmette, acanthus, and other such ornaments have maintained a timeless, classic importance, even into the recent period of realism. The line of development exemplified by certain stylized blossom forms such as the palmette did not essentially deviate its course even through the latest stage of antiquity, and we may as well extend this claim to cover the late Middle Ages.[15]

Having expounded Riegl's arguments at length, it is now time to offer a critical review of them. First, it is possible to take issue with a number of important details in Riegl's analyses of specific motifs. In this respect, both Castriota (in his annotations) and Gombrich have found difficulties with Riegl's attempts to derive the Greek acanthus motif from Egyptian precedents. However, even allowing for a few specific problems of this sort, Riegl has certainly succeeded in laying the foundations for a formalist and historicist account of the development of ornament. He shows how a specific aspect of art might be understood in historical terms as a series of stylistic transformations whose impetus is fundamentally internal to art itself. Whether these foundations are secure or not, is not so much a function of the general consistency of Riegl's narrative concerning style, so much as the basic concepts and assumptions which direct and orientate the narrative. It is these which I shall address.

A useful starting point is the framework of ideas laid down in Riegl's discussion of the Geometric Style. There, we will recall, Riegl proposes an 'a priori' schema where the Geometric Style is derived (through laws of symmetry and rhythm) from the line — set free in two-dimensional media, which is itself derived from the *prior* art form of sculpture. This theoretical transition from sculpture to Geometric Style finds its practical vindication for Riegl in the actual work of the Dordogne cave dwellers. Now this example raises a number of worries. For one thing its universality may be queried, in that whilst some development of the Geometric Style is to be found in all cultures, not all cultures have developed both sculpture and that transition to two-dimensional representation in which Riegl sees the origin of geometrical abstraction. Indeed, it may well be that the mastery of material involved in tool-making itself, or the experience of animal tracks, or a sense of territorial boundaries is involved here.

Related to this is Riegl's rather superficial treatment of the function and structure of, on the one hand, extra-artistic factors, and, on the other hand, innate human propensities. In relation to the former, for example, Riegl does not address the question of why people should want to represent images of animals at all. Neither does he consider the possibility that the transposition of the image into two dimensions may be prompted by magical beliefs pertaining to the control of that which the image represents — rather than the working out of some intrinsic art drive alone.

This, of course, brings us to the question of innate human propensities. In *Problems of Style* generally, Riegl seems to be operating with four key notions of this kind: a) the urge to adorn or decorate, b) laws of symmetry and rhythm, c) *horror vacuui*, and d) the 'feast for the eye'. Now what this in effect means is that the art drive is itself complex — a function of these propensities in concert. However, it is a moot point as to whether such propensities in themselves are simply given, and unamenable to further analysis (as Riegl himself suggests on occasion).[16] In fact, an analysis of each of these four terms in the context of the Geometric Style, and then in the overall trajectory of Riegl's arguments, proves extremely illuminating.

To show this, I will first consider the urge to adornment which Riegl sees as preceding the need to cover the body. Riegl tends to see this urge as something enjoyed for its own sake and which is, in effect, synonymous with the urge to decorate. It is surely neither. One might just as well trace the urge for adornment to a survival-oriented need to compel recognition and/or fear in other persons or animals, or to exert a magical influence over them. If adornment is to mean anything more than this, and if, in particular, it is to be equated with the urge to decorate, then this necessarily entails the involvement of factor b) noted above, namely laws of symmetry and rhythm. Indeed, what constitutes the artistic or aesthetic object is precisely the capacity to give form and order to sensible material on the basis of such laws. Now, of course, a hard-headed neo-Semperian might argue that the pleasure we take in seeing material ordered in this way can be further analysed as a function of our admiration for the skill or patience required in carrying it out. Doubtless this can be involved. It is not, however, fundamental. Rather the ubiquitous human predilection for symmetry and rhythm is tied to some of the profoundest constants in human experience itself. There are a number of aspects to this. The one which I shall develop here is loosely derived from Slavoj Žižek's reading of some ideas in Lacan's later work.[17]

At the heart of self-consciousness is the capacity to signify, i.e. to deploy signs so as to communicate specific meanings. Now the ability to do this presupposes various capacities for recall and comprehension; it also controversially presupposes something else — a capacity to take pleasure in achieving signification. For whilst it is all very well having the cognitive and receptive mechanisms which make language-use possible, these would remain inert, if it did not, in some sense, pay us to deploy them. Such usage, in other words, must have a positive affective value. This value might, of course, be seen to lie in the way it initiates us into forms of life with all the dimensions of recognition from the Other which this involves. But again, why should this recognition matter to us if we did not, in some way matter to ourselves? To be a self-conscious being entails taking a pleasure in our sense of self, and to take a pleasure in the self, in its most minimal form, is to take a pleasure in the achievement of significance.

These points help explain why, for Lacan, this pleasure is absolutely primal — the basis of consistency in the individual's experience. It arises from (in Lacan's neologism) 'sinthome', i.e. recurrent behavioural traits which are ordered and meaningful without the subject being able to explain them in any terms deeper than their ostensible pattern and structure. (They are thus a kind of 'normal' version of hysterical symptoms.) Sinthome, in other words, is significantly activity whose pleasure consists in nothing other than the act of signification. Now whereas our pleasure in signification is normally woven into (and thence lost in) the symbolic networks of everyday interactions in the experience of sinthome we encounter it in its primal form.

It is in this light that we must view Riegl's treatment of the innate artistic laws of rhythm and symmetry, and, in particular, the significance of the Geometric Style. To signify on the basis of rhythm and symmetry, is to exemplify (in the purest and most schematic way) the organizational axes of signification itself. In poststructuralist discourse it is customary to regard these as the metonymic and metaphoric axes respectively. These are not entirely apt terms, but what they mean are the rule-governed physical conjunction of signs (in the former case); and (in the latter case) the rule-governed recurrence of signs, or the substitutability of one sign for another. Rhythm and symmetry *vis-à-vis* visual signs in the Geometric Style instantiate these axes through the exactness of their individual spatial contours and recurrent distribution. The Geometric Style is prototype for signification itself. It exemplifies the possibility of lawlike articulation at a level which engages both our capacities for cognitive recognition and sensory receptiveness. Given this, it is easy to understand why a pleasure in the Geometric Style is of fundamental significance in the human experience and thence why its occurrence is so ubiquitous. One could even argue a case for its phylogenetic significance, as a necessary correlate of linguistic competence *per se*, i.e. if human beings had not engaged in geometric pattern-making, they would not have developed language in a full sense.

These points have further important ramifications for Riegl's central line of argument in *Problems of Style*. To see why this is so let us now consider the other two innate propensities noted earlier (as c) and d) respectively), namely *horror vacuui* and the 'feast for the eye'. The former notion is, in fact, the obverse corollary of the urge to decorate on the basis of rhythm and symmetry. For if, as I have argued, this urge is an expression of primal pleasure in signification, then, in visual terms, an empty space is both a challenge — something which *needs* to be filled, and a threat — of the absence or death of signification. This, however, is where the question of the 'feast for the eye' must be raised. Consider the following crucial remarks by Riegl:

> . . . the kinds of things that make history, that immediately capture our attention, and save us from the monotonous pace of everyday life tend to be the exception to abstract laws. The Geometric Style strictly considered in accordance with the highest laws of symmetry and rhythm, is from the standpoint of regularity the most perfect of styles; on our scale of values, however, it occupies the lowest rank.[18]

What makes these points so crucial is that Riegl is pinpointing the origin of history itself. Some cultures are severely restrained by the physical conditions of their habitat or the depredations of hostile forces. Their level of cultural development accordingly is static, and characterized by simple repetition of patterns of existence already laid down. In the context of visual culture, the rigid persistence of the Geometric Style alone would be one symptom of this. However, there are, of course, other cultures, who are not as severely restricted by the physical conditions of their habitat. They are able to expand the scope of their activity in both cultural and geographical terms, for example, by trade or migration. In particular, they establish changing patterns of belief and value through contact with other cultures. Now in a situation such as this, the Geometric Style no longer suffices. As one's human situation changes, existing patterns of sinthome can seem dead or inert. They cease to exemplify signification in any adequate sense. One would expect, therefore, that notions of rhythm and symmetry would be varied in new and more complex directions in response to the challenge of environmental and cultural change. This diversification of sinthome would very much involve a complex 'feast for the eye' incorporating elements of that polar structure which Riegl describes as involving, on the one hand, formal variety *per se*, and, on the other hand, the expression of ideas and feelings. Once a dialectic between these two elements is in play, then we have, in the visual context, history — in the sense of a narrative of change rather than inert chronological succession.

It is, of course, just such a narrative which constitutes the central trajectory of Riegl's history of vegetal ornament from Egypt, through Greece, and the rise of Islam. However, in the foregoing points, note how I have broadened Riegl's notion of 'feast for the eye' to encompass *both* elements of the polar structure, i.e. content as well as merely formal variety. This is a consequence of thinking through the deeper implications of the Geometric Style. For if the urge to rhythm and symmetry is to be revitalized in parallel with changing conditions of existence, then this must be through the infusion of complex elements from outside the field of art. Riegl himself shows this throughout *Problems of Style*. An implicit example is his point that before sculpture is the desire to imitate. In the case of the Dordogne cave dwellers, the objects of this desire are creatures which are sources of food or danger. Here, in other words, the sequence of events leading to the Geometric Style has its original (at least in part) in factors external to art. Similar considerations hold, of course, when on the basis of religious meaning, the Egyptians subject vegetal motifs to the laws of rhythm and symmetry. Now, Riegl himself, of course, stresses that the major motif in question — the lotus — is one with considerable artistic potential in terms of possibilities of formal development, but whether this potential is known in advance or not, is a point of debate. Oddly enough, it is to some degree irrelevant. For even if this motif was simply taken up by artists on religious grounds, the extraordinary diversity of its subsequent developments is enough in itself to evidence the workings of an art drive, striving to articulate rhythm and symmetry in more complex ways. We do not, in other words, have to conceive the art drive as purely teleological, following a predetermined course determined by formal considerations alone.

The point which I am making here is one which simply asks Riegl to be true to his own insight concerning the poles of art, i.e. formal variety, *and* the expression of ideas and feelings. For if the former aspect is to be *fully* developed, it will be so through enrichment from the realm of the latter. Matters in respect of what this involves come to a head in relation to both Riegl's treatment of Greek art, and the arabesque. We will recall, for example, that for Riegl the key innovation of the Greeks is the introduction of the undulating tendril. This formal innovation solves a problem implicit from the beginning, namely how to distribute visual elements over a flat surface in a satisfying way. However, the means to the solution of this problem are surely in part again provided by the extra-artistic context. For the undulating tendril is one which is infused with life. It exemplifies a vision of form which is at home with — indeed, committed to nature — in a way that is specifically Greek (or, at least was, at that time). This should hardly surprise us. For whilst the world-view of Egyptian culture involves a rich sense of life beyond the grave, ancient Greek culture does not. There is such a life, but it is a domain of shadows and yearnings for what was. The point is, therefore, that the Greeks possessed exactly the right means — a yea-saying to the world of nature — which enabled them to solve the formal problem of unifying pictorial space by means of the undulating tendril. A similar logic applies in the case of the arabesque. The formal device of infinite rapport as a unifying principle is as old as the Geometric Style itself. However, as Riegl himself notes, the device only becomes interesting when Islamic artists apply it in relation to the organization of vegetal motifs. Again, whilst the motive to do this is presented by a formal problem, the means adopted for its solution draw on factors external to art itself. The Islamic world-view is one which sees the world of nature as sustained by a unifying but (from the finite viewpoint) abstract Godhead. The device of infinite rapport sets up a sense of constant generation and transition, wherein natural forms point towards an ultimate abstract unity which organizes and sustains them. Here, in other words, it is a specific world-view which lends itself to the solution of the artistic problem.

There is another related sense in which Riegl is slightly inconsistent in his reluctance to give due weight to extra-artistic factors. It consists of his willingness to evaluate formal transformations in terms of advance and progress, rather than mere difference *per se*. The most notable example of this, of course, is his treatment of Greek ornament as an advance on Egyptian modes through its harmonizing of the need for formal variety and the expression of ideas and feelings. Now it is important to make a qualification here. For whilst Riegl rates the Greeks higher than the Egyptians, this does not imply that the latter are in some global sense culturally inferior to the former. Riegl's point is that the art drive inaugurates a tradition of specialist practices surrounding a body of shared formal problems. Each step forward in the treatment of these problems is a framework on which subsequent exponents of the tradition can build. Riegl, unfortunately, tends to give this an unduly teleological thrust, as though we are dealing with a process of inevitable advance. Each stage in the process — no matter how formally restricted *vis-à-vis* the more advanced stages — has the dignity of being a necessary part of the whole. However, we must recall Riegl's own point that what makes history is deviation from given laws. There are perhaps two aspects to this. Let us call the first 'normal historical difference'. This consists of simple diversifications of refinements of existing motifs and formats. It can be a question of formal variation *per se*; or (as in the case of the Mycenaean incorporation of butterfly and cuttlefish motifs) it can draw on extra-artistic factors. These changes are essentially small-scale innovations within specialist practice. 'Effective historical difference', in contrast, involves stylistic or compositional shifts which transform the scope of practice within a medium or artistic genre. Examples of this include the undulating tendril and the infinite rapport of the arabesque (discussed a little earlier).

Now the key point to note from all this is not only that (as Riegl's own major examples show) the real principle of stylistic advance is usually bound up with factors outside art, but also that this is not simply a one-way flow. For when art transforms its means at moments of effective historical difference, it does so in a way which elevates the infusion from life or nature to a more universal dimension. The wavy tendril, for example, now bespeaks the vitality of nature and the possibility of feeling for it. It is not simply a manifestation of the Greek world-view. Rather, by being drawn into the art drive and being made into an artwork, it offers a permanent possibility of experience for all those who have continuity (at whatever point of distance) with the tradition of vegetal ornament. This means that effective historical difference is a function of both the flow from life into aesthetic object and from aesthetic object back into the continuity of existence. The worth of a body of aesthetic artefacts, in other words, consists not only of formal innovations, but how these innovations clarify and enrich the ongoing narrative of human experience. In this respect, the historian's present always has a privileged position *vis-à-vis* his or her precedecessors. Moments of effective historical difference only emerge through description and interpretation of bodies of artefacts and their continuing effects *qua* aesthetic objects on subsequent traditions of production and reception.

Riegl's positive assessment of Greek ornament in relation to Egyptian modes can, therefore, be justified. This, however, is not on the grounds of its higher place in a blind teleological process, or indeed through the former being in formal terms more pleasing. Rather we must justify it on the basis of the history is makes. This means both its patterns of breakage with existing stylistic precedents and its giving birth to new ones, with both formal and existential potency. Ironically, Riegl himself concedes this in effect through his point (noted earlier) that the Greeks harmonize that twin pole of art which involves both formal variety and the expression of ideas and feelings. Unfortunately, he chooses to focus his official account of artistic change on the former, with the latter (at best) a mere mysterious accompaniment. This rigid account of artistic development is bought at the price of a degradation of that broader relation to life which enables the achievement of effective historical difference, i.e. the building of tradition itself.

In conclusion, it could be said that Riegl offers us a complex jigsaw of the truth. He is right to identify an art drive in human beings, and I have sought to bolster that view through linking it to the need for sinthome. Riegl is also right to argue that ornament's satisfaction of this need (as indeed is the case with all art) involves patterns of formal transformation. His main mistake is to see these transformations as almost exclusively internal, rather than as a complex dialectic between the art drive, life and tradition. His narrative, indeed, would actually have read more consistently if his account of artistic autonomy had been a relative rather than absolute one.

Now, of course, the problem of the relation between art's claims to autonomy and extra-artistic factors is a recurrent problem in Riegl's subsequent works, and one which is never satisfactorily resolved. This problem (amongst many others) surfaces in Margaret Iversen's new book on Riegl — a work which considers the development of Riegl's thought in its original intellectual context, and in terms of its more general relevance. I shall now offer a survey of Iversen's book.

The first chapter broaches the notion of the *Kunstwollen*, and gives some emphasis to the broadness of Riegl's use of the term. In particular, it is argued that the broadness of this application is one which offers criteria for the analysis of art which avoids the narrow focus of traditional methods and approaches. This is not only manifest in the diversity of art forms which Riegl relates to the *Kunstwollen*, but also in the complexity of the subject–object relation involved at different historical stages. Iversen pays particular attention to the developing way Riegl deals with this relation, and to the ways his ideas have informed the work of other art historians and cultural theorists in the twentieth century.

Iversen then goes on to consider Riegl's thought in the context of its original production, namely Vienna at the turn of the century. Especially useful is her exposition of the ideas of Semper and neo-Semperians such as Otto Wagner. Indeed she seeks to establish that 'Otto Wagner must have been one of the people Riegl disparagingly referred to as the "sub-Semperians", or at the very least he represented the latest and most prominent exponent of a theoretical position to which Riegl was implacably opposed.'[19]

This relating of Riegl to the original context of his writings is continued in the next chapter. Here Iversen emphasizes Riegl's own emphasis on the importance of stylistic '*transformation*', and relates this in some detail to the controversy surrounding Klimt's design for the *Philosophy* mural in the Great Hall of the University of Vienna. She also relates Riegl to an 'aesthetics of disintegration' which has a (putatively) distinguished lineage in German thought. (In this respect Iversen cites figures such as Kant, Schiller, and Hegel.) Broadly speaking, this aesthetic is oriented towards a breakdown of natural (and especially tactile forms) in a way which demands much more imaginative activity on the part of the viewer and even, to some degree, a loss of self. Traditionally, the tactile ideal of art is one which is active, involving an effortless mastery of materials. In the *Late Roman Art Industry* and (even more so) in *The Dutch Group Portrait* Riegl argues that this ideal is transformed into a more optical or subjective one, which involves an element of passivity. Iversen sees this as a positive understanding of modernity itself. Indeed 'Riegl's highly original inflection of the aesthetics of disintegration was a new way of thinking the connection between artistic achievement and the attainment of freedom.'[20]

These first chapters open out some of the major themes and possibilities which inform Riegl's work in general. In the next chapters Iversen addresses the major arguments of *Problems of Style, The Late Roman Art Industry*, and *The Dutch Group Portrait* in turn. Given my own earlier exposition of the first of these, I will not dwell on the topic except to say that Iversen's treatment of Riegl on ornament is one which focuses much more closely on the debate with the neo-Semperians and Goodyear, and, indeed, on some *possible* sources of Riegl's ideas, notably in the psychology of Herbart.

The Late Roman Art Industry recommences the battle with the neo-Semperians, with two major trajectories. The first is to show that the Late Roman art world is not in decline or in a state of decadence, but is rather a necessary element in the transition from ancient to modern. A more general direction of argument is described by Iversen as follows:

> In *Late Roman Art Industry*, the *Kunstwollen* became the basis of a whole theory of art history. It is a fundamental intent common to all types of art, which insures the integrity of artistic production and the continuity of art's history.[21]

One of the most interesting aspects of this is the way it leads Riegl to affirm the primacy of how a form or subject is represented rather than what it is explicitly intended to mean. Iversen follows this up (having first traced the influence of Hildebrand on the formation of Riegl's position). Broadly speaking, the impetus of antique art's *Kunstwollen* is to isolate single individual entities, in order to present them in clear 'self-contained unity'. This involves visual data being individualized within the plane, with only a minimal use of depth. At its most basic or 'haptic' level such representation takes the form of a near- or close-sighted view of objects which emphasizes a clear outline against a material ground. (Egyptian art, and hollow relief, in particular, manifest this). Such works avoid any detailed particularizations of the subject matter — as might be entailed, for example, in foreshortening or shadow, or attentiveness to particular facial expressions.

The second phase of antique art involves a haptic-optic conception of things, and is exemplified in classical Greek art, notably relief. Here the optical viewpoint is, comparatively speaking, a normal one. However, the amount of depth in such pictorial fields is severely restricted — even in relief, where plastic figuration is firmly locked into the ground plane.

In the third — 'optical' — phase of antique art (exemplified in Late Roman culture) objects appear in fully three-dimensional terms. Space between material bodies is understood as 'measurable'. Objects are still organized in relation to a plane, but no longer have any tactile connection to it. This is because the plane contains 'interruptions' achieved by deep shadowing. Objects appear to the viewer from a long-sighted distant position, and tend to blur into their environment. Such works have a primarily optical orientation. Having made this exposition, Iversen follows up some of the problematic implications of Riegl's treatment of this third phase, with especial reference to architecture. She pinpoints both particular difficulties of application (for example, the *Temple of Minerva Medica* in Rome), and the general problem of how the dissolution of tactile coherence can have intrinsic aesthetic value.

For Iversen, *The Dutch Group Portrait* goes *some* way towards resolving this latter difficulty. She (and Riegl) set out the continuity between the latter's earlier and later work as follows:

> Both early Christian and Dutch art strive to make space embrace disparate elements and to create psychological bonds. Riegl sets out to show these unifying elements were perfected in Dutch group portraiture; 'The general developmental tendency appears here to be directed toward binding the figures physically with the surrounding free space and psychologically with the external world: both subjective tendencies.'[22]

Iversen gives special emphasis to the psychological 'attentiveness' involved here, and traces its ramifications in both Riegl's treatment of specific examples (notably Rembrandt), and the intellectual sources on which Riegl may have been drawing (notably Hegel).

Iversen's final chapters attempt to develop the more general implications of Riegl's theory of spectatorship in relation amongst others to Michael Fried on Absorption, Wolfgang Kemp on Constitutive Blanks, and Michael Foucault on *Las Meninas*. The work concludes with a consideration of Riegl's complex relation to Panofsky.

Iversen's book is written with grace and lucidity throughout and has two particular strengths. First, it traces Riegl's development by detailed reference to easily overlooked short writings (as well as his major works); and secondly, it offers extremely valuable insights into the intellectual context in which his thought was generated. The work is also of use through its indication of new contexts in which Riegl's key concepts might be developed. Here, however, a crucial caveat must be entered. Like many art historians, Iversen's tendency is to approach theory as if it were a work of art. By this I mean that considerable emphasis is placed on how the theory came to be generated; who it was originally addressed to, etc. Now, as has already been noted, this is of some value in understanding Riegl's work as a historical product, but it severely restricts Iversen's capacity to negotiate that work's status as a body of truth-claims. For example, after inaugurating a critical discussion of Riegl's treatment of the transition from Egyptian to Hellenistic ornament, Iversen then launches into the influence of Hildebrand, and parallels with Wölfflin's treatment of the triumphal arch. Indeed, throughout the book, just when the going is getting critically good, we are returned to a discussion of Riegl's sources. As a result one feels that Iversen does not get to grips with issues of decisive theoretical interest.

One further example of this is her consideration of the relation to Hildebrand — which was important in forming Riegl's account of the interplay between haptic and optic in antiquity. Clearly there is a formal transformation of the type broadly described by Riegl, but whether it is really to be explained as a change of perceptual framework is another matter entirely. Iversen indicates her unease with Riegl's derivations from Hildebrand, but this unease is not, as it were, fully chased out in a critical discussion where Riegl's formal transformations might be explained in more viable terms. This particular worry is symptomatic of a broader unease concerning Iversen's treatment of the relation between formal transformations, *Kunstwollen*, and extra-artistic factors. Riegl himself never really sorts this out, and, given its recurrent importance, it would surely have been worthy of a chapter (perhaps even the concluding one) in itself.

My major grumble with Iversen then is that she tends rather too much to address secondary issues concerning Riegl's source material, rather than negotiate the continuous trajectories of his arguments in depth. Clearly she has the intellectual means to do the latter. In the final analysis her book is simply much too short. It could have been double its existing length, without exceeding standard monograph size. Perhaps she will be able to offer us a further volume . . .

Paul Crowther
University of St Andrews

Notes

1 Riegl, *Problems of Style*, p. 5.
2 ibid., p. 14.
3 ibid., pp. 14–15.
4 ibid., p. 15.
5 ibid., p. 29.
6 ibid., p. 30.
7 ibid., p. 32
8 ibid., p. 33
9 ibid., p. 50.
10 ibid., p. 81.
11 ibid., p. 82.
12 ibid., p. 82.
13 ibid., p. 117.
14 ibid., p. 272.
15 ibid., p. 299.
16 See, for example, Riegl ibid., p. 40.
17 See, for example, Žižek's 'The Enlightenment in Laibach', *Art and Design*, April 1994.
18 Riegl, ibid., p. 16.
19 Iversen, *Alois Riegl: Art History and Theory*, p. 25.
20 ibid., p. 47.
21 ibid., p. 72.
22 ibid., p. 94.

The *Ignis Fatuus* of Colour

Barbara Saunders

Colour and Culture. Practice and Meaning from Antiquity to Abstraction by *John Gage*, London: Thames and Hudson, 1993, 335pp., 120 col. plates, 103 b. & w. illus., £38.00

Though contested, one foundational story in the Euro-American tradition tells of the achievement of painting as progress in the representation of Nature or the world. It is part of a bigger story according to which all forms of inquiry, whether art, philosophy or science, exemplify the representational theory of *mimesis*. Briefly this theory is concerned with the abstract entities which are extracted from, or correspond to, the physical or moral constants and invariables immanent in Nature, and which are represented in painting as an illusory whole or limited unity (Murdoch, 1992).[1] *Mimesis* in painting represents what is above being, which is non-personal, non-contingent and not of a particular thing, as a vision of an exemplary slice of life. Once thought to be the imitation of static forms, the favoured theory now considers *mimesis* to ascend to 'the end of inquiry', to fulfil its evolutionary *telos*. These issues are central to any discussion of colour — not only in painting but also in anthropological linguistics, psychology and cognitive science — as I will show.

In painting, the vehicles or ultimate constituents of *mimesis* have been held to be line and colour.[2] Lines and colours are considered not only the elements of the optical principles of visual experience as well as the structure of the work of art, but also the elements of explanation of how all this hangs together. Line and colour on this account are the means to the duality of picture perception, being at one and the same time both of reality and of depicted reality. Clearly theories of perception and depiction are interlocked here. Consequently, discussion of either line or colour will be saturated by favourite theories, consciously or otherwise. It is therefore important what stance is taken at the outset. Lack of clarity about such foundational issues has diminished what is otherwise the admirable work of Martin Kemp's *The Science of Art. Optical Themes in Western Art from Brunelleschi to Seurat* (1990), as well as the complementary work of Gage's *Colour and Culture*. As a result, although candidates for the status of canonical works of Euro-American art history, both suffer from a particular kind of limited vision: ambitious in scope, but ambivalent in their theoretical resources and aspirations.

Despite such shortcomings, *Colour and Culture* is a very welcome addition not only to art-historical literature, but also to research on colour in general. Gage adroitly produces an historical survey of the dialectic of colour theory and practice from Antiquity to Abstraction. His course can be seen as a microscopically detailed chart of how significant works are structured and realized in and through their physical medium. But it is also an account of how artists have struggled with diverse theories, trying to rhyme them with the constraints of the palette, the unpredictable interactions of materials and their properties of hue, tone and texture, the scale of the work, the complex behaviour of light, and the collusiveness of the spectator. Whether or not artists have been so profoundly indebted to natural philosophers and scientists as Gage might be read as suggesting is a moot point. But the presentation in *Colour and Culture* certainly would have supported, if not reproduced, the time-honoured priority of science, were it not that science has failed — and failed dismally — to provide a unified theory of colour. Had science not reneged on its ideal image, the story of colour might have gone something like this: just as the two-dimensional depiction of proportional relations, occlusions and edges of three dimensions (various kinds of perspective) is held to model how we see 'space', so too the palette is held to be a (partial) model of how we see 'colour'. However, despite the best attempts of science, a unified theory of colour is as remote as ever. From beginning to end, colour remains 'one of the worst muddles in the history of science', as Gibson (1968; also 1986) put it, and Gage offers nothing to dispel that judgement.

He shows in *Colour and Culture* how, from Democritus to Goethe, from Newton to Hering, the myriad attempts to discover the natural system of colour were defied by the phenomenon itself, as illustrated by a diversity of beautifully reproduced colour charts and diagrams. The only systems to gain more or less general respectability were developed in the twentieth century when business and industry demanded the standardization of colour samples. From around 1950 onwards, the most popular model, the *Munsell Color System*, organized by the three coordinates of hue, saturation and brightness, was coopted by psychology, anthropology and linguistics as a model of the purportedly innate 'colour space' in the human brain. It provided a tool for the experimental investigation of the cybernetic view of language and cognition. Developed during the Cold War to 'crack the code of thought', and worked up with some precision by Chomsky (1965; 1968) and Fodor (1983; 1987), this tool was used by Berlin and Kay (1969; repr. 1991) to test the cybernetic view cross-culturally. Colour was held to be an innately specified, autonomous and mandatory substratum in the brain, automatically issuing perceptuo-linguistic basic categorizations. The assumption was that underlying the (symbolic-) mind is the (literal-) brain, in which an inner eye reads the information that is encoded in the neurons from the world 'out there' (as Plato might say). In this story, physical, neurophysiological, phenomenological, syntactic and semantic aspects of 'colour' form a unified, mimetic whole, the particular balances of computations historically and cross-culturally determined by levels of evolutionary development (Hardin, 1988; Kay, Berlin and Merrifield, 1991; MacLaury, 1992). However, as I will argue below, the picture is mistaken.

In the first part of this review I will show why it is important to be clear about foundational issues with regard to colour and will be critical of Gage's refusal to address these issues explicitly. In the second part I will show how nevertheless his work contains many resonances crucial to a more foundational approach.

What is meant when art historians (or philosophers for that matter) talk about the part played by the mind or culture in characterizing a work of art? What, for example, is 'the period eye'? Is it a system of representations produced by and reflecting wider social conditions under which a work was produced? Perhaps mind or culture, formed by an abstractly characterized historical ethos or cultural tradition determines the nature of the work? This opens up talk of the 'genius' of a people or age once debated by Herder and Heidegger, and investigated by anthropologists such as Boas, and linguists such as Whorf, and which has now resurfaced in multicultural studies (Turner, 1993). But irrespective of what position is taken here, explanations assume that either a system of representations is in place (Boas's *Elementargedanken*; Whorf's *cryptotypes*), as rationalists since Plato have said, or the brain is equipped with neurons triggered by the appropriate stimuli, as proposed by various brands of physicalist scientism. Either way, on this account representations in some way are wired in, ultimately to be explained by the genes or neurons. Along these lines, linguists are already mapping the spatial prepositions of the world's languages onto, as it were, Mercator projections, in search of the 'spatial' neurons (Landau and Jackendoff, 1993).[3]

This suggests that the proper question to ask about 'the period eye' is: Do people, at different times and places, see differently when looking at the same thing? Do they 'see' space and colour in different ways?[4] Are there self-contained, autonomous, mental models or world-views underpinned by genes or neurons governing vision which anthropologists and art historians must translate into — well, into what? The meta-language of Anglo-American or the formulations of the geneticist?

With regard to colour, an answer has been offered by Berlin and Kay (1969). They ask: does a particular historical tradition or culture — specifically in the form of language — mediate colour vision? Their answer is that the evolution of the perceptuo-linguistic 'organ' determines colour categorization in a linear and cumulative way leading to eleven basic colour categories at the highest stage of evolution. With this we are back to the story of *mimesis* with which we began.

The basic thesis is that 'color categorization is not random and the foci of basic color terms [categories] are similar in all languages.' Thus the colour 'space' and its categorization, is a universal. Colour categories are governed by 'species-specific, biomorphological structures' (1969, p. 109) later identified as neuronal 'opponent processes' (Kay and McDaniel, 1978; Hardin, 1988).

On this model it is assumed that vision is veridical, providing anchors to reality. Such anchors are built out of atomic elements — space and colour — to reveal a universal aspect of vision: beneath the apparent chaos of appearances (the congealing and sedimentation of culture) lies the deep structure or universal law of colour (and space). As an ultimate constituent, colour may stand as a *pars pro toto* for reality. Consequently, what goes for colour goes for the rest of vision too. Primitive colour categories imply primitive consciousness and culture.[5]

At this point, with a not-so-willing suspension of disbelief, let us follow through the implications and development of this line of thought. If colour is a *pars pro toto* for reality, then provided the constant — the colour space — is accurately modelled, it is a short step to designing experiments which measure the degree of cultural input (usually the variable of language, but by implication, culture, mentality, or world-view). On this account, Gage's *Colour and Culture* is just more grist for the mill, filling in the paucity of historical detail for the Western tradition, for most research has been conducted cross-culturally. It is a rich and detailed case study and inevitably presents a chaotic and cluttered impression, as does all raw data. According to this argument, Gage's book can be read as supporting that painters too in their investigations of the atomic elements of reality have hit on the structure of the colour space; it is no accident that black/white, red/green, blue/yellow have emerged as the significant colour categories in modern painting. Similarly nineteenth- and early twentieth-century theorists and painters might be said to have rediscovered the basic laws of colour (see Gage p. 207 and references to Hering *passim*). Thus the history of Western art might be seen as confirmation of the exhaustive protocol of Berlin and Kay's evolutionary law. Naturally there is much 'noise' in the system and counter-examples abound — so pinks, purples, oranges and greys, being 'wildcard' colours, may turn up at any stage of evolution (Kay, Berlin and Merrifield, 1991). It is not surprising, therefore, to find these colour categories used in ancient painting. However, while contemporary Euro-American painting uses all the basic colour categories, few are found amongst peoples who 'exhibit relatively primitive levels of economic and technological development' (Berlin, 1970). Colour use amongst such peoples is limited to the stereotypical black, white, red (Turner, 1967), which is Berlin and Kay's Evolutionary Stage II, or is absent. If fortuitously blue is found in use, though without an appropriate linguistic label, as in ancient Egypt (see Baines, 1985), it is just an anomaly.

Although Gage is semi-dismissive of Berlin and Kay (chapter 5, p. 79) he enters no substantial debate with them. Instead, confusingly, he accepts that colour vocabularies develop ontogenetically in children. In addition he suggests that the black/white/red triad is fundamental not only in Africa and Asia but also in Europe. But any close examination of the African examples shows this categorization cannot be thought of as 'colour' in the ordinary (English) sense of black, white and red, the uses of the relevant terms being extremely polyvalent, raising questions about the wisdom of their translation as *colour* terms (see, for example, Kirby, 1988; Jacobson-Widding, 1979; Zahan, 1974; Whitely, 1973).[6] What pigments and dyes are used has depended on local resources (hues and textures achieved with ochres, charcoal and plant dyes — hardly the stabilized, saturated samples of the *Munsell Colour Chart*) until contact with missionaries and traders made the availability of European paints and dyes widespread. Talk of 'colour' in such situations follows from applying a model of 'symbols and meanings' and the assumption that the chromatic world must necessarily be lexicalized or used.

Kemp (1984) has suggested that the ability of an image to modify our subsequent perceptions, and the whole question of the feed-back from representation to how we see has largely been excluded from discussion of painting. It is this insight that I find helpful when applied to colour. Images and their theories are fed back into the world to modify both what the world looks like as well as our ways of looking. Hence, once the idea of, say, the closed system of basic colour categories is in place, metaphysical theories, optical habits and daily practices tend to combine to incorporate back into the visual universe, with a particularly snug 'fit', just that which they were developed to organize and describe. Anything can therefore be 'seen' in terms of eleven basic colour categories. This is not exceptional, for theories, concepts, findings and images are routinely re-incorporated into their originating universe of processes and events. This is a source of what Bourdieu (1977) has called the '*habitus*' dispositions acquired through a myriad of mundane processes of training and learning (Gibson's 'education of attention'), which are ingrained in, and literally mould the body, operating in such a way that they endure throughout life history, preconsciously, and hence are not readily amenable to reflection. Such dispositions are structured in the sense that they unavoidably reflect the social conditions within which they were acquired, though nonetheless nurturing the individual (Petit, 1993; Ingold, 1991). Once durably installed, the *habitus* tends to generate practices, perceptions, works and appreciations which concur with the conditions of existence of which the *habitus* itself is the product, creating thereby the mirage of naturalism.[7] The 'period eye', perspective and colour I believe to be examples of this. Elsewhere (Saunders, 1992) I have argued that Berlin and Kay's theory of *Basic Color Terms* is a paradigmatic example of the process.

Although generally held to be the case, it is a mistake to think that science has much to say about seeing colour. It can tell us a great deal about light waves, about the chemical structure of pigments and dyes, about such wavelength responders as avian and aquatic beings, and about the structure of the human eye and visual tract.[8] But there is next to nothing on the human proclivity to 'see colour', the question of whether 'seeing colour' is strictly amenable to scientific methods rarely being broached. I say 'proclivity' deliberately: some peoples fail to talk about colour at all, as linguists and ethnographers have shown (Hickerson, 1971, 1975; Conklin, 1955, 1973); some biologists (Maturana and Varela, 1988) suggest that in normal activity colour is invisible.[9] Space and colour as Gibson (1986) might say, are figments of fallacious theories of vision if not schemes of false metaphysics. We should stop trying to extract from the behaviour of pigments, dyes and light something we call colour. There *is* no single phenomenon to be captured by an all-embracing theory of colour.

Enough has now been said to show that the old idea of *mimesis*, the problem of the imitation of Nature or reality as applied to colour, is not discussed by Gage in a thorough-going way (though touched on in chapter 10: The Palette: 'Mother of All Colours'). The question of whether the world is viewed in the same way as depictions of it — the heart of the matter — remains unchallenged. Until it is, and a clear stance taken, everything becomes 'data' amenable to the Berlin and Kay theory (and its successor theories) — even *Colour and Culture*. The basic fallacy of such a stance is that samples on a colour chart are taken to be reality itself. The experience of living in a chromatic world is conflated with two-dimensional representations held to model how external physical colour is conceptually reconstructed in terms of categorized sensory input delivered by our biological equipment. Rejecting this theory reverberates into many areas of inquiry: it means, for example, that innummerable experiments in psychology, including those of Berlin and Kay, are just nonsense. Until the lessons of the ancient story of birds pecking painted grapes is thoroughly sorted out, the theory it contains will be played out again and again as a true theory of perception, the world being taken, for example, as a colour chart (Bousfield, 1979).[10]

However, in terms of an overall assessment of *Colour and Culture*, Gage should be congratulated for not falling for more of this nonsense. Indeed he has produced an honest book, presenting the enigmatic way that pigments interact in all their complex diversity — perhaps in a 'disjunct' way as philosophers might say, or in ways not available to perception, as some psychophysicists suggest (Lockhead, 1992). He shows that it is helpful to think of colour not as a self-contained form (in the brain or Plato's heaven) to which all samples refer via a naïve token-type relationship, but instead, to be a little Aristotelian, that the form of colour is immanent in the particular. The shiny pinky red lollipop, the setting sun, the mottled greenish-orange of the mango skin, the 'golden-rust' lipstick, and the lego bricks might all be referred to as 'red' but they are five different types reducible only at the expense of destroying the phenomenon. How can they belong to 'red' *sub specie aeternitatis* — the deep claim of the category 'red'? Conversely, why is it that some peoples when presented with a prototypical red (Munsell 5R 4/14, for example) categorize it with what in English is called brown, orange, yellow, white, pale green, pale blue, purple, black, as the Dani people did. These kinds of examples challenge the universality or Form of colour; instead they return it from 'out there' to the particularity of this bit of scumbled pigment here, or that relatively stable dye there. The merit of such a relational account is that it is not susceptible to charges of relativism or subjectivism. I think this characterization captures something of Gage's approach, and is a considerable advance on Berlin and Kay.

Gage's *Colour and Culture* does not reduce colour to the effusions of some perceptuo-linguistic or cognitive-modular function, nor to neural constraints; nor does he treat 'culture' as an autonomous domain, as systems and symbols of meaning essentially unconditioned by material, social and political processes. Instead, true to its subtitle, *Practice and Meaning, Colour and Culture* must be located in the tradition of inquiry wherein art historians such as Baxandall, sociologists such as Giddens, psychologists such as Gibson, and philosophers such as Wittgenstein are to be found. Gage is concerned with the practical aesthetics and ethics of colour (see especially chapter 3: Christian and Byzantine mosaics; and chapter 11: Goethe and Turner). He is concerned with the psychology of intention and effect (see chapter 4: the Dyonisian aesthetic in medieval thought; and chapter 14 on De Stijl and the Bauhaus); he shows the structurations of intentionality and agency, resulting from the dialectic of colour theory and painterly practice (see chapter 1 on the classical inheritance, and chapter 9 on the influence of Newton). Throughout he is concerned with the shaping of the environment by the use of colour in a thoroughly intentional way. His discussion is permeated by pigment and dye lore and the (political) economy of taste. He pleads for the inseparability of colour-use and style or meaning in characterizing the work. He accounts for the vicissitudes of pigments, dyes and coloured lights as metaphysical precept, colour theology, or science as heeded, ignored or transformed in practice. And he avoids essentializing and overemphasizing the idea of culture.

Gage makes colour responsive to a hurly-burly historical and social comprehension (without becoming engulfed by sociality and 'collective representations'), offering an alternative to the physical, neurophysiological, linguistic and essentialist accounts. Cogently summarizing his intent he states that he has tried:

> . . . to isolate techniques such as mosaic and stained glass, drawing or oil painting, which were clearly responses to particular aesthetic needs and to discuss their transformation as these needs themselves changed. Some chapters focus on these techniques; others look at more theoretical questions, such as the continual reinterpretation of an ancient text on four-colour painting, or the problem of how to see the rainbow, or the function of the palette, or the paradigm of music, all of which recur in many historical periods. Several themes return repeatedly, such as the feeling that verbal language is incapable of defining the experience of colour, or the notion from Antiquity to Matisse of an 'Orient' which was an exciting and dangerous repository of coloured materials and attitudes. (p. 10)

Throughout each of the fourteen chapters, these themes tack back and forth sketching out the conditions of possibility under which particular aesthetics and values are made manifest — nurtured by society — at particular times and places to issue in individual works. Specifically, the discussion of the 'Orient' as the source of colour (and attendant moral configurations) complements Said's *Orientalism* (1978), and the detailed chronicling of the mismatch of colour and colour words throughout Euro-American history shows the Berlin and Kay theory (1969) to be a mere catalogue of dead forms.

Although focusing on the constitution of colour in the Euro-American tradition (except for the brief *excursus* into Islamic sensibilities), Gage does not commit the solecism of conflating Culture (with a capital C) with Civilization, and thence Civilization with the West and Modernity (the Rest being *cultures* — small c, plural), for his message is not that the West has fully evolved the full categorization of the colour space. Instead, the currency of colour is saturated by practical (material, social, political) sensibilities. Whilst avoiding anything rigidified or reified, each of the sensibilities with which he engages is the bearer of specific socio-cultural intentions, in specific environments both natural and social (the separation of these two being quite artificial). For example, in the early Renaissance, the Virgin's robe could be scarlet, purple, vermilion, crimson lake, or ultramarine, all of which were cognate colours, united in value by their beauty, rarity and extraordinary cost, modern discriminations between them being quite foreign (p. 131).[11] That they were cognate is not ascribed to a lower level of evolutionary consciousness, but to their availability and desirability. Similarly, the Latin and medieval French use of the terms *glaucus, ceruleus* and *bloi* (p. 90) could signify either blue or yellow (later thought to be a neuronally based contrast).[12] Gage argues that medieval sensibilities depended on the physical as well as the metaphysical attributes of raw materials. Thus, the fluidity of colour names in all probability owed something to the production of pigments and dyes. Just as medieval glassmakers used the same copper oxide to manufacture red and green glass (considered as the median terms on the colour scale wherein resided beauty and harmony), so a comparable chemical colour change from yellow to blue would have been noticed in the manufacture of the blue vegetable dye-stuff *woad* whose leaves shielded from light were intense yellow, but on exposure turned blue.

Colour concepts might thus be considered embodied skills of judgement (the *habitus*), drawing their lives from the currency of local values. To understand a particular colour concept then is to locate it within local activities, norms and institutions. And as with any practice of any importance, they have a history within which they come to be, are sustained and transformed, and sometimes perish as parts of the histories of those practices and societies — a High Renaissance example being the split between the aesthetics of artists and patrons (Gage, p. 144). Thus, in a sense (and as Vasari saw), colour concepts are much like moral or value concepts. To abstract colour concepts from the contexts of the traditions which they inform and which inform them, is to risk a damaging misunderstanding, for those contexts and practices are constitutive. It is in the process of living interaction that colour-use is given stylistic shape. Every chapter of *Colour and Culture* contains this story.

But how can we get round the dilemma that colour is 'objective' (all normal humans are capable of seeing it) and that is *not* 'objective' (the states of affairs in the world do not force one unique description — taste, profile, accent, inflection, timbre, register — of colour onto us)? The way to approach the problem is, as I have suggested above, to stop confusing mental representations or samples (the picture theory of natural perception) with living in a chromatic world, and to offer a better theory of what it is to dwell in that world. It is also to recognize that picture perception is much harder and requires skills different from visual awareness of the surroundings, from which it is set apart, being a surface which specifies something other than what it is. Apart from that broad strategy, one might also consider that if the objectivity of colour is not considered a single or simple phenomenon, but a complexity sustaining a variety of descriptions, then it is necessary to recognize that asking what is the case requires a set of concepts[13] to be in place, without any one set being privileged in describing the world. This is to dissolve the subject–object distinction of Western thought and to take seriously what many non-Western peoples (and counter-currents in Western philosophy) have been trying to tell us.[14] So, for example, we should resist the separation of the physical from the social aspects of colour; we should not try to separate the surface of the painting from what the picture is about any more than we should attempt to separate sense and reference in language. Thus we should re-read the Berlin and Kay data divest of its scientistic and evolutionary claims, and look to history, as Gage has done, without being fooled by any illusions of naturalness (correspondence with Nature) about colour. We might understand colour then, not as something separate, distinct and given, but as something to which, if it matters, we may actively and intentionally attend, bringing to it certain skills, which in turn may bring into being new features or affordances, which in turn require new skills.

I would therefore have welcomed even more discussion of the ways pigments, dyes and hued lights (Flavin's fluorescent tubes, for example) have been used to present themselves as 'representing' (the duality of picture perception); what their style of presence and address is; how they articulate modes of relativizing the local norm or system to offer unexpected effects (for example, Gainsborough's or Turner's subversion of the warm/cool distinction); what their capacity to undermine claims to universality is; and in what ways they are oriented both towards their object of depiction and the viewer in a mobile context as a visual, ideological field of signifiers. (Gage's discussion of mosaics comes closest.) I would also have liked to have seen even more discussion of the contexts of practical appraisal, attendant organizational contingencies and moral orders.

Gage is concerned with painterly practice and the social and metaphysical conditions constitutive of individual works. His achievement is to show how minds in action, culture or life penetrate so deeply into what we call reality or the environment that the very project of presenting practitioners (whether in the Euro-American past or cross-culturally) as mappers of something mind-independent is fatally compromised from the start. Each and every one of his chapters can be read as evidence sustaining this vista. However, little of this complex programme is fully spelled out in the text of *Colour and Culture*. Indeed, the reader must make do with concentrated and tantalizing hints, as, for example, when Gage states that aesthetic intent gives value and coheres colour relationships, and hence art is of central importance for the study of colour in the larger social context (p. 9); or when he worries about how much of the past can ever be seen at all — alluding to the effects of time on pigments and dyes, to the indeterminacy of colour words, and perhaps to debates about cleaning and restoration. It is a pity that no chapter returns to discuss more fully these important theoretical issues. Nevertheless Gage effectively makes his point that there is no simple relation between vision and depiction.

Finally, I will add a couple of very trivial criticisms. First, the evidence for taking van Eyck's Arnolfini marriage portrait *also* as the 'coming-together of water and fire' (p. 143), as an allegory of alchemy in other words, might support taking it as an allegory of *colour* too. Plato, in *Timaeus* 68a, says that a particular variety of fire dilates the rays right up to the eyes and forcibly thrusts apart and dissolves the very passages in the eyeball, to cause a discharge of a mass of fire and water which we call a tear. Meeting with another variety of fire from the opposite direction (the centre of the eye), which leaps out like a flash to lightning, the ingoing fire is quenched in the moisture (fire and water commingled). He says that 'in this confusion all manner of colours arise.' Clearly there is more to say about the relation of colour and alchemy, though further evidence and interpretation must be adduced.

Second, I am not quite sure this is a book for non-academics as Gage asserts (p. 7). As I have argued, he needs no disclaimers for lack of 'system', for system in colour is an *ignis fatuus*. Rather, the book charts intimate interconnections between disciplinary specialities, and sub-specialities, working on many levels: to inspire undergraduates *and* advanced researchers (in a variety of academic disciplines); to decorate the coffee table *and* make a move in the bloody politics of colour (categorizing) research. Conversely, Bourdieu or Gramsci might be tempted to view the scholarly apparatus with which this volume is richly endowed as a signifier of distinction and power within art-historical discourse, and to regard it therefore as an academic book *par excellence.*

A review of this length cannot do justice to the richness and subtlety of such a work. I will merely recommend that it be read not just by everyone with an interest in the visual arts, but also by a wider public. For example, anthropologists and linguists unbeguiled by Berlin and Kay will welcome such a timely book, as will sociologists of culture. And philosophers now have a superb bouquet of examples. Perhaps, after reading this book, many will appreciate more fully Wittgenstein's prescient comment in his *Remarks on Colour* [73] 'There is no such thing as *the* pure colour concept'.

Barbara Saunders
University of Utrecht

References Cited

J. Baines, 'Colour Terminology and Color Classification: Ancient Egyptian Color Terminology and Polychromy', *American Anthropologist* 87, 1985, pp. 282–97.

E. Beaglehole and P. Beaglehole, 'Ethnology of Puka Puka', *B.P. Bishop Museum Bulletin* 150, 1938, Honolulu.

B. Berlin, 'A Universalist-Evolutionary Approach in Ethnographic Semantics', in A. Fischer (ed.), *Current Directions in Anthropology Bulletins of the American Anthropological Association*, vol. 3 (3), part 2, 1970.

B. Berlin and P. Kay, *Basic Color Terms: Their Universality and Evolution*, Berkeley, 1969.

M.H. Bornstein, 'Cross-cultural Developmental Comparison: The Case of Japanese-American Infant and Mother Activities and Interactions', *Developmental Review* 9, 1989, pp. 171–204.

P. Bourdieu, *Outline of a Theory of Practice*, Cambridge, 1977.

J. Bousfield, 'The World Seen as a Colour Chart', in R.F. Ellen and D. Reason (eds.), *Classifications in their Social Context*, New York, 1979.

N. Chomsky, *Aspects of a Theory of Syntax*, Cambridge, Mass., 1965.

N. Chomsky, *Language and Mind*, New York, 1968.

H. Conklin, 'Color Categorization' (review of Berlin and Kay 1969), *American Anthropologist* 75, 1973, pp. 931–42.

H. Conklin, 'Hanunoo Color Categories', *Southwest Journal of Anthropology* 11, 1955, pp. 339–44.

D. Davidson, 'On the Very Idea of a Conceptual Scheme', in *Inquiries into Truth and Interpretation*, Oxford, 1984, pp. 183–198.

D. Davidson, 'Mental Events', in *Actions and Events*, Oxford, 1980, pp. 207–25.

J.B. Deregowski, 'Real Space and Represented Space: Cross-cultural Perspectives', *Behavioral and Brain Sciences*, 1989, pp. 51–119.

J. Fodor, *The Modularity of Mind*, Cambridge, Mass., 1983.

J. Fodor, *Psychosemantics: The Problem of Meaning in the Philosophy of Mind*, Cambridge, Mass., 1987.

E. Gellner, *Nations and Nationalism*, Oxford, 1983.

J.J. Gibson, *The Senses Considered as Perceptual Systems*, London, 1968.

J.J. Gibson, *The Ecological Approach to Visual Perception*, New Jersey, 1986.

C. Hardin, *Color for Philosophers. Unweaving the Rainbow*, Indianapolis, 1988.

G. Herne, *Die slavischen Farbenbenennungen: Eine semasiologisch-etymologische Untersuchung*, Uppsala, 1954.

N. Hickerson, Review of Berlin and Kay (1969), *International Journal of American Linguistics* 37, 1971, pp. 257–70.

N. Hickerson, 'Two Studies of Color: Implications for Cross-Cultural Comparability of Semantic Categories', in M.D. Kinkade, K.L. Hale and O. Werner (eds.), *Linguistics and Anthropology: In Honour of C.F. Voegelin*, Lisse, 1975, pp. 317–30.

D. Hymes, 'Lexicostatics So Far', *Current Anthropology*, vol. 1, 1960, pp. 3–44.

T. Ingold, 'The Art of Translation in a Continuous World', in G. Palsson (ed.), *Beyond Boundaries: Understanding, Translation and Anthropological Discourse*, Oxford, 1993.

T. Ingold, 'Becoming Persons: Consciousness and Society in Human Evolution', *Cultural Dynamics* IV (3), 1991, pp. 355–78.

A. Jacobson-Widding, *Red-White-Black as a Mode of Thought*, Uppsala, 1979.
P. Kay, B. Berlin and W. Merrifield, 'Biocultural Implications of Color Naming', *Linguistic Anthropology*, vol. 1, 1991, pp. 12–25.
P. Kay and C. McDaniel, 'The Linguistic Significance of the Meanings of Basic Color Terms', *Language*, vol. 54, 1978, pp. 610–646.
M. Kemp, *The Science of Art. Optical Themes in Western Art from Brunelleschi to Seurat*, New Haven, 1990.
M. Kemp, 'Illusion, Allusion and Collusion: Perspective and Meaning in the Historical Context': Paper presented at the Royal Institute of Philosophy Conference 'Philosophy and the Visual Arts', Arnolfini Gallery, Bristol, 1985.
M. Kemp, 'Seeing and Signs. E.H. Gombrich in Retrospect', *Art History*, vol. 7, 1984, pp. 228–43.
J.P. Kirby, 'White, Red and Black. Color Classification and Illness Management': Paper presented at the Symposium 'Ethnomedical Systems in Sub-Saharan Africa: a Cultural Perspective on Traditional Medicine and the Concept of Disease', Leiden, 1988.
A.L. Kroeber and C. Kluckhohn, 'Culture: A Critical Review of Concepts and Definitions', *Peabody Museum Papers* 47, Harvard, 1952.
B. Landau and R. Jackendoff, ' "What" and "Where" in Spatial Language and Spatial Cognition', *Behavioral and Brain Sciences*, 16 2, 1993, pp. 17–66.
E. Lang, 'Primary Perceptual Space and Inherent Proportion Schema: Two Interacting Categorization Grids Underlying the Conceptualization of Spatial Objects', *Journal of Semantics* 7, 1990, pp. 121–41.
G.R. Lockhead, 'Psychophysical Scaling: Judgments of Attributes of Objects?', *Behavioral and Brain Sciences* 15, 1992, pp. 543–600.
R. MacLaury, 'From Brightness to Hue: An Explanatory Model of Color-Category Evolution', *Current Anthropology* 33 (2), 1992, pp. 137–86.
H.R. Maturana and F.J. Varela, *The Tree of Knowledge. The Biological Roots of Human Understanding*, Boston, 1988.
N.B. McNeill, 'Colour and Colour Terminology', *Journal of Linguistics*, vol. 8, 1972, pp. 21–33.
I. Murdoch, *Metaphysics as a Guide to Morals*, London, 1992.
Petit, P., *The Common Mind. An Essay on Psychology, Society and Politics*, Oxford, 1993.
H. Putnam, *Representation and Reality*, Cambridge, Mass., 1988.
E. Rosch, 'Probabilities, Sampling, and the Ethnographic Method: The Case of Dani Colour Names', *Man* 7, 1992, pp. 448–66.
E. Said, *Orientalism*, Middlesex, 1978.
B. Saunders, *The Invention of Basic Colour Terms*, Utrecht, 1992.
B. Saunders and J. van Brakel, 'On Translating *The World Color Survey*', in D. Raven and J. de Wolf, *Contemporary Anthropology*, Assen, forthcoming.
B. Spencer and F.J. Gillen, *The Arunta*, vol. 2, London, 1927.
D. Summers, *The Judgment of Sense. Renaissance Naturalism and the Rise of Aesthetics*, Cambridge, 1987.
D.Y. Teller and E.N. Pugh, 'Linking Propositions in Color Vision', in J.D. Mollon and L.T. Sharpe (eds.), *Colour Vision: Physiology and Psychophysics*, London, 1983, pp. 577–89.
T. Turner, Anthropology and Multiculturalism, *Cultural Anthropology* 8 (4), 1993, pp. 411–29.
V. Turner, 'Color Classification in Ndembu Ritual: A Problem in Primitive Classification', in his *Forest of Symbols: Aspects of Ndembu Ritual*, Ithaca, 1967.
E.B. Taylor, *Primitive Culture*, London, 1871.
J. White, 'Antique Perspective Theory and Pompeian Practice', in *Perspective in Ancient Drawing and Painting*, London, 1956, pp. 43–69.
W.H. Whitely, 'Colour-words and Colour-values: The Evidence from Gusii', in R. Horton and R. Finnegan (eds.), *Modes of Thought. Essays on Thinking in Western and Non-Western Societies*, London, 1973, pp. 145–61.
R. Williams, *Culture*, London, 1981.
L. Wittgenstein, *Remarks on Colour*, Oxford, 1990.
D. Zahan, 'White, Red and Black: Colour Symbolism in Black Africa', in A. Portman and R. Ritsema (eds.), 'The Realms of Colour', *Eranos*, 1974, pp. 365–95.

Notes

1 According to White (1956), Vitruvius might be considered one of the first to have formulated a version of the *mimetic* principle for line (perspective). The principle requires that 'artifical' perspective (on the picture plane) corresponds to, or extracts from, or models 'natural' perspective.

2 For example: 'the task of the painter is this: to describe with lines and tint with colors, on whatever panel or wall is given him, visible surfaces similar to any body whatever . . .' (Alberti, quoted by Summers, 1987); and again, painting 'is an imitation in line and colour of everything under the sun' (Poussin,

quoted by Kemp, 1990).

3 As Lang (1990. p. 121) puts it, 'Within the realms of cognitive studies, spatial structure is one of the few domains where attempts to trace mental representations from the level of sensory input conditions through conceptual structure to their lexical and grammatical organization seem to be feasible and revealing.' See, however, Deregowski (1989) for a different approach.

4 Are all humans biologically speaking, the same? Or are they biologically different? According to Bornstein (1989), we are stuck with the question of whether there is one 'genome' of which there are many variants (cultures), or many genomes, each sustaining, as it were, one hermetically sealed 'culture'. Obviously many genomes support relativist doctrines, one genome, universalist doctrines. Formulated this way, the problem is at an *impasse*.

5 Lack of a *mimetic* tradition has been explained in terms of an evolutionary register in which key types of perceptions — colour and space — are considered below the par of those of Euro-American siblings: for just as languages cannot be thought of as evolutionarily equal (Hymes, 1960), so too the capacity for *mimesis* is not equal. Where *mimesis* has not developed in a manner comparable to that of the Greek and Renaissance tradition, 'representations' are 'conceptual', not illusionistic, or if illusionistic, then 'primitive', or its cognate, 'exotic'. Kemp (1985) may like to dismiss this line of thinking as stemming from 'primitive researchers', but it is unlikely to change while the Berlin and Kay thesis and similar work in cognitive science maintains its ascendancy.

6 The same point can be made for Greek and Latin and perhaps for medieval germanic, romance and slavic languages. Our decontextualized concept of primitive or basic colours is a very recent invention of the Western tradition, which stabilized only when the technological production of dyes and pigments was standardized through industrial production methods. Technology, as it were, created a new ontology of colour.

7 This 'naturalistic fallacy' is a version of William James's 'psychologists' fallacy' which converts consequences of interactions of events into the causes of the occurrence of these consequences.

8 Teller and Pugh (1983) say 'Color science employs terms from two logically disjoint universes of discourse — that is, the one set of terms cannot be reduced to the other or vice versa by logical analysis alone. In the one universe of discourse there are subjective reports of the nonidentity or identity of sensations, as well as reports of subjective qualities of sensations, such as redness, greenness, etc. In the other universe of discourse there are the terms of physics, physical optics, photochemistry and cellular physiology.' I suggest there are more disjoint universes: for example, the use of colour in ordinary life; the use of colour in depiction.

9 'We do not see 'space' in the world; we live our field of vision. We do not see the 'colors' of the world; we live our chromatic space' (Maturana and Varela, 1988, p. 23).

10 *Pace* the old stories of *mimesis*, paintings are pre-eminently not 'real' in the sense that they may be confused with their referents, but profoundly ambiguous, exploiting their capacities to maximum effect. In this they are claimed to differ from psychological experiments which are intended to be transparent. In contrast, in one sense (though not exhaustively), I am inclined to see paintings as very complex psychophysical experiments, illustrating what Davidson (1980) has called 'anomalous monism'.

11 A telling example (not mentioned by Gage) might be the absence of the precious ultramarine blue in Fra Angelico's frescos at San Marco on the cell Walls, for the Dominican friars were dedicated to poverty.

12 Similarly, the old Serbo-Croatian term *plav* is used to refer to things blue or yellow (Herne, 1954), as is the Aruntan term *tierga* (yellow, green, blue [Spencer and Gillen, 1927]), and the Pukapukan term *yenga* (Beaglehole and Beaglehole, 1938). McNeill (1971) discusses how *purple, woad, safflower* in the ancient world, and *ao* in Japan present casts where a single colour name designates a wide variety of different hues. The *World Color Survey* (see Kay, Berlin and Merrifield, 1991) although withdrawn from circulation, ostensibly because of ingenuous comments by experimenters, is full of such so-called anomalies of colour naming. See Saunders (1992) and Saunders and van Brakel (forthcoming) for discussion.

13 Something like 'culture' is meant by this, though its slipperiness has been noted by writers as diverse as Tylor (1871), Kroeber and Kluckhohn (1952), Williams (1981) and Gellner (1983). Ingold (1993) has suggested that anthropologists may have to abandon the notion.

14 This is a position made familiar in philosophy by *inter alia* Putnam, Davidson, Kuhn, Wittgenstein and Heidegger; in psychology it is found in Gibson (1968; 1986) in his theory of affordances and the education of attention.

Art History ISSN 0141-6790 Vol. 17 No. 3 September 1994 pp. 505–512

SHORTER REVIEWS

Toil and Plenty: Images of the Agricultural Landscape in England, 1780–1890 by *Christiana Payne*, New Haven and London: Yale University Press, 1993, 219pp., 34 col. plates, 142 b. & w. illus., £30.00

Agricultural landscape imagery in England of the period 1780–1890 is defined here as the representation of arable farming, usually including the depiction of labourers at work in the fields. Such images, which seem obviously to pose questions of truth and idealization, of élite attitudes towards the countryside and the rural poor, have become, as Payne notes, objects of interest to academics from a range of disciplines. Mindful of the cultural theorists at her back, the author states that she aims 'to combine the traditional discipline of art history with some of the insights offered by the "new" art historians', and has 'tried to adopt a truly "interdisciplinary" approach' (p. 3).

In the first third of the book, Payne deals successively with social and economic changes in the English countryside, the myths and values attached to it, and how 'stylistic developments' in agricultural landscape imagery were related to these concerns. The major watersheds in the evolution of the genre are identified as political ones. The ending of the Napoleonic Wars and the subsequent rural distress and unrest was associated with a lessening of interest in patriotic, productivist imagery, and a growth in the demand for more sentimentalized rural genre. The repeal of the Corn Laws in 1846, ending the most serious division in the ruling class over issues affecting the countryside, and the avoidance of revolutionary crisis in 1848, meant that patriotic harvest scenes once more became credible and that it became easier to depict and draw attention to rural poverty without appearing subversive. Payne notes that merchants and manufacturers were buying agricultural landscapes from the 1820s, but follows Andrew Hemingway[1] in arguing that there were no significant differences in taste in this regard between landowners and the urban bourgeois in the early nineteenth century (p. 47). Later, however, without modifying her earlier conclusions, she observes that Peter De Wint, many of whose patrons were landowners, depicted neat and diligent ' "model labourers" ', whereas David Cox, who was a Radical and whose patrons were more often urban bourgeois, tended to represent rural workers as free individuals (p. 54).

Payne manages to condense her survey of this major topic into seventy-seven pages, the remainder of the volume being occupied by the exhibition catalogue. Overall, the strength of this work lies in its conscientious comparison of the actuality of socio-economic conditions and working practices in the countryside with the images that were portrayed. Ideology is also discussed in greater depth than the cautious eclecticism of the introduction might have led one to suppose. Nevertheless, social, political and ideological factors sometimes seem to be invoked merely in order to provide a kind of sociological 'interest', while the aesthetic realm retains much of its autonomy and privileged status. Thus Barrell[2] is criticized for 'overemphasizing the effects of capitalism and the belief in industriousness as the chief working-class virtue while underestimating the importance of aesthetic factors such as the Picturesque' (note on p. 67). I would argue that the Picturesque functions as an essential foil to notions of industriousness and 'improvement' in capitalist ideology, much as the travel section stands in relation to the business section in a newspaper. It is significant that topographical engravings, which had less status than landscapes in oil and watercolour, and which more often combine picturesque and productivist elements, are not given much attention. Moreover, the few photographs which appear at the end of the catalogue are not examined as representations, but solely as documentary evidence. Finally, there is little explanation of the role of these images in the construction of national identity,[3] of why depictions of arable farming in southern and eastern England are still viewed as symbols of Englishness and, indeed, of Britishness.

Andrew Kennedy
Courtauld Institute of Art, University of London

Notes

1 Andrew Hemingway, *Landscape Imagery and Urban Culture in Early Nineteenth-Century Britain*, Cambridge and New York, 1992.
2 John Barrell, *The Dark Side of the Landscape: The Rural Poor in English Painting, 1730–1840*, Cambridge, 1980.
3 See, in this respect, Stephen Daniels, *Fields of Vision: Landscape Imagery and National Identity in England and the United States*, Oxford, 1993.

Thomas Eakins and the Heart of American Life edited by *John Wilmerding*, London: National Portrait Gallery, 1992, 212 pp., 61 col. plates, 110 b. & w. illus., £25.00

While the recent Eakins exhibition at the National Portrait Gallery was an event to be applauded and welcomed, the way in which it presented Eakins's work requires a rather more critical stance. The exhibition, entitled 'Thomas Eakins and the Heart of American Life', worked with a very superficial view of American history, and this simplistic and reductive approach is repeated in the catalogue of the show.

There are two major essays in the catalogue. In the first of these, John Wilmerding attempts to marry what he sees as the two types of approach taken to Eakins's work: the biographical and the visual-analytical. The result is an historically shallow and methodologically unrigorous mish-mash which falls between the two poles of discussion and simply recycles standard ideas about the artist and his canvases. For instance, the unhappy demeanour of Eakins's wife in his portrait of her is explained by Wilmerding as a projection of the artist's own unhappiness, with neither an explanation as to the role of style, nor an account of the psychology of transference as a determinant of the art object. Most alarming of all is a passage towards the end of the essay where Wilmerding works with the notion of a *Zeitgeist*, placing Eakins side by side with Freud, Einstein and Marie Curie. These figures, Wilmerding tells us, make Eakins's late work more comprehensible; the late paintings apparently operate according to similar psychic, spatial and theoretical paradigms! This breathtaking claim displays not only a methodological naïveté, but also a misunderstanding of science.

The second essay, by John Hayes, the outgoing director of the NPG and the mastermind behind the exhibition, is concerned with Eakins and his European contemporaries. Hayes makes no claims to be an Eakins scholar, but even allowing for this, his essay is disturbingly unsophisticated. What is most interesting here is the attempt to recuperate Eakins as a modernist of sorts, an attempt that is staged elsewhere in the catalogue too. Hayes is clearly embarrassed that Eakins ranked Couture and Gérôme so highly, and seems to have had so little interest in Courbet and Manet, but nonetheless he makes strenuous efforts to implicate Eakins in the great tradition of modernism. For instance, in comparing Eakins's work to various European styles of portraiture, Hayes declares at one point that the only real point of comparison can be Degas (p.45). Not only does this point to a determination to hang on to modernist values in the face of visual evidence and important revisionist histories, but it also suggests that Hayes is unaware of American taste and aesthetics of the period.

The catalogue entries for the paintings exhibited are variable in quality. Many are historically shallow and rely exclusively on secondary sources. An engagement with issues of race, gender and social class, all of which one would presume to lie at 'the heart of American life', is frequently absent. This blindness to difference is in many instances symptomatic of a tendency to discuss Eakins's works as transcendent of their specific social and historical locations. To cite an example, the entry on the sketch of boxer Billy Smith sees the painting as 'a celebration of humanity' and of 'the heroism within all men' (p.135), and the writer's refusal to engage with class seems born of a complete lack of acquaintance with the history of boxing, its role in urban culture, and its relation to contemporary gender and ethnic identities. There are occasional gems: Bryan Wolf's fine essay on the portrait of Professor Henry A. Rowland is the only place in the catalogue where one is offered a critical account of the relation between art and science, and Michael Fried's *Baby At Play* is characteristically interesting (and provides a brief discussion of realism as a style *producing* effects of character, countering the more naïve definitions elsewhere). The bulk of the other entries are somewhat undistinguished, and many bear a distinctly undergraduate stamp. In the burgeoning field of Eakins studies, this catalogue is something of a non-intervention.

Michael Hatt
London

The End of the Salon: Art and the State in the Early Third Republic by *Patricia Mainardi*, Cambridge: Cambridge University Press, 1993, 210pp., 51 b. & w. illus., £30.00

This lucid and thorough study explores further the relationships between artists, government and society and their roles in the creation and exhibition of art products, concerns which Patricia Mainardi so effectively examined in her last book concerning the preceding period of the Second Empire.[1] The focus of these works upon the politics of exhibition and sponsorship provide a vital counterpoint to the modernist, anti-historical obsessions with aesthetics and avant-garde heroes still rife in so much of the conceptualization of contemporary exhibitions and scholarship, yet her tone bespeaks a welcome pluralist tolerance and accessibility lacking in so many of the reductively entrenched oppositions of contemporary debates.

Our understanding of the complex reasons for the restructuring and eventual collapse of the Paris Salon and concurrent variations in the independent and commercial forums of this period is deepened by her distinction of 'pictures to see and pictures to sell' and its ground-breaking elucidation in terms of the failed (and thus?) forgotten attempt at a Triennale Salon for morally improving art. This analysis describes the arts education policy which sought to revive industry through universal training in geometric drawing, the influence of commercialized display techniques, the repercussions upon the privileging of public and private experience resultant from national aesthetic and economic protectionism. The frequent elision of political and artistic stances which crudely ascribes liberal or reactionary art policies to regimes or even parties or individuals is avoided in favour of a recognition of the panoply of social, political, aesthetic and popular phenomena. The book's gold mine of citations and references to debates in the Chambre des Députés and the Ministries reveals the over-simplistic and anti-historical assumptions implicit in such paradigms. The wise yet melancholy reminder of the preface of the disturbing reactionary 'turns of tide' without our own fin-de-siècle's quashed liberalism resonates throughout the work and in the thoughts of many of us.

This framework provides a rich context for future studies seeking to reverse the exclusion of a huge swathe of Third Republic decorative mural painting which has been enacted within even the most revisionist canons of art history.[2] One cannot help wishing Mainardi had examined these schemes and their reception at more length herself, though admittedly this might well have blurred the sharp focus of her study, which is one of its greatest merits. The book with its plain prose style and legible structure is a worthy and readable voice of the most promising trends of art history. It is to be hoped its inclusion in the curriculum of the discipline at all levels will be prompt. Can students of the late 1880s and '90s hope for the next instalment soon?

Claire Richmond
Courtauld Institute of Art,
University of London

Notes

1 Patricia Mainardi *Art and Politics of the Second Empire The Universal Expositions of 1855 and 1867*, New Haven and London, 1987.

2 The studies of Marie Jeannine Aquilino and Debora Silverman and the 1986 Petit Palais exhibition have also been crucial in bringing the neglected areas of decorative arts and mural painting to light.

Stanley Spencer: A Complete Catalogue of the Paintings by *Keith Bell*, London: Phaidon Press, 1992, 544 pp., 314 col. plates, £95.00

In 1974 the Tate Gallery acquired at Sotheby's, for a mere £8,500, Stanley Spencer's 1937 *Double Nude Portrait: the Artist and his Second Wife*, one of his outstanding works, although it is true that the frankness of its gaze had not then been put in context by the phenomenal rise in reputation and popularity of Lucian Freud. In 1990, admittedly at the very peak of the 1980s' art boom, Spencer's two-metre square 1958 *Crucifixion* sold for £1.2 million in the same rooms. In spite of the circumstances which might respectively have depressed and raised the price of these paintings, there clearly has been a massive shift in the market view of Stanley Spencer, and one which would seem to justify the claim in the jacket blurb of this book that Spencer's 'contribution to British art and his true stature as an artist are now internationally recognized'. This stature is that he 'is one of outstanding painters of the twentieth century' (note, not just British painters). Nevertheless, in an earlier review of the book (*Guardian*, 1 December 1992), James Hall felt able to conclude that the market was a fool and that Spencer's paintings were 'the ludicrous alibis of a wasted talent', thus lining up with the late Sir Alfred Munnings, PRA 1944–9, who attacked (in a letter to *The Times*) *The Resurrection, Port Glasgow* as 'intentionally abnormal' when it was purchased by the Chantrey Committee in 1950, and in the same year declared one of Spencer's paintings (probably *Age* from the 'Beatitude' series) to be pornographic, initiated a police inquiry, and when this failed, advised that the painting be destroyed, which apparently it was.

Spencer clearly continues to cause confusion and unease, as Keith Bell shows he did throughout his career, but particularly from the time of his first marriage, in 1925, when sex became a driving force, sometimes explicitly so, of Spencer's art. Extreme traditionalists such as Munnings saw Spencer as a dangerous modern, while modernists equally disapproved. Fry, for example, found him 'not plastic' and mostly 'dull and inexpressive' and even when not so, as in *The Resurrection, Cookham*, concluded the total effect 'to be a distinctly unpleasant and disagreeable stimulation'.

Spencer is indisputably a massive, inescapable presence in twentieth-century British art, but what kind of presence? Who and what is 'Stanley Spencer'? Publication of this exhaustively researched book substantially adds to the most recent view of Spencer's art, presented by the 1980 exhibition at the Royal Academy, and at last provides the complete catalogue and battery of references that should enable the art history industry finally to get to grips with Spencer and sort him out. Bell has found 455 paintings (about the same oeuvre as Turner, and Spencer's paintings are almost all finished) but it is the structure of this book that makes it especially valuable, effectively a complete portable retrospective, or as near a definitive monograph as we are going to get.

The catalogue is at the back, preceded by a succession of critical essays dividing Spencer's career into four major phases of figure painting, with separate sections devoted to his landscapes and portraits. This commentary is lavishly illustrated in colour, 314 plates, as well as some black and white, and adds up to an unprecedented overview of Spencer's career which more than compensates for the inconvenience of having to cross refer from the essays to the catalogue for illustrations of works not reproduced in colour, and for the catalogue information which complements the main text. Most notably, this structure brings into new focus Spencer's practice as a landscape painter and excitingly reveals him as a portraitist, although I would quarrel with putting the extraordinary nudes of the mid-1930s in this category. The book is beautifully designed, by David Hillman and Karin Beck of Pentagram, with a jacket of tightly controlled drama, and proportions and typography to satisfy Whistler, or Donald Judd. Its production costs must have been frightening and the support received from the Henry Moore Foundation and from Christie's should be acknowledged. Books like this must continue to be published.

Simon Wilson
Tate Gallery, London

Art Criticism since 1900 edited by *Malcolm Gee*, Manchester: Manchester University Press, 1993, 240pp., 17 b. & w. illus., £35.00

The title *Art Criticism since 1900* gives nothing away. You could be forgiven for thinking that this was a collection of pieces of criticism that would provide a variety of examples of dominant, alternative and oppositional ways of writing and thinking about art. Or else that it might be a book detailing the way that art criticism (in all its various guises) provides part of what reception theorists would call the 'horizon of expectations', that heterogenous and historical set of cultural, political, ethical and aesthetic expectations which would frame a viewer's commerce with art. This book, however, offers only a very limited range of art criticism for analysis — it is mostly northern European, and mostly from the specialized press. It also seems relatively uninterested in the way art criticism in general might function, about how general meanings for modern art become available to both specialized and non-specialized audiences, and how certain ideas of art come to 'win out' over others, *Art Criticism since 1900* wears its title as something of a false promise.

The thirteen essays that make up this book began life as contributions to a session for the 1990 Conference of the Association of Art Historians. The editor, Malcolm Gee, has arranged them into four parts, kicking off part one ('Issues in Criticism') with his own piece, which acts as an overview to the field of specialized art criticism and as a partial introduction to the essays that follow. There is much here that would be worth extending. Especially suggestive is the discussion of art criticism as a rhetorical strategy that negotiates contradictions: the art criticism that champions a particular work manages to construct it as both utterly new *and* a continuation of tradition, while seeing it as both the unique outpouring of the artistic personality *and* as universally relevant. For the most part, the essays that follow concern themselves with the micrological study of particular critics (Lhote, Reverdy, Zervos, Benjamin, Restany, Read, etc.) and their interpretations and constructions of the artists and art practices with which they are associated.

There are, however, moments that break through this insularity. Sarah Wilson's essay (in part four, 'Issues in Modern French Criticism') raises the problem of the lack of fit between Anglo-American and French usage of a term like 'modernism'. This should alert us to the wider problems of geographic differences; what is the relationship between a country's global position and the way it writes the cultures of others? What would be the story if there was a section on 'Issues in Mexican Criticism'? The theme of nationalism is also touched on by Patricia Hills and Margaret Garlake (both essays in part three, 'Britain and America'), but the issue needs extending outside the cultural triangle of this book: London, Paris, New York (with the emphasis on Paris).

Gerard Mermoz's dense essay (in part one) tackles the philosophical and practical question of what critics and historians do when they attend to objects using such categories as 'art', 'modernism' and 'postmodernism' — it offers a rigorous basis for further investigations. Chrisopher Green (in part two, 'Criticism in France Between the Wars') discusses a construction of Picasso as social phenomenon and 'genius' which, he argues, follows an ethnographic model. This essay demonstrates how a notion of self-expressive value can be secured using forms from a discipline that, on the face of it, would be critical of such value.

Art Criticism since 1900 offers thirteen different essays unhampered by the idea of a shared project, or common issues of debate. The book's gaps and evasions might tell us something about the discipline of art history, about its self-understanding as autonomous. It seems to me that art criticism as practised in daily newspapers, on TV and radio, as well as in the specialized press, is part of the process of securing general meanings (ideologies) about selfhood. It is also part of the process of consolidating cultural capital. Art criticism, to my mind, operates in much more dispersed and everyday ways than *Art Criticism since 1900* would have us believe.

Ben Highmore
Bristol

Making The Modern: Industry, Art, and Design in America by *Terry Smith*, Chicago and London: University of Chicago Press, 1993, 528 pp., 166 b. & w. illus., £39.95

For those of us familiar with Terry Smith's earlier work, for example his essay on Frida Kahlo in *Block* magazine[1] during those heady days when there was a strong sense of a job to do in matters of art, design, representation and cultural politics, *Making the Modern* has been a long time in the making. It has, however, been well worth the wait.

My main reason for this assertion lies with the fact that relatively few attempts have been made to draw together wider critical and theoretical work on cultural representation with the problematic of modernism, in a way which has such a high use-value to the student of the visual; of an accessible 'iconology of modernity' as Smith will have it, without collapsing the project into a chronological category. This task is made none the easier as the result of the breadth and scale of his work.

Smith's rejection of modernity as an historical given, by proposing an iconology which 'actively produce(s) meanings and knowledges in its social reception' with its consequent emphasis upon 'processes of visualisation', provides the framework for his ambitious and scholarly book. Smith draws into conceptual focus an impressive diversity of representations of American modernity including Charles Scheeler's industrial landscapes, Margaret Bourke-White's photographs, Albert Kahn's factory designs and the work of Frida Kahlo and Diego Rivera, to mention but a few, in a critical articulation of the visual rhetoric of American modernity between the world wars.

In posing 'the very question of modernity to a particular time and space' (p. 2) Smith has to steer round, if not elide, the 'paradoxical doubling or inherently dialectical quality that makes modernity both so irresistible and so problematic a category',[2] as Peter Osborne has remarked. It is Smith's emphasis upon the social relations of modernity, represented, as he puts it, by 'something like an ensemble of *processes of visualisation*' (my emphasis) which enables him to escape the trap of seeing modernity solely as a category of historical periodization, by engaging with the dialectic of 'modernity's drive to perpetual renovation'. This most clearly seen with Smith's critique of Fordism and the American automobile industry. Here he produces a stimulating analysis of the assembly-line process as a mode of cultural representation, where questions of time and 'new form / new content' are intertwined in a temporality characteristic of modernity, one which embraces both built-in obsolescence and the desire for the new. With critical acumen Smith traces the construction of the consumerist 'life style modernity' and the American Way of Life.

Against the technocratic factory aesthetic, an abstract background not unlike the 'classical' industrial landscapes of Charles Scheeler, Smith brings to life the productive processes and drives of a modernizing America through an engagement with the social relations of everyday life. In parts 2 and 3 of his volume, the social, political and economic issues behind a continuously reforming modernism are laid bare. The Depression and the response by New Deal agencies are illuminated through incisive critical studies of, for example, *Fortune* business magazine, the murals of Diego Rivera, and 'documentary style' New Deal publicity. Most especially, the photographic representations of the contradictions of class, the dual injustices of the division of labour and unemployment, integrate with Smith's text, to impact powerfully upon the reader. Here, 'picturing poverty' through the images of Dorothea Lange, Russel Lee and Lewis Hine, we become witness to the price paid for the modernizing zeal of America's commercial and industrial elite.

The major achievement in all of this lies with the way that Smith in *Making The Modern* is always accessible to his audience as a wider constituency. Perhaps for the more demanding reader of theoretical perspectives on modernism, this openness may be seen to invite conceptual slippage; I think that this risk is a price well worth paying, especially at a time when some are suggesting a move backwards to exploring the level of autonomy of the individual artist or designer. With this well-illustrated and well-presented volume Terry Smith has made a substantial contribution to the social history of modernism and modernity in twentieth-century America.

David Firth
Falmouth School of Art and Design

Notes

1 T. Smith, 'From The Margins', *Block*, no. 8, Middlesex Polytechnic, 1985.
2 P. Osborne, 'Modernism is a Qualitative, Not a Chronological, Category', *New Left Review*, no. 92, March–April 1992, p. 73.

Expressionism Reassessed edited by *Shulamith Behr, David Fanning* and *Douglas Jarman*, Manchester and New York: Manchester University Press, 1993, 232 pp., 5 col. plates, 30 b. & w. illus., £40.00 hdbk, £12.99 pbk

Though it is notoriously difficult to turn a series of conference papers into a book, the editors of *Expressionism Reassessed* have managed to convert the disparate papers of the *Manchester International Conference on Expressionsim 1992* into a coherent volume through the concept of reassessment, summed up in the final sentence of the Introduction: 'From the disputed origins and chronological and aesthetic demarcations of the term, to the lack of cohesiveness of the movement, the complexities of Expressionism invite, and no doubt will continue to invite, reassessment.' (p. 7)

Both the geographical range of the volume and the variety of media discussed (painting, sculpture, literature, theatre, dance, music, cinema and architecture) are invitations to reassessment. Colin Rhodes and Manfred Kuxdorf seek to bridge gaps between different media in their essays, while Marit Werenskiold and J.M. Ritchie delineate the broader geographical influences of Expressionism in Scandinavia and Britain respectively. Arguably, these essays add to the scope of the term Expressionism, but the main thrust of reassessment in the volume lies elsewhere — in shaking Expressionist shibboleths and destabilizing traditional definitions.

In an excellent essay, Gill Perry challenges time-honoured assumptions about the relationship between 'Nature' and Expressionist painting, arguing for a more critical approach to such an 'ideologically loaded' (p. 53) category. Both Peter Vergo and Christopher Hailey explicitly reconsider the notion of the *Gesamtkunstwerk* in their essays, whilst that particular term also surfaces in the concerns of other writers, such as Erich Ranfft. No reassessment of Expressionism would be complete without questioning the spiritual and political overtones of *Geist* and *Utopie* and these are duly considered in the volume by David Elliott, Peter Franklin and Raymond Furness in their very different essays.

If there is one recurrent theme in the project of reassessment, however, it must be the tension between finding a meaningful definition of Expressionism applicable to a multiplicity of artistic practices and turning the term into a tautology. Werner Sudendorf addresses this with regard to cinematic Expressionism: 'It is not my intention to condemn this list of films as incoherent; it does, however, lead to a quite arbitrary set of rules, to the point where the term becomes devoid of any real meaning.' (p. 92) This sentiment is echoed by Dennis Sharp in his essay on architecture and by Stephen Hinton when he writes of musical Expressionism. The problem has beset Expressionism from the beginning and indeed necessitates reassessment. Perhaps Shulamith Behr, describing 'conflicting themes' (p. 186) and Rhys Williams speaking of the 'co-presence . . . of reactionary and progressive ideas' (p. 210) in Expressionism are closest to surmounting this dilemma by allowing Expressionism its self-contradictory nature. As John Willett asserts in the Foreword, 'Sometimes it is a bonfire, sometimes a jellyfish' (p. ix); doubtless this fascinating volume will stimulate further debate on the question.

Marsha Meskimmon
Staffordshire University